VIETNAM CRISIS

STEPHEN PAN, PH.D. • DANIEL LYONS, S.J.

PUBLISHED BY THE EAST ASIAN RESEARCH INSTITUTE
86 RIVERSIDE DRIVE, NEW YORK, N.Y.

CONTENTS

PREFACE

by

Stephen C. Y. Pan, Ph.D.

Viet Nam demands the close attention of the entire world today. It is of the utmost concern both to those who are still free, and to those who are already behind the Iron and Bamboo Curtains. The outcome of the Vietnamese war will not only decide the fate of the people in that area, it can greatly affect the rest of Asia, as well as Africa and Latin America. Secretary of State Dean Rusk told the NATO Council in December, 1965, that Europe's fate may also depend on the outcome in Viet Nam.

Many reports have been written about the fighting and the political changes in Asia, but they have usually been fragmentary. Books have appeared that present personal accounts and views of current happenings in that war-torn part of the world. Yet there remains a serious need for a systematic account of Viet Nam from the standpoint of history and political science.

I have been interested in the history, culture, geography and politics of Viet Nam for almost thirty years, especially in regard to her relations with China, France, and the United States. My personal contacts with Ngo Dinh Diem, Nguyen Ngoc Tho, Duong Van Minh, and Nguyen Con-Vien, and my acquaintance in my youth with Ho Chi Minh and other leaders of An Nam's revolutionary movement have impelled me to watch closely the developments in Viet Nam, particularly since 1936.

My extended visits over the years to both North and South Viet Nam have caused me to be very sympathetic with the Vietnamese. For many centuries they have fought, off and on, against Chinese overlordship. Never in all that time did they lose their national identity or their will to resist. Freed from Chinese domination, they were subjected to the colonial empire of France, and again they resisted. Their determination to rid themselves of the French was both admirable and brave. In recent years the tenacious patriotism of these idealistic nationalists has been grossly abused by the Communists in their relentless quest to further the cause of Communism.

During its long history, Viet Nam has been divided at times into two parts, at times into three. Such divisions were artificially brought about for reasons of political administrations. These divisions have so long existed, however, that nationalist feelings arose within the separate areas. To some extent, feelings of dislike also developed. These feelings still exist today. Americans unfamiliar with Vietnamese culture, civilization, history, geography and politics often paint a picture of Viet Nam as they imagine it, or as they would like to see it. Many books and articles have been written about Viet Nam and its people, about its politics and its policies.

No book is written without a purpose. Based on an extensive study of Viet Nam and long associations with the Vietnamese, it is our desire to present a rather comprehensive picture of Viet Nam from an historical and political viewpoint. This we have done as impartially as possible. As the Director of Area Studies and Dean of Human Affairs at the University of the Seven Seas from 1963-1965, I was repeatedly urged by both students and faculty to write a popular-size book on the current situation in Viet Nam. I have tried to answer their many questions herein, as well as the questions put to me by audiences throughout the United States. In this I was greatly encouraged by the Reverend Daniel Lyons, S.J., who visited Viet Nam with me several times in recent years. Father Lyons is nationally known as a writer and lecturer, and is a serious student of Southeast Asia. He is the chairman of the Free Pacific Association, Inc., for the United States, and the Asian Speakers Bureau. E. Ray Nichols, Jr., former President of the University of the Seven Seas, also urged us to write a book on Viet Nam, using some of the materials from my lectures over the past two years on the floating university.

Numerous persons have helped us gather documents and materials from various sources. Among them, Thomas C. Brennan, my former student at Seton Hall University, now Chief Counsel, Subcommittee on Patents, Trademarks and Copyrights of the Senate Judiciary Committee, furnished us wtih many Congressional documents. John B. Tsu, who succeeded me as Director and Professor of the Institute of Far Eastern Studies, Seton Hall University, permitted me to use the file concerning my correspondence with Ngo Dinh Diem, before he returned to Saigon to become Prime Minister and later President of the Republic of Viet Nam.

Reverend Raymond J. de Jaegher, a close friend and personal adviser to President Diem from 1955-1963, furnished us with valuable documents and many useful comments on Viet Nam. He studied the entire text prior to its publication. Pauline Clauston, Kenneth Rhodes, and the staffs of the British Information Service Library not only afforded us the facility of using their library, but supplied us with many published documents concerning Viet Nam and Indo-China. Hsia-Chen of the Chinese Mission at the United Nations gave us many documents concerning China. Li-Huan of the Chinese Division of the United Nations Secretariat supplied many U.N. documents, and Messrs. Gene I-cheng Loh, Ting-Yung Hang, S. K. Li, and Yu-liang Wu of the Chinese News Service furnished us with valuable information concerning the situation in China, Viet Nam, and other parts of East Asia. Hansen Oxholm raised many valuable questions and contributed constructive comments on the presentation of our writing to American readers.

Reverend Louis Tchang, who was in Viet Nam for many years, gave us valuable Vietnamese documents prior to the death of President Ngo Dinh Diem. Nguyen Quy-lien, Observer and Ambassador of the Vietnamese Mission at the United Nations, supplied us with many current Vietnamese documents and much official information about that country.

I had the opportunity to talk with the late President Ngo Dinh Diem at length on many occasions, as well as with Vice-President Nguyen Ngoc Tho, General Duong Van Minh, Ambassador Nguyen Con-Vien, Nguyen Duy Lien and many of the other leading officials of the Vietnamese Republic. All of this enabled me to comprehend the views of these responsible men and to weigh their opinions carefully.

General Duk Shin Choi, the Ambassador of the Republic of Korea at Bonn, and Choi Woon-sang, Minister-Councilor of the Mission of the Republic of Korea at the U.N., gave us information about President Diem's visit to Korea.

Jerry N. Farmer, the Executive Director of the Asian Speakers Bureau, has helped with the gathering of material. Sandra Krebs helped with the proof-reading of the manuscript. Maureen Matthiesen helped with the typing.

The original draft of this book was thoroughly documented. As this is to be a popular edition, annotations and footnotes have been reduced to the minimum and the material itself has been greatly condensed. In all fairness to the authors, it should be pointed out that every statement has its documentary or otherwise reliable source. The entire book has been written as objectively and impartially as possible.

Although we have obtained much assistance and information from many sources, governmental and individual, we wish to assume full responsibility for whatever is contained in the book. Opinions expressed in this book are purely personal and do not represent the policies of the organizations with which we are connected.

Stephen C. Y. Pan, Ph.D.
East Asian Research Institute
86 Riverside Drive
New York City
March 27, 1966.

PREFACE

by

Daniel Lyons, S.J.

It has been a pleasure to write this book with Dr. Stephen C. Y. Pan. He is not only a prodigious worker and an excellent researcher, he knows Asia like a book, and has been closely acquainted with many of its major personages for many years. As a student he knew Ho Chi Minh, Mao Tse-tung, and Chou En-lai. He has personally known Chiang Kai-shek for most of his life. When the late President of South Viet Nam, Ngo Dinh Diem, lived in this country before becoming President, he stayed with Dr. Pan for several months.

We wish to acknowledge our indebtedness to the Most Reverend Paul Yu-Pin, exiled Archbishop of Nanking, who encouraged us to write the book, and who over the years introduced us to many influential people in the Far East. One of these was the Reverend Raymond de Jaegher, who has lived in China and Viet Nam since 1930. Father de Jaegher eye-witnessed many of the events in Viet Nam we have attempted to describe. He not only shared his detailed knowledge with us, but carefully checked the book for accuracy. Like the authors, he is now available in this country for speaking engagements, through the Asian Speakers Bureau in New York City.

We wish to thank Mr. Patrick Frawley, Jr., for having the book translated into Chinese, German, Italian, and Spanish. We extend our sincere appreciation to Mrs. Phyllis Schlafly for her generous offer to help substantially with its distribution.

Viet Nam is the most discussed subject in the world. It is of the greatest concern to the free world, and it is of the greatest concern to the Communist world as well. To the free world Viet Nam has become the symbol of aggression. To the Communist world it is the test case for wars of liberation.

There has been a great deal of pessimism, a lack of realism, and a lot of propaganda about the war in Viet Nam.

There is ample room for criticism of our basic policy, but there are those who disagree with it completely, who would have us lose in Viet Nam. These critics, it seems to me, can be reduced to three: 1) the misinformed or uninformed; 2) the unrealistic; 3) those who have a different set of values.

I have spoken and debated on the subject of Viet Nam as much as almost anyone in the United States. Every year I journey there, to learn all that I can. An example of misinformation occurred when I was engaged in a debate with one of the professors on the Berkeley campus in February, 1965. He maintained that the war was completely indigenous to the South. The North Vietnamese regime has sought to confuse the issue by making its aggression appear to be an indigenous revolt, but we should not be deceived by such a subterfuge. As Secretary of State Rusk pointed out to the Senate Foreign Relations Committee, this is a familiar Communist practice.

Few say that it is predominantly a civil war any longer, but many argue that it was a civil war until 1960. Since America helped South Viet Nam before then, they say that we provoked the North into the war. The fact, of course, is that the eight nations of SEATO have all condemned the aggression of North Viet Nam against the South every year since 1954, and no one has come up with any reasonable evidence to show that these eight nations in their unanimous condemnation of the North's aggression were uninformed or lying. The National Liberation Front has been held up as truly representative of the South Vietnamese, but this is a distortion of the facts.

Not only is the NLF completely directed and controlled by North Viet Nam, the two leading figures of this Communist front, Chairman Nguyen Huu Tho and Secretary-General Nguyen Van Hieu, have been known Communist agitators for over twenty years. The National Liberation Front has been forced to put such men in its top jobs because ever since Viet Nam was divided in 1954, not a single significant non-Communist leader has been willing to associate with the Front. The rumor about a civil war ignores the fact that Ho Chi Minh was appointed in Moscow by the Communist International in 1924 to head the Communist Party in Indo-China, and has headed it there ever since.

Groups like the World Council of Churches call for an immediate cessation to the bombing of the North, not realizing that such an action would mean certain defeat for South Viet Nam. America was not even able to stop the

Mexican bandit, Pancho Villa, until we stopped granting him sanctuary and went after him into Mexico. America is not so superior to North Viet Nam on the ground, as long as Peking is in the picture, nor can any country defeat aggression if it grants sanctuary to the enemy. Church groups call for an immediate cease-fire, and even want a unilateral cease-fire. But peace cannot come to South Viet Nam until the North Vietnamese Communists pull out. The United States has no intention of destroying the government of North Viet Nam, nor do we demand surrender. All we have ever asked is that the North leave South Viet Nam alone. There is no just compromise to that.

Pope Paul VI is constantly being quoted in favor of peace, and pacifist groups like the *Fellowship of Reconciliation* and the *Catholic Worker* keep twisting what he said. But in all his peace appeals he has consistently distinguished peace from pacifism. Pacifism means surrender in the face of aggression, and surrender is neither Christian nor American. Pacifism is not Christian because it fails to distinguish between who is right and who is wrong. Pacifism fails to protect the innocent because it fails to distinguish between defensive and offensive war.

A lack of realism is exemplified by a question I heard at Princeton University. Several of us had talked on Viet Nam, when a Korean veteran in the audience asked a young man from the State Department why we did not bomb the industry around Hanoi. The future diplomat gave what he thought to be a realistic reply. He said because some innocent people might be killed. The questioner pointed out that American soldiers were being killed each day in South Viet Nam, and said: "What is your ratio in the State Department? How many Americans are you willing to see killed in South Viet Nam in order to save how many people in the North?" Unfortunately, innocent people are killed in any war on either side, nor can one presume that because a soldier in either army wears a uniform he must be guilty. The realities of war are harsh, though the realities of Communist conquest of a country are infinitely harsher.

Another instance of a lack of realism was in a debate I had with Dr. John Oliver Nelson, former national director of the *Fellowship of Reconciliation*. Dr. Nelson urged complete pacifism, but also advocated defending the enclaves. He kept pointing out that the money spent in defense of South Viet Nam would be better spent on material aid. How this was to be accomplished in the face of a Communist takeover was not explained.

A pamphlet by the *Center for the Study of Democratic Institutions* complains that the American press never describes a Communist as altruistic, or genuinely committed to the well-being of his fellow man. This is a complaint that Senator Fulbright makes. It brings up the question of a different set of values. As Linus Pauling, who is attached to the *Center,* has bragged on television: "I am godless. What's wrong with that?"

If a person is an atheist, then Communism is not so bad. Because he does not believe in a Creator, he cannot speak about inalienable rights. The Communist does not believe in them. As a government official he denies the people the right to worship God, the right to family integrity, the right to personal morality, the right to freedom of thought or speech or assembly, freedom of movement or employment, freedom of ownership, all those freedoms we take for granted. If a person does not value any of these things, then Communism is tolerable. This is the explanation to those who wonder if Communists are altruistic. They have no belief in human rights. Similarly, people who subscribe to the theory of "better Red than dead" are either defeatist or they figure that their country is not worth fighting for.

George Kennan, former U.S. Ambassador to Russia, maintains that even if America were attacked by Soviet Russia, we should not retaliate. He argues that nothing is more important than physical survival. But this is not the spirit of our Founding Fathers. They started this country by signing the Declaration of Independence. In signing it they pointed out that they would probably lose their lives by doing so— and some of them did. But, they said, "our grandchildren will have freedom." And so we have. We will continue to have it as long as we value it sufficiently. But freedom isn't free. It has to be fought for, and it has to be defended.

When I testified on February 16, 1966, before the House Subcommittee on the Far East and the Pacific, I declared that if our predominant policy was based on fear, we should surrender. I pointed out that when we send young men eighteen years of age to Viet Nam, they are liable to get shot at any time, no matter where they are. We expect them to have courage beyond their years, and I reminded the Congressmen that those young men have the right to expect courage from their government in Washington, D.C. I told the House Subcommittee that our policy in Viet Nam is basically correct, that it is not only justifiable but morally commendable. It is a combination of Christian charity and enlightened self-defense. In the past, I pointed out, we failed to apply the Truman Doctrine to Asia, except for South Korea, and that led to our problems in Viet Nam today. I indicated that our present policy contained the following dangerous errors, in varying degree:

1) Fear of Red China dominates all of our other policies, e.g. whether we should use the troops from Taiwan, and what target areas should be hit. It seems to take us a year or more to overcome our fears at each step, and the losses from this are incalculable.

2) We think that weakness, rather than strength, will discourage aggression. Exactly the opposite is true, and our history of dealing with the Communists proves it, e.g. Greece, Turkey, Korea, the Berlin blockade, the Cuban missile crisis.

We are told that America's power is resented around the world, but just the opposite is true. The only consternation you find as you travel around the world is that we seem so reluctant to use our power in defense of freedom. The rest of the world is terrified of one thing only, the military might of Communism, and its ability to weaken our resolve through its cold-war tactics. Dean Rusk was right when he testified before the Senate Committee on Foreign Relations that "a hundred small countries all over the world will clap their hands in relief" if we succeed in defending South Viet Nam. No free country wants to see the Red monster of Communism win out. Whether even the majority of the people behind the Iron and Bamboo Curtains want to see Communism win in South Viet Nam is very questionable.

3) We let our diplomats override such basic military decisions as blockading or mining Haiphong.

4) We underestimate the importance of the cold-war front within the United States. For example, the government often fails to send speakers to teach-ins when they are requested, or it sends unqualified speakers. We have not presented the wonderful story of American aid in South Viet Nam to the American people.

5) We base our policy on the mistaken notion that Communist Russia is secretly on our side. The testimony of ex-Ambassador Kennan to the Fulbright Committee on February 10, that it is more important to have a "detente" with Russia than it is to win the war, is typical of this sad mistake.

6) We fail to recognize that Ho Chi Minh is not "Titoist," as Hans Morgenthau maintains, and neither is Tito. The persecution of religion is as strong under Tito as it is in the other countries behind the Iron Curtain.

7) We think the UN Secretary-General, U Thant, is impartial, that he is really interested in working toward a just peace, and that he is against "wars of liberation." Yet his whole policy has clearly favored a Communist takeover in South Viet Nam. For example, when we started to win the war, he declared that "war is not the answer." Experts realize how dangerous it would be to return to the 1954 Geneva Agreements. But U Thant maintains: "I think this is the clue to the settlement of the Vietnamese problem." He also has advised us to "gracefully withdraw."

8) We think that North Viet Nam will give up easily, so we keep on granting sanctuary to Haiphong and Hanoi. The enemy knows that we have superior air and naval power, but he is counting on us not to use either one effectively.

9) We are under the illusion that a stalemate is somehow going to make the enemy withdraw all of his troops, and give up all that he has been fighting for. We are asking them to admit defeat, but we seem to have no intention of defeating them in their desire for conquest.

10) We fail to realize the great danger of having other wars of liberation commence while this war drags on interminably, even though we are committed to defend 41 other nations at the same time. If we cannot defend South Viet Nam, how can we hope to defend Europe, or anywhere else? This is the question in the minds of people all over the world, on both sides of the Iron Curtain.

11) We fail to realize that missiles can never replace bombers against small-scale aggression. This is not only a physical problem, it weakens us psychologically in the mind of the aggressors.

12) We fail to realize that only Soviet Russia has the power to destroy us, and that we tempt the Kremlin by prolonging the war.

13) We fail to realize that Communists can justify anything they want to. We keep thinking they have bound themselves to our code of ethics.

14) We fail to realize that we can win the war within a year, but we underestimate our enemy if we think that negotiations can be had just for the asking. On the other hand, it is foolish to think that we will grow tired, but they never will.

15) We fail to realize that if we compromise in Viet Nam, like we did in Laos in 1962, it will be the beginning of the end of the United States as the leader of the free world, and that without a leader, it will be the beginning of the end of the free world itself. If we lose in Viet Nam we will

suffer the greatest defeat in all of our history. The repercussions will reverberate around the world. We have deeply committed ourselves, and rightly so.

16) We think that this is primarily South Viet Nam's war, instead of the free world's. It is the free world that has the most to lose.

17) We fail to see that recognition of the Viet Cong, i.e., any discussion with them as a group, will mean a postwar coalition government, something that would destroy all that we are fighting for. Yet people like U Thant, Lippmann, Fulbright, Harriman, and Robert Kennedy have come out in favor of a coalition.

18) We fail to realize that we are not the government of South Viet Nam, and that we cannot negotiate for them. South Viet Nam has already said they will not negotiate with the Viet Cong as a separate political entity. We have no right to sabotage their position. For years we have kept saying: "Unless they want to win . . ." They are more anxious than we. They favor a stronger policy. The policy of stalemate-negotiate is ours.

19) We foolishly propose military advantage to the enemy in exchange for "talk, talk." We forget that two-thirds of all the American soldiers killed in Korea were killed after negotiations started. Yet our Ambassador-at-Large, Averell Harriman, said on his return from Moscow in June, 1965: "I told the Russians we would not stop bombing North Viet Nam until negotiations started." We should not grant military concessions in order to have negotiations.

20) We labor under the illusion that the last Geneva Conference was satisfactory, and that another one would be desirable. It was an Asian Munich, and we refused to sign it then. Why should we put ourselves in the shoes of a defeated France by reverting to it now?

21) We seem convinced that if we try to win the war within a year, China will enter, but if we take five years to win, she will not enter. Just the opposite is true. In five years she will be more able to enter. Nor can South Viet Nam hold out for five more years.

22) We fail to realize that the critics of our basic policy are either uninformed or unrealistic, or that they may have a different set of values. We fail to see that there is no reasonable alternative to our basic policy in Viet Nam. There will always be excuses for pulling out, or for not winning the war, but there are no good reasons for doing either one. I have debated dozens of professors and others who dis-

agreed with our basic policy, but I have never encountered a reasonable alternative.

The greatest danger facing us is recognition of the Viet Cong, or letting the Communists get control through undemocratic elections. We recognize it when we face military disaster. We may not recognize it when we are confronted with political or economic disaster. Yet they can be just as disastrous and defeating.

A recent survey by the national edition of the *Denver Register* was announced on May 8, 1966. Out of 969 responses from forty-eight different states, 609 indicated they wanted us to use "whatever added force is necessary to win." Another 103 wanted to "bomb the North as necessary, even at the risk of war with Red China." Only 38 wanted to keep on as we are, and only six favored retreat to the coastal enclaves. "Get out now" was indicated by 179, but a great number of these had the impression that we are not wanted in Viet Nam, which is untrue, or they favored getting out because "we aren't in seriously to win."

The vast majority of American citizens want us to win in South Viet Nam, and they want it done with all deliberate speed. So do the vast majority of people throughout the world.

The President keeps referring to his critics as though they were all on the side of withdrawal or undue restraint. Yet the great majority are critical only because we are losing American lives unnecessarily with our crippling policy of stalemate. I travel constantly throughout the country, addressing every type of audience. My questioners have thoroughly convinced me that a policy of winning with reasonable dispatch would be the most popular policy we could have. The notion spread by a small but vociferous minority that most Americans do not want to win is a grave distortion of the facts. Never have so few imposed so much on so many.

This preface can hardly be concluded without referring to Senator Fulbright's remark that "American servicemen have made a brothel out of Saigon." One could say the same thing about government officials in our nation's capital, or about any group of persons anywhere. The 250,000 men in Viet Nam have left their families to risk their lives in defense of Southeast Asia and the whole free world. It ill behooves the Senator from Arkansas to pass judgment on our servicemen abroad, or to insult their families from whom they are separated. To condemn them all because of the actions of some is extremely un-Christian. In the words of the Divine Master: "Let him that is without sin cast the first stone."

As this book goes to press I was requested by the White House to re-visit Viet Nam in mid-June, accompanied by the Rev. Calvin Thielman of Montreat, North Carolina. The concern of President Johnson for the civilian casualties and the war refugees in South Viet Nam prompted the request. Our Chief Executive is not only the President of the United States but the leader of the whole free world. He deserves the loyalty, support, and unqualified cooperation of us all.

Daniel Lyons, S.J.
Asian Speakers Bureau
New York City
Memorial Day
May 30, 1966.

CHAPTER I

VIET NAM: ITS HISTORY AND GEOPOLITICS

1. *Introduction*

To the Communist world, Viet Nam represents the current phase of its war for world domination. It is of the greatest importance. No other international problem since the Korean War has caused so much concern to the rest of the globe. For the United States there are two fronts to the war in Viet Nam: the home front and the foreign front. The home front consists of conflicting ideas, the outcome of which will decide Americas' policies. The foreign front deals with the actual fighting in View Nam, as well as with the diplomatic battles in the United Nations and in the various capitals of the world. These two fronts are closely related, and through the various media of communication, as well as in the halls of Congress, the great debate goes on.

The undeclared war in Viet Nam is a new type of war. Hanoi, Peking, and Moscow call it a "war of liberation." It is an unconventional war, both hot and cold, both military and political. It has no front, yet the front is everywhere. President Johnson termed it "the new face of an old enemy." American policy today aims at the containment of Communist China, just as America decided to contain Soviet Russia under the Truman Doctrine.

A Communist victory in Viet Nam would pave the way for a quick take-over of all Southeast Asia. When Peking, Moscow, and Hanoi feel the time is ripe, they will resort to the conference table to accomplish their aims. A cease-fire could play into their hands very easily. It could lead to peace terms like those in Laos in 1962 which the west found impossible to enforce. Viet Nam is a much more difficult country for policing a cease-fire than a country like Korea. The free world may again be defeated at the conference table.

2. *Historical and Political Background*

A basic understanding of the historical and political background of Viet Nam is essential. Viet Nam was first known to the western world as *Cochin-China*. It has been called *Giao Chi* or *Chiao Chi,** *Nam Viet* and *An Nam* for about 4,000 years, its boundaries varying from time to time. Early Chinese history refers to this area during the reign of Emperor Yao, about 2,300 B.C. At that time, *Giao Chi* was a small kingdom in southwest China. In 1,121 B.C., during the 6th year of Emperor Cheng, in the Chou Dynasty, a prince from *Giao Chi* or *Nam Viet* (meaning South Viet) came to ancient Cathay to pay tribute to the Chinese Emperor. When the Viet prince could not find his way back to his native land, the Duke of Chou presented him with a mariner's compass to guide him safely home.

The first Emperor of the Tsin dynasty, the Great Dictator of China (247-221 B.C.), conquered Viet Nam. His suzerainty was lost after the death of his son. In 183 B.C. a Chinese duke named Chao Tao proclaimed himself the Emperor of Viet Nam, but his troops were defeated by the Vietnamese. Chao Tao then sent his own son to win the confidence of the Viet king. A Vietnamese princess fell in love with the Chinese prince, and from her he learned the secret weapon of the Vietnamese troops—poisoned arrows. These were then used by the Chinese to defeat the Viet Army. The international romance ended with the resentment of the Viet people. As a result of Chao Tao's victory, Viet Nam found itself dominated again by the self-proclaimed Emperor of Viet Nam.

By the year 30 A.D. the Viet King paid tribute to the Chinese emperor. Chinese influence on the politics and culture of that part of the world had commenced. In 98 A.D. General Ma Yuan, also known as General Ma Fu Po, directed a large expeditionary force against Viet Nam. Relations between these two ancient countries were usually friendly, but the courts often plotted and warred against each other. In the third century A.D. Viet Nam became known as the *Prefecture of Giao Chi,* a term that lasted for several centuries. The name *An Nam,* for what is now the general area of

* *Giao Chi* or *Chiao Chi* was an ancient term referring to the area in southwest Cathay where the people wore sandals separating the big toe from the others. It means "big, separated, but still attached toes." Some writers speculate that the people who lived in that area were referred to as living in the "toe of the Asian mainland," a term similar to calling Italy the "boot of Europe."

both North and South Viet Nam, was first used during the Tang dynasty (629-957). *An Nam* means "Safety South" or "Peaceful South." It replaced the former names of *Giao Chi* or *Nam Viet*.

In the 12th and 13th centuries, during the Sung dynasty, there were about twelve independent kingdoms in what later became known as *Indo-China*. Each ruler tried to dominate the others. Some of them invaded Southwest China, particularly Kwangtung, Kwangsi, and Yunnan provinces. When China faced internal troubles, An Nam was often treated as an independent state. During the Mongol or Yuan Dynasty (1278 to 1346) under Ghengis Khan, the Mongol-Chinese forces again invaded An Nam. But these expeditionary forces in An Nam did not last long in Viet Nam, and Viet Nam maintained her autonomy. During the Ming dynasty (1370 to 1663), there were more armed conflicts between China and An Nam. Chinese forces invaded such areas as Hanoi and Tonkin Bay, and the An Namese forces occupied parts of the Kwangsi, Kwangtung, and Yunnan provinces of China.

An Nam at times included both North and South Viet Nam. But when France assumed her protectorates in Indo-China, Viet Nam was divided into three parts for administrative purposes. These were Tonkin, An Nam, and Cochin-China. Tonkin means "East Capital," the old name for Hanoi. An Nam was the central part of what is South Viet Nam today. Its capital was at Hue. Later Cochin-China covered the southern part of modern Viet Nam. In other words, when France controlled Indo-China she controlled all of the present North and South Viet Nam, plus Laos and Cambodia.

France governed on the principle of conquer, divide and rule. She divided Viet Nam, keeping it in two or three divisions from 1885 to 1945. The division between North and South was between the 16th and 17th parallel. Although Japan occupied Indo-China during World War II, Emperor Bao Dai united Tonkin and Cochin-China under the name of the Vietnamese Empire in March, 1945. This nominal unity of Viet Nam lasted only a few months. Bao Dai was forced to abdicate on August 24, 1945, and Ho Chi Minh declared himself President of the *Democratic Republic of Viet Nam.* It was not until September, 1945, that France was able to return to Indo-China. By then Ho Chi Minh had been able to entrench his forces in Hanoi, and Viet Nam was again divided into two separate countries. Some Chinese Nationalist forces were fighting against Ho Chi Minh, but they withdrew at the insistence of France. The French felt they could drive Ho Chi Minh out of the North in short order.

In South Viet Nam the French forces controlled Saigon and many of the cities and villages. But there was much opposition to French colonialism, particularly on the part of Cao Dai and the Hoa Hao religious sects. Later the Hoa Hao elements cooperated with the French. After World War II, Ho Chi Minh pretended that he was not a Communist but a patriot against colonialism. He called his group the "Viet Minh," meaning "Alliance of the Viets." The Viet Minh was the predecessor of the Viet Cong. Ho Chi Minh had been a Marxist since before 1920, and never ceased to be one. His forces did not extend to the southern part of Viet Nam from 1941 to 1954, because that area was principally under Japanese and then French protection. In June, 1954, Ngo Dinh Diem became Prime Minister of the State of Viet Nam. Due to his stern measures against Communist infiltration and subversion, South Viet Nam enjoyed a certain order and stability. This did not mean there were no Communist troubles in that part of the world, but between 1954 and 1962, South Viet Nam was much more stable than it has been since.

3. *America's First Diplomatic Mission to Cochin-China* (1832-1833).

By the early 19th century Great Britain had extended her influence in India, and by 1826 she had signed a treaty with Siam. It was the age of colonialism, and France was also extending her influence in Indo-China very rapidly. The United States, too, became interested in Cochin-China. Her first diplomatic mission to East Asia was in 1832.[1] Edmund Roberts, a former consul, was sent by the American Government to negotiate treaties with Cochin-China and Siam.[2] His negotiations with the authorities of Cochin-China were of no avail.*

The failure of this first American diplomatic mission to East Asia was due to the following factors:

i. The letter by President Andrew Jackson, which Roberts carried, was addressed to the King of Cochin-China, when it should have been addressed to the Emperor.

ii. When the Vietnamese officials suggested to Roberts that he write a letter to the Minister of Foreign Affairs, Commerce and Navigation, he told them that the wording they suggested

* The United States sent Caleb Cushing to China in 1843-1844, and sent Commodore Matthew C. Perry to Japan in 1852-1854. The U. S. succeeded in signing a treaty with China in 1844, with Japan in 1854, and with Korea in 1882.

was humiliating. They explained that it was merely the Oriental manner of courtesy.

iii. Roberts drafted his own letter to the Minister of Foreign Affairs, Commerce and Navigation at Hue, asking for an interview with the Emperor of Cochin-China "with the least possible loss of time." The Minister's deputies asked Roberts to state his purpose in asking for an audience with the Emperor. They also requested a Chinese translation of President Jackson's letter to the Emperor. Roberts' representative, a Mr. Morrison, replied that "letters of the rulers of Nations ought not to be read by their Ministers."

iv. Morrison insisted that the letter to the Emperor could not be opened, but must be carried directly to the Emperor at Hue, or be carried back to the President.

v. Roberts then denounced the Vietnamese officials as "rude" and "uncivil," criticizing their lack of cooperation. The Cochin-Chinese officials maintained that certain etiquette, protocol and customs should be respected. They pointed out that any envoy from a foreign country should do business through officials deputized by the Emperor, and should not directly approach the Emperor himself merely by sending the Emperor a letter, without revealing the real purpose of the Imperial visit.

vi. Roberts finally secured a Chinese translation of his letter and revealed the purpose of his mission, but the contents of President Jackson's letter to the Emperor were not revealed, so the Cochin-Chinese deputies declined to forward President Jackson's letter to the Emperor.

vii. When the Vietnamese officials asked whether or not Roberts had complied with the usual sign of respect in East Asia by bringing a gift for the Emperor, Roberts refused to answer.

viii. The native officials told Roberts that he should *kow tow* to the Emperor, i.e., touch the ground with his forehead as a sign of respect. He strongly objected to this. For these reasons Roberts was not permitted to go to Hue, and the first efforts by the United States to make a treaty in East Asia ended in failure. Roberts did succeed, however, in making treaties in Siam on March 20 and in Muscat on September 21, 1833, on behalf of the United States.

The Roberts mission proved that as early as 1832 the United States was interested in establishing friendly relations and commercial intercourse with the area later to be known as French Indo-China.[3]

4. Early French Influence in Indo-China

The first missionaries to Indo-China were French Jesuits who arrived in 1615. No description of French colonization of Indo-China would be complete without mention of Monsignor Pigneau de la Behaine, Bishop of Adran (1741-1799). As a member of the Society of Foreign Missions of France, he was sent to the Far East at the age of 25. He arrived in Ha Tien, Southwest Viet, in 1767, and was appointed Bishop of Adran in 1770, but actually consecrated in 1773. He returned to Cochin-China in 1775, after the ban of 1750 against foreign religions was lifted. He published his first catechism in Vietnamese that same year.

This scholarly and politically oriented Bishop of Adran met Nguyen Anh, a young Prince of Cochin-China in 1777. Shortly after there was a revolt against the Court of Nguyen. By hiding the young prince in his purser's office, he saved him from massacre. He then sent him to the Gulf of Siam. The prince regained his throne, and since Bishop Pigneau had gained his confidence, whatever advice he gave the prince was usually accepted. In 1784, the prince, who was now Emperor, authorized him to negotiate an agreement with France for military support by promising to pay for it. In February, 1795, the Bishop of Adran returned from Pondicherry, then French India, to Cochin-China, as French Ambassador. As King of Cochin-China, the former prince was happy to receive this priest-diplomat as the French Ambassador to his court. The Emperor had so much confidence in Bishop Pigneau that he allowed him to teach and take care of his five-year-old son, Prince Canh.

The newly appointed French Ambassador did not get the necessary support from his higher authority in Pondicherry, so he went to Paris to appeal in person in 1786. From February, 1786, to November, 1787, he argued his case in the ante-chambres of the French King. His eloquence and determination obtained what he needed for Cochin-China. He argued that if France succeeded in influencing Cochin-China, "France would be able to dominate the Seas of China and the Archipelago", as well as "the commerce of this part of the world." He was finally authorized by the French Court to become "Royal Commissioner of France for Cochin-China," with a Treaty of Alliance between the King of France and the King of Cochin-China.

As a result of Bishop Pigneau's negotiations, Cochin-China agreed to give France the port of Tourane and the island of Poulo Condore, plus the privileges of freedom of religion and freedom of trade in Cochin-China. After four days, however, the French Minister of Foreign Affairs secretly instructed the Governor of Pondicherry not to furnish Bishop Pigneau with the necessary military aid for the Cochin-China campaign. He did not inform Pigneau of this until more than a year later, in April, 1789. The determined Episcopal diplomat reportedly replied: "I shall make the revolution in Cochin-China alone." He had the support of French merchants and volunteers, and was able to secure two ships with weapons for carrying on the expeditions. Meanwhile the French Revolution, which began in July, 1789, caused the French Government to take a new look at its policy in Indo-China.

With little French military advice and weapons, Pigneau's protege succeeded in winning battle after battle, and the Nguyen Dynasty crushed the rival Tay Son Family. By 1802 both Hue and Hanoi were under the domain of the victor, who proclaimed himself Emperor of Cochin-China under the name of Gia Long. Bishop Pigneau's thirty-two years in that country allowed him to play an exceptionally important role in the government, and in Viet Nam's subsequent relations with France.

Bishop Pigneau's pupil, Prince Canh, died twenty years before his father did. After Emperor Gia Long's death, his immediate successor, Minh Mang (1820-1841) became anti-Christian and anti-foreign, after the waves of European encroachment in the Far East. The Vietnamese Government feared the growing French influence, and the Court asked the French missionaries to leave. Relations worsened as Emperor Thieu Tri came to the throne (1841-1847). He insisted that all French and Spanish missionaries leave Viet Nam. Some he persecuted; others he killed.

Spain then joined France in sending expeditionary forces to An Nam in retaliation. This precipitated the French conquest of that part of the world, which was just the opposite of what the various Cochin-China emperors had hoped for. By 1862, An Nam was forced to sign a treaty with France, ceding three Eastern Provinces and an island to her. The right of foreign missionaries to work in Cochin-China was also conceded.

An Nam (Viet Nam) was then a vassal of China, but China faced internal troubles herself, especially the Taiping Rebellion, and had been repeatedly defeated by various western powers. For several years the courageous An Namese continued to resist further French encroachments, but by 1867 France occupied from Hue in the north to Saigon in the south. Finally the An Namese Emperor felt compelled to recognize French authority in that area. By 1868 France extended west of An Nam, setting up the protectorate of Cambodia. In 1874, France was given the right to navigate the Red River leading into Hanoi, with special privileges in that area. By 1884, France took the Red River delta, forcing the An Namese Emperor to accept the French protectorate.

During the French military campaign against An Nam, Chinese forces under General Liu Yi (Liu Yung Fu) helped fight the French invaders, defeating them at Hanoi. France, in retaliation, increased its troops and crushed the Chinese general's forces. From October, 1884, to May, 1885, undeclared war existed between France and China. A group in Peking under Li Hung-chang favored "peace at any price," and insisted on making peace with France. China requested the mediation of the United States, but France rejected it.

G. Detring, a British national serving in the Chinese Government as "Commissioner of Customs in Canton," talked with the French naval command on the war situation between China and France. Detring urged the Viceroy at Canton to cable Li, asking him to urge the Chinese Court to make peace with France. Li instructed Detring to go to Peking with M. Fournier, the French naval commander, who was given credentials *ad hoc* by the French Government. These two negotiators met and signed the Li-Fournier Provisional Truce Agreement on May 11, 1884, with the understanding that a more detailed treaty would be signed later. Before this could be negotiated, fighting broke out between the Chinese and French forces. Both the Chinese and the French accused each other of violating this agreement, and while fighting was going on, a provisional agreement was finally signed which called for the cessation of hostilities between the Chinese and the An Namese on the one hand, and the French on the other. The French Minister at Peking, M. Patenotre, signed a separate agreement at Hue with the Vietnamese Foreign Minister, Nguyen van Tuong, on June 6, 1884. This agreement legally and factually made An Nam a French protectorate. Article I stated that "An Nam recognizes and accepts the protectorate of France. France shall represent An Nam in all her foreign relations. An Namites abroad shall be placed under the protection of France." [5] France next made peace with China on June 9, 1885. This peace treaty provided that An Nam no longer remained a Chinese vassal state, but a French protectorate.

With Viet Nam and Cambodia now French protectorates, France next occupied Laos, adding her as a protectorate in

1893. All these territories formed French Indo-China. These colonies were of great strategic importance to France, and they also proved profitable. Viet Nam was by far the largest and most populous colony in the whole of Indo-China, containing 70 to 75 percent of its total population. It was also the richest in agricultural and mineral resources.

5. *The Geopolitical Factors in Indo-China*

How did geographers and political writers come to call the southeastern part of this huge peninsula in Southeast Asia "Indo-China?" It is situated somewhat between India and China, particularly as far as sea routes are concerned, and in the centuries before Christ there may have been rumors or reports of a land beyond India yet not part of China, a land easily known because it was so accessible by water.

The first European exploration of "Indo-China" was made by Mendez Pinto, a Portuguese in 1540. The first Frenchman to set foot on the Mekong delta was M. Louvet, forty years later. After French exploration and conquest had been completed in 1885, it was controlled by the Colonial Office in Paris. A governor-general was put in charge, with residences in both Saigon and Hanoi. Under the governor-general were the provincial or prefectural governors living at the provincial headquarters: Hanoi for Tonkin; Hue for An Nam; Luang Prabang for Laos; Pnom-penh for Cambodia; and Saigon for Cochin-China.

More than half of the French Indo-China area is mountainous, with mountain chains that tend to run from the northwest to the southeast. Along the Chinese frontiers adjoining Kwangsi and Yunnan are the mountains of Tonkin. The highest peak is 7,880 feet. The An Nam cordillera is composed of ranges and plateaus. The mountains still obstruct communications between the Mekong River and the east coast of South Viet Nam, with peaks as high as 10,000 feet. Cambodia's mountains reach only 4,150 feet. The plains of Indo-China are partly in the interior and partly along the sea coast. The interior plains lie along the Mekong River, mostly in Cambodia but partially in Laos. Coastal plains are found in North and South Viet Nam.

In north Viet Nam, the Red River and its tributary, the Black River, cover an area of 5,400 square miles. Hanoi is at the head of the Red River delta, with a 15-foot elevation. Floods there rise to 35 feet, and dikes are employed to protect the lowlands.

The Mekong River, one of the ten largest in the world,

originates in Tibet. Its delta in South Viet Nam covers 26,000 square miles. The coast range separates the Mekong basin from the numerous short streams that flow into the South China Sea. The Saigon River accommodates ocean-going ships as far as Saigon, 40 miles up-river.

Saigon, the former capital of Cochin-China, is the present capital of the Republic of Viet Nam. It was formerly a twin city with Cholon, but they have recently merged into a metropolis of two million people. The French had planned it for a maximum of one-half million.

Hanoi, the former capital of Tonkin, is now capital of the *Democratic Republic of Viet Nam,* the headquarters of the Viet Communists. They control both the government of the North and the "National Liberation Front," a political and military arm of the Communists in South Viet Nam. Hanoi is about 60 miles inland from the port of Haiphong, in the Gulf of Tonkin. In 1902 the capital of Indo-China was moved from Saigon to Hanoi. Most of the industries and factories built by the French were centered around this capital city. Until the end of World War II, Saigon and the whole of South Viet Nam had very little industry. French withdrawal in 1954 left North Viet Nam far more industrialized than the South.

Viet Nam is the heart of Southeast Asia. It borders on China, Thailand, Laos, and Cambodia. Viet Nam is of strategic importance to every country interested in the Pacific. It can be used by an unfriendly power for aggressive purposes in every direction. The area itself is rich in such agricultural products as rice, rubber, hemp, copra, tea, coconuts, timber, and vegetable oils. It contains coal, iron, tin, tungsten, chromite, bauxite, and other mineral resources in abundance. Fishing is also a principal income for the natives in this area.

Viet Nam, Laos, and Cambodia occupy about 285,000 square miles, and have a population of about 38 million. Between 30 and 32 million of these are in Viet Nam, North and South. The Vietnamese, like the Chinese, are of Mongoloid origin. They mainly follow the pattern of Chinese culture and mode of living. French colonization lasted about seventy years, and its influence on the culture was very strong. French is still widely spoken, and in the Republic of Viet Nam, most government officials still speak French.

Among the Vietnamese people themselves there are certain differences between the Northerners and the Southerners. The average Northerner is a little taller, lighter-skinned, and more energetic than the average Southerner. Of course, there are many exceptions. The principal written language was Chinese, as far back as the Chin Dynasty (211-207 B.C.). In 1832-1833, when Edmund Roberts presented President Jackson's letter to the Emperor of Cochin-China, the Imperial officers insisted on a Chinese translation. This practice continued until the early part of the 20th century. After the French occupation in 1885, the Vietnamese still used the Chinese language as their own. Even during the French colonial period, both French and Chinese were used as the official languages and in official documents.

The first catechism was in Latin and *Quoc Ngu,* the spoken national language. It was printed in Rome in 1649. This was the work of the great French linguist, Father Alexander of Rhodes (1591-1660), who also published the first Vietnamese-Latin-Portuguese dictionary. *Quoc Ngu* was a revolutionary linguistic invention for the Vietnamese. It freed the Vietnamese people from the difficulties of the Chinese written language, and was the result of the collective efforts of the Portuguese and Italian Jesuits. Father Rhodes perfected it, and employed it as a means of communication between the Confucian mandarins and the Catholic missionaries in order to teach the Vietnamese people.

In 1895 a dictionary was published in both the Chinese and Viet languages. The present Vietnamese language is similar to the Chinese. It is monosyllabic, but its grammar has been subject to both Chinese and French influences. The Chinese written characters have been largely replaced by the Romanized alphabet of the Viet language.

The social customs and manner of living of the Vietnamese people, both North and South, were quite similar to those of the Chinese people in the Kwangtung, Kwangsi, and Yunnan Provinces before the Communist take-over. Their diet, cooking, houses, lodging, and manner of dressing are essentially the style of old China. By and large, the Vietnamese adhere to Confucian ethical codes. Professor Russell H. Fifield wrote that in Viet Nam or An Nam, "the degree of Chinese influence was so pronounced that the people actually became Sinified." [6] It is inaccurate to say that the majority of the Vietnamese are Buddhists, because there are no accurate statistics about Buddhists in North and South Viet Nam, and anyone can claim that he is a Buddhist or a Buddhist monk.

During the 70 years of French rule in Indo-China, the French did not govern as well as the British might have. France did make substantial cultural contributions and certain material progress, as well as providing a strong Christian influence. Thousands of Vietnamese studied in France, and some good French schools and hospitals were built in Indo-China. The French constructed a system of highways and railroads, and established water supplies, electricity, telephones and postal service. But even these were mediocre.

The French made no serious effort to train the Vietnamese to manage their own government, and did not strive very diligently to improve their mode of living. The French colonialists, with some exceptions, were primarily interested in commerce, in their plantations, and in strengthening France's position in Indo-China. Gambling, opium dens, and prostitution were legally established in Viet Nam, and flourished particularly in the main cities of Saigon-Cholon, Hue, and Hanoi. Other illegal traffic was sanctioned by the French colonizers, and political and moral corruption were common. This was the picture from 1885 to 1954, and these myriad evils caused the Vietnamese to despise French rule.

In World War I, French Indo-China furnished France with both manpower and war material to resist the Germans. After the Nazi attack on Poland led to the Anglo-French declaration of war against Germany, the American Government tried every possible way to keep French Indo-China from being used by the Axis powers for aggression in Asia. This effort was not entirely successful, but Japan did recognize the technical independence of the Bao Dai Government until 1944. Japan used Saigon and other parts of Viet Nam, however, as a springboard for conquering Malaya, Singapore, the Philippines, and the Dutch East Indies. She also made a puppet state out of Siam. During the Japanese occupation of Indo-China there was unrest and open rebellion against Japan. The Chinese and Vietnamese Communists took full advantage of this situation to further the cause of Communism under the guise of nationalism and liberation. The strategic importance of French Indo-China has been fully borne out in two world wars.

Concerning Viet Nam, the political division of North and South has been repeatedly recognized by Ho Chi Minh himself. Since Ho Chi Minh proclaimed himself President of the *Democratic Republic of Viet Nam* in September, 1945, his control and jurisdiction never extended to the South, although the Viet Communist guerrilla forces existed there. From the autumn of 1945 to the beginning of 1946, French forces regained their control in the South. But in March, 1946, France gave provisional recognition to Ho Chi Minh as the President of North Viet Nam. In December, 1947, the former An Namese Emperor became Chief of State of Viet Nam, which was somewhat autonomous in Saigon's internal affairs.

In 1950, when the State of Viet Nam officially became a member of the French Union, Ho Chi Minh did not lodge a protest. Ho Chi Minh and his regime tacitly admitted the independence of South Viet Nam. The Geneva Agreements of July, 1954, which were signed by a delegate of Ho Chi Minh, openly and officially recognized the political division of Viet Nam at the 17th parallel, pending a national election under international supervision for a possible unification of Viet Nam, North and South. The Republic of Viet Nam existed as a quasi-independent state from 1947, and as a completely independent state from 1954. Fifty-two nations have given *de jure* recognition to South Viet Nam, while eight have given *de facto* recognition. Troops from the Republic of Korea, Australia, New Zealand, Thailand, and the United States are helping the Vietnamese fight for their freedom. The Republic of China has offered troops. Material or technical aid is being given to South Viet Nam by more than 30 countries, particularly the Republic of China, West Germany, Japan, and the Philippines, in addition to the United States.

6. *South Viet Nam Today*

South Viet Nam is 700 miles long, with a coastline of 1,500 miles. It is 40 miles wide at the north and 120 miles wide in the south. It is bordered by the South China Sea on the east, and by the Gulf of Siam on the south. It has a 1,000 mile border on Laos and Cambodia. North Viet Nam would have had to give up long ago, had the Communists not taken most of Laos after the U.S. negotiated for its "neutralization" in 1962. Most of the infiltration since then has come through Laos, with the close cooperation of the *Pathet Lao*, the Communist forces in Laos, which are also directed by Ho Chi Minh.

The population of South Viet Nam today is between 14 and 15 million. Eight million people live in the Mekong delta area, south and west of Saigon. There, too, is the heaviest concentration of Viet Cong, although substantial progress has been made in 1965 and 1966 in uprooting them. The Mekong plain rises only one foot every 20 miles, and much of the area is inundated much of the time. There is a 12-month growing season, with three or four crops a year. The country supplies more than enough food for all its inhabitants. Four years ago South Viet Nam was exporting 300,000 tons of rice each year. The United States now imports 100,000 tons of rice annually, as internal transportation is so disrupted by the Viet Cong. They can ambush almost any road in the country, and if they do let trucks pass it is often only after payment of "taxes" to the Communists. Such taxes are paid even on supplies shipped to American bases.

The delta is intensely cultivated, especially with wet rice. The Communist troops in that area have an abundant food supply. They move freely on the 2,500 miles of waterways, attacking mostly at night. All over the country, much of the land is held by the government in the day time, and taken over by the Viet Cong at night.

Two million people live in the Saigon area, about 40 percent of them Catholic. Another three million people live along the coastal plain north of Saigon. They depend mainly on the sea for food, plus rice from the delta. Only 500,000 live in the central inland part of the country north of Saigon to the 17th parallel. West of them, on high plateau area, live one million Montagnards in a semi-primitive state. At least ten thousand of these are Protestant. Roads throughout the country are scarce, particularly in the northern areas. The roads as well as their users are subject to Viet Cong attack at any time. The *White Paper*,[7] published by the State Department in the spring of 1965, as well as much of the evidence since, has established the fact that most of the Viet Cong weapons were furnished by Red China. There are no Viet Cong who are not under the command of North Viet Nam. Recent reports indicate that Red Chinese Commissars are working in every Viet Cong regular regiment in South Viet Nam, and Peking has increased its military and economic help to the Viet Cong. The Hanoi regime, largely through its political arm, the National Liberation Front, is doing everything it possibly can to conquer South Viet Nam, which is a highly strategic area.

The next step in Communist aggression will be to take Cambodia, Thailand, the one-third of Laos that Hanoi has not already seized, and then other areas in Southeast Asia, all of which are an essential part of the Communist program to take over the free world. The American, British, and other statesmen who keep trying to get Soviet Russia on the side of the free world seem to ignore the fact that Moscow is closely tied to the Communist world, that she considers the free nations her only real enemy, and that she is helping North Viet Nam just as much as Peking is. The U.S.S.R. has sent thousands of weapons to the Viet Cong, and sufficient anti-aircraft artillery have already shot down more than 250 U. S. and South Vietnamese planes. The SAM missiles Russia has given Hanoi are among the most modern in the world.

She has also provided Soviet technicians to operate them effectively.

Through Presidents Eisenhower, Kennedy, and Johnson, the United States has repeatedly promised to aid the *Republic of Viet Nam* in preserving her territorial integrity and the right of her people to self-determination. Though not a signatory of the Geneva Agreements of 1954, the United States has declared that any violation of the terms of the agreements would be considered by her as a threat to the peace and security of the world. The Southeast Asia Treaty Organization, in September, 1954, also provided for the protection of the free state of Viet Nam, collectively and individually.

The Joint Congressional Resolution of August 10, 1965, Public Law 88-408, has authorized the President of the United States "to take all necessary steps, including the use of armed force, to assist any member or protocol state of the Southeast Asia Collective Defense Treaty requesting assistance in defense of its freedom." By the commitments of its presidents, by its treaty obligations, as well as by acts of Congress, the United States is bound to help the Republic of Viet Nam repel aggression in that very stragetic area of the world.

The defense of Viet Nam is not only a matter of concern to the people of Viet Nam themselves, it is of the utmost importance for the peace, order, and security of the world. Secretary of State Dean Rusk, on December 14, 1965, told the NATO Council that Europe's fate may be decided by the outcome of the war in Viet Nam. The war there has brought about certain differences in opinion among the nations of the free world, and even among the American people themselves. The world stands at the crossroads in Viet Nam.

FOOTNOTES

CHAPTER I: VIET NAM: ITS HISTORY AND GEOPOLITICS

1. Tyler Dennett, *Americans in Eastern Asia,* (New York, rev. ed., 1963), pp. 128-129.
2. Samuel Flagg Bemis, *A Diplomatic History of the United States,* (New York, rev. ed., 1961), p. 344.
3. Edmund Roberts, *Embassy to the Eastern Courts of Cochin China, Siam, and Muscat in the U.S. Sloop-of-War Peacock,* (New York, 1937), p. 6, pp. 192-193, p. 194, pp. 197-198.
4. A. Faure, *Les Francais en Cochinchine au XVIIe Siecle: Mgr. Pigneau De Bahaine, Eveque d'Adran,* (Paris, 1891). E. Louvet, *Mgr. d'Adran, Missionnaire et Patriote,* (Paris, 1900).
5. Maritime Customs of China, *Treaties, Conventions between China*

and Foreign States, (Shanghai, 2 vols., 1917), Vol. I, pp. 885-900, pp. 908-909.

6. Russell H. Fifield, *Southeast Asia in United States Policy,* (New York, 1963), p. 7.

7. Department of State *Aggression from the North: the Record of North Viet Nam's Campaign to Conquer South Viet Nam* (Washington, February, 1965).

CHAPTER II

VIET NAM: FROM WORLD WAR II
TO DIEN BIEN PHU (1939-1954)

1. *Viet Nam in World War II.*

Viet Nam constitutes around 75 per cent of the population of Indo-China. It is rich in mineral and agricultural products, and of great strategic value. Both France and Japan attached great significance to Viet Nam during World War II. It was not only strategically important to the Japanese advance in Southeast Asia, it furnished Japan with manpower and raw materials, both mineral and agricultural. Viet Nam was France's only foothold in East Asia.

Japan's aggression in Manchuria, starting in 1931, was the actual beginning of World War II. The Japanese heralded their policy of dominating East Asia by calling it the "New Order," and the "Co-Prosperity Sphere," "Japan's Guidance," "Asia for the Asiatics," and "Pan Asia." [1] On January 22, 1934, Japan's Foreign Minister, Koki Hirota, declared that Japan "bears the entire burden of responsibility for East Asia." Indo-China, and especially Viet Nam, fell into the Japanese "Greater East Asia Co-Prosperity Sphere."

Article 2 of the German-Italian-Japanese Axis Alliance, signed on September 27, 1940, proclaimed that Germany and Italy recognized and respected the leadership of Japan in the establishment of the New Order in Greater East Asia. On the eve of the attack on Pearl Harbor, the Japanese Government, as an excuse for war, charged the American Government with obstructing Japan's efforts to establish the New Order and Co-Prosperity for Greater East Asia.

Shortly after Germany's attack on France, the Vichy regime under Marshal Pétain controlled French Indo-China. This regime tried to cooperate with the Japanese militarists in order to preserve nominal French sovereignty in that region. But since Japan had been preaching the doctrine of "Asia for the Asiatics," it was difficult for her to ask the people in Indo-China to cooperate with the French colonial-

17

ists. However, Japan technically recognized the French position in Indo-China by playing down the theme of independence, and by dealing with Admiral Jean Découx, the French Governor General in Hanoi.

In 1940, when France surrendered to Germany, the Vichy Government agreed to the Japanese military occupation of Indo-China, with the understanding that the French still continue to administer the colonies in the same way they had done previously.

The American Government was seriously concerned about the French surrender of Indo-China to the Japanese. Secretary of State Cordell Hull considered it impossible for the American Government to continue talks with the Japanese envoys if Japan insisted on keeping Indo-China in a state of military occupation. The American Government insisted that Japan should "withdraw all military and naval aid, and police forces from China and from Indo-China." [2] As early as September 22, 1940, President Roosevelt cabled Prime Minister Churchill, cautioning him that the invasion of Indo-China was imminent.[3] On December 8, 1940, Mr. Churchill pointed out that Japan was thrusting southward through Indo-China to Saigon, and that this would enable Japan to attack the Philippines, Singapore, and the Dutch East Indies.[4]

In April, 1941, Prime Minister Churchill admitted that Japanese sea and air power in Indo-China were threatening the Dutch East Indies, Siam, Malaya, Ceylon, and the Bay of Bengal.[5] On January 31, 1941, Japan negotiated an armistice with Vichy and Siam, as the Japanese Navy became increasingly active around Indo-China.

When Hitler invaded the Soviet Union in June, 1941, the Japanese Government did not have prior information, although there was a Berlin-Rome-Tokyo Axis treaty signed in April that same year. The Japanese Cabinet considered this a case of "losing face." Japan did not want to enter the German-Soviet war. The Japanese Cabinet did agree, however, "to go ahead in the southern seas and to complete the occupation of South Indo-China." [6] This occupation of Indo-China was a prelude to attacking the British and Dutch colonies in Southeast Asia.[7]

On July 21, 1941, the Vichy Government yielded to Japanese pressure for military bases in southern Viet Nam. By the end of July, Japanese forces occupied Saigon and Cam Ranh Bay. By the fall of 1941, Japan had lost 70 to 80 per cent of her trade with the United States and Great Britain. Hence she tried to create a sphere in Asia that would make her self-supporting. But when France gave Japan the right to air bases in Indo-China, Britain realized that Malaya and Singapore were seriously threatened.

2. Ho Chi Minh's Strategy

Concerning the Indo-Chinese themselves, a small but important movement for independence started there about 1925. It was begun by a small group of An Namese including a Lee Shui, or Lee Shun, whose real family name is Nguyen. He later became known as Ho Chi Minh. Lee Shui had helped found the Communist Party in 1923. In 1925 he went to Canton, China, and formed a group of about thirty people. This group was called the An Nam Revolutionary Association. A sign to this effect was put in a small apartment at Man Min Road in Canton, where the group held its meetings. Lee (Nguyen at that time) worked with Michael Borodin, a Soviet citizen of Jewish descent from New York, who was the official representative of the Soviet Union in Canton from 1925 to 1927. Borodin represented the Comintern, and was in charge of activities in South China.*

Borodin also worked closely with Chou En-Lai, Mao Tsetung, Liu Shao-Chi and other Chinese Communists in Canton.

Between 1938 and 1945, Lee Shui changed his name to Yuong Son Nhi, Houng Son, or Wong San Yi. During this time he received economic and military aid from both the National Government of China and from the Chinese Soviet Communists. From 1937 until about 1943 the Chinese Communists were still cooperating with the Chinese National Government, when it was to their advantage. Both the Nationalist Chinese and the Communist Chinese gave substantial aid to Ho Chi Minh and his followers in order to ward off the Japanese aggressors in Indo-China. By 1941, Ho's group was called the *Viet Minh*, which means "the League of Alliance of the Viet for Independence."

From 1941 to 1943, most of the aid obtained by Ho Chi Minh came from Chunking, China. Even as late as 1944, most of America's aid was going to Great Britain and the Soviet Union. But in 1944, U. S. military aid began flowing to Ho Chi Minh. Japan announced the independence of Viet Nam from the French in March, 1944. Japan declared Bao Dai, the former emperor of the French protectorate of An Nam, chief of state. The kings of Laos and Cambodia were also made chiefs of these newly independent states. The establishment of an independent Viet Nam was denounced by

*See Chapter V: Bao Dai, Ngo Dinh Diem, and Ho Chi Minh.

the Viet Minh as a "puppet government." Ho Chi Minh immediately created a "liberated zone" in the North. By so doing he hoped to seize power from the Japanese and establish his own government before the allied troops arrived.

Free France was then headed by General Charles de Gaulle. In the spring of 1945, de Gaulle announced that Viet Nam, Laos, and Cambodia would become members of the French Union, after the war. This was taken to mean that these nations would acquire a quasi-independent status. From July 17 until August 2, 1945, President Truman, Marshal Stalin, and Prime Minister Churchill (later replaced by Prime Minister Atlee) met at Potsdam. They decided that Japan must accept unconditional surrender, and that the Allies should work for the liberation of Asia through the Chinese in the North and the British in the South. This meant that the liberation of Indo-China was to be accomplished by the British under Admiral Louis Mountbattan. The French felt slighted by this, but they were powerless to recapture their former colonies.

The strongest elements of the Vietnamese liberation forces after 1944 were headed by Ho Chi Minh. He was supported for awhile by both the Chinese Nationalists and the Chinese Communists, and later by the United States. In September, 1945, just after the Allied victory in Asia, Britain and the United States helped France reestablish her authority in Indo-China. Meanwhile the Chinese Nationalist troops were occupying many parts of Viet Nam, both North and South. But they were asked to withdraw in favor of the British and French. A vacuum was left behind which enabled the Viet Communists to control most of North Viet Nam. Ho Chi Minh also sent military and political personnel to help the people in Laos and Cambodia eliminate French rule.

Through Communist sources, Ho Chi Minh was told about the imminent surrender of Japan right after the Potsdam Conference, and he organized a provisional government for Viet Nam. On September 2, 1945, Ho Chi Minh proclaimed himself the President of the "Democratic Republic of Viet Nam," just one day before the Japanese surrender took place on board the *U.S.S. Missouri*. The preamble to his declaration included the following: "All men are created equal. They are endowed by their Creator with certain inalienable rights," etc. His statement went on to condemn the French for their "political brutality and economic enslavement." Ho remained a Communist all the time. He forced Emperor Bao Dai to abdicate in favor of the Provisional Government of Viet Nam.

France recognized Cambodia's autonomy under the herditary monarch on January 7, 1946. China agreed on February 28, to withdraw her forces from Indo-China completely. On March 6, General de Gaulle agreed to recognize Viet Nam as a free state within the French Union, and French troops were to re-enter the northern part of Viet Nam. On August 27, Laos succeeded in obtaining recognition of its autonomy. None of the three states of the French Union— Viet Nam, Laos, and Cambodia—were really independent. While French forces were re-entering North Viet Nam, Ho Chi Minh went to Paris to see General de Gaulle. He had arranged for a *modus vivendi* with France in September 1946. It was his last agreement with France until the Geneva Conference in 1954.

Ho Chi Minh called his group the *Association for the Study of Marxism*. He continued to lead the Communist Party in Viet Nam secretly. After obtaining a temporary agreement with France, he reverted openly to the use of the name *Viet Minh*. He also used *Lao Dong* (the Workers Party).

Ho Chi Minh returned to Hanoi in 1946 as a hero. He had convinced France to give provisional recognition to his *Democratic Republic of* Viet Nam. He advocated less taxes and no forced labor. He promised more food, better housing, better schools, and medical care for the people. Above all, he promised to give everybody land. He soon began to attack French military installations, and accused the French of violating their pledges. By December, 1946, he increased his attacks on the French wherever he could. The French began to realize that Ho Chi Minh was not merely an agrarian reformer but a strong Communist leader who was supported continually by both the Soviet and the Chinese Communists.

By 1947, France wanted to fight Ho Chi Minh, but she was doomed to failure. First of all, France was fighting as a colonial power to suppress the national feelings of the Vietnamese for independence. The latter not only wanted independence, but were led by a well-organized Communist Party with international support. France was hardly strong enough at that time to win a war in Viet Nam. The Communists, together with the doctrinaire liberals throughout the world, condemned the French actions in Viet Nam as opposing the Vietnamese in what was called a "war of liberation." America was soon to be engaged in the Berlin Airlift, which served as a diversionary tactic. In additon, the Chinese Communists, with Soviet military aid, were fighting decisive battles in Manchuria and North China. Viet

Nam was not Amerca's principal concern. Last but not least, American aid given to France to resist the Viet Communist threat was too late and too little. In the fall of 1949, The Chinese Communists made rapid advances on China's mainland. By October they occupied the Yunnan, Kwangtung, and Kwangsi provinces, all of which are adjacent to the borders of Viet Nam. The loss of China to the Communists radically altered the balance of power between the Communist and the democratic countries. It created a very favorable situation for the Communists in Viet Nam, both militarily and politically. Indirectly, this was a fatal blow to the French forces who were fighting there.

After the establishment of the "People's Republic of China" on October 1, 1949, Ho Chi Minh appealed to Mao Tse-tung for more military aid. In 1950, the Chinese Communist Chairman sent General Lo Kwei-po as military adviser to the Viet Cong army. Many types of experts from Communist China served in Hanoi and other Viet Minh cities. Red China also supplied the Viet Minh with foodstuffs, arms, and ammunition. Large numbers of Viet Minh officers went to Communist China to receive political and military training.[8] With the advance of Mao Tse-tung's army on South China, "Vu Hong Khanh formed an army of ten thousand men, most of whom were Chinese, and led them to Viet nam." [9]

The Chinese Communist general directed the Viet Minh forces to attack the rear of the French forces in Viet Nam and Laos, as they lay behind the protection of the An Namese mountain chains. The French made aerial bombardments with napalm, inflicting heavy losses on the Viet Minh. But the Red Chinese Command advised the Viet Minh forces to change their strategy. They attempted to lure the French into jungle fighting, using favorable geographical settings.

In December, 1950, the French persuaded Bao Dai to resume the role of chief of state in South Viet Nam, with headquarters in Saigon. By this time Bao Dai had become a notorious playboy, and was no match for the cunning of Ho Chi Minh in Hanoi. Soviet Russia, Red China, and most of the Communist bloc had already recognized Ho's regime in the North, and the United States hastened to recognize South Viet Nam and the kingdoms of Laos and Cambodia as independent states within the French Union. Some American economic aid and a small amount of military assistance was sent to the new government under Bao Dai.

When Bao Dai again assumed the position of chief of

state of Viet Nam, he was more interested in his own pleasures and enjoyment than in the well-being of his people. His administration soon became known for its corruption. The black market was rampant, and the old ways of life under the French administration were resumed. Bao Dai left the fighting of the Viet Cong forces to the French. He tried to gain more independence from France but his efforts brought little fruit. Meanwhile, both French and Vietnamese soldiers were dying in battle, and the Viet Cong forces were terrorizing the countryside. Both Bao Dai and the French officials were much too complacent. They refused to believe that the poorly equipped Viet Cong could possibly overcome the superior forces of France.

Bao Dai tried to acquire more independence from France, but his efforts with the French Government did not produce much fruit. His government remained far from independent. This semi-autonomous rule was condemned by Ho Chi Minh and his followers as subjugation to France. French complacency and the lack of support of Bao Dai's government gave many advantages to Ho Chi Minh's regime.

Ho Chi Minh and his fellow Communists seized their opportunity and aroused the people against the Bao Dia Government. They followed the pattern of the Chinese Communists, using the formula:

(1) "fight, fight, talk, talk, and fight," and

(2) "two steps forward, one step backward, one step sideward and another step forward in order to advance."

The Viet Minh wore down the resistance of the people to Communism, at the same time building up in the people a hostility to colonialism.

Familiar with conventional warfare, the French still believed in the Maginot Line type of defense, despite its utter failure against Hitler's armies. They did not realize that the Communists had adopted a new type of warfare, one that was without a front, yet had a front everywhere; a war of attrition, subversion and terror. This new face of war also involved religion, psychology, politics, economics, and the whole gamut of culture. It is a completely unconventional type of war, and is deliberately designed to frustrate modern forces.

The guerrillas retreat any time it is to their advantage. They do not engage in competitive firepower unless they feel sure to win. They avoid getting pinned down. They achieve local victories by surprise and terror. They trade in casualties if it is to their advantage. The number of guerrillas killed or wounded is not of prime importance to them. Evaluation has

23

to be made in their terms. More men, more supplies, less lives lost, will not win by themselves. What is more important is winning over the civilians, for they supply the enemy with food, intelligence, and potential recruits.

Mob demonstrations are helpful to the Communists, especially if they turn into riots and bloodshed. Death arouses sympathy, and that is what they want most of all. The communists expended lives callously, but hatred was stirred up against the French and Bao Dai. Then armed attacks were launched. The step sideward had gone forward.

The war of liberation is a combination of invisible Communist spies, saboteurs, terrorists, propagandists, political commissars, military experts, technicians, patriot, liberals, and common soldiers. This is the type of war that was fought against the French and which is now being fought against the South Vietnamese and the Americans. It stresses propaganda to win the hearts of the people. A battle costs lives and equipment, whereas propaganda costs very little and is often far more effective.

Mao Tse-tung has said that he would never fight a battle he was not sure to win. Only when the enemy is suffering from attrition and weariness, and when his supply lines are weakened, does the guerrilla attack. Later the enemy may challenge his opponent, and he may finally launch a counter-offensive that will bring victory. But it is more likely that he will merely force his enemy to the conference table, in order to win his final battle there. This was clearly demonstrated at Dien Bien Phu in 1954. The French still had the military power to continue to fight, but they preferred to negotiate because of internal weakness and lack of international sympathy and support.

The Chinese Communists have had over forty years of experience, and they have passed on this experience to the Communists in Viet Nam. China's Reds understand the Vietnamese, and many speak their local dialects. Their plan has been to occupy more and more space, and finally to squeeze the supply lines until they become so small and sluggish that they can take them over. The large cities are only their final goal.

3. *Red China and the Viet Minh*

It is often thought that during the Korean War, from June 25, 1950, to July 27, 1953, the Viet Cong forces had to rely on their own strength to fight against the French. Actually this was not the case. While the Chinese volunteers were fighting in Korea, and while Soviet munitions were being sent to Korea, both China and Soviet Russia sent men and arms to help their fighting comrades in Hanoi. A few interesting but little-known facts are cited here as examples of Sino-Soviet assistance given to Viet Minh forces:

i. On August 20, 1950, about 150,000 Chinese soldiers, traveling in civilian clothes, arrived in Kun Ming. Yunnan Province, to help the Viet Minh. This was reported by the *Chinese United News Agency* in Hong Kong. The report was confirmed by other neutral Chinese news sources.

ii. On October 28, 1950, a news dispatch issued by the *Kwong Wah News Agency* in Hong Kong reported that two Chinese ships left Kwong Chau Wan for Haiphong, North Viet Nam, loaded with munitions for Ho Chi Minh.

iii. On June 28, 1950, the *China Tribune* of New York City reported that two ships by the names of *S.S. Kuo Tai* and *S.S. Kuo Young,* from Whang Pu, a port near Canton, Kwangtung, China, were about to leave for North Viet Nam with a load of munitions.

iv. On August 13, 1951, according to a Chinese pro-Communist newspaper in New York City, the *China Daily News,* a large Viet Cong delegation of about fifty persons went to Peking to attend the *Chinese Political Consultation Conference.* Seven hundred Chinese Communist officials greeted the Viet Minh at the train station. It was resolved at the conference that all possible aid should be give to the Viet Minh in order to make their revolution a success.

v. On August 24, 1951, the *Chinese United News Agency* in Hong Kong reported that General Lin-Piao sent his own chief-of-staff, General Shao Keh, from his mission in Korea to Nan-ning, Kwangsi Province, China, in order to establish a "Sino-Viet Minh joint staff group," with six Soviet military advisers. The mission of this joint staff was to coordinate the efforts of the Chinese and Viet Cong forces.

vi. In September, 1951, it was reported that Chinese Communist demonstrations in various parts of China advocated sending volunteers to help their comrades in Viet Nam in order to liquidate their adversaries. Editorials in several Chinese Communist newspapers said that China was powerful enough to defeat the imperialist countries on two fronts, namely the Korean and Vietnamese fronts. By September 20, Chinese Nationalist intelligence sources, as well as others, reported that 150,000 Chinese Red volunteers were ready to disguise themselves as Vietnamese and participate in the liberation of the Vietnamese people.

vii. On September 21, 1951, the *Chinese United News Agency*, Hong Kong, reported that about 450 Soviet advisers had already arrived in Viet Minh headquarters. It was known to the Chinese Nationalist intelligence sources and to others that two-thirds of the Communists were Vietnamese, the other third being Chinese Reds.

viii. On May 29, 1963, the *China Daily News* reported that Ho Chi Minh went to Peking, where he and Liu Shao-Chi, the President of the *National Congress* at Peking, issued a joint communique in which Ho Chi Minh acknowledged the previous Red Chinese aid, while the Red Chinese regime pledged its full support to the Viet Communists.

From the above quoted news dispatches it is evident that during the Korean war, while the Chinese and Soviet forces were helping the North Koreans fight the United Nations forces in Korea, the Chinese and Soviet Communists also helped the Viet Minh very extensively in their fight against the French. After the armistice in Korea had been reached, sixteen nations that had given military forces to the United Nations in its fight against the aggression in Korea feared that Chinese Communist forces might be shifted to other parts of Asia.[10] These nations signed a declaration in Washington, attached it to their report to the United Nations, and released it to the world.

The declaration stated, in part, that the Korean Armistice "must not result in jeopardizing the restoration or the safeguarding of peace in any other part of Asia." They thereby declared that they would not tolerate the shifting of Chinese Communist forces from the cease-fire in Korea to the war in Viet Nam and other parts of Indo-China. Defying the warning, Red China increased its political and military support to the Communists in Viet Nam, Laos, and Cambodia, in order to help overthrow the existing governments there. This was easy for Red China because of her geographical propinquity. Chinese Communists could easily cross the border lines of Viet Nam from several directions in Kwangsi, Kwangtung, and Yunnan provinces. They could readily supply the Viet Minh with political and military advisers and material. They could disguise themselves as natives of Viet Nam, Laos, and Cambodia without much difficulty. The United States realized the necessity of helping free nations to strengthen their defense against aggression, particularly in Indo-China. America began to supply the embattled French forces with substantial military support. This was done in accordance with the provisions of the amended Mutual Security Acts of 1949 and 1951, which provided mutual assistance, self-help, and technical assistance to Europe, the Near East, Africa, the Far East, the Pacific, and the American Republics in the New World.

While the French were trying their best to combat the Viet Minh with American aid, the Communists intensified their revolutionary warfare. With Ho Chi Minh's approval, Vo Nguyen Giap, who was trained by the Chinese Communists, divided Viet Nam into two major theaters, one in the North and the other in the South. In the North, the Viet Minh built a regular Red Army in the Red River delta (Tonkin) from 1945 to 1948. By 1949, the Viet Minh were prepared to attack the French from all directions. In 1950, Vo Nguyen Giap, as a disciple of Mao Tse-tung, wrote his military guide for the Viet Communist forces. The title of his book is *La Guerre de la Liberation et l'Armee Populaire*.* This book in fact is a revision of Mao Tse-tung's book: *Strategic Problems in the Anti-Japanese War*, published in 1938. The basic principles of the "war of liberation," as outlined by Giap, are to win the support of the people against the enemy, to consolidate the revolutionary forces, and to implement the guerrilla forces with general movements of war. The Viet Minh leader divided his strategy into three stages:

a. Passive resistance, to consolidate and increase political and military strength;
b. Active resistance, to attack all of the enemy fronts and to prepare for a counter-offensive;
c. The general counter-offensive, which is intended to defeat the enemy and make him sue for peace.

In the South, the Viet Minh spread their forces in the Mekong delta and adopted the combined tactics of passive

*Cf. Vo Nguyen Giap: *People's War, People's Army: the Viet Cong* New York, 1962; Mao Tse-tung: *On Guerrilla Warfare* New York, 1961.

and active resistance to the French up to 1954. When the Viet Minh were weak, they fought mildly in order to engage the enemy in a protracted war, and to gain time and strength. From 1945 to the beginning of 1947, the Viet Minh were engaged in the first stage of the war of liberation. But from 1947 to 1950 they entered into the second stage against the French in Viet Nam and other parts of the French Union. From 1950 to 1954, they entered into the third stage of the war, which meant they were engaged in a general counter-offensive against the French in all of the theaters of war throughout the French Union. The Viet Minh forces under Ho Chi Minh and Vo Nguyen Giap wanted to be sure of the following factors before they actually launched the general counter-offensive against the French:

(1) The absolute superiority of the revolutionary forces;
(2) Considerable improvement in their supplies;
(3) A more favorable international situation;
(4) Strong indication that the Viet Minh would win the war.

The above conditions could be improved for the Communists by consolidating their hold on the population through revolt within South Viet Nam and through propaganda abroad; through diplomatic maneuvers, strikes, and demonstrations for peace in various forms.

The French commanding forces may have known about this political-military strategy of the Viet Minh, but they could not believe it would be successful. France's General Marcel Carpentier relied mainly on mobile units for offensive operations. He was succeeded in 1950 by Marshal Jean de Lattre de Tassigny, who regrouped his troops and mobile units. His tactics in 1951 proved quite successful. He captured Hoa Binh and cut off the north-south route of the Viet Minh, causing heavy losses. Vo Nguyen Giap was then criticized by some of his comrades and by the Chinese Communists, but he consolidated his forces for future attack. The French forces held on to Hoa Binh without pressing the Viet Cong forces further.

By Ausust, 1952, the Communist Party of the *Democratic Republic of Viet Nam* admitted their mistakes at Hoa Binh, stressing the need for guerrilla warfare before they could attack the French. They further emphasized the importance of the support of the population both in the rear and within the enemy's territories. The Viet Minh wanted their own rear absolutely secure, and they wanted to create insecurity in the enemy's territories. Such tactics would serve two purposes:

i. to obtain food and supplies from the rear;
ii. to get food and information from civilians in the enemy's territory.

From 1952 to 1954, the Viet Minh tried in every way possible to indoctrinate their own people in the rear, to undermine the Bao Dai Government in Saigon by calling it a French puppet regime, and to intensify their propaganda against the French colonists in Viet Nam and other parts of the French Union. They further tried to sabotage the French war efforts, and to have the Viet Minh in both the North and South join the army of Bao Dai in order to sabotage it and cause revolt. They increased their propaganda in other parts of the world, and attacked the weaker parts of the French positions, e.g. the mountainous regions where the French forces were undermanned.

In the autumn of 1953, the French signed an agreement with Laos providing membership for Laos in the French Union. Vo Nguyen Giap tried to send troops into Laos, but this was actually a diversive action to deceive the French forces. General Henri-Eugene Navarre decided to occupy Dien Bien Phu in order to ward off the Viet Minh forces invading Laos and to create a stronghold there against the Viet Minh.

During the autumn of 1953, the United States started to realize the seriousness of the French situation in Viet Nam. American transport planes began to transport French troops from France to Viet Nam. The United States also sent in ground crews to help maintain and repair U.S. military aircraft given to the French. But such belated American effort was insufficient to turn the tide of the war in Indo-China.

The Viet Minh and the Chinese Communists learned in January, 1954, that both the French and the British were willing to attend an international conference to be held at Geneva to discuss the problems in Indo-China. The Communists wanted to win a big battle in order to put themselves in a better bargaining position. They resolved at all costs to attack the strong French position at Dien Bien Phu, in order to make conclusive political gains at the conference table. The 308th Division of the Viet Minh forces were re-routed from their original plans to go to Laos, and dispatched to surround the French at Dien Bien Phu.

On April 26, 1954, with the Geneva Conference already in session over Korea, the bloody Viet Cong assaults on the French position were intensified, with large military forces and superior gun emplacements. The French had lost about 15,000 men, but the loss of French prestige was much greater than their military defeat. Above all, the French lost heart. The defeat itself was not necessarily fatal to France. She could still have continued to fight. But France had been spending a third of her budget for the war in Viet Nam, and losing more military officers than she could replace. She simply lacked the will to continue fighting.

Red China had poised a large army near the Vietnamese border. This too was a political, military, and psychological threat to the French forces. France also knew that more American military aid was not immediately forthcoming, while further Viet Minh and Red Chinese efforts could be expected. Therefore, on May 8, 1954, the French command in Indo-China surrendered to the Viet Minh forces. This was the greatest defeat of the French since World War II. It created a threatening new international situation in Asia, a situation whose impact is still being felt, and will continue to be felt for many years.

FOOTNOTES

CHAPTER II: VIET NAM FROM WORLD WAR II TO DIEN BIEN PHU, 1954.

1. Stephen C. Y. Pan, *China Fights On,* (New York, 1945), Ch. IV: "Japan's Monroe Doctrine".
2. Cordell Hull, *The Memoirs of Cordell Hull,* (New York, 2 vols., 1948), Vol. 2, pp. 982 ff, pp. 1018-1020;
   Foreign Relations of the United States: Japan, 1931–1941, (Washington, 2 vols., 1943).
3. Anthony Eden, Earl of Avon, *The Memoirs of Anthony Eden; the Reckoning,* (Boston, 1965), p. 160.
4. Winston S. Churchill, *The Second World War: Their Finest Hour,* (Boston, 1949), p. 592.
5. *Winston S. Churchill, The Second World War: The Hinge of Fate,* (Boston, 1950), p. 172.
6. *Winston S. Churchill, The Second World War: The Grand Alliance,* (Boston, 1951), p. 194.
7. *Op. Cit.,* p. 195.
8. Von Chi Hoang, *From Colonialism to Communism: A Case History of North Viet Nam,* (New York, London, 1963), pp. 63-64.
9. *Ibid.,* p. 26.

10. The 16 nations were: Australia, Belgium, Canada, Columbia, Ethiopia, France, Greece, Luxembourg, the Philippines, Netherlands, New Zealand, Thailand, Turkey, Union of South Africa, United Kingdom, and the United States.

CHAPTER III

VIET NAM AND THE GENEVA AGREEMENTS, 1954

1. *The Background*

Following the Korean truce, in July, 1953, the Foreign Ministers of the Big Four Nations, Britain, France, the United States, and the Soviet Union, met in Berlin. They decided to call a meeting for January 25, 1954, to discuss a peaceful settlement for Korea. The meeting included Britain, Soviet Russia, the United States, the Chinese People's Republic (Red China), the People's Democratic Republic of Korea (North Korea), the Republic of Korea, and the other countries engaged in the Korean war.*

U. S. Secretary of State John Foster Dulles felt that Red China and Communist Korea should not be invited to attend, since they had been condemned by the United Nations. But Soviet Russia and the United Kingdom insisted that no peaceful settlement could be made without them. Although the United States was consistently opposed to the recognition of Red China, she had no definite policy against discussions with her. The American Government had already negotiated on many occasions with Red China without affecting its policy of non-recognition. Secretary Dulles consented to including the delegates from Peking and Pyongyang (capital of North Korea) at the conference, with the understanding that this did not imply recognition of those governments. The same theory was later applied to the Hanoi regime.

The conference started in Geneva on April 26, 1954. Nineteen nations attended the first phase, which dealt with

*These nations were: Australia, Belgium, Canada, Columbia, the Democratic People's Republic of Korea, Ethiopia, France, Greece, Luxemberg, the Netherlands, New Zealand, the People's Republic of China, the Philippines, the Republic of Korea, Thailand, Turkey, the Union of Soviet Socialist Republics, the United Kingdom, and the United States.

Korea. The discussions over Korea ended on June 15, without any agreement.

After the start of the Geneva Conference, in the latter part of April, 1954, the Indo-China war became more and more intensified, with both sides suffering heavy losses in men and material. The defeat of the French forces at Dien Bien Phu, on May 8, shocked the French public and Government. The Viet Communists had also suffered severely, but the morale of the French was even more injurious than their military disaster. The French had lost their spirit and will to carry on the war. With them it had never been a fight on behalf of the free world against Communism, but merely a struggle to impose a firm grip on their former colony. As soon as the defeat at Dien Bien Phu was known at the Conference, the delegates began to discuss Viet Nam and Indo-China as a whole. Most of these discussions were conducted informally and in secret. The proceedings were also kept in great confidence and secrecy. Only part of them have ever been published. Delegates from Red China, South Viet Nam, Communist Viet Nam, Laos, and Cambodia were included in the discussions, in addition to the Big Four: the United States, Great Britain, France, and the U.S.S.R.

The principal conferees were men of great experience in diplomatic and military affairs. Soviet Russia was represented by V. M. Molotov. Even he was overshadowed by Red China's Premier and then Foreign Minister, Chou En-lai, a seasoned and cunning politician who had been a leader of the Chinese Reds for almost forty years. Since Communist China had entered into an alliance with the Soviet Union in 1950, Chou and Molotov made a very formidable team. Chou En-lai had been trained as an actor in his youth and he could always act, under any conditions.

France was represented at first by her Foreign Minister, Georges Bidault, who was replaced on June 17 by Pierre Mendes-France.* Sir Anthony Eden, representing Great Britain, exerted considerable influence on the Conference. America was represented by Under Secretary of State Bedell Smith, her former Ambassador to Moscow, and by Walter S. Robertson, Assistant Secretary of State for Far Eastern Affairs. They were instructed to declare that they were simply observers. The American Government did not wish to be associated as a signatory, as the agreements were considered

---

* Georges Bidault later became Premier of France. After he disagreed with de Gaulle, the General tried to arrest him. Bidault fled to Switzerland and then to South America.

by American public opinion as "surrender to Communism," and "an Asian Munich." This was the reason why the U.S. delegation did not sign the Geneva Agreements. The Democratic Republic of Viet Nam was represented by its Foreign Minister, Pham Van Dong, the present Premier of the Hanoi regime. He is a hard core Communist with much experience in military and political affairs. The delegate for the State of Viet Nam was Tran Van Do, who is the Foreign Minister of South Viet Nam today.

Having just met with a terrible defeat at Dien Bien Phu, France was anxious for peace at any price. Britain wanted to see the war over before it spread to any of her colonies. The American delegate did not like the agreements being made, but was more of an observer than a participant. Red China, Soviet Russia, and the Viet Communists all had a common and definite purpose: to get the French and any other foreign influence out of Viet Nam, and to put all of Veit Nam, Laos, and Cambodia under Communist control.

The French delegate, Georges Bidault, opened the discussion at the first plenary session on Indo-China on May 8, 1954. He laid down two principles for the truce: (1) to restore peace in Indo-China; (2) to guarantee that peace. Bidault declared that France was ready to end the hostilities in Indo-China immediately, and prepared to recognize the independence of Viet Nam, Laos, and Cambodia. He also presented concrete proposals regarding peace terms for Viet Nam, Laos, and Cambodia. Before the Conference could actually discuss the merits of the French proposals, Pham Van Dong, the delegate from Hanoi, injected a new proposal. He proposed that the representatives of the *Resistance of Khmer*, of Cambodia, and the *Pathet Lao of Laos*, be invited to attend the Conference. Both are Communist groups. The American delegate strongly objected to this. He was supported by the delegates of Laos and Cambodia, on the grounds that such underground Communist forces could not constitute governments. The Conference ruled that the Hanoi proposal be rejected.

At the second plenary session on May 10, the delegate from Hanoi persisted in his demand that France recognize not only Viet Nam, but also the independence of the *Pathet Lao* and the *Khmer*. The Communists wanted control over both Laos and Cambodia. The Laotian delegate pointed out that there had been no civil war in Laos, just a foreign invasion by the Communists. He demanded the withdrawal of these invading forces.[2] The Communists accused the United States of being an "imperialist." Sir Anthony

Eden replied that "no one in the world has been enslaved by the United States."

In the Third Plenary Session, on May 12, Tran Van Do of South Viet Nam suggested that adequate guarantees of independence must be given to his country. The British, the French, and American delegates expressed their sympathy for this idea and were in favor of international supervision of the Agreements. When the Fourth Plenary Session was convened, Molotov charged that the United States was forming a Southeast Asian military bloc, and extending its colonial war into that region. He also charged the American Government with intervention in the war in Indo-China. His position was strongly supported by Chou En-lai. From May 14 to 29, there were many informal and restricted meetings of the delegates and staffs. On May 29, a communique was issued by the Conference.[3] It authorized the respective commands to meet immediately at Geneva to discuss ways and means of ending hostilities, to establish the determined areas, to dispose of the troops, and to report their findings to the Conference.

Georges Bidault pointed out that France favored an International Commission to supervise the agreements. He amplified his views at the Fifth Plenary Session on June 8, endeavoring to be very conciliatory towards the proposals made by the Communist delegations.[4] The Soviet representative suggested that the International Commission be composed of Czechoslovakia, Poland, India, and Pakistan. The first two of these were Communist, and the latter two leaned more toward the Communist bloc than toward the democracies, if one may judge by their voting records in the United Nations. Molotov also declared that France must give complete independence to all of Indo-China immediately. He denounced the government in South Viet Nam as unrepresentative of the people, and declared that the Communist government of Ho Chi Minh was the only true representative government in Viet Nam, both North and South.

The Laotian delegate, having pointed out that there was no civil war in Laos, demanded that the question of Laos be settled first. He pointed out that Laos was already independent, but that she wanted to remain within the French Union in order to strengthen and safeguard her independence. He also maintained that Laos had a constitution and was already a democratic monarchy. He insisted that the so-called "Laos Resistance Government" was merely a fabrication of the Communists. Red China's Premier and Foreign Minister, Chou En-lai, echoed Molotov's proposal by recommending that the Neutral Nations Supervisory Commission include Czechoslovakia, Poland, India, and Pakistan. He further suggested that decisions made by the Neutral Nations Supervisory Commission should be by unanimous vote. In other words, each member nation of the Commission was to have veto power.

Anthony Eden, the British Foreign Secretary, then told the conference that the Viet Minh forces invading Laos and Cambodia were no more justified than was Hitler's invasion of Czechoslovakia. He pointed out that the Vietnamese Communists "not only crossed a political boundary, they crossed the frontier that divides two great cultures of Asia, the Indian and the Chinese." [5] Molotov then blamed the conference for delaying, and for stalling about the formation of an international commission to supervise the proposed ceasefire.[6]

At the final plenary session, Bedell Smith supported the British suggestion that the Viet Minh forces in Laos and Cambodia must be immediately withdrawn, and that the sovereignty and independence of both nations must be preserved. The American delegate then insisted on the immediate and complete withdrawal of the Viet Minh forces from that country. No further agreement could be obtained, and this plenary session was called to a halt.

The cessation of hostilities in Indo-China and the future political settlements for those countries were thus left to under-the-table agreements among the delegates, although the Soviet and British delegates were to act as co-chairmen of the conference when it came to calling a future meeting. On this note the first phase of the formal conference on Indo-China ended, having lasted from May 8 to June 10.

For forty-one days there were no formal meetings, just secret consultations and off-the-record talks. After the main points had been agreed on, the eighth and final plenary session was held on July 21, 1954. With Anthony Eden presiding, the three most important agreements regarding a cessation of hostilities were made: (1) for Viet Nam, (2) for Laos, (3) for Cambodia.

There were other documents, such as the declarations of Laos, Cambodia, and France. But these were not revealed to the public, on the grounds that the armistice would come into force at different times. Pierre Mendes-France had just assumed the new French premiership on June 17, and was eager to find a way to end the war in Indo-China at any cost. The delegates from the three Communist countries knew that they had acquired what they wanted for the moment, and that they would need more time for making further gains. The British delegate wanted the war in Indo-China ended without sacrificing British interests, and the role played by the United States was weak and insignificant. Thus the final declaration of the Geneva Conference on Indo-China was signed, on July 21, 1954.

2. *The Essence of the Agreements:*

1. The establishment of an international control commission to supervise the cease-fire agreements in Cambodia, Laos, and Viet Nam.
2. Cambodia, Laos, and Viet Nam were henceforth to be fully independent and sovereign nations.
3. General elections were to take place in Cambodia and Laos in 1955.
4. The introduction into Viet Nam of foreign troops or arms was prohibited.
5. No military base was to be established in Viet Nam for aggressive purposes.
6. The military demarcation line was to be provisional, and was not to be interpreted as a political or territorial boundary.
7. The territorial integrity and political independence of Viet Nam was to be guaranteed. Free general elections were to take place throughout all of Viet Nam in 1956, under the International Supervisory Commission, later known as the "International Control Commission" (ICC).
8. The Vietnamese were to have the right to choose which zone they would live in for a period of three months.
9. There would be no individual or collective reprisal against persons who had collaborated with any of the parties in Viet Nam, Laos, or Cambodia.
10. The French troops were to withdraw from Viet Nam, Laos, and Cambodia at specified times by fixed agreement.
11. France was to operate on the principle of respect for the independence, sovereignty, unity, and territorial integrity of Viet Nam, Laos, and Cambodia.
12. No member of the Geneva Conference was to interfere in the internal affairs of Viet Nam, Laos, or Cambodia.
13. The members of the Conference agreed to consult one another on any question which might be referred to them by the International Supervisory

Commission i.e. ICC, regarding the cease-fire terms.

The Geneva Conference provided that a cease-fire was to be effected and that a demilitarized zone on either side of the 17th degree north latitude was to be established. North of this line was to belong to the *Democratic Republic of Viet Nam,* while south of this line was to belong to the *State of Viet Nam.*

No person was to cross the demarcation lines unless authorized by the Joint Commission, or for the civil administration of the buffer zone. Pending the general elections for the unification of Viet Nam, the political and administrative measures of both sides were not to interfere with each other. Civilians of either side who might choose to go to the other side during the three months allowed for this were to be assisted by the authorities on their original side. A ban was placed on the introduction of fresh troops, arms, and munitions, except for normal rotation of units. Reinforcements were prohibited. A Joint Commission was formed between the French and the Viet Cong to enforce the cease-fire. An International Commission was formed with a representative from Poland, a representative from Canada, and a chairman from India to report any violations of the truce. This commission was to report its findings to the Geneva Conference, but its decisions had to be unanimous. Otherwise it could merely file a majority and a minority report. Since one of the commissioners was from a Communist country, the Reds knew that they could commit all the violations they wanted without ever being censured.

The whole arrangement left South Viet Nam with little protection against subsequent activities. The authors were told by President Ngo Dinh Diem, and later by Prime Minister Nguyen Ngoc Tho, and by General Duong Van Minh that the International Control Commission was not only of no help, but that it created considerable trouble for South Viet Nam. The Commission kept insisting on inspecting all of the Vietnamese armed forces, personnel, and military installations, and then handing the information over to the Communists in the North.

The Geneva Conference placed the American delegation in a very embarrassing position. France had already surrendered at Dien Bien Phu in May 1954; Britain was anxious to see the war in Indo-China ended before it spread to where she would be involved; the Sino-Soviet Alliance of 1950 was still a continuing threat to Southeast Asia. Under such circumstances, the United States was not willing to break up the conference. Yet Moscow, Peking, and Hanoi kept pressuring the Conference for a quick conclusion, since the situation was so favorable to the cause of Communism. American public opinion at that time did not want the United States to be a party to an Asian Munich, so Bedell Smith announced, on July 21, 1954, at the final plenary session, that the United States would not sign the conference declaration. This unilateral action by the U.S. is of such importance that it should be quoted at length, as follows:

3. *The Declaration*

The government of the United States being resolved to devote its efforts to the strengthing of peace in accordance with the principles and purposes of the United Nations,
Take note
of the Agreement concluded at Geneva on July 20 and 21, 1954 . . .
The Government of the United States of America
Declares
with regard to the aforesaid Agreements and paragraphs that (1) it will refrain from the threat or the use of force to disturb them, in accordance with Article 2 (Section 4) of the Charter of the United Nations dealing with the obligations of members to refrain in their international relations from the threat or use of force; and (2) it would view any renewal of the aggression in violation of the aforesaid agreements with *grave concern* and as seriously threatening international peace and security. (Italics added.)

In connection with the statement in the Declaration concerning free elections in Viet Nam, my Government wishes to make its position which it has expressed in a Declaration made in Washington on June 29, 1954, as follows:

'In the case of nations now divided against their will, we shall continue to seek to achieve unity through free elections, supervised by the United Nations to insure that they are conducted fairly.'

With respect to the statement made by the representative of the State of Viet Nam, the United States reiterates its traditional position that peoples are entitled to determine their own future and that it will not join in an agreement which would hinder this. Nothing in its declaration just made is intended to or does indicate any departure from this traditional position.

We share the hope that the agreement will permit Cambodia, Laos, and Viet Nam to play their part in full independence and sovereignty in the peaceful community of nations, and will enable the people of that area to determine their own future.[7]

4. *U. S. and South Viet Nam Not Signatories*

These agreements also gave international recognition to the division of Viet Nam into two separate and independent countries, pending a free and fair election for the unification of Viet Nam. The United States also declared that it was against the use of force to disturb the peace in Viet Nam. The American Government made it clear that any renewal of aggression or threat of force would be viewed with grave concern. The actions of the United States in Viet Nam from 1954 to the present are not a departure from the above declaration. They are merely defensive acts against aggression from the North.

Since the signing of these Agreements, the North Viet guerrilla forces have never ceased to operate within the territories of South Viet Nam. The *State of Viet Nam* (since 1955 it has been the *Republic of Viet Nam*) has been under constant attack, and these attacks are still becoming more serious every day. Under these aggravated conditions it would be extremely difficult, if not impossible, for the people of South Viet Nam to participate in a plebiscite to determine whether or not there should be a unification. Under the Communist regime in the North, on the other hand, there is no freedom of speech or assembly, and it would be a farce to hold an election in that country, where they have never even held a free election. There are about one million more people in the North than in the South, and in Communist countries elections are won by 99 per cent. Even Stalin, who was so bitterly condemned later, was never defeated in a Soviet election. Concerning the International Control Commission, which is composed of Canada, Poland, and India, the Communist representative would cause great trouble in any Vietnamese election. He has already made the ICC one of the least effective of all international bodies.

The representative of the State of Viet Nam, Tran Van Do, refused to sign the Geneva Agreements. His objections and reservations were based on the fact that at the conclusion of the truce there were still many regular and irregular Viet Minh forces left in South Viet Nam, and that there were neither legal barriers against their remaining there, nor effective means of checking their further invasion of his country. The sad truth of this has been subsequently proven. The chairman of the conference, Sir Anthony Eden, commented on these remarks of South Viet Nam's Foreign Minister, and asked the conference to take official note of them.

The net results of the Geneva Conference were as follows: (1) The Communist state under the name of the *Democratic People's Republic of Viet Nam* was recognized by all the signatories at Geneva: (2) Red China, through her spokesman, Chou En-lai, achieved great prestige; (3) the Sino-Soviet Alliance of 1950 was proven to be effective; (4) France, once a great colonial power, lost her colonies and influence in Southeast Asia, and her loss in prestige was even worse than her material losses; (5) South Viet Nam received very little protection under the cease-fire terms, and the International Supervisory Commission, with Poland as a member, was used later as an instrument for obtaining military information for the Communists; (6) though they were represented at the Conference, Laos and Cambodia were consigned to neutral positions, and subsequently became the victims of Communist pressure, infiltration, sabotage, and guerrilla warfare, until they became largely Communist dominated and controlled; (7) Communist forces began working steadily toward the overthrow of the Government of South Viet Nam, through the Laotian corridor.

The efforts of delegate Tran Van Do of South Viet Nam to modify the terms of the Agreement were of no avail. Communist regular and irregular forces were permitted to stay in Viet Nam.

5. *Comment on the Agreements*

At the close of the conference on July 20, 1954, Tran Van Do cabled Prime Minister Ngo Dinh Diem:

> Absolutely impossible to surmount the hostility of our enemies and perfidy of false friends. Unusual procedures paralyzed the action of our delegation . . . All arrangements were signed in privacy. We express our deepest sorrow on this total failure of our mission.

On the following day President Eisenhower declared:

The United States has not itself been party to or bound by the decisions taken by the Conference, but it is our hope that it will lead to the establishment of peace consistent with the rights and needs of the countries concerned. The agreements contain features which we do not like, but a great deal depends on how they work in practice.[8]

Three weeks after the close of the conference, Senator William E. Jenner told Congress: "The United States was outthought, outtraded, and outgeneraled."[9]

The Geneva Truce was summed up by a noted writer on American diplomatic history:

After the rise of Hitler and the Nazis in Germany came Munich and the Second World War, Yalta, and the Soviet harvest. After Yalta came the cold war in Europe, the Chinese Revolution in Asia, and the Communist victories in Korea and Indo-China. Most Americans accepted the Indo-Chinese Armistice as once they had looked on Munich, something better than going to war themselves to prevent, without fully reckoning the consequences.[10]

Another writer on Southeast Asia commented: "For France, the Geneva settlement marked the end of its role as a great power in Southeast Asia. For Peking it constituted a major achievement in its rising international stature."[11] The American delegation's declaration that "any renewal of Communist aggression would be viewed by the United States with grave concern" justified America's action in giving military aid to Viet Nam for repelling aggression. The United States could also invoke the Protocol of SEATO, which included Viet Nam in the "treaty area" of the collective defense of Southeast Asia. The SEATO Treaty bound the United States to respond to the request for aid from South Viet Nam.

The Communists had it all their own way at Geneva. They agreed to the division of Viet Nam only because they were not prepared to conquer all of the South immediately, and because they had ever reason to expect that South Viet Nam would soon collapse like a house of cards. Undoubtedly it would have, had it not been for the new Prime Minister, Ngo Dinh Diem. Statements have recently been made in Moscow, Peking, and Hanoi, and even in Paris, that the various parties should return to another conference like the one in Geneva in 1954. That is to be expected, at least from Moscow, Peking, and Hanoi, as they know that in any conference like the one held in Geneva in 1954 they are bound to win again.

What is surprising is that Secretary of State Rusk stated that the United States would not object to another such Geneva Conference as a basis for discussions for a cease-fire in Viet Nam today. Senate Majority Leader Mike Mansfield has taken the identical position. On January 7, 1965, in a press release issued by the State Department, the American Government, in laying down the 14-points, agreed to use the Geneva Agreements of 1954 and 1962 as a "basis for peace in Southeast Asia." Even President Johnson himself, on March 25, 1965, declared: "We seek no more than a return to the essentials of the agreements of 1954—a reliable agreement to guarantee the independence and security of all Southeast Asia."

In a major speech in the Senate in June, 1965, Senator J. William Fulbright, the chairman of the Senate's Foreign Relations Committee, urged that both sides make "major concessions." He, too, suggested that the United States return to the Geneva accords of 1954, adding that America return to them "not just in their 'essentials' but in all their specifications." Yet American public opinion was very much against American agreement to the 1954 Geneva Conference because the public realized that it was a surrender to Communism.

The Geneva Conference required that all foreign troops be withdrawn, and that general elections would be held to decide who would rule all of Viet Nam. The Communists in the North would be certain to win such an election. The International Control Commission that would supervise the election is not only one-third Communist and one-third pro-Communist, it is rigged in favor of the aggressor. All major reports had to be unanimous, and even then there is no way to enforce its findings, as the last twelve years have abundantly proven.

The Geneva Conference put in writing the defeat of France, and the unwillingness of both Britain and the United States to stand up to Communism at that particular time and in that particular place. The checks against Communist aggression proved to be worthless in practice. Even in theory the United States and South Viet Nam had refused to sign them. Why should America put herself in the position now of accepting what she found so unacceptable in the face of allied defeat?

It is rather difficult to understand why some of America's top policy-makers would now be willing to accept the Geneva Agreements that the United States and South Viet Nam refused to accept twelve years ago. The agreement with the Communists has meant nothing. Agreements with them seldom have, and this was one of the most meaningless and least effective of all. The only agreement worth making with the Reds is an agreement to cease-fire, an agreement like Korea where the cease-fire is enforced with military strength. The free world cannot afford another agreement like the Geneva Conference of 1954, which enabled the Reds to capitalize on America's patience and forebearance, while they constantly strengthened their position by aggression and terrorism. The 1962 Agreement over Laos is a perfect example of how the Communists use an agreement to disarm their enemy while they wage guerrilla war.

Senator Fulbright criticized both former President Diem and the United States for "violating" the Geneva Conference. How could either country violate an Agreement which both countries had not only strongly objected to, but which both had adamantly refused to sign? Senator Fulbright went on to call for "restraint" on the part of the United States, including a permanent halt to the bombing of North Viet Nam. He complained that America's suspension of bombings in May, and during the Christmas season of 1965, were not long enough, even though such suspensions gave advantages to the enemy and produced no beneficial results. Senator Fulbright failed to mention that South Viet Nam and the United States should try to win the war. He insisted, instead, that the U.S. should offer the Communists "a reasonable and attractive alternative to military victory." To offer an attractive reward to the Communists for their aggression seems strange enough on the face of it, but it is even stranger to think that they will be satisfied with anything less than what they have been trying to achieve for twelve years: the complete subjection of South Viet Nam, as the beginning of the subjugation of all of Southeast Asia. There is no "attractive alternative" that Washington can offer, unless the United States tells the Communists to take over some other country instead. America's only hope is in convincing the Communists by military force that they cannot have what they are trying so ruthlessly to seize.

From every point of view, it is highly doubtful that either the Republic of Viet Nam or the United States is obliged to adhere to the Geneva Agreements. Those who have not signed a treaty or contract are usually not bound by it. The Geneva Conference created the division between the two countries, and provided that the State of Viet Nam be separated from the regime in Hanoi by the 17th parallel. The Viet regular and irregular forces were supposed to be withdrawn from the South, since they represented a foreign power. Yet since the conclusion of that Conference, the Viet Communists from the North have violated the Agreement they signed by attacking the South with military force, terrorism, and subversion.

According to a well-established principle of international law, known as *"Rebus sic Stantibus,"* this change in conditions rendered the treaty subject to alteration, in accordance with Article 19 of the Covenant of the League of Nations. Although the League is dead, its principle, as used in international law, remains valid. Regarding a national election for the possible unification of Viet Nam, because of the military and political situation in both the North and the South, such an election cannot be either free or fair. Concerning the possibility of having an international commission supervise such a national election, it would not be practical to have the members of that commission act on the basis of a unanimous vote. The Polish representative would certainly act in favor of the Hanoi regime. If such an election were to be supervised by the original Co-Chairmen of the Geneva Conference, namely the United Kingdom and the Soviet Union, neither the conditions nor the outcome could ever be agreed on.

Section I, Article 6 of the Geneva Agreement states that "no person, military or civilian, shall be permitted to cross the provisional military demarcation line unless specifically authorized to do so by the Joint Commission." The *White Paper* published by the State Department pointed out that the Viet Cong have sent tens of thousands of unauthorized persons to launch guerrilla warfare in South Viet Nam.[12] In addition to personnel, the Vietnamese and Chinese Communists have continually sent large amounts of the latest and most advanced weapons from Red China to support their guerrilla forces in the South. The Communists from the North have not only invaded the South by the tens of thousands, they are currently doing so at an increasing rate. South Viet Nam and the United States finally took to bombing limited targets in the North, but only after enduring for twelve long years a brutal onslaught from the North.

Article 14. Chapter 11. of the Agreement ruled that the

Vietnamese were entitled to live either in the North or in the South, and that they were to be permitted to move freely across the border in either direction. As a result of this provision, and despite persecution by the North against those who wanted to leave Communist rule, nearly one million political refugees came from the North to South Viet Nam, while only a few thousand chose to go to the North. The agreement also stipulated that both sides must refrain from any reprisals or recriminations against persons or organizations on account of their activities during the hostilities. All were to be guaranteed their democratic liberties. Despite these provisions, many thousands of persons who had been anti-Communist before 1954 were kidnapped and tortured by the Communist guerrillas. Many more thousands were murdered. Since the signing of these Agreements it was the Communists from the North who carried on subversive activities against the South, and not vice-versa. It was the Communists who turned these same subversive activies into aggression.

It was the Viet Cong who first violated the Geneva Agreements, even though they had accepted and signed them. Even if the Republic of Viet Nam had signed the Agreements, it would no longer have been bound by them after the flagrant violations of the Communists. The decision by South Viet Nam and the United States not to grant sanctuary to the North any longer was based on the realization that otherwise the war would soon be lost. In any war, declared or undeclared, the country that has been attacked is not bound to grant sanctuary to the enemy. This is just as true whether the aggressor makes a direct attack, or whether he attacks through infiltration, tyranny, sabotage, or subversion. The allies would never have defeated Hitler if they had been unwilling to attack German territory. The United States was not even able to defeat the Mexican bandit, Poncho Villa, until it invaded his country.

FOOTNOTES

CHAPTER III: VIET NAM AND THE GENEVA AGREEMENTS, 1954

1. British Foreign Office, *Documents Relating to the Discussion of Korea, and Indo-China at the Geneva Conference, April 27 to June 15, 1954.* (London: Her Majesty's Stationery Office, 1954).
2. *Ibid.,* p. 122.
3. *Ibid.,* pp. 136–167.
4. *Ibid.,* pp. 137–142.

5. *Ibid.*, p. 167.
6. *Ibid.*, p. 168.
7. British Foreign Office, *Further Documents Relating to the Discussion of Indo-China at the Geneva Conference, June 16–July 21, 1954,* (London: H.M. Stationery Office, Cmd. 9239, 1962), pp. 6-7.
8. Department of State, *Bulletin,* August 2, 1954, p. 163.
9. *Congressional Record,* August 14, 1954.
10. Samuel Flagg Bemis, *A Diplomatic History of the United States,* (New York, rev. ed., 1955), p. 955.
11. Russell H. Fifield, *Southeast Asia in the United States Policy,* (New York, 1963), pp. 24-25.
12. Department of State, *Aggression from the North: The Record of North Viet Nam's Campaign to Conquer South Viet Nam,* (Washington, February, 1965).

CHAPTER IV

VIET NAM AND SEATO

1. The Concept of SEATO

According to Article 1 of the United Nations Charter, the U.N. was created for "the removal of threats to the peace, and for the suppression of acts of aggression or other breeches of the peace . . ." Many people maintain that the U.N. is the only hope for peace in the world. Yet it was founded on the theory that all of its member nations agree, that all nations are basically on the same side. When the U.N. was being founded, it was decided that only peace-loving states would be admitted. That is why the veto did not seem unrealistic. But hardly was the U.N. Charter between the free and the Communist worlds signed before the cold war began. A continual stream of hot wars followed on the China Mainland, in Korea, Iran, Greece, Malaya the Philippines, and Indo-China. The United Nations has never even been able to agree on what constitutes "aggression." Therefore it has been all but helpless. Even the old League of Nations had been able to take action by condemning Italy, Japan, and Soviet Russia as aggressors.

The free world has seen countries like Lithuania, Latvia, and Estonia disappear from the political maps of the world. Not even the pretense of calling them colonies is observed by the "anti-imperialist" bloc. The Geneva Agreements of 1954 are incapable of enforcement because they have no teeth. Gradually the United States came to realize that the world-wide organization of the United Nations, the "hope of the world," was not sufficient to check threats of war or breaches of the peace. Under the leadership of Secretary of State John Foster Dulles, the U.S. and other non-Communist nations began to form regional agreements. This was not done in any violation of the letter or spirit of the United Nations Charter. Article 52, Section 1 of the Charter recognizes the right of nations or groups to form "regional arrangements or agencies for dealing with such matters relating to the maintenance of international peace and security as are appropriate for regional action. . . ." The Charter further stipulates in Section 2:

"The Members of the United Nations entering into such arrangements or constituting such agencies shall make every effort to achieve pacific settlement of local disputes through such regional arrangements or by such regional agencies before referring them to the Security Council."

In order to check the sweeping tide of Communist forces throughout the world, and particularly in East Asia, the United States cooperated with other nations and entered into bilateral and multilateral agreements for the maintenance of peace and security in their respective areas.[1] America was slow to learn about the Communist menace. In 1947, for example, a friend of the authors, who had been lecturing to the Nationalist troops in China, told President Truman that if Manchuria fell, all of China would fall to the Communists. The President replied: "What could the Communists do with China anyway? They couldn't even feed them." Stalin, however, called the fall of China "the greatest event in the world in the 20th century." The additional Communist takeover of North Korea, North Viet Nam, and most of Laos and Cambodia threatened the whole of Asia.

The United States had already signed the Rio Pact of 1947, the North Atlantic Treaty of 1949, and the bilateral Mutual Defense Agreements with various nations in Asia and in the Pacific. The U.S. also entered into a Tripartite Treaty with Australia and New Zealand on September 1, 1951. The Mutual Security Pact between the U.S. and the Republic of China was signed on December 2, 1954, and ratified in January, 1955.

All these treaties and agreements signed by the U.S. with various countries, especially those in East Asia, indicated that the American Government considered Southeast Asia vitally important to its own security. This was not only because the area contains rich agricultural land and valuable mineral resources, but because it is in a very strategic position, one of the most important crossroads in the world.

The Communist nations were even more aware of the vital importance of Southeast Asia, and they realized that Viet Nam is its gateway. This they learned from the Japanese during World War II. Communist China and the Soviet Union, through their instrument, the Viet Cong, have continuously tried to launch a campaign of subversion, terror, sabotage, and guerrilla warfare in order to conquer South

Viet Nam. It would provide them with a direct route to Thailand, Burma, Malaysia, Singapore, Indonesia, Australia, New Zealand and the Philippines. The increasing signs of Communist design in Southeast Asia, especially in Viet Nam, caused the policy-makers in the United States and other countries to try to find ways of coping with the situation. It has been reported that Ramon Magsaysay, then President of the Philippines, strongly advocated that there must be an anti-Communist alliance in Southeast Asia in order to deter the spread of Communism from the China Mainland. He communicated his idea to the American Government, especially to the then Secretary of State, John Foster Dulles, who had the same idea and was willing to crystallize this idea into a reality. Thus Secretary of State Dulles travelled far and wide in Asia, Australia, and New Zealand, seeking a multiple guarantee for the peace and security of that west Pacific area.

SEATO, the Southeast Asia Treaty Organization, was formed for the peace and security of the countries concerned, and was signed to deter aggression by Communist China in the Southeast Asian area. Dulles outlined the basic concept of SEATO on January 13, 1954, when he declared:

"At the north, the Korean mainland; and in the south, . . . Indo-China . . . In between are the islands themselves—Japan, the Ryukyus, embracing Okinawa, Formosa, the Philippines, Australia and New Zealand . . . The United States has a security tie, of one sort or another, with each of these areas, not formalized in some cases in the form of a treaty, but nevertheless very real and very actual." [2]

The Eisenhower-Dulles idea of SEATO constitutes an enlargement of the containment policy of the Truman-Acheson administration, a part of the Truman Doctrine.

The idea of a collective security pact in the West Pacific and Southeast Asia, along the lines of the North Atlantic Treaty Organization, had little support in Washington, London, and Paris before 1954. But when the French surrendered at Dien Bien Phu in May of that year, these capitals realized the Communist danger in those areas. Several countries, such as India, Indonesia, and Ceylon, followed the policy of nonalignment, and would not take part in such an organization. The Republic of China and the Republic of Korea were not invited to join SEATO because of French and British opposition. The alleged reason for such opposition was on the ground that these two countries are not located in Southeast Asia, but neither are Australia and New Zealand. Their objection was based on the fear that the admission of the Republic of China and the Republic of Korea into a multilateral defense pact would aggravate Red China. South Viet Nam was not permitted to join because of the Geneva Agreements of 1954, although she had never signed them. Japan was not permitted to join, as she had been demilitarized, and already had a security pact with the United States.

The American, British, and French diplomats made all of these exclusions, only to have SEATO derided later by the Communists because it represented so few countries. The three Asian signatories were Thailand, Pakistan, and the Philippines. The five non-Asian countries were the United Kingdom, France, the United States, Australia and New Zealand. The delegates of these eight states met in Manila and signed the Pacific Charter and the Southeast Asia Collective Defense Treaty, known as the Manila Pact, on September 8, 1954. It should be broadened to become a collective security treaty among all the non-Communist nations in East Asia.

The Pacific Charter stressed the right of self-determination, peaceful means for promoting self-government and independence, and effective measures for insuring the principles of self-determination.[3] Economic, social and cultural cooperation among the signatories was also provided. Lastly, the signatories were to use "appropriate means" to counteract any action which might endanger their freedom, sovereignty, or territorial integrity. As a supplement to the Pacific Charter, the Southeast Asia Collective Defense Treaty was immediately signed by the same eight nations.

The Southeast Asia Collective Defense Treaty, together with its protocol and the Pacific Charter, are known as the Manila Pact.[4] Their treaty area covers Southeast Asia and the Southwest Pacific. It includes Pakistan, Thailand, Australia, New Zealand, and the Philippines, and by its protocol includes Laos, Cambodia, and South Viet Nam. It does not include Hong Kong, Macao, the Republic of China, Japan, or Korea.

2. The SEATO Treaty

(1) Invoked the principle of the regional arrangements as provided by the United Nations Charter, and the use of "peaceful means to settle any international disputes." (Article I)

(2) Stressed the necessity of using effective means to resist not only aggression but also subversive activities. It provided

that "in order more effectively to achieve the objective of this treaty, the parties, *separately* and *jointly,* by means of continuous and effective self help and mutual aid, will maintain and develop their individual and collective capacity to resist armed attack and to prevent and counter *subversive activities directed from without* against their territorial integrity and political stability." If any of the signatories encounters any armed attack or subversive activities directed from the outside, any of the nations attacked or involved, or any other signatory, can separately and individually employ appropriate measures to resist the aggression. (Article II. Italics supplied.)

(3) SEATO emphasized the importance of free institutions, and of economic cooperation and technical assistance between and among the nations that signed the pact. (Article III)

(4) It left each nation to decide what constitutes aggression. In the case of the Manila Pact, it was declared that "each party recognizes that aggression by means of armed attack in the treaty area against any of the parties or against any state or territory which the parties by unanimous agreement may hereafter designate," would "endanger its own peace and safety," and agreed that it would in that event "act to meet the common danger in accordance with its constitutional processes." (Article IV, Paragraph 1.) The signatories also agreed to consult each other immediately if, in the opinion of any one of them, "the inviolability or the integrity or the sovereignty or political independence of any party in the treaty area or of any other state or territory should be threatened . . ." in any way other than by armed attack, "or by any fact or situation which might endanger the peace of the area." (Article IV, Paragraphs 2 and 3.)

Each signatory "undertakes not to enter into any international engagement in conflict with this treaty" (Article VI). By unanimous agreement, "the signatories may invite a nonsignatory to adhere to the provisions of this treaty." (Article VII.) Such adherence must be accepted by all the original signatories. If any of the signers wants to withdraw from its treaty-obligations, one year's notice must be given to the government of the Philippines.

Besides the Pacific Charter and the Manila Pact, a very important protocol was adopted by all of the participating parties. The protocol of this treaty particularly stipulated that "the parties to the Southeast Asia Collective Defense Treaty unanimously designated that Articles III and IV are applicable to Cambodia, Laos, and the free territory under the jurisdiction of Viet Nam. These three states, though they were not signatories to the pact, thereby benefited from the protection and collective security of the eight nations. The inclusion of the former French Indo-China within the protocol area of the treaty was suggested by the French delegate and adopted by the Manila Conference.

The American delegation made one reservation. If the United States deems that a situation sufficiently endangers the security, sovereignty, and independence of any of these countries named in the treaty or protocol, the American Government may act individually or jointly to take appropriate measures to resist the subversion or aggression. In the case of purely local civil wars, or an armed conflict between non-Communist countries, however, the United States would consult her allied signatories before taking any action.

The American delegation originally intended to check the spread of Communism from Red China, and to include this concept specifically in the treaty. This idea was supported by the delegations from the Philippines and Thailand. Because of the British and French objection, however, the term "Communism" or "Red China" was eliminated. As a compromise, the terms "subversion" and "subversive activities" were put into the document. This was the first international agreement to declare that subversive activities amount to aggression and should be resisted. The treaty was aimed at checking the spread of Communism, something the United Nations could not be counted on to do. Unfortunately, the U.S. agreed to the removal of Laos from the protection of the SEATO Treaty, in 1962.

The main provisions of the Manila Pact are similar to some of the traditional concepts of American diplomacy, e.g., the Inter-American Treaty of Reciprocal Assistance (The Pact of Rio de Janiero) signed on September 2, 1947, and also the Vandenberg Resolution of June 11, 1948. The principles of the Rio Pact and the Vandenberg Resolution constitute a prototype of the North Atlantic Treaty Organization of 1949. The main difference between NATO and SEATO is that NATO is better organized. One of the weaknesses of SEATO is that it has no armed forces or joint command.

At the Manila Conference, Dulles supported Prince Wan Waithayakon, then Foreign Minister of Thailand. The Prince advocated a combined mobile force for SEATO in order to cope with any unexpected aggression within the treaty area. This idea was opposed by some of the other delegations. As a compromise, the Conference decided to set up a political committee to make recommendations to the

53

Council of Foreign Ministers of SEATO. Each year there have been annual military maneuvers in which the eight signatory-nations have participated, except that in 1964 and 1965 France only sent observers to the military exercises. Pakistan was unable to participate in the maneuvers on one occasion because of insufficient time to prepare.

SEATO is different from other American defense treaties. The American treaties or pacts with Korea, Japan, and the Philippines, for instance, provided for resistance to armed aggression. But SEATO stipulated that the signatories should *individually* or *collectively* resist armed aggression or subversive activities directed from without against the territorial integrity or political independence of any country within the treaty area. SEATO is also different from NATO in other respects. In the case of NATO, "an attack on one is an attack on all." This is not the case with SEATO. NATO has a standing army and a joint command; SEATO does not. The concept of the Monroe doctrine is embodied in Article IV of SEATO. This was stressed in Secretary Dulles' testimony given at the Senate Foreign Relations Committee Hearing on November 11, 1954.

SEATO also provided that in case the signatories face common danger they should act in accordance with their constitutional processes. This removed any fear from the U.S. Congress that the Chief Executive would take arbitrary action in dealing with the SEATO signatories and protocol nations. Despite the weakness in SEATO, *Radio Peking* and the *New China News Agency* assailed it as "a warlike device contrived by the United States to get Asians to fight Asians," immediately after the Treaty was signed. Peking termed SEATO "a military bloc opposed to the Asian peoples." Red China also attacked Secretary Dulles, pointing out that he "made no bones about the fact that the pact was directly against the Asian peoples." SEATO was aimed directly at Communism in Asia.

3. *Reactions to SEATO*

On September 14, 1954, less than a week after the Manila Pact was signed, the Soviet Union made a lengthy and detailed radio broadcast to the world denouncing the treaty. Soviet Russia attacked the Pact as a military bloc "against the countries in Asia in general and against China in particular." She said it was against "the national liberation movements of the peoples of that area and their fight for national independence." Soviet Russia described it as an "anti-Comintern Pact," and said it was an "old method" used against the U.S.S.R. and the People's Republic of China. Moscow also charged that the inclusion of Laos, Cambodia, and Viet Nam in the protocol of the Manila Pacts was a violation of the Geneva Agreement of July, 1954. In the United States, there was strong bipartisan support for the treaty and the ideas underlying it.

The general public labors under the misconception that there is an East-West conflict, that the eastern countries are Communist and the Western countries anti-Communist. Such a concept is misleading. Most of the countries in the East, such as Japan, South Korea, the Republic of China, the Philippines, Thailand, Malaysia, and the Republic of Viet Nam are very anti-Communist. On the other hand, the West has nations within the Communist bloc, e.g., East Germany, Yugoslavia, Czechoslovakia, Hungary and Cuba.

An American military writer considered the Manila Pacts the result of "an agonizing reappraisal" of American policy in the light of the world situaton. He felt that its impacts are mainly psychological, but that it provided a basis for a broad Asian security organization. It is not formally an alliance against Communism, but an alliance against aggression from any source.[5] Enacted to counteract the Geneva Conference, it contains no veto.

When the Senate Foreign Relations Committee, on January 19, 1955, considered the ratification of the Manila Pact, it voted 14 to 1 to approve it. When presented to the Senate for approval, on February 1, 1955, it was approved by a vote of 82 to 1. The exchange of the ratifications took place in Manila on February 19 of the same year.

Dulles' concept of American strategy in the whole of East Asia consisted of three fronts: (1) the Korea-Japan front; (2) The Taiwan Strait front; (3) the Southeast Asian Front. He hoped that ultimately the U.S. would be able to tie these three defense links into one solid front against Communist aggression and subversion. He argued that because of her inferior weapons, Red China would not risk a general war. Peking has already demonstrated its unwillingness to fight on three fronts. When the Korean war was on, Peking gave only limited military aid to the Viet Minh forces in Indo-China, and did not want to be engaged in large scale fighting in the Taiwan Straits at the same time. Peking is well aware of the immense retaliatory power of the United States, and does not want to take the chance of risking war with her. America's superiority is in her equipment, in her ability to produce, in her air power, and in her power of nuclear retaliation.

Since the Communist nations hated the provisions of SEATO, Peking and other Communist and "neutralist" countries used the Bandung Conference in April, 1955, to denounce America's role in the formation of SEATO. Even the eloquent defense by the delegates from the Philippines, Pakistan, and Thailand could not counteract the condemnation of Uncle Sam. Despite the Communist denunciations of SEATO, however, the treaty area enjoyed a comparative quiet from 1954 to 1958. The only exception was in Viet Nam, where the Communists increased their subversive activities and prepared the way for future aggression.

4. Viet Nam and SEATO

The rather soft policy toward the non-Communist countries by the Communist bloc at that time in East Asia was partially due to the fact that SEATO was serious in its defense against Communist subversion and aggression. In 1957, for instance, at the annual meeting of SEATO in Canberra, the U.S. delegation proposed to increase the military effort of the Asian member states in order to deter Communist aggression in that area, and to foster economic development in the hope of destroying the breeding ground of Communism. The proposals were accepted by the Canberra Conference. By March, 1958, the Moscow-Peking Axis tried to play down their revolutionary programs. Instead of large scale armed aggression, the Communists attempted to ally themselves with whatever groups they could in order to pursue their programs along the lines of social, economic and political "reforms." They also tried to intensify Asian feelings of nationalism or patriotism against the Americans and the British.

Concerning Communist subversion in Asia, the Secretary General of the Council of Foreign Ministers of SEATO declared in March, 1958, at Manila:

Asia, as well as the Middle East, has always been regarded by the Communists as a particularly favourable target for early expansion of their influence . . . they continue to work toward the eventual domination of free Asia . . . the Communist bloc and local Communist parties and movements *seek by every means to subvert, to isolate and to divide the free peoples* of South and Southeast Asia and thus to weaken their will and capacity to defend themselves individually and collectively.[6] (Italics added)

In 1959 there was no substantial change in the Communist subversion in Southeast Asia except for Viet Nam, where such activities were greatly increased and extended. In speaking before the National Press Club in February, 1959, Pote Sarsin, the Secretary General of SEATO, warned about the increasing threat of Red China. He predicted:

> Communist China represents a very dangerous element and potentially powerful force over the next five years. No evidence can be found that it is not working very closely with and contributing to the activity of Soviet Russia. There is no doubt that Chinese Communist subversive activities will be increased if any opportunity is afforded them.[7]

In 1960, whle Nikita Khrushchev was preaching "peaceful coexistence" in Europe and America, Communist subversion and aggression were increasing in East Asia. Quemoy and Matsu were attacked continually. The Republic of Korea was subject to sneak attacks, and in South Viet Nam, aggression was greatly increased and terrorism was intensified.

Admiral Harry P. Felt, then U. S. Commander in Chief in the Pacific, warned the other members of the Military Committee of SEATO in May, 1960:

> Communist political leaders on the enslaved mainland of China have agitated themselves to a point where once more they may set off further encroachments upon their neighbors.[8]

A few days later, the admiral further stated that the situation in Viet Nam was "worsening," and that the "bandits" had succeeded in continuing their harrassments of the Vietnamese Government activities, despite the fact that the Vietnamese Government had a "pretty good army" of 150,-000 men, comprising seven divisions. He further said that the Viet Cong had been organized by infiltration from the North into the Delta regions near Saigon.[9]

Every year the SEATO nations have held conferences, and every year North Viet Nam has been unanimously condemned, with the exception of France in 1964 and 1965, and Pakistan in 1965, who refrained from voting. Joint military training programs of member nations have been held annually. Red

China charged that SEATO's military exercises were intended to bring Asia to the "brink of war," and that the maneuvers were being held to "conduct provocations against the Chinese and all the Asian peoples." Radio Peking further charged that these exercises were "a provocation to heighten international tension in line with Dulles' brink of war policy." The criticisms leveled at Dulles are proof of his effectiveness.

At another annual meeting of SEATO in Bangkok on March 29, 1961, the conference issued a communique pointing out the seriousness of the situation in Viet Nam and Laos. It adopted the following resolutions:

(1) The SEATO Council has noted with grave concern the continued offensive by rebel elements in Laos who are continuing to be supplied and assisted by Communist Powers in flagrant disregard of the Geneva Accords.

(2) SEATO is a defensive organization with no aggressive intentions and reiterates, in the words of the treaty, 'its desire to live in peace with all peoples and all governments.'

(3) The Council desires a united, independent and sovereign Laos.

(4) The Council also notes with concern the efforts of an armed minority, again supported from outside in violation of the Geneva accords, to destroy the Government of Viet Nam, and declared its firm resolve not to acquiesce in any such takeover of that country.

Again in 1962, the Secretary General of SEATO reported:

"The Communist movement adopts various disguises in its drive for world power. It creates front organizations which ostensibly seek to carry out reforms; it joins groups of political parties in a 'united front.' It creates secret cells within societies of nations; it engages in revolutionary warfare. Always the Communists are seeking to create conditions which they can exploit. And always they take their orders from the Central Communist authority. Communists owe their allegiance to the Communist Parties either in Moscow or Peking rather than to the country in which they were born." [10]

The communique of the Ninth Council Meeting of SEATO, issued on April 15, 1964, is perhaps the most significant in the history of the Southeast Asian Collective Treaty Organization. This communique reiterated the fact that SEATO has been "a most important stabilizing influence in Southeast Asia." It declared that "world domination remains the aim of Communism, and thus vigilance must not be relaxed," and that in order to deter overt aggression and active insurgency, "there should continue to be emphasis on the development of economic and social conditions which strengthen national resistance to subversion." It further declared that "material support and encouragement should be given those nations which, in defending themselves, need and request such support."

This communique made special reference to the Republic of Viet Nam. It stated that the Council of SEATO noted "the efforts made there to check increasing subversive and aggressive activities, and expressed its continuing deep interest and sympathy for the government and people of Viet Nam in their struggle." It also expressed "grave concern" about the continuing Communist aggression against South Viet Nam. It charged that "documentary and material evidence continues to show that this organized campaign is directed, supplied and supported by the Communist regime in North Viet Nam, in flagrant violation of the Geneva Accords of 1954 and 1962." It highly praised the government and the people of the Republic of Viet Nam, "for they have given eloquent testimony to their determination to fight for their country." The SEATO Council also agreed that the defeat of the Communist campaign is essential not only to the security of the Republic of Viet Nam, but to all of Southeast Asia.

In explaining the U.S. role in Viet Nam, Secretary of State Rusk declared, on April 25, 1964:

"The statement of the SEATO allies that Communist defeat is 'essential' is a reality. To fail to respond . . . would reflect on our honor as a nation, would undermine world-wide confidence in our courage, would convince every nation in South Asia that it must bow to Communist terms to survive. . . . Let no one doubt that we are in this battle as long as South Viet Nam wants our support and needs our assistance to protect its freedom. Our appraisal of the morale and capabilities of the government and people of South Viet Nam is not exclusively American. Seven members of SEATO—all of whom have representatives in South Viet Nam—joined in saying: 'The government and people of the Republic of Viet Nam have given eloquent testimony to their determination to fight for their country.' " [11]

Secretary Rusk moreover stated that "between the end of the Indo-Chinese war in 1954, and 1959, South Viet Nam made great economic and social progress. Its achievements left the vaunted Communist paradise in North Viet Nam far behind. Almost certainly that is why Hanoi reactivated the assault on South Viet Nam in 1959." [12]

The U.S., Australia, and New Zealand in July, 1964, declared that the defeat of Communist aggression against South Viet Nam is necessary "not only to the security of Southeast Asia and the Southwest Pacific, but as a demonstration that Communist expansion by such tactics will not be allowed to succeed." In a communique issued in Washington on July 18, 1964, after its annual meeting, the ANZUS council (Australia, New Zealand, and the United States) noted "with grave concern" the continuing threat to peace in South Viet Nam and Southeast Asia "posed by the aggressive North Vietnamese and Communist Chinese regimes." [13] This Council also reaffirmed its determination "to cooperate with other countries equally determined to preserve their national independence by promoting the peace and security of the area." [14]

The ANZUS Council agreed that they should remain prepared to take further concrete steps within their respective capacities to assure the defeat of this aggression, and expressed the hope that other nations who prize freedom will join in assisting the valiant people of South Viet Nam to preserve their freedom, and to achieve peace, stability, and a better life "which presently are denied to them by the Communist aggressors." The SEATO Secretary General, Kontri Suphamongkon, declared on September 7, 1964, at Bangkok, that SEATO was willing and able to defend the freedom of Southeast Asia. He explained that "the centuries-long fight for freedom of mankind has been too painful for it to be lost by default or by blindness or by lack of determination or cohesiveness." He stated that SEATO member nations have for the past ten years held the fort in Southeast Asia, and that they will continue to do so until freedom is secure.[15] Southeast Asia, he said, has been a "testing ground against the Communist aim to overrun the region, and peoples and governments are for the most part standing firm in their determination to remain free."

The SEATO Secretary-General said that the situation in Laos and South Viet Nam was "particularly crucial. The Communists of North Viet Nam and Mainland China give military assistance to their agents, the Pathet Lao, and utilize the subjugated territory in Laos as a communication route to supply, support and direct the Communist Viet Cong in South Viet Nam."

Regarding the Communist rift, the Secretary-General believed that the two major Communist powers are agreed on their goal of world domination: "They differ primarily as to tactics and leadership." He felt that their threat to the free world might be intensified rather than diminished. In its twelve years of existence, SEATO has had many shortcomings, but it has also accomplished much.[16] Although it has no standing military forces of its own, it stages military exercises every year. These exercises furnish the participating nations with valuable experience in the combined operations of army, sea, and air forces. Concerning anti-subversion, its expert coordination efforts, such as the exchange of information and experiences concerning Communist strategy, tactics, and personnel, are especially beneficial. In the field of economic cooperation and assistance, various projects have been successfully accomplished, e.g., skilled workers have been trained, and a graduate school of engineering, plus a clinical research center, were established in Bangkok in 1959. Medical research centers were established in Pakistan and Thailand. Considerable cultural interchange has taken place by exchanging professors, research fellows, and students, and by sponsoring conferences and forums.

On April 20, 1965, the French Government announced that France would not send a delegate to attend the forthcoming SEATO conference in London. This constituted a blow to SEATO, especially when the Vietnamese war had developed into a very serious stage, calling for more team work on the part of the SEATO signatories. Yet President de Gaulle's attitude towards SEATO was not surprising, as his Government had once previously abstained, in 1964, from a SEATO decision against Communist subversion and aggression. De Gaulle's policy towards SEATO has been very uncooperative. He even urged a "neutralization plan" for Viet Nam in order to appease Hanoi, Peking, and Moscow, all of whom he has long since recognized, and with whom he trades as much as he can. He manages to reserve his criticisms for the United States.

Pakistan's policy towards the May, 1965, SEATO conference in London was rather paradoxical. As a member of

SEATO, Pakistan had supported the American policy from its inception in 1954 to 1963. In 1963, however, Pakistan got closer to the Peking regime. In 1964, it signed a military agreement with Red China. Zulfikar Ali Bhutto, the Pakistani Foreign Minister, visited Peking. During the undeclared war between India and Pakistan in the fall of 1965, Peking served New Delhi an ultimatum as a means of helping Pakistan. Peking's ultimatum turned out to be a bluff, but the Pakistani delegate to the 1965 SEATO Conference in London abstained from the declaration of the conference condemning Communist aggression in Viet Nam. Instead, the delegate urged the restoration of peace in Viet Nam through negotiations on the basis of the Geneva Agreements.[17] The Pakistani delegate did not object to the principles contained in SEATO's declaration, however, admitting that he appreciated the position taken by the conference.

The visit of President Ayub Khan to President Johnson in mid-December, 1965, may yet serve to draw Pakistan closer to Washington, without causing her to break away from Peking. There was some hope at first that Pakistan would be able to reconsider her attitude towards the Vietnamese war. Some commentators thought that Pakistan might consider sending military aid to Viet Nam, but this proved to be wishful thinking, at least for the time being. Pakistan's President is reportedly non-committal toward Viet Nam, hoping that he can stay out of the war.[18] Some observers feel that Pakistan and Cambodia both lost faith in SEATO when they offered to go to the aid of Laos in 1961, only to have the United States decline their offer. America had already decided to "neutralize" Laos, and to remove her from the protection of the SEATO Treaty. Averell Harriman told the Rev. Raymond J. de Jaegher in Saigon, in 1961: "We have to give some places on the government of Laos to the Communists." America's concessions over Laos in 1962 unquestionably encouraged Peking and Hanoi to escalate in South Viet Nam. America is paying the price in human lives for her past mistakes in Asia.

Although Pakistan did not support the position of SEATO in 1965, the delegates from Australia, New Zealand, the Philippines, Thailand, and the United Kingdom strongly supported the position of the United States. In their communique they expressed "grave concern" over the aggression "organized, directed, supplied and supported" by the Communist regime in North Viet Nam. Australia then sent 1500 troops to Viet Nam. This has since been increased to 4500. At the SEATO Conference on May 3, 1965, the British Foreign

Secretary, Michael Stewart, firmly denounced Communist aggression and subversion in Viet Nam, saying: "It is not asked of them that they should surrender any territory . . . It is asked of them simply that they should leave their neighbors alone."

The Communique further stated:

"History shows that tolerance of aggression increases the danger to free societies everywhere . . . and that defeat of this Communist campaign is essential not only to the security of the Republic of Viet Nam, but to that of Southeast Asia." The Communique continued: "Communist expansion by such tactics will not be permitted." The six Council members of SEATO all agreed to increase their assistance to Viet Nam. The United States has not yet formally invoked the Protocol of SEATO regarding Viet Nam, but the legal grounds for the U.S. to repel the aggression in Viet Nam on the strength of the SEATO Treaty are very strong.

The Republic of Korea, which is not a member of SEATO, has already sent 41,000 troops to help stem the aggression. Such international help is of great political and psychological importance. The Vietnamese Government has repeatedly said that it would welcome help from any friendly nation. It is difficult to understand why the forces of the Republic of Korea can be accepted, yet the United States apparently will not permit South Viet Nam to use the troops that have been offered by the Republic of China. There are 600,000 troops on Taiwan, far more than all of the American troops in Viet Nam, and they are among the finest troops in that part of the world. Is it fear on the part of the United States State Department that keeps these troops from being used, fear that Red China might not like it? It is courage, not fear, whereby wars are won. Communism attacks weakness, but follows a "hands-off" policy in the face of strength.

FOOTNOTES

CHAPTER IV: VIET NAM AND SEATO

1. The Mutual Defense Agreements signed by the U.S. with the various Asian and Pacific nations include the following: Korea, Jan. 26, 1950 (and also mutual security treaty signed in 1953); Iran, May 23, 1950; Indonesia, Aug. 15, 1950; Thailand, Oct. 7, 1950; Burma, Nov. 6, 1950; Pakistan, Nov. 29-Dec. 17, 1950 and May 19, 1954; Saudi Arabia, June 10, 1951; New Zealand, June 1951; the Philippines, Aug. 30, 1951; The Tripartite Security

Treaty: Australia, New Zealand and the United States (ANZUS), Sept. 1, 1951; and the Republic of China, Feb. 9, 1951 and Dec. 2 ,1954.

2. *New York Times*, Jan. 14, 1954.
3. British Foreign Office, *Pacific Charter, Manila, September 8, 1954,* (London, H.M. Stationery Office, Cmd. 9299, October 1954), p. 3.
4. U.S. Senate, *Hearing Before the Committee on Foreign Relations, etc., the Southeast Asia Collective Defense Treaty and the Protocol there-to signed at Manila on September 8, 1954,* Pt. 1, pp. 5-10; British Foreign Office, *The South-East Asia Collective Defense Treaty, in Treaty Series,* No. 63, (London, 1963), pp. 2-8.
5. Hanson W. Baldwin, "SEATO's Impact Now Mainly Psychological," *New York Times,* Sept. 12, 1954.
6. Southeast Asia Treaty Organization, *Collective Security: Shield of Freedom,* (Bangkok, rev. ed., 1964), p. 96.
7. *Chinese News Service Releases,* New York, Feb. 10, 1959.
8. *New York Times,* May 26, 1960.
9. *Loc. Cit.*
10. SEATO, *Collective Security: Shield, etc., Op. Cit.*
11. Reprint of an address on "The Situation in the Western Pacific," by U.S. Secretary of State, Dean Rusk, at the Valparaiso University, Valparaiso, Indiana, April 25, 1964. Also in *SEATO Record 10th Anniversary Year,* (Bangkok, Oct. 1964), Vol. III, No. 5, p. 21.
12. *Ibid.,* p. 22.
13. "ANZUS Council Cites Communist Threat," *SEATO Record:, Op. Cit.,* p. 19.
14. *Op. Cit.* pp. 19; 88.
15. *Op. Cit.* pp. 19-22.
16. *Op. Cit.* pp. 8-12.
17. *New York Times,* May 6, 1965.
18. *Ibid.* December 17, 1965.
19. *Loc. Cit.*

CHAPTER V

BAO DAI, HO CHI MINH, AND NGO DINH DIEM

Three very important persons have helped shape the fate of Viet Nam for many years to come. They are Bao Dai, Ho Chi Minh, and Ngo Dinh Diem. Each one represented a different political theory. Each one strongly influenced the policies of the other. The action of one often caused the reaction of another. In many ways the present struggle has largely been their doing. The problems of this tragic country can best be understood by understanding them.

1. *BAO DAI*

Bao Dai became the Emperor of Viet Nam in 1932 at the age of 19. Since 1955 he has lived in France. Ngo Dinh Diem, who succeeded Bao Dai in 1955 as head of the government of South Viet Nam, was assassinated in 1963. Ho Chi Minh, the eldest of the three, still controls North Viet Nam, and is constantly threatening to take over the South.

Bao Dai was the Boy Emperor of Viet Nam during the days of the French Protectorate. He continued on as Emperor during the Japanese military occupation of Indo-China in World War II. In August, 1945, he abdicated, but became "Chief of State" in the Associated State of Viet Nam within the French Union in 1947, and again from 1949 to 1955.

Bao Dai was born in Hue, the capital of An Nam, in 1913, the son of Emperor Khai-Dinh. His original name was Nguyen Vinh Thuy. Bao Dai is his dynastic name, meaning "the preservation of greatness." The heir apparent, he was sent to France to study at the age of nine. He succeeded his father ten years later. Defying tradition, he married a Vietnamese Catholic girl of ordinary birth the following year. The young Emperor wanted very much, at first, to govern his country well. But because of his limited capacity, because his authority was restricted under the French, and because of the shortage of experienced statesmen to serve him, he was unable to accomplish much for his country.

During most of World War II, Bao Dai still enjoyed the rights and privileges of an An Nam Emperor under the protection of the Vichy administration in Indo-China. The Japanese tolerated the French, allowing them to administer local affairs. On March 10, 1945, the Japanese militarists took complete charge of Indo-China from the French. The Japanese ambassador at Saigon announced in Hue that Bao Dai was the Emperor of the independent state of Viet Nam, both North and South. The next day Bao Dai proclaimed that the Franco-Chinese treaty of 1885, which recognized the French protectorate in Indo-China, was hereafter null and void. He expressed his adherence to the principle of "Asia for the Asiatics," and pledged his support to cooperate with Japan within the framework of the Greater East Asia Co-Prosperity Sphere. Bao Dai reorganized his cabinet, and in order to include every political element in his administration, he enlisted nationalists, socialists, pro-Communists, and some who were Communist Party members, unknown to him. On the advice of his new cabinet he ordered the release of all political prisoners, including some well-known Communists.

During this period of Japanese-occupied "independence," there was at least a symbol of unification between the North and South, as Cochin-China, Hanoi, Haiphong, and Tourane were returned to Viet Nam by the French. But from March to August, 1945, allied bombs destroyed railroads, highways, ports, and factories. There was famine in Viet Nam from May until August, yet the Japanese war lords continued plundering wherever they could. When the first atomic bomb was dropped in Japan on August 6, 1945, Tran Trong Kim, the Prime Minister of Viet Nam, resigned immediately, as did most of the cabinet. Bao Dai's quasi-independent rule under Japanese domination lasted for only five months.

The Soviet Union hastened to revoke her "Mutual Security Pact" with Japan, declaring war on her on August 8, 1945. The Japanese Emperor had already broadcast to the world that he would accept unconditional surrender terms from the Allies, and announced that he had ordered the Japanese armed forces throughout the world to cease fighting by August 7. According to the provisions of the Potsdam Conference in July of 1945, the British were to take over the surrender of the Japanese in Indo-China and assume responsibility for the security of that area until they could turn it over to the

French. Bao Dai was aware of the growing activities of the Viet Minh under Ho Chi Minh, and he saw the growing spirit of nationalism. On August 17, 1945, he appealed to President Truman, King George VI, Generalissimo Chiang Kai-shek, and General Charles de Gaulle to recognize his government in Viet Nam. He warned France:

> Even though you may be able to re-establish French administration here, it would not be obeyed any more. Each village would become a nest of resistance; every former collaborator would become an enemy of France . . .

> The only way to safeguard French interests and the spiritual influence of France in Indo-China is to recognize frankly the independence of Viet Nam and to renounce all thoughts of re-establishing French sovereignty or administration under any form whatsoever . . .

> We could easily be able to understand each other and become friends, if you would cease to pretend that you again want to become our masters.[1]

France, the United States, the United Kingdom, and the Republic of China did not pay much attention to this rising tide of nationalism. While these powers were standing by, Ho Chi Minh's forces gained the upperhand, and Bao Dai was forced to abdicate on August 21, just four days after his urgent and reasonable appeal. Perhaps it had already been too late to help Bao Dai counteract Ho Chi Minh, who had masqueraded as the leader of Vietnamese nationalism, and had been given substantial aid by the United States, Great Britain, and Nationalist China. Although the non-Communist countries did not see the political value of Bao Dai, the astute Ho Chi Minh appreciated the usefulness of the name to the Vietnamese, and even to the outside world. Immediately after the abdication of Bao Dai in August, 1945, Ho Chi Minh conferred on him the title of "Supreme Adviser" to Ho's *Democratic Republic of Viet Nam,* and added the title of "Citizen Prince" to precede his name. By so doing, Ho Chi Minh could gain the support of the royalists and many other non-Communists who supported Bao Dai. This also created the impression abroad that Ho Chi Minh's regime was not Communist, but only controlled by the Viet Minh.* Bao Dai accepted the title, only to find himself a virtual prisoner in Hanoi. Six months later, on March 18, 1946, he flew to Hong Kong and stayed there. It was during this long exile in Hong Kong that he acquired the new title of "Playboy Emperor."

By the end of August, 1945, substantial British forces arrived in Saigon, while a large number of Chinese Nationalist troops entered Hanoi. Soon the French army also arrived in Saigon. The Viet Minh* had quickly formed a provisional government under the name *Democratic Republic of Viet Nam.* On September 2, 1945, it pronounced Ho Chi Minh President of that "Republic," while the British, Chinese, and French were still discussing how to deal with him. President Franklin D. Roosevelt had told Stalin at Yalta that the French should not be allowed back in Indo-China. Britain opposed this, but it gave great encouragement to Stalin, who acted through his agent, Ho Chi Minh, to do everything he could to take over that part of the world.

In order to make the new Viet Minh regime legitimate and proper, the Communists had to get rid of Bao Dai. Combining promises and threats, they forced Bao Dai to abdicate on August 24, 1945, nine days before they inaugurated the *Democratic Republic of Viet Nam.* Bao Dai sent a message to the Vietnamese people saying that during his twenty years' reign he had accomplished very little for them, thereby discouraging them from fighting for him or for their independence. During all those years he had the French, then the Japanese, and then the Viet Minh to contend with, each of whom in turn, severely hampered his reign and did its best to limit his role to that of a figurehead.

After 1946 the Viet Minh became stronger and more arrogant against the French. Paris called in Bao Dai to form a government against Ho Chi Minh. Bao Dai requested Ngo Dinh Diem to come to Hong Kong for consultation. When Diem arrived, however, he found that Bao Dai had already signed an agreement with the French High Commissioner, Emile Bollaert, making Viet Nam a member of the French Union. Diem objected to the agreement, and Bao Dai found himself defending unpopular French colonial control while

---

* "Viet Minh" is an abbreviation of "Viet-Nam Doc-Lap Dong Minh," or "The Alliance of Leagues for the Independence of Viet Nam." Such a name was used in order to enlist the people of Viet Nam to join the organization under the assumption they would be working for independence. It was a Communist-front organization.

"Viet Cong" is an abbreviation of "Viet Cong-San," which means "Viet Communists." The term has been widely used since the defeat of the French at Dien Bien Phu in May, 1954.

Ho Chi Minh advocated complete independence from France. William C. Bullitt, the former American Ambassador to France, advocated support of Bao Dai, and the French made this suggestion their policy. Bullitt conferred with Bao Dai in Hong Kong in October, 1947, and in Geneva two months later.[2]

In the spring of 1948 the *Radical Socialist Party* in France was replaced by General Charles de Gaulle's *Rally of the French People*. The RPF was unwilling to lessen its control over the Vietnamese. Bao Dai then discontinued his talks with the French and went back to Hong Kong. Diem contacted the French High Commissioner to see if France would give more liberal terms to Viet Nam, but he was unsuccessful. Diem was opposed to Ho Chi Minh and the Viet Minh, but he did not want to cooperate with the French until actual dominion status was granted. By the end of 1948 it was clear to him that the French domination was no different from what it had been before. Meanwhile, the Viet Minh cleverly denounced the Bao Dai regime, and kept plugging the slogan, "Viet Nam for the Vietnamese."

While the desperate struggle between the Viet Minh forces and General Nguyen Van Xuan's provisional government went on, Bao Dai was still in France—from 1948 until the spring of 1949. Vincent Auriol, the French President, thus had to grant Bao Dai further power by signing an agreement at the Elysee Palace in Paris on March 8, 1949. Bao Dai then told the press that he would soon return to Viet Nam. He said further that the country would be given democratic institutions and profound economic and social reforms.[3] Finally, on March 8, 1949, Viet Nam formally joined the French Union as an associated state. Viet Nam still recognized France's right to control its foreign policy and its defense. Laos and Cambodia accepted similar agreements with France in the latter part of 1949. Viet Nam, however, was to have her own army, with French advisers and equipment. The French newspaper, *Le Monde,* reported from Washington that the United States believed that a national government under Bao Dai might be able to halt the spread of Communism in Viet Nam. The Viet Minh then immediately denounced the reported "American intervention." Leftist elements in France urged immediate negotiations with Ho Chi Minh. That same year, in the fall of 1949, Ho Chi Minh declared that "the center of gravity of the power in Asia had shifted." Communist China had a great psychological, political, and military impact on the Vietnamese. In December, 1949, the Chinese Communists reached the borders of Viet

Nam and hoisted their Red flag at International Bridge, connecting Tung Hing on the Chinese side and Mon Cay on the Vietnamese side. Peking extended its recognition to Ho Chi Minh's regime in the early part of January, 1950, and Moscow followed suit. In August, 1950, Ho Chi Minh took pride in the fact that Viet Minh was recognized "by the two biggest countries in the world—the Soviet Union and the People's Republic of China—and by the new democratic countries." [4] That same year, Chinese Communist troops were posted at the Vietnamese borders. The Viet Minh then commenced full-scale attacks on the French positions along the Chinese frontiers. Soon one Vietnamese village after another fell to the Viet Minh.

In 1950, Premier Rene Pleven informed the French National Assembly that large quantities of artillery, automatic weapons, mortars, and radio equipment had been brought into Viet Nam from Red China, and that more than 20,000 Viet Minh troops had been trained and equipped by the Chinese Communists. In 1951, Peking increased its military advisers and material to the Viet Minh. The Viet Minh, in return, sent tin, manganese, wolfram, rice, rubber, timber, and opium to Red China.

On March 3, 1951, a veteran Communist named Ho Tung Mau announced, in the presence of Ho Chi Minh, the formation of the Viet Nam Lao Dong (the Workers Party). He described it as the "vanguard and general staff of the working class and working people of Viet Nam." [5] As the Viet Minh pursued a more aggressive policy, Bao Dai's government began to realize that it had to build a national Vietnamese army in order to cope with the Viet Minh activities. By 1953 the Viet Minh army, composed of The People's Army, regional troops and the local militia, had from 300,000 to 400,000 men.[6] Bao Dai had the French Union forces, the Expeditionary Corps, the African Legionnaires, and the native Vietnamese forces and auxiliaries. Both sides had about the same number of troops. The build-up of the National Vietnamese Army owed much to General Jean de Lattre de Tassigny and to General Nguyen Van Hing, before the arrival of the American military advisers in Saigon in 1956.

In order to cope with the increasing demand for elections, local and national, Nguyen Van Tam, Prime Minister under the Bao Dai Government, submitted a proposal to the National Congress on October 16, 1953. As a result, the Congress adopted a resolution in qualified terms to repudiate the concept of the French Union. About the same time, Prime Minister Tam was involved in a scandal that brought his resignation in January, 1954, and the planned national election was postponed. Even if the complete independence of South Viet Nam had been acquired from Paris, and if the French forces had entirely withdrawn, it would have left the Bao Dai Government at the mercy of the Viet Minh and Red China. The confusion of Vietnamese internal politics, together with the Viet Minh pressures, had paved the way for the disastrous defeat of the French forces at Dien Bien Phu on May 8, 1954. France's seventy years of colonialism in Asia ended without any popular realization that the threat of Communism, not the overthrow of colonialism, was the critical issue.

Most of the American economic and military aid to France from 1950 to 1954 was used by the French Government for the support of the war in Viet Nam, though partially in Laos and Cambodia. It was up to the French Government, however, to spend the American money and material where it deemed fit. The United States defrayed about 80 percent of French military expenditures in Indo-China. The American Government paid about $500 million annually to France for her ammunition, aircraft, automatic weapons, hospital equipment, naval vessels and technical equipment, under the American Military Assistance Advisory Group (MAAG). In 1953, at the special request of the French, the United States gave France an extra $385 million. This was supposed to aid the plan drafted by General Henri Navarre to force the Communists to fight out in the open instead of in hiding. But the Communists continued to infiltrate and penetrate by stealth into the French areas of defense until they were strong enough to challenge openly the French forces.

2. *Ho Chi Minh*

Now in his late seventies, the outstanding Communist in Viet Nam's history is a man of many aliases. As a political refugee in China, he used various aliases to suit the occasion. The name given him by his father is Nguyen Sang Cong. In school, at the age of ten, he was called Nguyen Bih-sinh. While in exile abroad he called himself "Nguyen Ai Quoc," which became his name for many years. Nguyen is his real surname; "Ai Quoc" means "love of his country." When he was a political refugee in Canton, China, in 1925 and 1927, he used the names of "Ly Thuy," "Ly Suei," "Lee Shun," "Vuong Son Nhi" or "Vuong Son," and various other appellations. One of the authors, as a student, used to see Ho Chi Minh in Canton, where he observed him using the names "Ly Thuy," "Lee Suei," and "Lee Shuk" during the years 1925 to 1927.

Ho Chi Minh studied the Chinese classics as a boy. For awhile he studied French subjects at the same Lycee in Hue where Diem was to study ten years later. This Lycee was founded by Ngo Dinh Kah, the father of Diem. Later it became a national college for Vietnamese students. When Ho Chi Minh was in Canton, China, he spoke and wrote Chinese to students who encountered him. One of the authors of this book was among them. Ho learned English as a seaman. He embraced the philosophy of advanced Socialism, then Communism, after going to France in 1911. He was trained in Soviet Russia in 1924 and 1925. Besides his native Vietnamese, he speaks the French, Russian, and Chinese languages. He also has a good knowledge of conversational English.

It was reported in 1933 that "Nguyen Ai Quoc" was dead. On several occasions he denied that he was "Nguyen Ai Quoc," but in the August, 1960, issue of *Viet Nam Dan Chu Cong Hoa* (the Democratic Republic of Viet Nam), a picture of Ho Chi Minh was published with the caption: "Comrade Nguyen Ai Quoc at age 30, carrying out his revolutionary activities abroad." This was the first time that Ho Chi Minh had been officially identified as the same person as "Nguyen Ai Quoc." But the name Ho Chi Minh was generally used in Southwest China, adjacent to what is now North Viet Nam, where he spent most of the time from 1941 to 1945. Ho lived with a Chinese woman for many years, but because of his revolutionary activities he often had to flee, and finally lost contact with her. When he did try to find her, he was unable to do so.

Ho Chi Minh's father was a practitioner of Chinese herbs in Viet Nam. His influence over his son seems to have been slight, and after Ho qualified as a teacher in Viet Nam the father helped him get a job on a French ship, the *SS La Touche-Treville*, sailing from Saigon to Marseilles. After working on board the French ship for two years, Ho worked in the kitchen of the Carlton Hotel in London from 1913 to 1917. During that time he was very active in the Overseas Workers Union, an anti-colonial and anti-imperialist organization established by Chinese and Indian seamen. During World War I there were about 60,000 Vietnamese soldiers and seamen in France, but only a few hundred in London. So he went to France to promote revolutionary activity among his countrymen. Soon Ho Chi Minh was working with Nguyen The Truyen, a well-known left-wing Vietnamese leader in France.* Together they decided to publish a magazine called "Viet Nam Hon" (The Soul of Viet Nam). It was a small periodical, printed in Vietnamese. It advocated the abolition of the colonial system. The Socialist movement at that time was quite strong in France, and the little magazine, with its very limited circulation, was not molested.

While in France, Ho became acquainted with the French Socialists. He joined the party and was a delegate to the Socialist Congress in 1920, where he voted for the Third International and for "Scientific Socialism—Communism." In 1922 he attended the 4th Congress of the Communist International, which decided to increase its efforts for revolution in East Asia by establishing an Asian Section of the Communist Party in Moscow. In 1923 he attended the Peasants International Congress. In 1924 he studied at the Eastern Workers University in the Soviet Union. Ho studied the works of Marx and Lenin, Communist tactics and party machinery. He claimed that he was a Chinese citizen and obtained a Chinese passport to go to the Soviet Union.

Ho Chi Minh is one of the most experienced conspirators alive, and has had to escape from police traps many times in China, France, England, and Indo-China. He possesses the qualities of a leader, and has long been austere, perserving, determined, and devoted to the cause of revolution. Family ties were of little interest to him. Although his physique has always been fragile, he has always worked diligently and relentlessly.

In 1925, while the Soviet Union was cooperating with the Nationalist Party in China, Ho Chi Minh was sent to Canton to direct anti-French colonial activities in China. He became secretary to the well-known Communist, Michael Borodin, a Soviet agent who was then the Supreme Political Adviser of the Chinese National Government and the Kuomintang in Canton from 1925 to 1927. Ho Chi Minh was known in those days to the young Chinese students at various colleges and at Whang-Poa Military Academy. He cooperated closely with Chou En-lai, Liu Shao-chi, and other Chinese Communists in Canton. He also organized the Association of the Vietnamese Revolutionary Comrades in Canton at that time.

There was a movement for closer cooperation between China, Japan, and Viet Nam, called *Dong Du* (Trip to the East), under the leadership of a Vietnamese scholar, Pham Boi Chau. Ho Chi Minh was one of the followers of Pham Boi

---

* Nguyen The Truyen was a presidential candidate against Ngo Dinh Diem in 1961, but was defeated by an overwhelming majority.

Chau, but in 1925 Ho betrayed him, selling him to the French security force for more than 100,000 piasters. Five or six piasters at that time could buy an ox or a water buffalo. Chau was told by Ho Chi Minh to meet him at an address in Shanghai. As prearranged, Chau was immediately arrested by the French. The explanation given by Ho Chi Minh was that Chau's arrest would be good for the revolutionary cause because it needed the money to function. When Ho Chi Minh received the money, he used part of it to organize the League of Revolutionary Youth of Viet Nam in Canton. What Chau had to say about the matter has not been recorded.

Ho Chi also acted as informer to the French Consul in Hong Kong, reporting the movements of conservative and patriotic Vietnamese who were about to leave or return to Viet Nam. By so doing he got rid of his political rivals and got paid for doing so. Through the French and otherwise, Ho Chi Minh saw to it that most of the patriotic Vietnamese leaders who were not Communist were liquidated. This also forced the Vietnamese to choose between Ho Chi Minh's Communist organization and the activities of the French colonialists.

In 1929, Ho Chi Minh was sent to Siam (Thailand) where he worked under a French Communist agent, Hilaire Noulens. Together they communized the Vietnamese emigres in that country. Later the Comintern sent Ho Chi Minh to Hong Kong, where he stayed until he was arrested on June 6, 1931. He then went to Singapore where he was again arrested and sent back to Hong Kong. There he was admitted to St. Paul's Hospital for treatment of tuberculosis. After a year's recuperation, Ho Chi Minh again spent some time with the Chinese Communists, learning their political and military tactics, particularly guerrilla warfare. Occasionally he returned to Viet Nam and directed the *Popuar Front* against French colonialism.

In the spring of 1941, Moscow ordered Ho Chi Minh to come to Moscow, and then sent him back to South China, near Viet Nam. It was at this time that he began to use the name *Ho Chi Minh*. Although he worked directly under the Kremlin at all times, he claimed to be a patriot and said that he had no other purpose except to deliver his country from Japanese occupation. He formed a united front by enlisting the various elements that were against French and Japanese imperialism. This is how the Viet Minh front was formed. From 1942 until 1945, Ho Chi Minh received financial and military aid from American, British, and Chinese military authorities in exchange for his information about the Japanese military movements in Indo-China.

Ho Chi Minh was quick to learn that Japan would soon be defeated. In August, 1945, he forced Bao Dai to abdicate as the Emperor of An Nam and created the *Democratic Republic of Viet Nam*. He persuaded or compelled Bao Dai to become the Supreme Adviser to the newly created "republic," in order to win over the support of the Royalists and many non-Communist citizens of Viet Nam. He still had many political rivals, and he used one group against the other, liquidating most of them in one way or another before the end of 1945. His terrorism was well known to the better informed, and gradually most of the people of Viet Nam became aware of it. Later on he killed as many as 100,000 peasants from 1954-1956 in order to destroy the resistance in North Viet Nam, in the traditional Communist manner of getting control over agriculture.[7]

In 1946 Ho Chi Minh and his coalition government were still in a desperate position. They were attacked by Vietnamese who were supported by the Chinese Nationalists and by the French troops. But to Ho Chi Minh's surprise and good fortune, France succeeded in convincing Chiang Kai-shek that he should withdraw all of the Chinese Nationalist troops from northern Viet Nam, even before the French arrived. France thought she could make short work of Ho's forces. Instead, France gave him a respite during which he could strengthen his position immensely. After the withdrawal of the Chinese Nationalists, Ho Chi Minh soon defeated almost all the Vietnamese forces that were opposed to him.

Ho Chi Minh today is the head of the Communist Party of Viet Nam, and is in charge of the Communist movement in Laos and Cambodia. He is President of the *Democratic Republic of Viet Nam,* which is the Communist government of North Viet Nam. Whether to extend the war or negotiate peace is still largely his decision. But he is also very dependent on Communist China and Soviet Russia. His government thus far has both refused to go to the conference table and to stop its prolonged and brutal aggression against South Viet Nam. Until Peking, Moscow, or both give their approval to end the fighting at the time they consider most favorable, or until he faces defeat, Ho Chi Minh will continue his war against the Republic of Viet Nam, and indirectly against the whole free world.

3. *Ngo Dinh Diem*

Concerning the man who was the only President South Viet Nam has ever elected and who headed that government for approximately nine years, it is difficult to say which are more widespread about him, the facts or the fallacies. He has been called "The Last of the Mandarins," * a dictator, and the only democratic leader his country ever had. The Communists called him a puppet of the United States, while U.S. State Department officials often thought him too Asian and too independent.

His full name was Jean-Baptiste Ngo Dinh Diem. He was known throughout America simply as Diem. His life was bound to be controversial, for he assumed leadership of a country that was torn apart by war, economically ruined. politically disintegrated, and facing Communist subversion and aggression. Neither his friends nor his foes expected him to form a lasting government. When the Viet Minh accepted the French surrender at Dien Bien Phu in May, 1954, and signed the Geneva Agreements two months later, the Communists were convinced that within two years they would be able to unite North and South Viet Nam under Communist Rule without much trouble. That was one of the main reasons why the Communists agreed to the Geneva Agreements.

Diem has been both highly praised and severely condemned. To understand him it is necessary to know his background. His father was a scholar and a mandarin, i.e., one of the officials of the An Nam Empire. His mother was a modest woman with rigid family training in the tradition of the Confucian Ethical codes. Ngo Dinh Diem was born on January 2, 1901, in his parents' modest home in Hue, the old capital of An Nam. One of the author's of this book visited Diem's aged mother in Hue in April, 1961. She was then 91 years old. Although semi-paralyzed, she was still very alert. Whenever her sons came home, including Diem and Monsignor Ngo Dinh Thuc, the former Archbishop of Hue, she invariably asked them whether they had done anything wrong. She had always maintained a strict maternal discipline and a lofty moral code for all the members of the Ngo family.

The ancestral family home was small, with a parlor, four sleeping rooms, and a small kitchen opening onto a courtyard

* The title of the book on the late President Diem by Anthony T. Bouscaren, Duquesne University Press, 1965. Dr. Bouscaren is employed by the Asian Speakers Bureau.

with flowers and trees. Diem's mother, like himself, was very fond of birds and she received many different kinds from various parts of the world. She died in Saigon at the age of 93, about a month after the assassination of her sons Diem and Nhu in 1963.

Ngo Dinh Diem had five brothers and one sister. His eldest brother, Ngo Dinh Khoi, a provincial mandarin, was murdered along with his son by the Communists in 1946. His second eldest brother, Ngo Dinh Thuc, was bishop of Vin Long and later became Archbishop of Hue in 1958. At the time of Diem's assassination he was attending the Ecumenical Council in Rome. After the assassination of Diem and his brother Nhu, Archbishop Thuc wanted to return to Hue, but he was asked by Pope Paul to await further developments in Viet Nam. He is now living a very quiet life in Rome. Still another brother is Ngo Dinh Luyen, who for some time was Vietnamese Ambassador to London. He now lives very humbly on the north coast of Africa, where he struggles to support his large family.

Of all the brothers, Ngo Dinh Nhu, the brother assassinated with Diem, was the most talked about and the most attacked. As a young man he was a trade union leader and organized a Congress of *National Union and Peace* which met on September 6, 1953, in Cholon, the twin city of Saigon. This Congress demanded unconditional independence for Viet Nam, the meeting of a national assembly, freedom of speech, reform of the army and administration, and an end to corruption. Nhu later formed a small political group in Saigon. He was considered progressive—even leftist—at that time. But after Diem became President of the Republic of Viet Nam, Nhu acted as an adviser to his brother. He was later the head of the Youth Movement in Viet Nam. He headed the Strategic Hamlet Program and the National Revolutionary Party of Viet Nam. Although he held no other official position in his brother's government, he was probably the most powerful man in the country from 1957 to 1963, next to the President himself. Nhu was about ten years younger than Diem. He was once imprisoned by the Communists, but escaped. His wife, Madame Nhu, and the eldest daughter were held by the Communists as hostages for several months, but were released after a ransom was paid.

Madame Nhu, who was born Tran Le Xuan, of a prominent Vientamese family, was head of the Women's Solidarity Movement in Viet Nam, an organization she founded and built into two million members. One of the most influential women in Saigon, she was elected to the National Assembly in 1956. When Diem first became President in Saigon, the head of the army, General Nguyen Van Hing, kept plotting against him. He threatened a coup almost daily, and said that he would exile Diem and his family, but would keep Madam Nhu "as a concubine." One day she confronted the general at a cocktail party in Saigon and told him plainly, so that all could hear:

"General, you are never going to overthrow this government because you don't have the guts. And if you do overthrow it, you will never have me because I will claw your throat out first."

No one had had the courage to challenge him before. It was because of such courage that Saigon first began to take notice of Madame Nhu.

After her election to the National Assembly she proceeded to upgrade the status of women, who until then had no legal rights whatsoever. The Vietnamese woman, she pointed out, was "an eternal minor, an unpaid servant, a doll without a soul." She put through the assembly a Family Bill outlawing adultery, polygamy, concubinage and divorce (except by presidential dispensation). Perhaps she was too strong in doing so, she commented later, but she said, "I have chosen to defend the legitimate family."

Madame Nhu was from an old Buddhist family. She became a Catholic at the time of her marriage. Some of her father's extensive land holdings were confiscated by the Diem Government as part of its land reform program. Her father became the Vietnamese Ambassador to the United States several years before her husband's murder, but in 1963 the Ambassador began to denounce Diem.

Madame Nhu served in some ways as the first lady of South Viet Nam since her brother-in-law, President Diem, had never married. Although she attended college for only a short time, she speaks French fluently. She first learned English when she lived in a convent for a few months in Hong Kong, and later from the wife of an American editor in Saigon. She became known for her outspokenness, although she was sometimes misrepresented by the press. The authors were together in New York City on October 21, 1963, when she was asked by reporters after her lecture, "If you were President of the United States, what three things would you do?" The New York newspapers next day ran pictures of her shaking her finger, with the caption: "Madame Nhu criticizes Kennedy." The pictures showed her wearing different clothing from what she wore at the talk, and were obviously not taken the night before, but they made her appear critical.

A fourth brother of Diem, Ngo Dinh Can, lived in Hue, in the northern part of South Viet Nam. His primary interest had been in labor unions, but he was very anti-Communist, and succeeded in keeping that area out of Communist hands. Can spoke no French and no English, although he had studied a little French in school. He very seldom received foreigners, and although he held no official position, he had more power than the governor in Hue. After the assassinations, Can took refuge with the Redemptionist Fathers, whom he had often befriended. For fear that he might cause them severe punishment from the leaders of the coup, he went to the American Consulate at Hue and asked for asylum. The consulate asked for instructions from the American Embassy in Saigon. Ambassador Henry Cabot Lodge replied that the consulate could not grant him asylum, but he ordered Can to be sent immediately to the American Embassy. Upon his arrival, the Embassy delivered Can to the Military Revolutionary Council for trial. It has been authoritatively learned by the authors that the American Embassy had the understanding with the Council that three conditions were attached to the delivery of Can:

    i. He was to receive a fair and public trial;
    ii. He was not to be ill-treated;
    iii. He was not to be shot or killed.

It was naive to think that a fair and public trial would be possible under the circumstances. Can did not even receive a proper diet and medical treatment, although he was seriously ill at the time with high blood pressure and diabetes. As a result of this maltreatment and lack of medical care in prison, Can would probably have soon died. Instead, too weak to stand, he was held standing by ropes to a post and shot. One can only recall that when a pro-Communist monk took refuge in the American Embassy in August, 1963, he was given comfortable asylum by Ambassador Lodge until Diem and Nhu were killed nine weeks later. It remains for history to pass judgment on such inconsistencies.

The only sister in Diem's family married a merchant, and they have a son who is a Catholic priest. This branch of the family have never participated in politics. Nhu's daughter, Ngo Dinh Le Thuy, was with Madame Nhu in Los Angeles when her father was killed in Saigon. The three sons, Din Trac, Dinh Auyen, and Dinh Quyh, were flown by chartered plane to Rome a few days after the coup. All of the Nhu children now live with their mother in Rome and attend school there and in Paris. They visit with their uncle, the Archbishop, as Pope Paul gave a modest residence for him and them to live in. Madame Nhu is still banned by the State Department from visiting the United States. She is caring for her children and working on her memoirs.

Diem's early education was in Chinese, and he was undoubtedly influenced by Chinese culture. When he went to visit in Seoul, Korea, for example, he wrote a poem in classical Chinese for the occasion. Diem's ancestors were

The following poem, originally in Chinese classical style, was written by President Ngo Dinh Diem while he was flying to Seoul, Republic of Korea, on September 18, 1957:

Accompanying the stars, I traverse
Ten thousand miles to Seoul.

The landscape of this storied place,
Its scenery and man-made things, my eyes admire.

Heroic memories linger here of Hwa-Rang's deeds*
And make this land a sight of Grandeur;
While ruins of Ki Tza's ** fortress stand alone
No trees or woods around.

Here, lofty aims of heroes past
By many a patriot are remembered.

The friendship of allies is strengthened
By the kindred cultures of peoples.

Blossoming will be the flowers of freedom,
Gone will be the forces of evil;

* "Hwa Rang" in Korean is not a name of an individual, but a title given to leaders of ancient knights known as "Hwa Rang Do," in the Silla Dynasty, which was founded in 57 B.C. The Hwa Rangs were the impetus and driving force to the unification of Korea under the Kingdom of Silla. They were chosen from noble families on the basis of their good looks, education, intelligence and good behavior. Their motto was: Loyalty to the nation, faithfulness to the parents, trustworthiness to friends, no retreat from battle, and fair treatment of the enemy in accordance with law. (This has become a guide or spiritual code of the present military forces of the Republic of Korea.) The biggest victory won by the "Hwa Rang" was in 562, when they were at war against the "Kara Kingdom."

** "Ki Tza" is pronounced in Korean as "Ki Gi," (in Chinese "Chi Tze") and is supposedly the founder of Korea.

United will be the whole nation,
Bright again, the Sun and the Moon.

Catholic since the 17th century. At the age of 15 Diem
began studies to become a Christian Brother. He soon left
the seminary, however, and attended a French school where
he prepared himself for civil service. It is interesting to
note that to Diem and to many Vietnamese and Chinese,
Confucian ethics and teachings are not in conflict with
Catholicism or the practice of Catholic doctrines. A good
Catholic may still adhere to the ethical codes of Confucius. Chinese Catholic bishops have taken part in public
ceremonies commemorating Confucius' birthday in Confucian temples. Diem declared Confucius' birthday a national
holiday in Viet Nam.

Diem's father was a very close friend of Nguyen Huu Bai,
the Prime Minister of the Imperial Court of An Nam. For
some time he raised Diem as though he were his own son.
Diem completed his studies at the Lycee, a French school
in Hue, just ten years after Ho Chi Minh attended there.
Diem then entered the School of Law and Administration at
Hanoi. He graduated in 1921 at the top of his class, then
entered government service as a District Chief in Hue. At
28 he became Governor of Phan Rang, a very poor province
where Ho Chi Minh had taught some years earlier. By
1932, Diem had gained a reputation as a capable administrator. The young Emperor, Bao Dai, appointed him to the Senior
Administrative Corps, and in the following year Diem was
appointed Minister of the Interior, the chief minister in the
government. With his uncompromising temperament, he felt
that the Emperor was not strong enough in resisting the
French, so he resigned, returning all his titles and decora-
tions to both the Emperor and the French colonial authorities just two months after his cabinet appointment. Diem
then spent several years in France. He kept in contact with
various Vietnamese national leaders from 1934 to 1941, both
in Viet Nam and in Europe. He returned to Viet Nam in
July, 1944, but left shortly after. In March, 1945, both the
Japanese and Bao Dai offered him positions in the Viet Nam
government, but he declined.

Shortly after V. J. Day, when Hue fell into the hands of
the Viet Minh, Diem escaped along the coastal road but
was recognized by the Viet Minh and arrested at Tuy-Hoa.
He was handcuffed and brought to Ho Chi Minh in Tuyen-
Quang. Knowing his administrative ability and his excellent

reputation among the Vietnamese, Ho Chi Minh offered Diem the same position he had held under Bao Dai; i.e., Minister of Interior. Although still a prisoner of the Viet Minh, Diem flatly refused to cooperate with Ho, even at the risk of his life. Diem told Ho that he could never cooperate with him. Diem demanded to know why his eldest brother, Ngo Dinh Khoi, had been killed by the Viet Minh, along with Khoi's little son. Ho Chi Minh replied that it had been a mistake, that the country had been in a state of confusion. Diem turned on his heel and walked out.[8]

Diem was sent back to prison by Ho Chi Minh, but was released after the French made an agreement with the Viet Minh which provided for the release of all political prisoners. He returned to Hue in 1946, and became head of the *National Union Front*, a conservative group. He refused to accept any official position from the French or from Bao Dai, devoting himself to the cause of independence for Viet Nam. His theory regarding Vietnamese independence was "all or nothing."

In 1947, Diem went to Nanking, hoping to get help from Nationalist China. He did not succeed in seeing President Chiang Kai-shek, although he did see a number of Chinese government and Kuomintang officials. He succeeded in obtaining pledges from the Chinese National Government that certain aid would be given him. Due to a delicate and complicated international situation, however, the help he received from the Chinese Government from 1947 to 1954 was very limited.

When Bao Dai again assumed his position as Chief of State of Viet Nam in 1949, he offered Diem the post of Prime Minister, since Diem had become the leader of the Nationalist majority. Diem refused, however, and organized a small political party in South and Central Viet Nam called *The Nationalist Movement*. The backbone of this movement were the Catholics and their friends and sympathizers. The French kept a watchful eye on Diem, but since he and his co-workers did not use violent methods, the French did not suppress them.

In August, 1950, Diem left Saigon for Hong Kong and Tokyo. He tried to see General Douglas MacArthur, the Allied Supreme Commander in Japan and United Nations Commander in Korea. He did not succeed, so he left Tokyo for Washington, D. C., in the hope of pleading the cause of his people there. He arrived in Washington with a letter of introduction to Archbishop Paul Yu-pin, who was then President of the Institute of Chinese Culture. Diem was asked to stay at the Institute. One of the authors of this book was then Vice-Director of the Institute. He gave Diem a room on the second floor, and Diem stayed there for several months. That was in 1950.

Diem made several visits to the Maryknoll Fathers at Lakewood, New Jersey, and Ossining, New York. He stayed with them briefly, then returned to the Institute of Chinese Culture in Washington. During his stay in the United States, he studied English, American history, and government. He tried to approach the State Department, but was told that since he had no diplomatic or official status, the Department could not discuss Viet Nam with him. Through the introduction of personal friends he did succeed in meeting Francis Cardinal Spellman, Richard Cardinal Cushing, Senator William F. Knowland, Senator Mike Mansfield, Justice William O. Douglas, the late Senator John F. Kennedy, and Congressman John W. McCormack and Walter Judd.

In 1951, when the United States began increasing its aid to France to combat the Communists in Viet Nam, Diem, who had been in Europe with the Reverend Raymond J. de Jaegher, returned to Washington, remaining in the United States until the spring of 1953. In May of that year, Diem again left for Belgium, where he stayed with the Benedictine monks at Saint Andre-les-Bruges.

Diem had first met Father de Jaegher in 1947.* He is a brilliant linguist with an extensive knowledge of Communism and the Orient. He became Diem's frequent companion and closest friend in China, the United States, and Europe. After Diem became Prime Minister of Viet Nam in 1954, he invited Father de Jaegher, an Asian expert, to help him. From 1955 until 1963, Diem consulted daily with Father de Jaegher, who served without any title or remuneration. After Diem's assassination, the Military Revolutionary President, General Duong Van Minh, consulted him frequently.

The French Government granted full independence to Viet Nam on June 4, 1954, less than a month after its defeat at Dien Bien Phu. Diem thought the time was ripe for him to form a new government in Viet Nam. At the suggestion of Georges Bidault, the French Premier, who was a close friend

* Father Raymond J. de Jaegher speaks and writes Chinese fluently. He is the author of "The Enemy Within" (New York, 1952) and is an authority on China and Viet Nam. He directed the Free Pacific Association in Saigon, founded several schools there, and edited papers and magazines in Chinese, French, and English. He is closely associated with the authors at the *Asian Speakers Bureau* and the *East Asian Research Institute, Inc., at* 86 Riverside Drive, New York City.

of both Bao Dai and Diem, Bao Dai made Diem his Prime Minister and gave him full power over the State of Viet Nam. Diem in turn gave allegiance to Bao Dai as the Chief of State. Bao Dai then took up residence in France and never returned to Viet Nam. Diem arrived in Saigon on June 26, 1954. He had no military forces, and was met by only a few close friends and officials at the airport. On July 7, the Double Seven of the same same year, Diem announced the formation of his first cabinet. The Double Seven (the seventh day of the seventh month) later became a national holiday.

Although Diem was Prime Minister, he did not have control of the army. General Nguyen Van Hing, the Chief of Staff, frequently disobeyed him and plotted to overthrow him. Bao Dai pleaded with General Hing from Paris to cooperate with Diem, and pressure was also put on him by the United States. Diem finally managed to dismiss the general.

On July 20, 1954, two weeks after Diem formed his cabinet, the Geneva Truce was signed between France and the Hanoi regime. This brought about the division of Viet Nam into two separate zones. Ho Chi Minh called his Communist Government in the North the *Democratic Republic of Viet Nam.* His capital is Hanoi, where he controls a population of between sixteen and seventeen million. In the South, with his capital at Saigon, with a population of between fifteen and sixteen million, Diem inherited the very weak government established by Bao Dai. Following the defeat of the French only two months before, the Diem Government was more than shaky. Nearly all the industries that had been established in Viet Nam were located in the North. The South was almost entirely agricultural. Most of the French officials returned to France, although many French businessmen remained in Viet Nam. Many of the European shops and stores in Saigon were closed. Throughout the countryside, the railways and public roads were destroyed or disrupted. Foodstuffs often could not be transported from one place to another. Rice factories in Saigon and Cholon could not get enough crops from the villages to polish and process the rice. The production of crude rubber had been greatly reduced, and the Viet Cong guerrillas still terrorized the villages.

The most effective weapons Diem possessed were his own integrity and his administrative experience. He appealed to the conscience and patriotism of the people, and the majority supported him. Even the Trotskyites backed him for awhile, since they were against Ho Chi Minh. Later, however, they turned against Diem.

Any government opposed to flourishing vice encounters opposition from monied interests, and Diem was no exception. He soon found himself opposed by General Le Va Vien of the Binh Xuyen. General Vien was known as the "vice king" of Cholon. The general controlled the gambling, brothels and opium dens in the Saigon area. Many of the Cholon police were being bribed by him. Diem, shortly after the formation of his cabinet, suppressed gambling, prostitution, and the use of opium. He publicly witnessed the burning of opium pipes in downtown Saigon. Gamblers and prostitutes were arrested and exposed to ridicule in public parades. It was a relentless war on the "dark society" of Viet Nam, and a war that was waged effectively. Diem used persuasion, determination, and strategy. He employed the press to arouse the population of Viet Nam and to win the people to his side. Even the Buddhists supported Diem's policies, realizing that he stood for absolute independence from France, that he was against Communist control from the North, and that he was determined to clean up the habits of vice that were enslaving his people.

In his first nine months as Prime Minister, Diem also had to cope with one million refugees who fled from the North after the Geneva Conference. Refugee camps had to be built, and food and jobs had to be supplied. Diem appealed to America for help. He was much consoled as various American charitable organizations, plus the American Government, the Catholic Relief Services of the National Catholic Welfare Conference, and the International Refugee Committee extended immediate economic aid and medical supplies for the refugees.

In spite of all the challenges to be met, the Diem regime succeeded in overcoming the seemingly insurmountable obstacles to the first six months of his government. His success in those first months was due to several factors:

    a. The majority of the Vietnamese realized the need for supporting the new government in order to keep their political independence.

    b. The high ranking French military officers and the French Expeditionary Corps remaining in Viet Nam were not opposed to the Diem regime, although the French remained divided in their attitude towards Diem.

    c. General Lawton Collins, America's Special Ambassador to Saigon, was initially sympathetic to the Diem Government.

d. Some of the Chinese who lived in Viet Nam for many years enlisted in the fighting forces of Viet Nam to help Diem suppress the armies of the various religious sects, as well as the Viet Cong guerrillas who opposed the Government.

Even with these conditions, it was almost a miracle that Diem survived from July until October in his first year as Prime Minister. America did not lend its support until Senator Mike Mansfield wrote a report favoring aid to Viet Nam in October, 1954. Senator Mansfield spent two months in Viet Nam. His *Report on a Study Mission to Viet Nam, Cambodia and Laos,* which he prepared for the Senate Foreign Relations Committee on October 15, 1954, concluded that Diem had a "reputation throughout Viet Nam for intense nationalism and equally intense incorruptibility." The Report established the fact that Diem was determined to suppress conspiracy and sabotage, and that he was vigorously opposed to corruption and social injustice.

Senator Mansfield highly recommended sending economic aid to the Diem Government, and his recommendations were accepted. General Collins arrived in Saigon the following month as Special American Ambassador, a move that strengthened the position of Diem considerably. General Collins' first act was to grant American aid for the resettlement of refugees. He also decided that economic and military aid to Viet Nam should be given the Diem Government directly, instead of through the French. He arranged for a U. S. Military Advisory Group to take over the training program of the Vietnamese army. Colonel Edward G. Lansdale, the C. I. A. agent in Saigon, supported Diem, as did Allen W. Dulles, then director of the C. I. A., who persuaded his brother, Secretary of State John Foster Dulles, to continue supporting the Diem Government.

The determination of Diem to destroy the armed religious sects which openly fought his government ended the divided opinions of both French and Americans in Saigon. Diem refused to compromise with the ultimatum presented him by the Cao Dai, Hoa Hao, and Binh Xuyen leaders on March 19, 1955; nor did he listen to those French who advised him to stop fighting in the streets of Saigon and Cholon against these sects.

While Diem was struggling to establish order out of chaos,

Bao Dai, who was still Chief of State, lived comfortably in France. But he and his advisers began to realize that he was losing control of the whole situation. On April 28, 1955, Bao Dai sent a cable to Diem asking him to come to Paris immediately. Diem replied that he could not leave Saigon at that time, but urged Bao Dai to return to Viet Nam. Bao Dai remained in Paris, and the imperial family gathered in Hue to proclaim the dethronement of Bao Dai on June 15, 1955.

On the first anniversary of the formation of Diem's cabinet on July 7, 1955, the Vietnamese Government declared that a national referendum would be held on October 23, to decide whether the people preferred a monarchy or a republic. Less than two percent voted for the monarchy, and 98.2 percent voted for the establishment of a Republic of Viet Nam. A Constituent Assembly was formed, composed of 123 members of five political parties and various independents. Fifteen members were selected to draft a Constitution, with the counsel of A. A. C. Grant, an American attorney, and Juan C. Orendain, a Filipino attorney. The General Assembly adopted the draft of the Constitution. Diem, as President of Viet Nam, signed it on October 26, 1956, a date that became Constitution Day in the new republic. The new Constitution resembled America's presidential form of government in many respects, although it differed in various ways from the English, French, or American forms of democracy.

As the national referendum showed more than 90 percent of the votes in Diem's favor, the charge was made by critics that the local officials had used pressure in Diem's behalf. Diem denied the charges and challenged his critics to prove them, which they were unable to do. This also proved that Diem was neither an American creation nor a puppet of the United States as some critics have charged.

At the time of the national referendum and election of the President, Diem had been back in Viet Nam for just a little more than one year. He still had no military power directly under his control, with which he might have coerced his people to vote for the ousting of Bao Dai and for his own election as the first President of the new Republic of Viet Nam. From all the evidence available, and from personal contacts with Viet Nam and the Vietnamese year after year, the authors can only conclude that in his two terms as President of Viet Nam, until the fall of 1963, Diem was popular among his own people, who considered him a national hero, the founder of their country, and the only President they have ever had. His accomplishments and his failures are discussed in the following chapter.

FOOTNOTES

CHAPTER V: BAO DAI, NGO DINH DIEM AND HO CHI MINH

1. *Viet Nam Tan Bao* (official Journal of Viet Nam), (Hue, Aug. 20, 1945).
2. William C. Bullitt, "The Saddest War," *Life*, Dec. 29, 1947.
3. *Le Monde*, March 9, 1949.
4. *Voice of South Viet Nam*, Aug. 16, 1950.
5. Viet Nam News Agency, *Releases*, April 10, 1951.
6. *L'Expres*, Feb. 27, 1954.
7. *Time*, July 16, 1965.
8. *Time*, Aug. 4, 1961.

CHAPTER VI

NGO DINH DIEM: HIS ACCOMPLISHMENTS AND FAILURES 1954-1963

"You can pass judgment on a man," says an old Chinese proverb, "only after he is in his coffin." Although nearly three years have passed since his death, many of the documents pertaining to his policies or leading to his assassination are still not available. Ngo Dinh Diem is bound to remain a controversial figure in world history. His enemies called him a dictator, an autocrat, and a totalitarian. The Communists labeled him "ruthless, corrupt, and reactionary," just as they did Chiang Kai-shek, Francisco Franco, Syngman Rhee, and anyone else who opposed them. Yet his admirers have been many. They have compared him to George Washington, and he was praised by no less a personage than Lyndon B. Johnson as the "Winston Churchill of Asia."

Ngo Dinh Diem assumed the prime ministership in 1954 when his country was facing economic chaos, political instability, and external subversion, not on a massive scale, but on a scale that kept increasing in intensity. He led South Viet Nam through its initial crises, changed it from a monarchy to a republic, and built up the first national loyalty its people ever knew. A rather neutral English periodical, the *Economist,* described the new republic a few months after it was founded:

"The ministers and civil servants of the new Viet Nam do not merely work hard—for ten to sixteen hours a day is common—but also with will, enthusiasm and brimming confidence . . . Out of a situation that seemed desperate eighteen months ago, President Ngo Dinh Diem has produced an order and calm that must be envied in Burma and Indonesia, and even in Malaya, yet it could be disastrous to underestimate the protracted and arduous job still to be done." [1]

What were some of his accomplishments?

1. Ngo Dinh Diem's Accomplishments

i. Agricultural Developments

The emergence from a colonial status into an independent state is never easy. In many countries "freedom" to the native means that he does not have to work any more. The problems were compounded in Viet Nam: (a) the country was divided, with most of the industry remaining in the North; (b) there were a million refugees who poured out of the North and flocked to Saigon; (c) many lines of communication were destroyed; (d) rice fields, rubber plantations, and other agricultural products were neglected; (e) prices of all kinds of consumer goods were inflated; (f) guerrilla activities of the Viet Cong endangered the whole country.

Immediately after the Geneva Agreement was signed in 1954, the refugees began flocking into the South. Diem ordered the construction of refugee camps in various places in order to give the refugees food and housing. Medical care stations and schools were built around the refugee centers. Jobs were provided as much as possible. Skilled laborers were sought out and employed. Handicraft industries were begun. Farming was resurrected and expanded. By July 7, 1957, President Diem was able to report to the nation: "The area of rice cultivated has been raised from 1,659,000 hectares in 1954 to 2,625,369 hectares in 1957," a 58 per cent increase. He further reported that the number of fruit trees had increased by 30 per cent in the same three year period. He pointed out that 300,000 tons of rice were being exported that year (1957).

From 1955 to 1962, rice production rose from 2,800,000 metric tons to 5,000,000 metric tons. In 1955, rice exports were 70,000 tons. By 1960 they had risen to 340,000 tons. Without America's economic aid since 1954, Viet Nam probably would not have survived. But without Diem's determined and untiring efforts, South Viet Nam would not have lasted beyond 1955 or 1956.

On May 13, 1965, President Johnson declared that, despite the ravages of war, South Viet Nam

"is one of the great rice bowls of the entire world. . . . Since 1954, South Viet Nam doubled its rice production, providing food for the people as well as providing a vital export for the nation." [2]

90

In spite of all the guerrilla attacks on the villages, the rubber production was much improved from 1954 to 1962. Most of the rubber was exported to the United States and France. The government headed by Diem also increased the production of other agricultural products, such as vegetables, peanuts, sugar cane, soybeans, palm and coconut oil, tea, coffee, citrus fruits, and tobacco. Kenaf, a fiber similar to jute, was also introduced into the country in 1957. Livestock, such as cattle, buffalo, pigs, chickens, and ducks, increased about 500 per cent during the first seven years of Diem's presidency.

Fishing is one of the principal occupations of the Vietnamese, as many of the natives live along the coastal villages. Sea food is one of their main dishes. Between ten and twelve per cent of the Vietnamese people are engaged in fishing. In South Viet Nam, about 50,000 metric tons of sea food were produced in 1955. In 1962, production was five times that figure. Production of "fish juice," a special Vietnamese product, also increased steadily since 1955.

At the end of 1955, the Mekong delta was recaptured from the Hoa Hao forces by the Government troops. Since then the new *Cao San* project helped provide a livelihood and space for additional resettlements for refugees from the North. By the end of 1957, more rice was grown in the Mekong delta for home consumption and export.

In the northern part of the Mekong delta there are plateaus and highlands that were previously uncultivated. With modern scientific methods, various kinds of products have been successfully planted there since 1956. These efforts increased the total of Viet Nam's agricultural products, and also helped to build up her foreign trade.

ii. *Land Reform*

Land reform played an important part in Viet Nam's basic economy and social structure under the Diem regime. During the French colonial period the peasants, who constituted the majority of the population, endured considerable hardship. Fifty per cent of all the cultivated land in the country belonged to three or four per cent of the people. Under French rule, 80 per cent of the land was farmed by the tenant peasants, who received little from the crops they raised.

Many of the guerrilla wars against the French, after 1945, and against the government troops after 1954, were fought in the rice fields. The peasants found their livestock killed, their irrigation ditches ruined, and their sons drafted into the army by both sides. Nearly a million peasants fled into the cities. Here they created unemployment problems, while the farms and rice paddies were neglected. The Diem government launched its land reform program along the following lines:

    a. Anyone holding more than 245 acres of land was to turn over the excess for redistribution to landless peasants.

    b. Landlords were to be reimbursed with 10 per cent of the value of the land in cash, and the rest in bonds, for a period of 12 years. The bonds could be used to buy government industries, and in payment of taxes.

    c. Land rentals were limited to 25 per cent of the main crop.

    d. Peasants or landless tenants who obtained land from the redistribution could pay for it in six annual installments without interest.

    e. The land tenure of the tenant was assured for five years.

    f. French-owned ricelands were to be bought with the help of subsidies from the French Government.

    g. A Farmers' Association was established.

The land reform programs, started in 1955, made rapid progress. Within two years, on July 7, 1957, President Diem reported to the nation:

"Over 600,000 lend-lease contracts have been signed between land owners and tenants . . . farmers and co-operatives have been granted loans totalling 250,000,000 piasters . . . 26,120 hectares of land have been allotted to tenants desiring to become landowners." ³

By the end of 1959, 436,700 hectares of land had been transferred, and 411,300 hectares (about one million acres) had been surveyed and assigned to 119,000 new owners. The redistribution of land in Viet Nam lessened many of the burdens of the peasants. It improved their livelihood, it reduced the effectiveness of Communist propaganda, and it greatly contributed to increased agricultural production.

President Diem reported to the National Assembly in October, 1960, that whereas 1,584 big landlords had controlled most of the private lands, by 1960 there were 1,228,002 landowners among the peasant families. By 1962, the distribution of land had been almost completed. Ninety-eight per cent of the peasants now tilled their own lands, keeping what they earned from their crops. Taxes were low, and the government loaned money to these peasants at special low rates. The entire land reform program greatly improved the living standards of the majority of the people, who were formerly peasants. With improved methods of farming and irrigation, animal diseases were reduced. The production of corn, potatoes, vegetables, sugar cane, and sundry agricultural products was increased steadily from 1955 to 1963, despite the fact that the country faced full scale subversion and guerrilla warfare from the aggressors in the North.

iii. *Industries*

The vast majority of the industries built by the French were in North Viet Nam. Except for public utility plants, street cars and railways, there was no large industry in the South. However, there were some rice mills, sawmills, and breweries in South Viet Nam when the French withdrew from that region. When Diem became Prime Minister in Saigon, there was only one coal mine under his jurisdiction. He first concentrated on the preservation and improvement of the land. By March, 1957, when the country had achieved more stability, President Diem began his first five-year economic plan. His government provided $500 million for this purpose, $286 million of which came from the American, French, and Japanese governments as war reparations. About $50 million was spent for industrial development, $233 million for electrification and public works, and $88 million for agriculture.

On the third anniversary of his accession to office, on July 7, 1957, Diem was able to report that prices and market conditions had been stabilized, and that economic rights had been assured. He further stated:

"Our people are now participating efficiently in the fields of domestic and foreign trade, industrial production, and handicrafts.

Over 750,000,000 piasters in loans were made available by the government for the benefit of our businessmen. In 1956 alone, local tradesmen and industrialists were granted government loans totalling 78,000,000 piasters. From July, 1956 to date, local products worth approximately 2.5 billion piasters have been exported.

Within the framework of the economic development program, the republican government has ordered the repair of over 2,800 kilometers (1,500 miles) of earth dredged from the waterways." [4]

It was the policy of the Diem Government to encourage foreign investors in Viet Nam in order to build up industry, as long as they were not from the Communist bloc. Foreign investors either received land free or at very low cost. They were also tax exempt for the first five years. Consequently a large French cement factory was built in Tu Duc and Ha Tien from 1958 to 1961. Cotton mills, textile plants, and plastic factories were built by investors of Vietnamese citizens of Chinese origin with some foreign capital during the same period. Lumber and textile mills, pipe, wood, glass, and paper factories, plus a huge print shop, were built by foreign industrialists between 1960 and 1962. Fishing enterprises were developed and electric power increased. Three sugar mills and a large factory for making milk products were also opened by American merchants. Canning and fertilizer factories were started near Saigon.

Viet Nam's textile industries produced about $47 million annually by 1960. Increased production in cement, wood, canned fish, and meat saved an additional $20 million in foreign exchange. Coal production was increased to 200,000 tons in the Nong Son area. The construction of a chemical complex based on the coal and coal-generated electricity of Nong Son was not completed before the death of Diem, but it was finished the following year. Raw silk, raw hemp, and their products were increased and improved, greatly aiding in foreign exchange. A factory for the production of hemp bags was completed in 1961, with a capacity of 3 million bags a year.

Lumber production was increased substantially. More and better highways and railroads were built for serving the countryside. More telephone equipment was installed, and more electric lights in the villages. Equipment destroyed or damaged by the Viet Cong was repaired. Dikes were repaired or newly constructed. Modern bridges and new airfields were built.

Up to the last, President Diem gave more guarantees to attract foreign investors. On February 18, 1963, he declared that there would be no nationalization on any foreign investment for twelve years, and that profits could be repatriated at the rate of twenty per cent of the capital investment each year. He was doomed to disappointment in his plans, however, since Ho Chi Minh's terrorism and subversion kept plundering his tragic little country. What he could have done without the constant Communist attacks is merely a subject for speculation.

With all of Diem's guarantees, American investments in Viet Nam from 1957 to 1962 were still relatively small. In 1959, for instance, only about one million dollars was invested by American companies, although French investments totaled 22 million dollars the same year. Under the American-Vietnamese Investment Agreement of November 5, 1957, the American Government guaranteed American investors against nationalization or war losses. This lessened the fears of American businessmen to some extent, and in April of 1962 a contract for 16 million dollars was signed between the Vietnamese Government and the Esso and Shell Oil Companies. It provided that the Vietnamese Government hold 40 per cent of the stock, and Vietnamese private investors hold eleven per cent.

South Viet Nam had had an unfavorable balance of trade from 1954 on, but the Vietnamese government continued to hold a large gold reserve. In December, 1960, the Saigon Government had more than $216 million in gold reserves in its treasury. The Government was strongly criticized for this by the British and American press. But it was Diem's way of achieving monetary strength, and the only way he could control inflation, a situation that would have hurt both the Government and the people.

iv. *Education*

The total enrollment in elementary schools rose from 477,-581 to 717,198, from 1954 to 1957, Diem's first three years in office. High school enrollment increased from 47,890 to 72,020. The number of students in the technical schools rose from 4,519 to 7,319. The number of students in universities increased from 2,109 to 3,823. The number of adult literacy courses and night classes also greatly increased.[5]

By 1960, there were 1,230,000 students enrolled in elementary schools, and 160,500 enrolled in high schools. There were 9,200 students attending universities at Saigon, Hue and Dalat. More than 2,200 of these were studying natural science. Several hundred graduate students were sent abroad by the Vietnamese Government for postgraduate studies. On October 26, 1963, hardly five days before his assassination, President Diem reported to the National Assembly that the enrollment of students in government elementary schools had been increased to 1,174,020; the enrollment of students in government high schools was 198,749; and the enrollment at Saigon, Hue, and Dalat universities was increased to 17,345—almost twice the number in 1960.[6] Under Diem's administration, emphasis was also put on technical training such as mechanics, agriculture, and electricity. Many such schools were established throughout the country. There were also many private schools,[7] with 416,809 students enrolled by the summer of 1963. The standard and quality of education was greatly improved. Qualifications of teachers at every level were carefully examined. Libraries, laboratories, and text books were also inspected. Mass education was imposed on the villages, and literally millions were taught at least the basic skills of reading and writing. By 1963 there were 265 private Chinese primary and high schools in the Saigon area alone. The French administrators had cared very little what these schools were doing. But by 1957 the Vietnamese Government had established rigid regulations governing them. Under the new regulations the Chinese schools had to teach the Vietnamese language.

v. *Public Health*

Prior to 1954, public health conditions in Viet Nam were very poor. The French had never built a medical school, and tropical diseases and epidemics were common in the villages. President Diem established a medical school in Saigon, despite the war, and the situation was greatly improved by 1962 and 1963, largely due to U.S. medical aid. Millions of people received injections against cholera and other diseases in the cities and hamlets. The *Catholic Relief Services* of the United States, with the help of the *Catholic Medical Missions Board*, also took care of hundreds of thousands of refugees. Medical and surgical units were established throughout the country.

vi. *Strategic Hamlets*

The Communist aggression, infiltration, and subversion in South Viet Nam had no front lines. The Viet Cong penetrated into the villages, into mountain areas, and along river banks. The American and Vietnamese politico-military strategists agreed on the adoption of the strategic hamlet idea which had worked so well in Malaya and the Philippines against the Communist guerrilla forces there. The project was approved by both President Diem and President Kennedy. They were encouraged by the island fortress of Father Nguyen Lac-Hoa, who had often defeated the Viet Cong invaders. This system, started in 1961, was a device to bring small isolated villages and solitary families together into larger units. The Viet Cong had been kidnapping or killing the leaders of small villages and terrorizing the inhabitants. By bringing a large group together, these tactics would not be so possible. The expense for the new homes, and transportation to them, was borne by the government.

It was decided that 11,864 strategic hamlets should be established by 1963. The hamlets had political and social significance, as well as military, as the inhabitants were mobilized against both the Communist propaganda and Communist attacks. Diem declared that when all of the hamlets had been established, the government would have reached an important stage in achieving its goal, but that it would then have to strengthen the social, economic, and cultural aspects of the hamlets. He lived to see 8,600 hamlets established, providing protection for nearly ten million people. Diem pointed out that the strategic hamlets had a very democratic base, through the election of officers. Before his death, elections were held in nearly all of them.

The hamlets were effective in combatting the Communists, although it often involved inconvenience to the villagers. Production was to be increased until each hamlet became as self-sufficient as possible. The system strengthened the social and cultural lives of the Vietnamese. Even the Montagnards, became part of the strategic hamlet organization. The Communists had tried every possible means to get them to oppose the government, but by October 1, 1963, about 217,000 mountaineers from 436 different areas had become part of 210 strategic hamlets. The Montagnards became all the more determined to fight the Viet Cong. Furthermore, 10,571 former Communists had defected by September, 1963, and joined the Vietnamese Government. The hamlets left practically no room for Communist infiltration, and Diem announced that the government would welcome all Communist defectors. Each hamlet had its own soldiers, its own well, and its own medical personnel.

In the beginning of his regime, Diem found that public health services were almost non-existent. Epidemics and tropical diseases often scourged the villages. But in the strategic hamlets medical aid, much of it American, was used with great effect. Medical and surgical help were established in remote areas for the first time.

The strategic hamlets improved living conditions considerably. But above all they were effective against the Communists. They unified the villagers, and united the villages with the national government. Previously a few guerrillas could kidnap a person and terrorize his neighbors. After the establishment of the hamlets, the Viet Cong had to attack the whole community. This was a strategy that was very distasteful to the enemy. The guerrilla generals wanted to avoid frontal attacks because they were too costly, both in terms of men and material.

Each hamlet was equipped with radio transmitters, and when an attack was imminent, a call for help would go out immediately, thus rendering the villages more secure. The government was also better able to help the inhabitants economically and in every other way. The hamlets not only kept the Communists out of the villages, they persuaded the natives that they had a government that stood for freedom and a better way of life. Diem made this program his primary weapon, and put his brother, the late Ngo Dinh Nhu, in charge. Robert Thompson, who had been in charge of the strategic villages program in Malaya, was loaned by the British Government to cope with the guerrillas. At first his plans did not seem to meet with success because it was difficult to concentrate the villagers into special areas, as he had done in Malaya. But under the guidance of President Diem and Councillor Nhu, and with the cooperation of anti-guerrilla experts, they worked out the program of "strategic hamlets," Vietnamese style.

Nhu played a very important part in the formulation and execution of this program. He set the goal of constructing 600 hamlets a month, with 300 families in each. He was told by Thompson and others that he was expanding the program too fast, that the Army could not possibly keep up with him. But Nhu kept on, with amazing skill and energy. By the spring of 1963, only one year after the start of the operation, Thompson notified the British Government that, to his astonishment, the Diem Government already seemed "to have turned the corner and was winning the country back from the Communists."

The main function of the strategic hamlet was to protect the people in the area, to isolate the enemy, to cut off his supply lines, and to inform the Government of the enemy's plans and activities. When the hamlets were established, the enemy had to attack definite fronts. The strategic hamlets also improved the relationship between the Vietnamese Government and the people. Before, a few guerrilla personnel had been able to kidnap a person from a small village, or terrorize the inhabitants. After the establishment of the hamlets, the Viet Cong had to attack the whole community. The villages were much more secure with the people concentrated in the hamlets, and the government was able to protect and care for them better, both materially and militarily. Mr. Frederick E. Nolting, Jr., the American Ambassador at Saigon from January, 1961 to July, 1963, agreed with the Thompson report. He declared that the strategic hamlets in Viet Nam were successful, and that Diem was doing a particularly good job in this regard.

Secretary of State Rusk praised President Diem just a few months before his assassination. He had been highly praised by Vice President Lyndon Johnson in 1961, and by Senate Majority Leader Mike Mansfield. Secretary of Defense McNamara described the accomplishments of Diem as "a near miracle". The House sub-committee on Foreign Affairs declared, a few weeks before Diem's death:

"In the eight years since Diem took power, Viet Nam has acquired full independence, written a constitution, and held the first four national elections based on universal suffrage ever conducted in Viet Nam."

South Viet Nam had enjoyed more than nine years of stable rule under President Diem, and both American and British officials had declared that the war was rapidly being won. When the Communists in Viet Nam heard about Diem's death, they exclaimed that it was "too good to be true!" Of the 8,600 strategic hamlets that President Diem had built to protect the peasants from the Viet Cong, 5,000 were lost to the Communists in the turmoil after his death.

vii. *The International Position of South Viet Nam*

Although not a member of the United Nations because of the division of the country, the majority of the non-Communist states recognized South Viet Nam. Fifty-two nations have given it *de jure* recognition. Forty-six nations deal with it officially and have representatives in Saigon. Many international conferences have invited the Saigon Government to attend. The Vietnamese Government under Diem was represented at the United Nations by an observer, as Saigon is still represented today.

In passing judgment on President Diem one must bear in mind that during his nine and one-half year rule he made substantial progress in the fields of economics, agriculture, industry, education, and defense. He conquered almost unsurmountable obstacles from the very first, and he did this despite internal subversion, external aggression, and international plots to overthrow him. He created order out of chaos, suppressed vice, established law, and did a great deal for the stability and prosperity of his country, despite the fact that it was constantly under attack. Above all, he gave his people the will to fight against Communist aggression, so much so that the South Vietnamese have been praised by Senator Thomas J. Dodd and others as being "among the most anti-Communist people in the world."

2. *The Failures of Ngo Dinh Diem*

The Communist regime in Hanoi had been established for about nine years before Diem assumed the Prime Ministership. Ho Chi Minh was a potent enemy in his own right, but the backing he received from Red China and Soviet Russia made him all the more formidable. Communist activities are international, and all Communist disturbances are part of the same war against the forces of freedom around the world. Anything that took place in Viet Nam had its reaction. In every democratic country there are Communists, pro-Communists, fifth columnists, uninformed liberals, and informed ultra-liberals. Under the pretense of freedom and democracy, it is to be expected that any policy or action that is unfavorable to the cause of world Communism is bound to be severely attacked, in the United States as well as elsewhere.

President Diem tried to please the American Government and people by establishing a reasonably democratic government. He endeavored to act democratically as much as the circumstances permitted. It would have been extremely difficult for his government or any other to exercise democracy in its fullest sense, while the government was engaged in a life-and-death struggle with Communist subversion and aggression. It was impossible to have complete freedom and democracy under those conditions. Diem also had poor relations with the press, partly because of his rather proud and unbending nature. Furthermore, it was extremely difficult for reporters in those critical times to cover stories accurately, when they were ignorant of both the language and the customs of the country.

It was one of Diem's weaknesses that he did not have a public relations program to support him. The left wing had well organized propaganda machines abroad which attacked him personally and condemned his policies. Diem himself seemed indifferent to propaganda in his own behalf. He had not a single news agency abroad for protecting his image or correcting false reports. Moreover, Diem and Nhu were often accused by the Communists of being "stooges" of Uncle Sam, and they both purposely tried to show that they were independent of the American Government.

Contact, understanding, and aid from the United States was found to be difficult. It was much easier for Red China to support the Viet Cong than for the United States to aid South Viet Nam. China is adjacent to Viet Nam, and they are basically the same people, with a similar culture. Peking can send men as well as material to Viet Nam without detection. Red China learned during the Korean War that bad publicity should be avoided, and that the United States would not tolerate armed aggression when it is done openly. Hence its strategy has always been to help North Viet Nam surreptitiously, and to threaten the American people that China might engage in an open large-scale war with the United States if the free world came to South Viet Nam's defense. The Communists were determined to use every possible means to destroy Diem and his Government. They even succeeded to a remarkable degree in getting some Americans to become pacifists, something that served the cause of Communist aggression.

i. *Compulsory Naturalization of the Chinese.*

President Diem made an unfortunate move when he announced that the million Chinese in Viet Nam would have to become citizens. About 200,000 had fled from the North in 1954. A presidential order was issued on August 22, 1956, declaring that all persons of Chinese parentage born in Viet Nam were now Vietnamese citizens. This sudden and drastic order was resented by many of the Chinese as "compulsory naturalization."

As soon as the order was made known, the Chinese in Saigon-Cholon asked their Ambassador, Yuen Tse-Chien, to lodge protests with the Diem Government. Spontaneous demonstrations occurred in front of the Nationalist Chinese Embassy in Saigon. Foreign Minister George Yeh declared in Taipei, on May 7, 1957, that the policy of the Republic of China had always been based on the principle of free choice of citizenship. According to the Chinese-French Treaty of 1930, the Chinese in Viet Nam or Indo-China enjoyed a special status, combining the privileges of foreigners with the advantages of being permanent residents. Supplementing these presidential orders, further regulations were issued by the Saigon Government stating that all the property of the Chinese schools, associations, hospitals, and other organizations had to be registered with the government. School masters had to be citizens of Viet Nam, and were allowed to teach the Chinese language and Chinese subjects only a few hours a week.

Another presidential order was issued stating that the previous order would be enforced by March, 1957. No alien would be allowed to conduct any retail business, including the selling or manufacturing of rice, meat, fish, groceries, charcoal, firewood, petrol, oil, scrap-iron, or clothing, or act as a broker. In particular, only Vietnamese citizens were to handle milling and transporting of rice after September, 1957.

The Vietnamese Government explained that it was an honor for the Chinese to become citizens of the Republic of Viet Nam. But most of the Chinese did not care to do so. Hundreds of Chinese students left Viet Nam for Hong Kong and Taiwan, where they pursued their studies. Many Chinese merchants took their money and left Saigon for Hong Kong and Thailand. The orders about the Chinese and their assets were never fully enforced, but many of them sent their money to Hong Kong, Switzerland, Britain, France, and the United States. Some left Viet Nam and never returned, the Communists having spread propaganda that Diem was against the Chinese.

Concerning the dispute between the Chinese and the Diem Government, the person who exerted the most influence on President Diem for modifying the government orders and delaying their execution was Father de Jaegher. A close personal friend of both Chiang Kai-shek and Ngo Dinh Diem, his role as an unofficial mediator of the Chinese-Vietnamese controversy was singularly important. President Chiang was anxious to protect the Chinese and their rights and interests in Viet Nam. But President Diem felt that the Chinese in Viet Nam, almost one million strong, should participate more fully in the construction of the new republic by becoming citizens.

The Communist propaganda urged the Chinese: "Don't support Chiang Kai-shek"; "Don't support Mao Tse-tung"; and "Don't support Ngo Dinh Diem". This line of propaganda was to "neutralize" the Chinese in South Viet Nam in the hope that they would not support the Diem Government. The Communists realized how important it was for the

Saigon Government to gain the support of the Chinese. In Saigon-Cholon the 600,000 Chinese residents owned or controlled most of the commerce and light industry. President Diem was told by some of his advisors that he should not have "a capital within the capital," or "a state within the state." Some extremely nationalistic Vietnamese officers wanted to dissolve all the Chinese organizations, and to confiscate all their property, including the Chinese schools and hospitals.

Father de Jaegher tried to mediate between the Chinese people and the Vietnamese officers. He discussed the problem with President Diem and his cabinet, as well as with the local authorities and the leaders of the Chinese community, and tried to work out an equitable solution. At one point, the Chinese Ambassador in Saigon was instructed by his Government to break diplomatic relations with Saigon. President Diem finally agreed to modify the Government orders and delay their enforcement. The Chinese resentment gradually subsided, and they became more cooperative with the Vietnamese Governement.

Many thousands of Chinese later became citizens of the new republic and helped the new industrialization plan of the Government. For example, Ong Tich, a prominent Chinese businessman in Saigon, formed the first large scale industry of the *Vinatexco* in Viet Nam. Several large factories were built by the Vietnamese of Chinese origin, even while the country was facing repeated attacks.

ii. *Diem's Weakness*

Ngo Dinh Diem was a deeply religious man. He was a scholar, not an orator; an administrator, not a politician. He was often too frank and to the point, especially for the Orient. He employed no stratagems. His outspoken opposition to Communism, plus his dedicated patriotism, made him a strong leader against the Viet Cong. His stubborn and uncompromising attitudes, however, partially explain why many influential Americans disliked him. Diem had survived many plots against himself, and when he learned he had fallen out of favor, he became more withdrawn, more uncompromising, and more distrustful.

When the co-author of this book, on a number of occasions, asked Diem why he did not establish a publicity agent in the United States, Diem replied that the truth will prevail, and that propaganda plays only a small part in world politics. By the time he realized that publicity was important, and what bad publicity had done to him and his government, it was already too late. Father de Jaegher on many occasions pleaded with the foreign press, particularly the American, to be less unfair in their reporting. He finally told Malcom Browne of the Associated Press, and others:

"You are distorting the facts about the Buddhist persecution. If you keep it up, you can get rid of Diem. You have the power to do it. But if you do, it will be American boys who will have to come and take his place, and they will die here!"

An example of bad reporting was when the press played up the split between Madame Nhu and her father, without giving the reasons. Her father, Tran Van Thoung, was one of the very wealthy landowners who lost part of his land to the peasants, as part of Diem's land reform program. In the latter part of August, 1963, while he was serving as the Vietnamese Ambassador to Washington, he made a special trip to Saigon to ask Diem to resign, and to turn the government over to him by making him Prime Minister. The Ambassador told the cabinet that he had returned to Saigon with the full support of the U.S. State Department.

At an emergency meeting of the cabinet, Thoung's proposal was rejected. The majority said it was an act of treason and that he should be arrested. Ambassador Thoung hurriedly left the meeting and took a special American plane to Washington. There he declared that it would be useless to help the Diem Government. Ambassador Thoung's actions against Diem from the end of August to the end of October, 1963, were calculated to curry favor for himself with the State Department at Diem's expense. Obviously he did not want to face his daughter, Madame Nhu, when she came to the United States. But the American press criticized her for not going to see her father, and was extremely sympathetic to the "kindly" old man, who shed public tears for his "wayward" daughter.

Diem was honest and incorrupt. Reserved and dignified, he was not the Dale Carnegie type of super-salesman with wide appeal. The majority of American newsmen found him too blunt. They did not understand him, nor he them. He was bitterly attacked by reporters from leading newspapers. Important officials, including President Kennedy, were strongly influenced by these reports. Diem expelled several hostile reporters, but did not realize how powerful the influence of the press was in the United States. When asked by a reporter of the *U.S. News and World Report,* on February 18,

1963, why he had expelled some foreign newsmen, he replied:

"They have gratuituously insulted the institutions of my country. . . . Why try to humiliate and defame us while we are fighting a terrible war for our survival and for the defense of a vital border of the free world!"

iii. *Ngo Dinh Nhu and His Wife: Assets and Liabilities*

From 1957 to 1960, Diem's brother, the husband to Madame Nhu, cooperated very closely with the representatives of the Central Intelligence Agency (CIA) in Saigon. His official position was advisor or counselor to the President, but he had indirect control of the nation's intelligence and security service. Although he had been a labor leader and progressive reformer, Nhu took a hard line against Communism, and the leftists hated him more than anyone else. This was partially due to his position and partially to his effectiveness. It is seldom a popular move for a ruler to give a top position to his brother, but Diem knew that he could trust him, and that he did not have many persons around him whom he could trust so completely. Nhu lived with Diem. Several times when *coups* were attempted, or when an attempt was made on Diem's life, it was mainly due to Nhu that Diem was spared. Diem also relied on Nhu for advice, and he gradually came to depend on him more than on any of his cabinet officials.

President Diem never gave cabinet rank to his brother, and Nhu remained officially in the background. Nhu used to say that he was not a member of the Vietnamese Government and therefore should not give newspaper interviews. Nhu was severely criticized by the press, particularly after the start of the Buddhist crisis. Some said that Diem should appoint Nhu Minister of the Interior in charge of Intelligence, rather than letting him appear to act behind the scenes, without sharing the responsibility. Nhu had had good friends with the CIA in Saigon, but the CIA replaced them with men who were unfriendly to him. The fact that Nhu often refused to see diplomats and reporters who wanted to contact him added to the growing criticism of the Government.

Diem's refusal to participate in a national election for the unification of the North and South was condemned by many of his foes, and is still criticized on many a liberal platform. Even Senator Fulbright, in a major speech to the Senate in June, 1965, criticized Diem for violating the Geneva

Agreement by not holding elections with the North, although Diem cannot correctly be accused of violating something he never signed. Yet many of the ultra-liberals use this as a justification for the increased aggression against South Viet Nam after 1956. Diem placed human rights far above civil rights, and he was not about to let the Communists in North Viet Nam take over the South under a Communist-type "election".

The Republic of Viet Nam has often been accused of refusing to hold a national election with the North for the unification of the country, and the United States has been attacked for supporting such a refusal. There were several good reasons why Diem was reluctant to take part in a national election, as suggested by the Geneva Agreements of 1954.

a. In July, 1954, at Geneva, the delegate from the State of Viet Nam, representing South Viet Nam, protested "against the hasty conclusion of the armistice and agreements by the French and Viet Minh Command alone." He pointed to clauses of the agreement that were liable "to compromise gravely the political future of the Vietnamese people."

b. The division of Viet Nam was out of proportion. While the North had a population of about 16 million at that time, the South had less than 14 million.

c. There has never been a fair, just, or democratic election under any Communist rule, either in Asia or in Europe. Even with the supervision of an international body, it is still not possible to have fair and democratic elections.

d. South Viet Nam was not bound by the Geneva Conference, since she had refused to sign it.

e. In 1955 and 1956, Diem requested the Hanoi regime to create conditions whereby *real free elections* in both North and South Viet Nam could become a possibility. Even as late as April, 1958, the Vietnamese Government sent a formal note to the Hanoi regime, asking it to grant basic democratic freedoms to the people living in the North. This official statement maintained that in the absence of basic democratic freedoms, such as freedom of speech, freedom of the press, and freedom of movement, any election would be meaningless. All of these requests and proposals were left unanswered by the Hanoi Government. Under any Communist regime, no such basic freedom can exist.

A respected professor in Viet Nam commented a few months after Diem and Nhu were assassinated:

"President Diem's greatest mistake during the spring and summer of 1963 was to listen to the Americans.

Washington forced Diem to dig his own political grave when it urged him in the summer of 1963 to be 'lenient' and allow that extreme wing of Buddhists and students to create turmoil in the streets . . ."

Diem had never wanted to be a puppet of the United States, yet he had tried to go along with American policy whenever he felt that was possible.

When it became known that some of the Buddhist temples had caches of explosives, it was an indication that an internationally organized effort was being made to destroy the Government. But Diem and Nhu seemed unwilling to believe that a *coup d'Etat* would occur, so they did not act. The officers of the Saigon Government took an indecisive and passive attitude, thinking they could wait until the dust had settled before they acted. They refused to believe that an effective *coup d'Etat* would occur, as several had already occurred without success. They felt that most of the generals still supported the Government of Viet Nam. Diem was also counting on the arrival of the United Nations Commission on October 28, which was to investigate, at his request, the reports of Buddhist persecution. He thought that no coup would occur while the Mission of the United Nations was visiting there.

Others felt that the coup was coming, but that nothing could be done about it. They felt that since the President of the United States had publicly declared there must be a change of policies and personnel in the Government of South Viet Nam, and that since the American Ambassador in Saigon, Henry Cabot Lodge, was hostile to Diem, the handwriting was on the wall. They felt that the fall of Diem was inevitable. Diem greatly feared that such a split in his Government would only benefit the Communists. He worried, not about his own life, but about the future of his country if he were killed.

Future historians should not pass judgment on Diem according to American or European criteria. They should judge him and his administration by Asian, and specifically Vietnamese standards. His policies and actions should be correlated with the circumstances and conditions at that time. R. G. Casey, the Australian Minister for External Relations, made an objective statement regarding the criticism of Diem and his administration as early as 1959, a statement that should be kept in mind:

"Two facts should be remembered in any criticism of Viet Nam's administration. First, Viet Nam is in the front line of the cold war . . . Its government cannot afford to leave any opening which its opponents could exploit. This would be fatal not only to Viet Nam, but most detrimental to the interests of freedom in Southeast Asia. Second, the exercise of democracy on a national scale is a totally new concept in Viet Nam, and it will take time for institutions, traditions, and habits to be developed which will enable democratic rights to be exercised in a constructive and responsible way." [8]

The Australian Minister's remarks indicate a basis that would be appropriate for evaluating the late President Ngo Dinh Diem and his administration, as well as for judging the leaders of the Republic of Viet Nam for many years to come.

More than anything else, the problem of Viet Nam is simply a matter of facing reality. Joseph Alsop, the nationally known columnist and a regular visitor to Viet Nam for over twelve years, has been clear and eloquent on this subject. Five weeks before the escalation of February 7, 1965, he wrote from Saigon:

"It is almost comically silly to try to organize the kind of government in Viet Nam that will win the august approval of American editorial writers who know nothing of Asia and always seem to forget that the alternative is the bleak and ruthless tyranny of Asian Communism. There is no way out any longer, except to try to deal with the war crisis first, and to leave the political situation for later consideration. Dealing with the war crisis is the only way to create the essential conditions for comparative government stability. The government is unstable precisely because the war is going badly." [9]

Premier Ky was later to remark that it does not pay to agree entirely with the Americans, because "they may change their mind. The Americans told President Diem not to worry about stability, that democracy is really what counts. But now," he observed, "they say, don't worry about democracy. Stability is what really counts."

FOOTNOTES
CHAPTER VI: NGO DINH DIEM: ACCOMPLISHMENTS AND FAILURES, 1954-63

1. *The Economist* (London, Dec. 22, 1956).
2. *New York Times,* May 14, 1965.

3. President Ngo Dinh Diem's speech to the Nation in 1957 on the third anniversary as head of the Vietnamese Government. The English version was made by the Vietnamese Information Service. At that time, the official rate of the piasters was 35 to US $1.00.
4. *Ibid.*
5. Saigon University and Hue University were established in 1957; Catholic University at Dalat was founded in 1958.
6. Diem's *Report to the National Assembly*, Oct. 26, 1960.
7. Diem's *Report to the National Assembly*, Oct. 26, 1963.
8. Quoted by Richard Lindholm in *Viet Nam, The First Five Years* (Ann Arbor, Michigan, 1959), p. 344.
9. *Time Magazine,* Jan. 1, 1965, p. 48.

CHAPTER VII

THE BUDDHIST CRISIS AND THE SAIGON COUP (1963)

When Ngo Dinh Diem was re-elected President of the Republic of Viet Nam in April, 1961, after completing his first six-year term, Communists throughout the world called him "the arch-enemy of the people of Asia." He had become the main obstacle to Communist expansion in Southeast Asia. Not only the Viet Cong, but Communists everywhere wanted to destroy him. Several *coups d'etat* were attempted, but without success.

No one realized the Communist threat to the existence of South Viet Nam as an independent state better than Diem himself. On March 31, 1962, he sent an urgent message to the heads of 93 non-Communist states, informing them that the Viet Cong attacks on the Republic of Viet Nam were about 400 per week, that his casualties were about 800 weekly, and that this Communist aggression "must be a matter of concern for all nations." He warned the free nations of the world that the Communists "are making another brutal attempt in their effort to achieve world domination." He appealed to the free world "for increased military assistance and support." He explained that world opinion would be an important factor in the future decisions of the Communist authorities in carrying on the guerrilla war. He urged the free nations to raise their voices "in defence of freedom and peace in this area of the world by condemning the Communist aggression against the duly constituted government of the Republic of Viet Nam."

The Communists knew how to cope with Diem's appeals. Highly skilled at spreading false propaganda, they created incidents, and launched demonstrations. Masters of cold war strategy, they decided that the Achilles heel in Viet Nam was the Buddhist associations. They realized the acute sensitivity of Americans, in particular, to the charge of religious persecution. There were other factors in the downfall of the Diem regime, but the Buddhist crisis was easily the deciding one. This was the only serious charge that was accepted by an unsuspecting world.

1. *The Buddhist Issue*

Buddhism varies in the different countries of Asia. It is far from being organized like the Christian churches in Europe and America. To infiltrate a Buddhist organization is a very simple matter. That is what the Communists did in Viet Nam.

Diem had twice issued Presidential decrees about flying the national flag and religious flags. Both decrees stipulated that the national flag should be hoisted above a religious flag. Religious flags were permitted to be flown in public, but they were to be a little below the national flag.

The Buddhists violated the law by flying their own flags over the national flag as they paraded through the streets of Hue, in celebrating the birthday of Buddha, as early as May, 1962. This was done apparently with the tacit approval of the Governor of Hue, who was a Buddhist himself.

In April, 1963, Monsignor Ngo Dinh Thuc, the Archbishop of Hue and second elder brother of President Diem, consecrated the Redemptorist Church. He himself did not like the Presidential decrees, but he had to obey them. He did not ask for any exemption from the ruling. On a previous occasion, when the Archbishop celebrated his silver jubilee as a bishop, the Papal flag was hoisted in front of the Redemptorist Church in Hue, contrary to regulations. Government officials thought this would be pleasing to the Archbishop and the President, but Diem requested that the Papal flag be lowered, and that the Vietnamese flag be put in its lawful place.

About four days prior to Buddha's 2,507th birthday on May 8, 1963, the Buddhists in Hue requested the Governor there to postpone the application of the Presidential decrees concerning the use of flags until Buddha's birthday was over. The Governor accepted this petition quietly, but some of the Buddhist leaders were not satisfied with the Presidential regulations, even though the Buddhist flags were already flying with special prominence that 6th of May. Some of the Buddhists, or at least some who posed as Buddhists, considered the law itself discriminatory, and claimed that they were being persecuted. They organized mass meetings, demonstrations, and parades in front of the Governor's office, in front of the Catholic Cathedral, and in front of the Archbishop's residence. They next attacked the national radio station, which was under the protection of the army, demanding that its programs be changed by inserting the statement of a Buddhist monk. This statement was a strong attack against the Vietnamese Government and President Diem.

Major Dang Sy, the officer-in-charge, did not know what to do, and referred the matter to his commanding officer in Da Nang for instructions. He was ordered to protect the government radio station at all costs, and to fire if necessary. The crowd was about to break into the radio station when the demonstrators attacked the soldiers with bricks, stones, and bottles. Major Sy then ordered his troops to fire several shots into the sky as a warning. Then a plastic bomb exploded, followed by turmoil, confusion, and rioting.

The Buddhists maintained that the army had started the trouble in the first place by shooting at the demonstrators. They asserted that all the demonstrators did was to strike back at the army. While they argued back and forth, there was another explosion, probably another plastic bomb, and seven or eight people were killed, two of them Catholics. The Government blamed the Buddhists for starting both the rioting and the bombing. The Buddhists retaliated by blaming the government, and exaggerated the incident in the world press in order to gain national and international support. The Buddhist crisis was on.

The families of the deceased protested against having big demonstrations during the funerals, but the Buddhists insisted on using the funerals as occasions for arousing the sympathy of the average citizen and peaceful Buddhists. The agitators charged that President Diem was trying to wipe out Buddhism in Viet Nam, and that they must be united against religious persecution. They again demanded that the "Presidential Decree on flying flags" be repealed. They further demanded that the victims' families be compensated, and that the officers involved be severely punished.

The Buddhist Association of Viet Nam called for support from various temples. Monks who were unwilling to participate were told that if they did not, they would all die from "persecution." Through pressures and promises, more and more Buddhists joined the "United Committee for the Defence of Buddhism." Agitation and demonstrations against the Government spread from Hue to Saigon. President Diem formed a special commission headed by Vice-President Nguyen Ngoc Tho, himself a Buddhist, to negotiate with the Buddhist leaders in order to reach an amicable agreement. Nhu objected on the grounds that the demonstrations were a serious threat to the security of the state, and felt that they should be met with sterner measures. Diem overruled Nhu's objections, and told Vice-president Tho to go ahead and negotiate with the Buddhist leaders.

Meetings took place in Saigon from June 15 to 18. Vice-President Tho, representing the Government, discussed a solution with his fellow Buddhists. The Government agreed to compromise on the issue of the flag, and paid compensation to the families of the victims. The Buddhists insisted that the Government also had to admit that it had erred, and that it was responsible for the incidents at Hue. The Vice-President pointed out that the very purpose of the Commission was to establish responsibility for the incident. The Buddhists threw the meeting into a deadlock. This was followed by a Buddhist "suicide" in Saigon.

The Buddhists chose Thick-Quang Duc, who was one of several older monks. Two Buddhist monks took him by car to the front of the Cambodian Embassy. They helped him get out of the car at the front of the Embassy. Then they poured two large cans of gasoline over him. He struck the match and set himself afire. The Buddhists prevented the police from rescuing the burning monk, and also refused to let the Government perform an autopsy. Whether Thick-Quang Duc freely desired to commit suicide, or whether he was drugged or intimidated, is not known. Several more suicides occurred in the ensuing weeks, about eight or nine altogether. The victims may or may not have sacrificed themselves voluntarily.

There are more than 20,000 official suicides in the United States each year. One can hardly conclude that they prove anything, except that the victim is often mentally unbalanced. But the world press made the suicides in Saigon sensational. The world, and particularly the United States, was filled with shock and horror. The Diem Government seemed unable to defend itself, even though the importance of the incidents was grossly exaggerated, and the conclusions made were out of proportion. President Kennedy himself exclaimed to Lodge excitedly: "Where is it all going to end?"

Buddhism is basically against the use of force or violence of any kind, to oneself or to others. They do not even believe in killing animals. That is why Buddhists in most of Asia do not eat meat. There are, however, some Buddhist sects which teach that suicide is a short-cut to reincarnation in Heaven. But the suicides in South Viet Nam were undoubtedly inspired by politically-minded Buddhist leaders, dedicated to the overthrow of the anti-Communist government in Saigon.

Prior to 1885, the majority of the Vietnamese followed Confucian ethical codes. These codes included ancestor worship, Buddhism, Taoism, or Animism. During the colonial period, Catholicism became a very well organized religion in the country. Out of a total population of about 15 million, the Buddhist Association of Viet Nam claims only one million members. The Hoa Hao sect, which originated from Buddhism, has about half a million members in South Viet Nam. The Cao Dai is a special native Vietnamese religion with about one million followers in that area. There are about two million Catholics and about 400,000 Protestants. Most of the population are Confucian, Taoist, Animist, or without any particular religion. Confucianism itself is more of a philosophy than a religion.

Some Buddhist monks or Bonzes in Viet Nam live in the pagodas and take a vow of celibacy, others marry and take care of the Buddhist pagodas or temples in the villages. The Buddhists of "Greater Vehicles" wear grey or brown robes, while the Buddhists of "Lesser Vehicles" wear saffron yellow robes.

Regarding the relationship between Buddhism and the Catholic Church in Viet Nam, it should be noted that from time immemorial there has been religious freedom and tolerance in that country. From 1885 until 1954, most of the Catholic missionaries were French. Some of the natives associated the Catholic Church with the French as sort of allies, and felt a certain resentment toward the Catholics. In most countries there is some feeling between out-groups and in-groups. Even in the melting pot of America, Protestants, Catholics, and Jews may at times look askance at each other. After World War II, and especially after Bao Dai again assumed power as Chief of State in 1947, the situation in Viet Nam was somewhat altered. Although many French missionaries remained, there were considerably more native priests and nuns.

President Diem was criticized for having too many Catholics in the Government. How much truth was there in this accusation? Although Diem was a devout Catholic, he never attempted to make the Catholics the dominant force in Viet Nam. He conscientiously tried to be fair to the Buddhists. For example, he made a substantial donation to the building of Xa Loi Pagoda in Saigon several years before Buddhism became an issue. He commented to Father de Jaegher: "I am the President of a country which is one-third Buddhist, so I should also help the Buddhists like I help the Catholics, and like I help the other religions."

Diem chose a Buddhist to be his Vice-President during his two terms in office. In his cabinet during the last year of his administration, the Vice-President, Nguyen Ngoc Tho, was a devoted Buddhist. His Foreign Minister, Vu Van Mau, was another outstanding Buddhist. Among the 18 members of Diem's cabinet in 1963, five were Catholics, eight were Buddhists, and five were Confucians. The military governor of Saigon-Cholon, General Ton That Dinh, and the Commander-in-Chief, General Le Van Ty, were also Buddhists. Among the top 19 generals, there were only three Catholics. The others were Buddhists, Confucians, and Taoists. Although many of the best schools were Catholic, there were only 12 Catholics among the 38 provincial governors. The rest were Buddhists, Confucians, and Taoists.

When President Diem discussed the Buddhist issue with a co-author of this book, he said that in making political or military appointments he gave no consideration to the appointee's religion. He maintained that religious prejudice did not exist in Viet Nam. Of the 113 elected members of the National Assembly, there were 75 Buddhists. Until the day of his death, there was no real evidence of government interference or persecution of the Buddhists.

In spite of the fact that there was no evidence of prejudice against the Buddhists, there were Buddhist leaders who desired to overthrow Diem. The propaganda against him was intensified. The anti-Diem elements, together with the efforts of world Communists and their followers, made an impact that was felt all over the world. In Washington, the Kennedy Administration decided, with the insistence of a few "Oriental experts," that Diem must be ousted. A Catholic himself, President Kennedy was embarrassed to hear that a Catholic president of another country was intolerant. General Paul D. Harkins, of the U. S. Military Assistance Command in Viet Nam (USMACV), Frederick E. Nolting, Jr., U. S. Ambassador in Saigon, and John Richardson, CIA Chief in Saigon, lost most of their influence in Washington because they were allegedly "pro-Diem." Ambassador Nolting's report on South Viet Nam at this time carried less weight than the reports of a young and inexperienced *New York Times* correspondent named David Halberstam.[1] Halberstam and other U. S. reporters influenced the Administration unduly, and prejudiced it against Diem. President Kennedy finally insisted: "There must be a change in policies and personnel in South Viet Nam."

2. *Ambassador Lodge in Saigon, 1963*

When Henry Cabot Lodge was appointed to replace Ambassador Nolting, it was known to the world that this was evidence of the displeasure of Washington towards the Diem Government. Ambassador Lodge was originally supposed to arrive in Saigon on August 26, 1963. Instead, he arrived there on August 22, the day after martial law was proclaimed and several Buddhist temples were searched.

Within a few days after Lodge assumed his duties in Saigon, he reported to the State Department that Diem must be ousted. There was a lack of understanding on Lodge's part from the very beginning, and a conflict of personalities between him and Diem. Lodge had little background in Vietnamese culture and politics, although he speaks French fluently. According to some of the Vietnamese he acted as though he were the French Governor-General in Saigon.

As the Buddhists grew bolder in their demonstrations against Diem, the Saigon Government tried to arrest several pro-Communist agitators among the Buddhist leaders. The main culprit was Thick Tri Quang, a Buddhist leader who had been trained by the Viet Cong, and whose three brothers are reportedly still active Communists in the North. Quang was twice arrested by the French for Communist activity. Quang fled from the *Xa Loi* Pagoda into the United States Overseas Mission building, which was adjacent to the American Embassy. From there he went to the Embassy, next door. The Saigon Government asked for the extradition of this left-wing Buddhist leader on the grounds that the U.S.O.M. is not the American Embassy. Ambassador Lodge, however, rejected the Saigon Government's request.

This incident, which occurred shortly after Lodge's arrival, made Diem angry and disillusioned with Lodge. When one of the authors questioned an official of the Embassy in Saigon about the right to grant asylum under the circumstances, he was told that it was justified in the same way that the United States Embassy in Budapest was justified in giving sanctuary to Cardinal Mindzenty when the cardinal escaped from prison. To compare the pro-Communist monk with the Cardinal, however, or to compare the Communist regime in Hungary with Diem's Government, was stretching the parallel beyond recognition.

The noted French journalist, Suzanne Labin, was an eye-witness to much of what transpired. In her book she quotes from a conversation she had with Diem's brother, just a few days before the assassination. Nhu told her:

"When he [Lodge] was appointed here, though we were very sorry to see his predecessor, Mr. Nolting . . . leaving, we comforted ourselves with the thought that Lodge was a 'Republican.' We thought that, more than 'liberal' Democrats, he would possess good anti-Communist feelings, and we greeted him as warmly as possible. Then little by little, we had to face the facts; he didn't in the least possess this feeling. His political views seemed to be dominated by the fashionable degrees of Linus Pauling in the *New York Times,* and the neutralist preachings of Walter Lippmann in the *New York Herald-Tribune.*

"Lodge never stopped working against us, with the cocksureness that a representative of a colonial power might have evinced, thirty years ago, toward a protectorate . . .

"Lodge does not bother with the normal business of an Ambassador, which would be to galvanize and to strengthen the friendship between our two governments. No, his only care is to intrigue against the legal government to which he has been accredited." [2]

From 1955 on, the Communists had tried to bring dissension between the Chinese in South Viet Nam and the Vietnamese. They were not successful in this, so they tried to turn the one million Montagnards in the mountains against the Vietnamese. In this they were also unsuccessful. They next determined to sow discord among the Buddhists, so they instructed their followers to stage demonstrations in order to widen their influence among the masses, and then to make the Government appear to be persecuting the Buddhists.

When Diem learned that some of the Buddhist temples were hiding places for explosives and munitions, he suddenly proclaimed martial law, on August 21, 1963. The proclamation stated:

". . . In the face of recent Communist-instigated international events, especially in Southeast Asia and Laos, which have had a direct influence on the Vietnamese frontier, while in our country the entire people and army are putting forth the utmost effort to struggle against Communist aggression, our compatriots have

117

seen clearly for three-and-a-half months the government's extremely conciliatory good-will towards settling problems raised by the General Buddhist Association.

"However, the efforts have not been answered by a number of political speculators who have taken advantage of religion, and the extremely conciliatory attitude of the Government, to carry out repeated illegal actions in order to create a confused situation to sabotage this policy and to hamper the doctrine of democratic jurisdiction. This is very prejudicial to the good name of Buddhism and is beneficial only to Communism.

"Therefore, by virtue of Article 44 of the constitution of the Republic of Viet Nam, I proclaim the promulgation of martial law throughout the national territory as of 21 August 1963, and I entrust the Army of the Republic of Viet Nam with using fully all means and taking all necessary measures specified in the decree promulgating martial law in order to restore public security and order, to defend the nation, to vanquish Communism and to build democratic freedom." [3]

Ambassador Nolting had been away from Viet Nam since May, and was replaced by Lodge on August 22, 1963, a day after the above proclamation. The United States Embassy did not know in advance of the declaration of martial law, nor of the search of some of the Buddhist temples, or of the arrest of certain Buddhist leaders. But when the Embassy and State Department heard about them, they were shocked, and immediately denounced both Diem and Nhu. It did not help to explain that guns, rifles, pistols, bombs, TNT and other arms and explosives were found in some of the Buddhist temples, because neither the Embassy nor the State Department would believe it. For months they had been saying that the Saigon Government exaggerated the problem of Communist infiltration. Diem was accused of seeing a Communist "under every bed."

Some of the Buddhist leaders, such as Thich Thein Hoa, President of the old *Sangka,* urged his fellow Buddhists to refrain from taking any action against the Government. He declared that the agitation of the Buddhists was politically instigated, and that it was not a religious issue. But such statements went unnoticed in the American press. There are about 3,500 Buddhist temples in South Viet Nam, and only about 14 of them became involved in maneuvers against the Government, but it was from these 14 that the *New York*

Times and the *Associated Press* seem to have taken all their information.

As soon as Ambassador Lodge arrived in Saigon, he tried to find out about the government's search of the temples. He reported to the State Department, expressing his sympathy for the Buddhists. He accused the Vietnamese Government of being autocratic. He reported that Diem had violated his promise of being conciliatory towards the Buddhists. He further deplored Diem's declaration of martial law, although this was an internal problem of Viet Nam with which no ambassador should interfere. Within three days, on August 24, 1963, the State Department sent a message to Lodge stating that perhaps the American Government would have to choose from several courses of action, including getting rid of Diem. On the nights of August 24 and 25, radio broadcasts from American sources were carried to the people and the armed forces of Viet Nam, criticizing Diem and his family.

On August 28, General Ton That Dinh, the military governor of Saigon-Cholon, who was a Buddhist himself and the son of a Bonze, reported to the press about what had been found in the temples. Along with the arms and the explosives were documents that revealed plans for assassinating some American and Vietnamese army officers. Again the American journalists who were anti-Diem were not interested in reporting the facts. Two notable exceptions were the late Marguerite Higgins and the Rev. Patrick O'Connor, S.S.C.,* both very experienced journalists, and known for their integrity. But by and large, the American news media had turned against the Diem Government.

3. Coup Fomented

On September 2, 1963, the *Times of Viet Nam,* a semi-official newspaper of the Vietnamese Government, published an astounding account of how the American Government planned to overthrow the Government of South Viet Nam. The paper, which was edited by an American, carried large headlines on page one: "CIA Financing Planned Coup d'Etat." The sub-title read: "Planned for August 28, Falls Flat, Stillborn." The story appeared in six columns on the front page, and continued on page six. The opening paragraph began: "U. S. Central Intelligence Agency was financing a planned

---

* Veteran correspondent of the National Catholic News Service in Saigon.

coup d'etat scheduled for last Wednesday, reliable foreign sources said yesterday." This published report stated in part:

> "CIA agents in the Political Section of the U. S. Embassy, the Public Safety Division of USOM and the G-2 Section of MAAG, with the assistance of well-paid military attaches from three other embassies, had prepared a detailed plan for the overthrow of the Vietnamese government. The CIA plan, it is said, had the blessing of high officials in the 'distressed' State Department."

The report also indicated that the Vietnamese authorities were well aware of the questionable actions on the part of American officials:

> "CIA efforts helped build the political agitation of the 'Buddhist Affairs' to a point of popular confusion and hysteria which would be fertile ground for the planned coup d'etat . . . The Vietnamese government though seemingly well aware of all this, apparently could not believe such action was possible from allies, at a time with victory so near."

The startling report further stated that the Vietnamese Government also knew about the CIA agents in Saigon who had contacted the Buddhist agitators in Xa Loi Pagoda, during the absence of Ambassador Nolting from May to July, 1963. This pagoda was the center of the Buddhist anti-government agitation. The report depicted the plan for the coup, which was to cost from $10 million to $24 million in United States currency. It outlined the seven steps as planned by CIA officials as follows:

i. Create unrest and discontent among the masses, provoking 'religious' inspired anti-government sentiment; sow discord among the population.

ii. Mobilize youth groups (a function of the CIA agents in USIS and USOM) particularly the following groups; Boy Scouts, Girl Scouts, Buddhist Youth, Buddhist student groups.

iii. Buy police, army, labor and civil servants with three months' advance salary and a bonus.

iv. Assure government officials that they will be allowed to stay in their present posts if they agree to resign when given the signal.

v. While agitating in the different groups, provoke the government at the same time to commit mistakes, such as killing innocent civilians or imprisoning large numbers of particular interest groups, such as the youth.

vi. When confusion has reached its peak, make sure that 'representatives' of so-called 'representative groups,' e.g., civil servants, army, etc., present an ultimatum to the President to (A) resign or (B) send his family into exile.

vii. If the President resigns . . . a 'military junta' should be prepared to take the reins of government until elections can be held.[4]

As to the $24 million (maximum) to be spent by the United States CIA for the *coup,* it was to be used for advances in salaries, bonuses for the army, police, and civil servants, and for the Buddhist organizations, the youth movements, propaganda, and other contingencies. As the coup was planned to occur between August 25 and 28, the Vietnamese Government declared martial law throughout the country, searched some of the Buddhist temples, and arrested some leaders on August 21, in order to ward it off.

Both the CIA and the American Embassy in Saigon denied the report of the *Times of Viet Nam* that the CIA was planning a *coup d'etat.* All the copies of the paper disappeared from the newstands within a few hours, however, and when 6,000 more copies were reprinted on September 9, they, too, disappeared almost immediately. The authors have one of the few copies extant. That night the presses were smashed by unknown forces.

The Vietnamese Government made no official comment on the report, but when one of the authors asked Diem about it a few days later, the President paused and said: "Do you think that the *Times of Viet Nam* would have printed it if it were not true?" He asked this, knowing that the authors realized that Diem's brother Nhu controlled the paper. Diem then produced substantial evidence to confirm the report.

The book entitled *The Invisible Government,* in commenting on the role of the CIA agents in Saigon, pointed out:

"Those very American agencies which had helped Diem stay in power for so long were accused by his supporters of having directed his downfall."

The American Government next told Diem that his brother Nhu should be removed from office. Diem rejected the request, considering it interference in the internal politics of Viet Nam. One of the highest officials in Washington then contacted a member of the Catholic hierarchy, asking him to advise Diem to remove his brother from office. Diem finally agreed that he would appoint Nhu as Vietnamese Ambassador to Washington. The American Government never replied to this suggestion. Diem concluded that his proposal was not acceptable, and so dropped the matter.

4. Buddhist Issue Reaches the United Nations

After eight or nine Buddhists had burned themselves to death, willingly or otherwise, the "Buddhist issue" caught the attention of many international leaders. At the end of August, 1963, sixteen Afro-Asian nations wrote to U Thant, a Buddhist himself, at least politically, and expressed their concern over the situation in Viet Nam. Apparently these nations had never felt any concern about Communist aggression in Viet Nam, but they now requested the Secretary General to urge President Diem to protect the rights of the Buddhists. On August 31, U Thant cabled President Kennedy to convey the message of these Afro-Asian nations to Diem. He also urged President Kennedy to intervene in the Buddhist issue, something U Thant had never asked regarding the defense of the 15 million people in South Viet Nam.

On September 4, 1963, these Afro-Asian nations officially requested the Secretary General to include in the agenda of the U.N. General Assembly their charge of "the Violation of Human Rights in South Viet Nam." Their letter was circulated, together with an explanatory memorandum, by the Secretary General to all the members of the United Nations. On September 20, the General Assembly adopted this item in its agenda. To the surprise of the United Nations, before the General Assembly took up this item, President Diem sent a letter to the President of the General Assembly, inviting the United Nations to send a mission to visit Viet Nam in the near future so that it might personally see "what the real situation is regarding relations between the government and the Buddhist community of Viet Nam." [5]

The Soviet delegate tried to have the United Nations assign the investigation to the International Control Commission, through the co-chairmen of the Geneva Conference. The British delegate pointed out, however, that the co-chairmen did not have the authority to do this.

On the following day the delegates from Costa Rica and Chile presented a joint resolution authorizing the President of the General Assembly to appoint a commission of representatives of member states to collect information from Viet Nam. However, the Soviet delegates objected to this joint resolution. Other delegates, with the consent of the American delegate, urged the Costa Rican and Chilean delegates to withdraw their draft resolution, which they did.

It was agreed that the President of the General Assembly should be authorized to appoint a commission of member states to go to Viet Nam. Delegates were appointed from Afghanistan, Brazil, Ceylon, Costa Rica, Dahomey, Morocco, and Nepal, to form the Mission. With the delegate from Afghanistan as chairman, the group arrived on October 24. After spending three days in Saigon, they went to various towns and villages. They interviewed government officers, listened to Buddhists with complaints, and visited pagodas, temples, and educational institutions. They insisted on scheduling their own program and conducting their own investigation, using their own methods.

The Foreign Minister of Viet Nam assured the Mission on the first day of their arrival that "they would be free to go anywhere they wished." [6] On October 28, the Foreign Minister presented an Aide-Memoire to the Chairman of the U. N. Mission which stated that the Vietnamese Government had no objection to the Mission's examining witnesses or receiving petitions from Buddhist personalities, including those who were detained by the government on charges of plotting against the state.[7] Prior to the departure of the Mission from Saigon, the members issued a statement giving the names of those they had interviewed in prison. They pointed out that they had interviewed persons in three categories: spokesmen of the Diem Government; persons selected by the Mission; and persons coming forward of their own accord. Written statements were also accepted. They did not interview Thich Tri Quang because he was in asylum at the U. S. Embassy. The United Nations Mission left Saigon on November 3, 1963, as scheduled.

After their return to the United Nations, the committee held several meetings to draft a report. The report was 254 pages long, plus 70 pages of related documents in the appendix. It went into minute detail, yet there was no indication of religious persecution, or persecution of the Buddhists, in Viet Nam.

At the time of the 1,280th meeting of the General Assembly, on the morning of December 13, 1963, when the item on the "Report of the United Nations Fact Finding Mission to South Viet Nam" was on the agenda, the President of the Assembly drew a conclusion on the alleged "violation of human rights in South Viet Nam." This was his conclusion:

> "In the light of the recent events in Viet Nam, the sponsors of item 77 have informed me that they do not believe it would be useful to undertake a discussion of this item at this time. Therefore may I take it that in view of the circumstances I have just outlined the General Assembly considers that it is not necessary to continue consideration of item 77." [8]

That was six weeks after the assassinations, and that was how the U. N. General Assembly disposed of the alleged violations of Human Rights in South Viet Nam. No violations were found, so the report was buried.[9] Through the efforts of Senator Thomas J. Dodd it was later printed, but the United Nations gave it no publicity.

During September and October, 1963, Saigon's relations with the United States deteriorated almost to the point of collapse. In order to clarify the murky diplomatic atmosphere in Saigon prior to November 1, a few facts should be set forth. There were many enemies of the Vietnamese Government among American officials, both in Saigon and in Washington. Paul M. Kattenberg, who had tried his best to oust Diem in 1955, was appointed Director of the State Department's Working Group in Viet Nam in July, 1963. Kattenberg, who was originally from Belgium, is a naturalized American citizen. In Saigon he continued to advocate the ousting of Diem, and seemed more interested in getting rid of Diem than in the defeat of the Viet Cong.

Doomsday for Diem seems to have occurred on August 24, 1963. On that day, which was a Saturday, a telegram was sent from the State Department to its Embassy in Viet Nam declaring that unless Diem capitulated to American demands, the American Embassy should turn Viet Nam's generals loose on a *coup d'etat*. These demands included exiling Ngo Dinh Nhu and releasing the anti-Diem Buddhist agitators from jail, an event which, as Marguerite Higgins observed, "would have meant restarting the turbulent episodes of the summer" [10] all over again. The telegram was concocted by Roger Hilsman. Both Defense Secretary McNamara and CIA Director McCone felt that the "get-Diem" group, led by Hilsman and Averell Harriman, had "pulled a fast one" on the other U. S. officials by sending the telegram.[11] McNamara and McCone felt that a *coup* would hurt the war effort. No doubt they were also concerned about this betrayal of an ally. Said a top aide in the Department of Defense: "We are convinced that Hilsman and Harriman deliberately rushed that telegram out when McCone and McNamara were out of town because they knew that otherwise such a document would never have gone out." [12] President Kennedy and Secretary of State Rusk were also out of Washington at that time.

Plotting against the government is a familiar practice of the Vietnamese, with their colonial background. But until that day no plotter could hope for success, because the United States would have opposed him. On August 24, plotters got their green light. The people in Viet Nam knew all about the telegram, because the American Embassy leaked it to the press.

Some of the American journalists had attacked the Diem Government almost incessantly. David Halberstam of the *New York Times* kept repeating that Diem was most unpopular, and that there was great discontent among the people in Viet Nam. Halberstam maintained that the Buddhists "constitute 70 percent of the population" and resented the "Catholic Regime" of Diem. The Buddhists actually constitute about 30 percent of the population, and Diem's Government was not "Catholic." Halberstam magnified the discontent of the people, and never mentioned the successes of Diem, for example, his land reform, his strategic hamlet program, or the economic progress that had been made. Malcolm Browne of the *Associated Press* wrote in a similar vein.

Halberstam kept insisting that the Vietnamese soldiers would not fight, but he himself was so young and inexperienced that he was not qualified to pass judgment on military matters. This was the opinion of the experienced war correspondent, Richard Tregaskis, and others. Even so, Tregaskis pointed out that President Kennedy relied more on the opinion of Halberstam than on any of his official sources. Tregaskis, who is the author of "Guadalcanal Diary" and "Vietnam Diary," stated that the *New York Times,* through Halberstam, had more influence on U. S. foreign policy than at any period in the *Times* history with one exception: its reporting on Cuba by J. B. Matthews. It is too early to say which case caused the more serious disaster. General S. L. A. Marshall, in commenting on Halberstam's reporting, explained young Halberstam's criticism of the White House, the Pentagon, the CIA, et cetera, by stating that "the boy has a love for shining targets." In commenting on Halberstam's praise of Lodge as a man "who really knew his job," Marshall pointed out that Lodge "must have been friendly to the young reporter." [13]

On October 5, 1963, a Buddhist monk was going to commit suicide in public. When the police tried to prevent him from doing so, David Halberstam of the *New York Times*, John Sharkey of the *National Broadcasting Company*, and several other American television representatives tried to prevent the police from acting. They told the police they wanted to take pictures of the suicide. A fist fight ensued between the police and the U. S. newsmen, who reported to the United States that the police had struck them and had seized one or two of their cameras. On instructions from the U. S. State Department, Ambassador Lodge strongly protested the incident to the Vietnamese Government. Meanwhile, most of the reporters got pictures of the burning Buddhist, plus another "proof" that Diem was persecuting American newspapermen as well as Buddhists.

In October, 1963 John Richardson, the CIA Chief in Saigon, who had shown himself cooperative to the Government, was recalled to Washington, probably because some thought him too close to Diem and Nhu. Those unfriendly to the Ngo brothers were left there, while men like the experienced U. S. Ambassador, Frederick C. Nolting, Jr., who highly respected Diem, had been replaced by uninformed and prejudiced persons. These changes in personnel also explain the change in U. S. policy whereby America's subsidy for the 2,000 special Vietnamese forces that were controlled by Diem and Nhu was cancelled. These were the forces used by Diem to protect the Presidential Office, the same forces that had defended him during unsuccessful *coups* in 1960 and 1962. By discontinuing these forces, the United States left the Vietnamese President with very little defense.

The United States Treasury next issued an order forbidding the sending of U. S. currency to Viet Nam. It also discontinued its program of paying $12 million per month for food imported from the United States. By another order, the United States forbade sending U. S. money to Viet Nam in payment for the crude rubber it bought from Viet Nam. These measures could only have been intended to cripple the Vietnamese economy, and in this they succeeded. When the Vietnamese learned of these developments, the value of the U. S. dollar soared from 102 piasters to 160, causing uncontrollable inflation.

Rumors spread that a *coup d'etat* might occur at any time. Such rumors were common in the *Hotel Caravelle,* the *Hotel Majestic,* and the *Hotel Continental* in Saigon, and in the bars and restaurants frequented by Vietnamese, Americans, and Europeans alike. It became more and more clear that America would shut down the economy until Diem was pulled down.

House speaker John W. McCormack and Congresswoman Edna Kelly reportedly cautioned President Kennedy not to be a party to the anti-Diem campaign. They urged the President to examine the situation in Viet Nam carefully, particularly the alleged persecution of the Buddhists. Congresswoman Kelly defended Diem's nine-year record against the Communists, and the constructive programs he had put forth. President Kennedy had already made it known on more than one occasion, however, that there must be changes in the policies as well as in the personnel of the Republic of Viet Nam, if that country was to continue to obtain American aid. This was a clear and definite warning. President Kennedy's opposition to the Diem Administration, and particularly to Diem and his brother Nhu, was clear to the entire world, including those who were the most concerned, the Vietnamese.

When Diem learned that the United States was withdrawing its aid, he was very worried about what would happen to his country if the Government were overthrown. He told Father de Jaegher on many occasions: "I am working for Viet Nam and the free world. I have fought Communism all along, and if we have to get along without American aid we will have to tighten our belts. But we have to keep on fighting." Diem's brother Nhu also remarked to Father de Jaegher: "If we have no more cars, no more money, we will have to go back to using bicycles. We will have to work hard and try to save our country without aid." These were dedicated men, determined to resist Communism to their last breath. True patriots, they were more concerned about their country than about themselves.

When the Vietnamese military and political leaders learned that America had made Diem the obstacle to obtaining further American aid, they felt they must find some means of getting rid of him. Meanwhile, the Communists approached Nhu, explaining they knew that there was great tension between his government and the United States, and urged Nhu and Diem to save themselves by going to the Communist side. Nhu talked with Father de Jaegher about this just a few days before the *coup,* when they conferred together for two hours about the situation. Said Nhu:

> "There is no question of us going on the Communist side. The Communists have made approaches to us, and are trying to get us to their side. But of course (here Nhu switched into French) the Communists are basically bad, but we know that the United States is not basically bad."

These, said Father de Jaegher, were the strongest words he had ever heard Nhu utter about the United States.

The generals held secret meetings and decided to overthrow the Government, but wanted to avoid bloodshed as much as possible. They tried to persuade General Ton That Dinh, who for some time had been Diem's favorite, to join them. Finally, after much flattery and many promises, General Dinh agreed to ask the President to send his four remaining Special Forces—about 1,500 men—to fight. He said he needed these forces to deter an impending attack by the Viet Cong to prevent them from entering Saigon, adding that he would need them only over night. This was something Diem had permitted before, whenever the need arose, and he consented. Only a handful of guards were left to defend the Presidential Palace, an old edifice left over from the French. The main obstacle to the *coup d'etat* had been removed.

On November 1, the day the *coup d'etat* began, an article appeared in the *Times of Viet Nam* reporting that the Buddhist leaders who had been held by the police for agitating and plotting against the Government, were about to be released through the intervention of Ngo Dinh Nhu, who had recommended to Diem that he set them free. It was during the process of freeing these Buddhists that the *coup* began. It was noon, and rumors of a possible *coup* had been circulating in Saigon for over two months. At about 10 a.m. that day, Ambassador Lodge had gone, together with Admiral Harry Felt, the Commander-in-Chief of the Pacific Fleet, to see Diem. They talked for almost an hour, mentioning rumors of a *coup,* but drew no conclusion.

The *coup* began with demonstrations by civilians and parades at 12:20 p.m. It was "the Feast of all Saints," a general holiday in Saigon. When the paraders and demonstrators approached the downtown section of Saigon, near the President's office, they revealed themselves as soldiers. The police forces, navy headquarters, telegraph offices, and radio stations were taken over by the rebellious forces. Some naval units were attacked by rebel airplanes. About 4:00 p.m. insurgent artillery began firing at the Presidential office-residence. (Both of the authors examined the building a few weeks later and observed very substantial damage.)

The one who was actually in command of the *coup* was Ton That Dinh, who was under the supervision of General Minh, General Kim, and General Don. Ambassador Lodge was informed of the *coup*. The U. S. Commander, General Harkins, was not, because he was loyal to Diem. After the Presidential Office was attacked, Diem telephoned Lodge. Lodge told Diem that the U. S. Embassy would give him asylum, and he assured Diem of his safety. The commanding generals also telephoned Diem and asked him to surrender before 8:00 a.m. the next morning. They said that if he accepted this offer, he would be guaranteed safety to leave Viet Nam. Lodge then telephoned Monsignor Francisco de Nittis, the Charge d'Affaires of the Apostolic Delegation, urging him to ask Diem to seek asylum at the American Embassy.

When Lodge first telephoned the Charge d'Affaires, the Monsignor could not believe that it was the American Ambassador calling, because Lodge said, "I told Diem to come over to the American Embassy, but he did not want to, etc." The Vatican diplomat questioned Lodge's identity because he referred to the President as "Diem." Lodge identified himself, however, and the Vatican diplomat told the American Ambassador that the Apostolic Delegate, Monsignor Asta, was away, and that he did not think that his personal call to President Diem would change his mind about not wanting to seek asylum in the American Embassy. Diem and Nhu were proud and uncompromising to the last. They adhered to traditional principles that would not permit them to run to safety.

That night at about 11:20 Diem and Nhu left the Presidential Office together, each with one bodyguard. The soldiers manning the tanks surrounding the palace were all loyal to the President, and Diem and Nhu, who left by the back door, took a little French car and drove to Cholon, the sister city of Saigon. Before they left they had an assistant telephone Father de Jaegher several times to inquire about the main road to Cholon. Father de Jaegher explained that this road was held by rebel troops, so they took a side road. They went to the residence of Ma Tuyen, a Vietnamese merchant of Chinese origin. From there Diem called various generals to see if any of them would help him. At least two had already been shot because they would not cooperate in the *coup*. So had the commander of the Vietnamese Navy, Ho Tuu-Quang.

After calling General Dinh, both Diem and Nhu realized that they had lost everything, and they prepared for death. Back at the President's Office, the defenders put up a heroic fight, but by 8:00 a.m. the following morning they surrendered. The absence of the President was then discovered. After staying in their friend's house overnight, at about 8 a.m. on the morning of November 2, Diem and Nhu were driven in their small French car to St. Francis Xavier's Church, a Chinese parish in Cholon. The President sent his driver to the rectory to telephone the rebel generals where he was. Then he requested the French priest at the church, Father Guimet of the Foreign Mission of Paris, to offer Mass for himself and his brother. But all the regular Masses had been offered and no other Mass could be said. So Diem and Nhu made their last confession, received Communion, and prayed for half an hour in the church, kneeling in front of the statue of the Mother of God. It was All Souls Day, a day for praying for the deceased, whom they were soon to join. The people in the church were greatly moved to see their President and Mr. Nhu praying with so much devotion.

The generals had still not sent a car for them, so Diem went to the rectory to phone. He could not get through on the telephone, but a few minutes later, as Diem and Nhu were standing in the churchyard talking with the people, an armored car came to get them, escorted by other cars. President Diem remained very calm as the soldiers saluted him and asked him to go. Nhu seemed unwilling, but Diem said, "Yes, let us go." Nhu went with his older brother, faithful and protective as long as he could be.

The Military Revolutionary Council sent General Mai Huu Xuan to get Diem and Nhu. This general had been a high-ranking police officer under the French and under the Vietnamese Government. He had received promotions from Diem, but he felt that if Diem were allowed to live and go into exile, he would return to power some day, and in that case he and others involved in the *coup* would have to face the consequences. Hence, he decided to get rid of both Diem and Nhu. According to eye witnesses interviewed by the authors of this book, General Xuan did not ride in the armored car with Diem and Nhu to the Generals' headquarters, but followed in another car. He apparently assigned the job of execution to Major Nguyen Van Nhung. With their hands tied behind their backs, Diem and Nhu were pushed into the car. As Nhu struggled for a short time, Major Nhung shot him in the back of his head, and he died almost instantly. Unable to stand this tragic brutality, Diem protested, upbraiding the guards for the murder. Diem was then shot by the major in the back of his head, and died almost instantly.

The assassinations took place about 9:30 a.m. in the armored car, between the Catholic Church and the Army headquarters. Many of the generals wept openly when they saw the bodies. Ambassador Hill of Australia drove up, flying the Australian flag. He asked the generals to let him give asylum in Australia to their President, but he was told that Diem was dead.

The first report issued by the press around the world was that Diem and Nhu had committed suicide. This story appeared on the front pages in America. Father de Jaegher was also told this at the military headquarters, but he refused to believe it, knowing that neither Diem nor Nhu would ever take his own life. The report was issued in order to cover up the murder, and was later changed to "accidental suicide." Father de Jaegher did not believe that the two brothers were dead until a former secretary of Diem called him that evening to say, "Father, pray for President Diem and Nhu. Both are dead, and it's for sure." Two nieces of Diem also told Father de Jaegher of the deaths after they had personally put the bodies into coffins, and had even taken pictures of them.

The Military Revolutionary Council would not permit a requiem Mass for their funerals, lest public sympathy be aroused. Both were buried secretly in unmarked graves about 150 yards from the headquarters of the General Staff. A Jesuit priest presided at the interment, but the exact spot was kept secret.

Thus died, unhonored, two patriotic and dedicated fighters against Communism, themselves victims of Communist propaganda and intrigue. Thus ended the only stable regime that South Viet Nam had ever had, nine years of duly-elected constitutional government under President Diem, a man who may, in happier times, be held up as a patriot, a statesman, and the father of his country. The following month, Halberstam of the *N. Y. Times* and Browne of the *Associated Press* received the *Pulitzer Prize* for their reporting on the Buddhist crisis. General Thomas A. Lane (Ret.) wrote in his book on President Kennedy that the prize "should have been awarded in Moscow, at a review of the Kremlin Guard."

Immediately after the *Saigon coup*, the United States emphatically denied being involved in any way in its planning or execution. But Madame Nhu, who was in California at the time, said: "No one . . . can seriously believe in the disclaimer that the Americans had nothing to do with the present situation in Viet Nam." She pointed out that "this was not the first time the U. S. Government had wanted to overthrow Diem," and added that no *coup* could occur there without American instigation and cooperation.

In its lead editorial, dated November 2, the *New York Times* observed: "The only surprising thing about the military revolt in Saigon is that it has not come sooner . . . The Buddhist revolt in May and subsequent non-Communist unrest in South Viet Nam made continuation of all-out American support impossible." In its second-place editorial, dated November 7, the *New York Times* stated that as a result of the *coup* "there is new hope in both Saigon and Washington that the anti-Communist war can be won and South Viet Nam serve as a bulwark against the anti-Communist conquest of all the Southeast Asia. . . . With the people apparently rallying behind the new regime there is a better chance for ultimate success."

The *Christian Science Monitor* said: "The most urgent need of South Viet Nam is to make a transition from military back to civil government at the earliest possible moment." The *Washington Star* pointed out that "a spokesman for the State Department denies 'categorically' that the United States government was in any way involved in this coup attempt." The same paper also commented: *"The people who will believe this can be comfortably housed in a telephone booth."* (Italics added.)

The *Washington Post* expressed fear that the Saigon *coup* would lead the country "to plunge into the unknown. It will remain to be seen whether its successor government will make that resistance sufficiently effective to warrant a continued effort." The *New York Post* declared that "what remains to be seen is whether this is a real step toward a democratic resurgence or merely another chaotic episode in South Viet Nam's ordeal."

The *Chicago Tribune* doubted the advisability of the *coup.* It stated:

"The military coup which put an end to the Diem regime in South Viet Nam could hardly have been unexpected in Washington. . . . There seems to have been a division of opinion of the American Government about the advisability of throwing the internal affairs of South Viet Nam up for grabs at a time when the United States was heavily involved in that country's war for survival against communism."

The *Oregonian*, in Portland, declared that the coup held in Saigon was unobjectionable, and would be a clear gain. The *Seattle Post Intelligencer*, objected to the coup, saying:

"We do not share the elation of some officials in Washington over the coup. President Diem was autocratic and authoritarian. He perhaps was blindly stubborn. But he was a courageous, even dedicated anti-communist who managed to stave off Communist aggression during his rule, and in that sense he was an heroic figure."

As to congressional reaction, most members refrained from commenting. Senators Fulbright and Dirksen later on considered the decision to get rid of Diem a mistake. Senator Mansfield declared on January 3, 1965: "We are paying for our sins in getting rid of President Diem." As late as January 26, 1966, Senator Mansfield told the authors of this book: "The worst mistake we ever made was in getting rid of Diem." Americans who knew the inner story did not refer to Diem's death as a "loss", but a "mistake", because they knew that the United States had brought it about.

President Kennedy did not seem to realize that some of his top officials had been fomenting a *coup*, and he was perplexed and concerned when it came about. The press later reported that President Johnson admitted privately that the killing of Diem was "one of the great tragedies of our era."

Vietnamese General Ton That Dinh, Commander of the Third Army in Saigon, who commanded the *coup*, told Father de Jaegher afterwards, when he was Minister of Interior, that they simply had to overthrow the government because of all the United States pressure. General Dinh wept when the *coup* had taken place, even though he had led it. He produced many documents that he had to substantiate his statement of U. S. pressure. The influence that leading American diplomats and officials have over a country is immeasurable. In countries like Viet Nam and throughout the Far East, national leadership cannot be built up nearly as easily as in the United States. In Viet Nam, a man's background, education, morality, integrity, age, and reputation, his record as a leader, and his contribution to his country must be taken into consideration before he can acquire the status of a national figure. Ambassador Lodge had said, during the Buddhist crisis, that Viet Nam had plenty of persons who could run the country, that they did not need Diem. But he recently told one of the authors: "We have to hang on to Ky!"

Through his family, his background, his education, and his service to his country, Ngo Dinh Diem became known to his people as an outstanding leader in the latter part of the 1920's and the beginning of the 1930's. He was noted for his honesty and integrity as a public servant of his province, and as the Minister of Interior in the An Nam Empire. He was also known for his devotion to the cause of national independence for Viet Nam.

Because of his integrity, determination, and dedication he did much for his country. A deadly foe of Communism, he gained the confidence of his own people in his fight for the cause of freedom. The vacuum left by Diem's sudden death has not been easy to fill. There were nine changes of government in two years. American statesmen and diplomats should be understandably patient with anyone who is at the helm of the Vietnamese Government. They should also be less gullible concerning Communist propaganda.

FOOTNOTES

CHAPTER VII: THE BUDDHIST CRISIS AND THE SAIGON COUP, 1963

1. David Halberstam and some other U.S. correspondents implied that everything in Viet Nam was bad under the Diem Goverment. They greatly influenced the Kennedy Administration, including President Kennedy himself, to insist "there must be a change of policies and personnel in Viet Nam."
2. Suzanne Labin, *Vietnam: An Eye-witness Account,* (New York, 1964), pp. 34-35.
3. The *Times of Viet Nam,* Aug. 23, 1963.
4. The *Times of Viet Nam,* Sept. 2 and 9, 1963.
5. The 16 nations were: Afghanistan, Algeria, Cambodia, Ceylon, Guinea, India, Indonesia, Mali, Mongolia, Nepal, Nigeria, Pakistan, Sierra Leone, Somalia, Trinidad and Tigoland.
6. U.S. Document: A 5630, *Report of the United Nations Fact Finding Mission to South Viet-Nam,* (Dec. 1963), p. 10.
7. *Ibid.,* Annex IX, pp. 1-2.
8. *Ibid.,* Agenda 77.
9. *Loc. Cit.,* Agenda 77.
10. Marguerite Higgins, "Ugly Americans of Viet Nam", *America,* Oct. 3, 1964, p. 380.
11. *Loc. Cit.*
12. *Ibid.*
13. Brig. Gen. S. L. A. Marshall, "Hindsight Has All The Answers In Viet Nam", *Los Angeles Times,* May 22, 1965.

CHAPTER VIII

VIET NAM: U. S. COMMITMENTS AND DILEMMAS

During World War II, Japan used Viet Nam as a spring-board to conquer Siam (Thailand), Singapore, Malaya, the Dutch East Indies (Indonesia), and the Philippines. Since World War II, the conquest of Viet Nam and all of Indo-China has been part of the Communist program for the conquest of Southeast Asia. Shortly after American recognition of Vietnamese, Laotian, and Cambodian independence within the French Union, in 1950, the United States Government gave diplomatic recognition and extended economic and military aid to the non-Communist part of Viet Nam.[1] An American military aid program was worked out in 1951. The Council of the North Atlantic Treaty Organization, on December 17, 1952, declared that "resistance to direct or indirect aggression in any part of the world is an essential contribution to the common security of the Free World," and agreed to give Indo-China, including Viet Nam "continuing support from the NATO governments."[2] Prior to the French defeat in Dien Bien Phu, Secretary of State John Foster Dulles declared, on March 29, 1954:

> "The imposition on Southeast Asia of the political system of Communist Russia and its Chinese Communist Ally, by whatever means, would be a grave threat to the whole free community. The United States feels that the possibility should not be passively accepted, but should be met by united action. . . ."[3]

Dulles further asserted that the risks involved for a determined effort against Communist expansion in Southeast Asia now would be "far less than would face us a few years from now, if we dare not be resolute today."[4]

From early in 1953 until the French defeat at Dien Bien

Phu in May, 1954, the United States increased her military aid to France and the French Union. Subsequent to the Geneva Agreements, President Dwight D. Eisenhower, on October 23, 1954, assured the Vietnamese that American aid would be furnished for "maintaining a strong, viable state, capable of resisting attempted subversion or aggression through military means." [5]

American involvement in Viet Nam, when it was still under France, consisted largely of military aid. U. S. aid of all kinds to French Indo-China amounted to about $1.2 billion.[6] After her defeat at Dien Bien Phu, France drastically reduced her commitment to Viet Nam, and the United States stepped into the breach. The American Government served, not in the former role of France, but in support of indigenous Vietnamese nationalists who came to the fore in South Viet Nam in the wake of the French withdrawal. Since then, American aid has become an indispensable factor in preventing that part of the world from falling into the hands of the Communists of North Viet Nam and Red China. The aid was given directly to South Viet Nam starting in December, 1954.

When Ngo Dinh Diem became President in October, 1955, after first serving under Bao Dai as Prime Minister, he assumed the main burden of keeping this young Republic alive. France continued to give more economic assistance than any other country except the United States. The Republic of China and several other nations also gave some economic and technical assistance to the Government in Saigon.

President Diem's visit to President Eisenhower in May, 1957, strengthened the ties between Saigon and Washington and increased American aid. The White House issued a statement on May 11, 1957:

"President Eisenhower assured President Ngo Dinh Diem of the willingness of the United States to continue to offer effective assistance within the constitutional processes of the United States. . . ." [7]

1. *Increased Aggression*

Both presidents agreed that in order to meet the continuing threat of the Chinese Communists to Asia, the United States and Viet Nam must "seek closer cooperation with the free countries of Asia." [8] On April 4, 1959, Eisenhower referred to "the importance to the United States of the security and progress of Viet Nam."

About $1.4 billion for economic assistance to Viet Nam was given from 1955 to 1962. Its primary purpose was to sustain the Vietnamese economy, to help maintain an army of 150,000, and to aid in economic development. Military aid to South Viet Nam for equipment, supplies, and training of army, naval, and air forces, amounted to $600 million during the seven year period. From 1955 to 1959, much constructive work was undertaken. Agricultural production increased under the land reform program. Communications were reopened and enlarged. Education and various social services expanded. From 1955 to 1959 American military aid to South Viet Nam was limited to an advisory capacity. But the intensity of guerrilla raids and terrorist activities increased greatly after 1959. The Viet Cong attacked the villages and kidnapped the administrators, local magistrates, and even children. They set plastic bombs in the theatres, bars, restaurants, and wherever the Americans were likely to go. They attacked the American military establishments, bombed various American Government offices, attacked and kidnapped American personnel, and dynamited roads, railways, convents, schools, and newspapers. Buddhist temples and pagodas were plundered by the Viet Cong terrorists, casting the blame on Catholics, and vice-versa. In 1960, about 1,450 local and government officials were assassinated by the Viet Cong, while about 7,000 officials were kidnapped.

2. *Vice-President Johnson Visits Viet Nam*

The Viet Cong became more and more aggressive in their subversive activities. President Kennedy reiterated that the U. S. should not abandon the people of Viet Nam, who had courageously fought the Communists, and who wanted to preserve their freedom and independence. President Kennedy requested Vice-President Lyndon B. Johnson to represent him in conferring with President Diem. Vice-President and Mrs. Johnson went to Saigon, accompanied by a sister of President Kennedy. A joint communique was issued by President Diem and Vice-President Johnson on May 13, 1961, strengthening the relations between their two countries. It declared:

"The independence and territorial integrity of Viet Nam are being brutally and systematically violated by Communist agents and forces from the North. Action must be strengthened and accelerated to protect the legitimate rights and aspirations of the people of free Viet Nam to choose their way of life. The United States is also conscious of its responsibility and duty, in its own self-interest as well as in the interest of other free peoples, to assist a brave country in the defense of its liberties against unprovoked subversion and Communist terror. It has no other motive than the defense of freedom." [9]

Both the Vietnamese and the American Governments agreed to take the following measures to insure the security of the people of free Viet Nam.

(1) Build up and extend the existing programs of military and economic aid.

(2) Increase the regular Vietnamese armed forces and provide them with additional American military aid.

(3) Support the entire Vietnamese civil guard force with American aid. (This aid was withheld during the Buddhist crisis in October, 1963.)

(4) Both Saigon and Washington were to collaborate in promoting health, welfare, and public works in the Vietnamese villages.

(5) Welcome any aid given by free governments for fighting the Communist guerrillas.

(6) A joint American-Vietnamese group composed of economic and fiscal experts would work out a financial plan for Viet Nam.

(7) New economic and social measures would be inaugurated against the guerrillas in rural areas.

(8) A long-range economic program providing for development in agriculture, education, fisheries, public health, highways, industrial development and public administration would be worked out. [10]

President Diem, on behalf of Viet Nam, and Vice-President Johnson, on behalf of President Kennedy, pledged their mutual confidence and respect for each other's effort to preserve the freedom of the people in South Viet Nam, and to deter the spread of Communism in Southeast Asia. Shortly after the Johnson visit, an economic mission under Eugene Staley was sent to Viet Nam with the hope of strengthening the economic situation in that country by making suggestions for economic improvements and economic aid. Supplementing this effort, President Kennedy sent General Maxwell Taylor to Viet Nam. The report of the Staley mission, though primarily economic, touched on some military questions. Similarly, the Taylor report, though primarily military, dealt with political questions, such as freedom of speech, and more effective decentralization of government. It also touched on economic problems, such as currency and trade.

When the recommendations of the missions were made public, neither the Vietnamese Government nor the Vietnamese press liked the way these missions had criticized their government. The American press published the reports of the missions and implied that the Vietnamese Government was at fault. The Vietnamese communications media then strongly criticized the reports of the two missions, especially the Taylor Mission. The Vietnamese argued that the reports amounted to interference with the internal affairs of the Republic of Viet Nam, and would impair the confidence of the Vietnamese in their Government. In Washington, some were of the opinion that in time of war not much in the way of democracy could be expected from Viet Nam. The recommendations of Staley and Taylor concerning the reform of the Vietnamese Government were dropped by the United States, but the decision to hold South Viet Nam at all costs was made in Washington in October, 1961, after General Taylor reported to President Kennedy.

The Viet Cong kept increasing their attacks, and on December 7 of that same year President Diem sent an urgent appeal to President Kennedy for immediate further help. He informed President Kennedy that Viet Nam was facing "what is perhaps the gravest crisis in its long history." He also stated that if Viet Nam loses this war, it will be "swallowed by the Communist bloc," and their "proud heritage will be blotted out by the 'Socialist society' and will lose its 'national soul.' " [11]

President Kennedy replied to President Diem on December 14, reiterating that Hanoi had grossly violated the Geneva Agreements of 1954 by using force and terror against the South. He solemnly assured Diem:

"In response to your request, we are prepared to help the Republic of Viet Nam to protect its people and to preserve its independence. We shall promptly increase our assistance to your defense effort as well as help relieve the destruction of the floods which you describe. I have already given the orders to get these programs underway." [12]

By 1962, Viet Cong military infiltration into the South had

increased from 10,000 to 25,000 annually, with over 100,000 supplementary irregulars. By 1962, about 25,000 Vietnamese from the South had been killed by the guerrillas. Viet Cong attacks averaged over one hundred per week, ranging in size from squad to battalion level. Against these Viet Cong forces, the Saigon Government at that time had 200,000 regular enlisted men, in addition to 170,000 in the self-defense corps and civil guards, plus 25,000 Montagnards in an irregular civil defense group. The Viet Cong still did not fight an open war, but used their favorable strategic positions and overwhelming manpower at special points to defeat the government forces.

3. America's Role Becomes More Active

Because of increasing Viet Cong aggressiveness, American pilots were flying combat missions in Viet Nam by March, 1962. Finally, in February, 1963, President Kennedy authorized American military personnel to "shoot first, if necessary." United States personnel, however, were still serving as "advisors." From January to May, 1963, both the military and economic situation in Viet Nam improved considerably. The Communists became all the more determined to get rid of Diem and they concentrated on this. The "Buddhist crisis" occurring in May of that year took on more importance throughout the world than the war itself. In the United States, the alleged religious persecution so inflamed the news media that President Diem, his brother Nhu, and Madame Nhu, were portrayed as more dangerous enemies to freedom than the Viet Cong, or even Red China. American officials told Diem to stop worrying so much about stability, and about Communist infiltration. Democracy, they insisted, was the most important thing he had to bring about.

After the *coup d'etat* on November 1, 1963, some political and military authorities, plus some editorial writers, thought that the chances of defeating the Viet Cong had increased greatly. Hans Morganthau and the *New York Times* were of this opinion. The Military Revolutionary Council in Saigon was supposedly preparing for a big battle with the Viet Cong within a short time. Under the leadership of General Duong Van Minh, the Chief of State, and Nguyen Ngoc Tho, the Prime Minister, startling plans for winning the war were reportedly being contemplated.

This rosy picture did not last long. The Viet Cong were quick to take advantage of the sudden death of President Diem. The country was officially governed by a Military

Revolutionary Council of fourteen generals, but the Council was inexperienced and obviously at a collective loss. At first, most of the generals thought that the strategic hamlets were of little use. Soon after the assassination of Diem and Nhu, over fifty per cent of the strategic hamlets were taken over by the Viet Cong, and there was grave danger that the Viet Cong might take over the rest of them. The Council soon reversed its decision and attempted to restore the system of the strategic hamlets in order to check Viet Cong gains.

On December 31, 1963, President Johnson wrote to General Duong Van Minh, the Chairman of the Military Revolutionary Council, and Chief of State:

"The United States Government shares the view of your Government that 'neutralization' of South Viet Nam is unacceptable.

"As long as the Communist regime in North Viet Nam persists in its aggressive policy, neutralization of South Viet Nam would only be another name for a Communist take-over. Peace will return to your country just as soon as the authorities in Hanoi cease and desist from their terrorist aggression." [13]

After Secretary of Defense McNamara and General Taylor conferred with President Johnson, a statement was issued by the White House on March 17, 1964, that the United States was again to increase economic and military aid to Viet Nam.[14] On March 26, 1964, Secretary McNamara made a lengthy statement of U. S. policy in Viet Nam, repeating American determination to defend its freedom. He admitted, however, that "the road ahead in Viet Nam is going to be long, difficult and frustrating. It will take work, courage, imagination, and—perhaps more than anything else —patience to bear the burden of what President Kennedy called a 'long twilight struggle'." [15]

On June 2, 1964, President Johnson stated:

"It may be helpful to outline four basic themes that govern our policy in Southeast Asia. First, America keeps her word. Second, the issue is the future of Southeast Asia as a whole. Third, our purpose is peace. Fourth, this is not just a jungle war, but a struggle for freedom on every front of human activity.

"On the point that America keeps her word, we are steadfast in a policy which has been followed for 10 years in three administrations. That was begun by General Eisenhower, in a letter of October 25, 1954, to President Diem. . . . We are bound by solemn commitments to help defend this area against Communist encroachment. We will keep this commitment. In the case of Viet Nam, our commitment today is just the same as the commitment made by President Eisenhower to President Diem in 1954—a commitment to help these people help themselves." [16]

In early January, 1964, shortly after the authors visited with General Duong Van Minh, he was overthrown as Chief of State by Lieutenant General Nguyen Khanh, on the grounds that Minh was not fighting the Communists strongly enough. A three-man National Committee was established as the highest governmental authority, but within a short time General Khanh was in charge. Since that time an array of changes in top leadership occurred, e.g. General Khanh was overthrown, then regained power, and was overthrown again. A civil government in Saigon under Prime Minister Tran Van Huong was overthrown by the revolt of the generals known as the "Young Turks". They arrested some members of the civil government for an alleged soft attitude towards the Viet Cong. Several generals were then included in the government. They finally formed the government with Phan Khac Suu as Chief of State, and Phan Huy Quat as Prime Minister, in February, 1965.

4. Changes of Government

The following are the principal characters involved in attempting to establish governments in Saigon:

1. General Duong Van Minh, former Chief of Staff under President Diem, who led the coup d'etat overthrowing the Diem Government in November, 1963.
2. Lt. General Nguyen Khanh, who after deposing General Minh in a swift and bloodless coup, proclaimed himself as President of the Military Revolutionary Council in January, 1964. Twice overthrown and twice resuming power, Khanh once declared himself "Chief of State," but later withdrew because of the Buddhist riots and other opposition. A Buddhist himself, he became an "Ambassador-at-Large" of the Republic of Viet Nam in 1965.
3. Brigadier General Lam Van Phat was against Khanh. He became the leader of the abortive coup in Sep-

tember, 1964, but was quickly overthrown by the "Young Turks."

4. Tran Van Huong, former Mayor of Saigon, was appointed Premier of a civilian government in October, 1964, but was deposed in January, 1965.

5. Lt. General Tran Thien Khiem, one of the generals participating in the overthrow of the Diem Government in 1963, became the Ambassador in Washington. He was one of the military triumvirate governing South Viet Nam for about a month after Khanh was forced to resign as Chief of State. (The present Vietnamese Ambassador in Washington is Vu Van Thai.)

6. Air Vice-Marshal Nguyen Cao Ky, the Air Commander, was among the young generals supporting Khanh in September, 1964. He was one of the three most important military leaders in Saigon. Since June, 1965, he has served as the Prime Minister of South Viet Nam. But in January, 1966, during the visit of Secretary Rusk and Ambassador-at-Large Harriman, he was almost overthrown by an abortive coup of some dissatisfied military officers.

7. Colonel Pham Ngoc Thao, a former military aide to President Diem, was a former Communist and had been consulted by Diem quite frequently on Communist problems. He was for some time in charge of training the young Vietnamese officers in the United States. He participated in the coup in 1963, later becoming press officer at the Vietnamese Embassy in Washington, D.C. He planned a coup against Khanh, but failed.

8. Phan Huy Quat, former Foreign Minister, became Premier in Saigon in February, 1965, while Khanh retained his military power. During his premiership, he dismissed almost half of the strong anti-Communist elements from the Government. Such actions offended the Catholics, the Cao Dai, and Hoa Hao elements.

9. Phan Khac Suu was Chief of State from February to June, 1965. He was weak in handling the Government. His dispute with his own premier, together with his slow progress in coping with the political and military problems of his country, caused him to resign with his premier simultaneously.

The Saigon Government was toppled in June, 1965, after

a political dispute between Phan Khac Suu, the Chief of State, and Phan Huy Quat, the Prime Minister, over whether the Prime Minister had the right to dismiss two cabinet members without consulting the Chief of State. The real reason for Quat's resignation was that he had been yielding to pressure from the Buddhists and leftists, and fired 50 anti-Communist leaders. The Catholics, Hoa Hao, and Cao Daists then quickly forced his downfall. This resulted in the resignation of both Quat and Suu on June 12, 1965. Their power was then turned over to the National Leadership Committee of ten persons, with Major General Nguyen Van Thieu, now Chief of State, and Air Vice-Marshal Nguyen Cao Ky heading it.

From November, 1963, there have been so many changes of hands at the helm of the Saigon Government, that one can easily deduce the kind of situation under the surface of the Diem Government: the rivalries, the ambitions, and the jealousies, in addition to increasing Communist aggression and subversion. Frederick E. Nolting, Jr., American Ambassador to Viet Nam from 1960 to 1963, penned the following on November 1, 1964:

> "I cannot let this month pass without my respects to the memory of a brave man who died for his country a year ago—Ngo Dinh Diem, former President of the Republic of Viet Nam.
>
> Events in Viet Nam since his overthrow and assassination last November throw light upon some of the problems he faced during his eight years as President of that turbulent country. His government's achievements under difficult conditions, the schools, roads, hospitals, airstrips, land reform, the creation of defense forces and instilling the will to resist, still stand as major obstacles to Communist victory there.
>
> The death of Ngo Dinh Diem casts a long shadow over his troubled land, a shadow that reaches far beyond his own country. But Diem was a patriot, and I am sure that his wish for his people now, as it was throughout the years I knew him, is for success in their struggle for national survival, political progress and human dignity." [17]

On August 2, 1964, the *U.S.S. Maddox* was attacked in international waters off the coast of North Viet Nam by

Viet Cong torpedo boats. Two days later, the destroyer *C. Turner Joy* and destroyer *Maddox* were attacked by Viet Cong PT boats. There was no alternative for President Johnson except to retaliate with air action against the Viet Cong gun boats and certain supporting facilities in North Viet Nam. An attack on warships is ordinarily an act of war. In order to whitewash the Viet Cong and also to threaten the United States, Red China, on August 6, issued a lengthy declaration accusing the United States of planning an escalation of the war. In substance, the following points were made by Red China:

North Viet Nam had the right to attack the ships because they had allegedly entered the territorial waters of the *Democratic People's Republic*. The first and second Tonkin incidents never occurred, Red China alleged; they were merely fabrications of the United States Government.

The United States, continued Communist China, has repeatedly used armed force against North Viet Nam: on July 30, and on August 1, 2, and 5, 1964. These are further evidences of the United States plot against the *Democratic People's Republic of Viet Nam,* indicating its intention to extend the war to China. Since the United States has already started her aggression in Viet Nam, which is a brother-country of the *People's Republic of China,* the *Democratic Republic of Viet Nam* has every right to counteract the aggression. An act against Viet Nam is also an act of aggression against China. Communist China cannot sit idly by without helping the Vietnamese against American imperialism. If the American Government does not immediately halt her naval and air aggression, the United States must bear all of the consequences.[18]

This was the reaction of Red China. She took no action, but made lots of charges and veiled threats. In the United States, the Viet Cong attacks on American warships were considered so outrageous that American public opinion, as reflected in the Congress, deemed such actions intolerable. The House of Representatives, by a vote of 416 to 0, and the Senate by 88 to 2 *, authorized President Johnson "to take all necessary measures to repel any armed attack against the forces of the United States and to prevent further aggression." A Joint Resolution was adopted in both the House and Senate on August 10, 1964, and became Public Law

---

* The two were Oregon's Senator Morse and Alaska's Senator Gruening. The floor manager for the passage of this bill was Senator William Fulbright. Later on he "wondered" if the United States had provoked the attack.

88-408. The title of this resolution is "To Promote the Maintenance of International Peace and Security in Southeast Asia." It condemns the naval units of the Communist regime in Viet Nam for "deliberately and repeatedly attacking United States vessels lawfully present in international waters, thereby creating a serious threat to international peace."

The United States declared:

> "These attacks are part of a deliberate and systematic campaign of aggression that the Communist regime in North Viet Nam has been waging against its neighbors and the nations joined with them in the collective defense of their freedom."

The Communist world has often accused the United States of political, military, and territorial ambition throughout the world. This Congressional Resolution makes it clear that in assisting the peoples of Southeast Asia to protect their freedom, the United States "has no territorial, military or political ambitions in that area." The real purpose of giving assistance to the people there is so they may be "left in peace to work out their own destinies in their own way."

The Resolution in unmistakable terms provides "that the Congress approves and supports the determinations of the President, as Commander-in-Chief, to take all necessary measures to repel any armed attack against the forces of the Unied States and to prevent further aggression." (Section I)

The joint session of Congress further resolved that "the United States regards as vital to its national interest and to world peace the maintenance of international peace and security in Southeast Asia." Both Houses thereby declared that unless the United States stayed in Viet Nam, chaos to the free world might well result. This Resolution also provided that:

> "Consonant with the Constitution of the United States and the Charter of the United Nations and in accordance with its obligations under the Southeast Asia Collective Defense Treaty, the United States is, therefore, prepared, as the President determines, to take all necessary steps including the use of armed force, to assist any member or protocol state of the Southeast Asia Collective Defense Treaty requesting assistance in defense of its freedom." (Section 2)

This section of the Resolution is most important in the

light of the present situation in Viet Nam. It clearly shows the constitutional and legal basis for authorizing the President to use his discretionary power to "take all necessary steps, including the use of armed force, to assist any member *or protocol state* of the Southeast Asia Collective Defense Treaty." Since South Viet Nam is within the protocol or treaty area, the President of the United States has both the right and duty to help the Republic of Viet Nam defend its freedom, in response to its request for help.

As to when this Resolution shall terminate, it provides that it "shall expire when the President shall determine that the peace and security of the area is reasonably assured by international conditions created by action of the United Nations or otherwise, except that it may be terminated earlier by concurrent resolution of the Congress." Since this Resolution is still valid, the President of the United States has ample authority to invoke it to repel aggression, subversion, and infiltration in South Viet Nam, as long as, and in whatever way, he deems proper.

From different standpoints and for different reasons, both the United States and the Communist bloc fully understand the political, economic, and military importance of South Viet Nam. The United States from 1954 to the present has been trying to help the Republic of Viet Nam preserve her political and territorial independence, and to improve the living standards of her people. The Communist nations, on the other hand, are determined to conquer and control South Viet Nam, and to use that region as a stepping stone for further communization of Southeast Asia. According to the *White Paper* issued by the State Department in February, 1965, the essence of the Vietnamese situation may be summed up as follows:

> "South Viet Nam is fighting for its life against a brutal campaign of terror and armed attack inspired, directed, supplied and controlled by the Communist regime in Hanoi. This flagrant aggression has been going on for years, but recently the pace has quickened and the threat has now become acute." [19]

The *White Paper* further reported that "in Viet Nam a Communist government has set out deliberately to conquer a sovereign people in a neighboring state. . . . It has used every resource of its own government to carry out its carefully planned program of concealed aggression." [20]

In more detail, the same document elaborates on the following items:

Hanoi supplies the key personnel for the armed aggression against South Viet Nam, such as military personnel, infiltration of native North Vietnamese, and Viet Cong agents. Hanoi supplies weapons, ammunition, and other war material to its forces in the South. North Viet Nam is the base for conquest of the South. The organization, direction, command, and control of the attack on South Viet Nam is centered in Hanoi, including the political, military, and intelligence organizations. The National Liberation Front is a political arm of the Viet Cong.

The *White Paper* gives a brief history of Hanoi's campaign of aggression against South Viet Nam. After presenting the facts, the State Department substantiated them with figures and photographs, and presented its conclusion in the following words. The *White Paper*

"establishes beyond question that North Viet Nam is carrying out a carefully conceived plan of aggression against the South. It shows that North Viet Nam has intensified its efforts in the years since it was condemned by the International Control Commission. It proves that Hanoi continues to press its systematic program of armed aggression into South Viet Nam. This aggression violates the United Nations Charter. It is directly contrary to the Geneva Accords of 1954 and 1962 to which North Viet Nam is a party. It shatters the peace of South Asia. It is a fundamental threat to the freedom and security of South Viet Nam." [21]

Some critics of the Republic of Viet Nam have declared that the people in South Viet Nam do not want to fight, and that they are indifferent towards the war. The State Department denies the allegation.[22] The Communist nations have repeatedly accused the United States of having political, military, and territorial designs in Southeast Asia. The State Department repudiates the charge, pointing out that "the United States seeks no territory, no military bases, no favored position. But we have learned the meaning of aggression elsewhere in the post-war world, and we have met it." [23]

American convoys have been ambushed; the American Embassy and American hostels and barracks have been attacked; American civilian and military personnel have been killed; American military and civilian ships have been bombed and sunk. The dilemma posed to the United States

148

is not whether she should continue to help Viet Nam repel the aggression from the North, but for how long and to what extent. If the United States does not fulfill her commitments and obligations and withdraws from Viet Nam, where will the United States make a stand? And to what extent will United States commitments be valued in the eyes of the world?

Writers, commentators, professors, students, a few members of Congress, and others have criticized President Johnson's actions in repelling the aggression from North Viet Nam. Some even question whether the President has the authority to do so. Some maintain that the United States should not be in Viet Nam at all, and should "get out" immediately. Some think that the United States is now engaged in a "bloody and wanton stalemate," a "dirty war" or a "quagmire." Their theory is that since France was defeated at Dien Bien Phu in 1954, the United States cannot hope to avoid a similar defeat in Viet Nam. Others think that Viet Nam is not essential to the security and vital interests of the United States. These critics of the present policy of the United States would simply withdraw from Viet Nam by yielding to Viet Cong aggression, regardless of the consequences. The thinking behind such statements is usually something like the following:

1. Peace is always preferable to war.
2. Communism is "the wave of the future," or it is "not so bad," or, as Hans Morgenthau argues, a Communist conquest of South Viet Nam would be "Titoist," and therefore tolerable.
3. The United States should not get involved in such a war, in Asia or anywhere else. No non-Asian country can win there, says Walter Lippmann.
4. The fighting in Viet Nam today is a "civil war," and therefore the United States should not be involved. Senator Stephen Young of Ohio contended that it was a civil war as late as January, 1966.
5. Ho Chi Minh best represents the people of Viet Nam, and should be allowed to unite his country.
6. This is not a Communist take-over, but a grass-roots social revolution.

These are some of the main arguments of the critics, the pacifists, and the defeatists.

After the escalation of the war in February, 1965, a survey was taken of the members of the U.S. Senate Committee on Foreign Relations, and the Committee on Armed Services.

Twenty-five of the 35 members of these two committees gave their answers, with the following results:

a. Twenty agreed that the U.S. should not pull out of Viet Nam. None flatly favored withdrawal.
b. Eighteen agreed that the U.S. should not seek a settlement now, because no successful negotiation could be obtained from a weak position. Five favored immediate negotiations.[24]

5. Senatorial Opinions

The Senators expressed their opinion as follows:

Senator Russell B. Long (D-La.):

"We have a fair chance to win in South Vietnam. . . . We ought to bear down, try harder, and make victory our goal."

Senator Bourke B. Hickenlooper (R-Iowa):

"If a stable government can't be established in South Viet Nam, we would then have to decide whether we want to put a tremendous amount of additional American military power in there or whether we want to get some kind of a negotiated peace. . . . I would have no faith in a negotiated peace with the Communists."

Senator Wayne Morse (D-Oreg.):

"We should be seeking some kind of settlement that will carry out the 1954 objective of removing foreign domination from the old Indo-China, but this time with an effective guarantee of international enforcement."

Senator Leverett Saltonstall (R-Mass.):

"I believe we must make it clear that we intend to stay and assist the South Vietnamese if they are willing to help themselves. . . . I doubt if now is the time to seek a negotiated settlement."

Senator Thomas J. Dodd (D-Conn.):

"I don't think there is any possibility of a settlement with

Ho Chi Minh. What he wants is open surrender, or at least veiled surrender."

Senator John J. Williams (R-Del.):

"If we are going to keep American men in there, then we must put enough of them in so that we don't turn it into a slaughterhouse. The first order of business is to make up our minds as to policy."

Senator Stephen Young (D-Ohio):

". . . We must not escalate the war by invading North Viet Nam, if there is any chance at all that this action might draw the Red Chinese into the war. . . . I think the time has come for negotiations, if neutralization can be worked out. . . . We should try to neutralize both North and South Viet Nam and hope the Communists will abide by their agreements."

Senator George A. Smathers (D-Fla.):

". . . I don't think we should try to negotiate at present. We must first demonstrate the capacity to bring about a military stalemate. Only when it becomes clear to Ho Chi Minh that he cannot win the war in South Viet Nam—only then will it be opportune to find ways to work out a political settlement."

Senator Frank Carlson (R-Kans.):

"This is the poorest time we could select for any such move as seeking a settlement. If you are winning, you can work out arrangements and settlements. We certainly are not winning."

Senator Frank J. Lausche (D-Ohio):

". . . A coalition government in South Viet Nam will not work out. It would be the means for a takeover by the Communists. No coalition or so-called neutral government has ever worked out. The Communists have never kept their word. Negotiate what? When you enter into negotiations you should have in mind the subjects to negotiate. Is it for North Viet Nam to quit infiltration and subversion and inducement to riots? If negotiation means surrender, then of course my answer is: No."

Senator Jack Miller (R-Iowa):

"Our long-established policy has been that we will assist any government that requests assistance in stopping Communist aggression. . . . We should take such action as is recommended by our military advisers to implement this policy."

Senator Strom Thurmond (R-S.C.):

"It is impossible to defeat an enemy under self-imposed rules which limit the conflict to a specific geographical area and permit sanctuaries to the enemy. Do I favor making whatever effort is needed to win that war and get it over with? Yes.
"I do not believe there will ever be a time when a negotiated settlement with a Communist aggressor such as Ho Chi Minh will be in the interests of the United States."

Senator Joseph S. Clark (D-Penn.):

"I believe that neutralization of the entire area is not an unworthy goal, and I would support such a policy provided that the action was not just a sham to cover up further Communist take-overs in nations which are now independent."

Senator Daniel K. Inouye, (D-Hawai):

"We should never be afraid to either talk or fight, but any negotiations should be from a position of strength."

Senator Thomas J. McIntyre (D-N.H.):

"I presently understand that the loss of South Viet Nam woud be a prologue to future losses in Southeast Asia. I favor added effort by the U.S. on all fronts, including specialized combat troops to show how it can be done. . . . With some military successes as bargaining tools, negotiations could well be the way with honor at a later date."

Senator Robert C. Byrd (D-Va.):

"As to whether the time has come to seek a settlement with Ho Chi Minh, my answer is: No. Should the war be continued as now? I can't see any alternative at the moment."

Senator Daniel K. Inouye, (D-Hawaii):

"The presence of a stable government is the most important key to victory at this time. Militarily, we're in good shape."

6. *Arguments Against Withdrawal*

The main reasons for the rejection of American withdrawal from the Republic of Viet Nam are the following:

i.) If United States forces withdraw from Viet Nam, the inevitable result will be a Communist take-over of the whole country, and this will be a further threat to Thailand, Malaysia, and other parts of Southeast Asia.

ii.) If the United States abandons her commitments to Viet Nam, no matter what the excuse, or if she fails to keep them sufficiently, or if she shows, by accepting defeat, that she is either unable or unwilling to win the war, no country would trust the promises or treaties of the United States. Instead, they would be compelled to throw themselves at the mercy of Communism.

iii.) If the United States should withdraw from Viet Nam, it would mean an actual surrender to Communist aggression and an encouragement to Communist expansion in Asia and elsewhere.

iv.) The United States has sacrificed many human lives and much money to halt the Japanese aggression in Southeast Asia, and the North Korean and Red Chinese aggression in South Korea. Withdrawal from Viet Nam could easily result in the complete nullification of these efforts.

v.) Withdrawal from Viet Nam would not solve the basic problems in Viet Nam, nor would it stop Communist aggression in that part of the world, but rather increase it. The Thai government has already expressed grave concern over the growing Communist guerrilla forces on the northeastern borders of Thailand, and the recurring acts of terrorism there.

vi.) If the United States withdraws from Viet Nam in the face of greater Viet Cong successes, she will have a much more difficult time establishing a defense perimeter else-where.

vii.) The United States would not be able to hold successfully the coastal enclaves, if these enclaves were surrounded by hostile forces and population. It resembles the theory of the Maginot Line.

In addition to the theories of escalation and withdrawal, there is the theory proposed by France's President Charles de Gaulle, the "neutralization of Viet Nam." This has the support of many "non-aligned nations," including India, Ceylon, and the United Arab Republic. Neutralization is a treacherous policy, as the Communists consider it merely an interim device to enable them to consolidate, dominate, and finally control. When Defense Secretary McNamara visited Hue on an inspection trip, he was greeted by Vietnamese with posters, warning: "Neutralize, today, Communize tomorrow." The Communist idea of "fair play" is expressed in the saying: "What is mine is mine; what is yours is negotiable."

At a press conference on February 7, 1964, Secretary of State Dean Rusk was asked for his opinion of de Gaulle's "neutralization plan" for Viet Nam. Mr. Rusk reiterated his statement made in 1962: "The only problem of peace in Viet Nam came from the North, and if the North would leave her neighbors alone, there would be peace. Neutralization is simply a device for the Communization of all Southeast Asia, and that we cannot accept." [25] As late as March 1, 1966, however, Senator Fulbright in a Senate speech proposed that the Viet Nam conflict be resolved by an agreement with Communist China for neutralization of all Southeast Asia.[26]

On May 3, 1965, in the telecast on Viet Nam in which Maurice Schumann, President of the Foreign Relations Committee of the French Chamber of Deputies, Sir Alex Hume, former British Prime Minister, Michael Stewart, British Foreign Secretary, and former Senator Barry Goldwater participated, Secretary Rusk reminded the audience that the neutralization of Laos in 1962 was a failure, and a very sad experience. The Communists violated the pledges they made in Geneva in 1962, and the United States could no longer depend on an empty plan of neutralization for Viet Nam.

The United States has rejected withdrawal, unlimited escalation, and neutralization of Viet Nam. She hopes to make the Viet Cong sit down to a conference table, independent from the domination of Peking or Moscow. She has also promised Hanoi substantial economic aid, once a cease-fire is accomplished. Hanoi, Peking, and probably Moscow, have chosen thus far not to negotiate with the United States. The Viet Cong, instead, have greatly increased their infiltration from the North, and have intensified their war efforts. The principal reasons why Hanoi, Peking, and probably Moscow prefer to continue their fight in Viet Nam are the following:

The Communist nations want to take full advantage of the cold war in the United States. America has to combat opposition at home in the form of demonstrations, petitions, teach-ins, and other attacks against government policy in Viet Nam. The Communists believe that the leftist influence in the United States can prey on the soft hearts of Americans to prevail on their government to stop the bombing in North Viet Nam, and to agree to withdraw from Viet Nam in order to get the government of Hanoi to the conference table. The most important factor in the Communist denunciation of American peace offers is that both the Viet Cong and Communist China believe they can win. In this they are largely the victims of their own propaganda.

The Communists emphasize the impatience of the American people and their government. The Communists also count on their many friends, sympathizers, and "fellow-travelers" throughout the United States. America, on the other hand, has no significant influence behind the Iron Curtain. The Communist bloc counts on support within the United States, while the U.S. cannot rely on support from those under Communist rule.

The Communist bloc counts on the fact that the United States will never permit the government forces of South Viet Nam to cross into the North, just as the United States does not permit Nationalist China to attack the China Mainland. For some reason the United States has never even let the Chinese Nationalist troops fight the Communists in South Viet Nam. For sixteen years American policy in Asia has been dominated by fear of war with Red China. It is still the conviction of the Communist nations that, by dragging on the war, the various diplomatic pressures, the problems of trade, the increased loss of life, and the disruption to the American economy will cause the United States to withdraw. Whether it is done under the guise of coalition, or neutralization, or a new word, such as "non-alignment," the Communists hope to be able to take over South Viet Nam after a cease-fire is arranged.

FOOTNOTES

CHAPTER VIII: VIET NAM: U. S. COMMITMENTS AND DILEMMAS

1. U. S. Senate Committee on Foreign Relations, *Background Information Relating to Southeast Asia and Viet Nam* (Washington, 1965), pp. 21-22.
2. *Op. Cit.*, p. 25.
3. *New York Times*, March 30, 1954.
4. *Op. Cit.*
5. *Background Information, Op. Cit.*, (1965) pp. 67-8.
6. Report of Senators Mike Mansfield, J. Caleb Boggs, Claiborne Pell and Benjamin A. Smith on *Viet Nam and Southeast Asia to the Committee on Foreign Relations, United States Senate* (Washington, 1963), p. 3.
7. The White House, *Press Release*, also in the Department of State, *BULLETIN*, (Washington, 1963), p. 3.
8. *Ibid.*
9. Department of State, *BULLETIN*, (Washington, June 19, 1961), pp. 956-7.
10. *Loc. Cit.*
11. *BULLETIN, Op. Cit.*, January 1, 1962, pp. 13-14.
12. *Op. Cit.*, p. 13.
13. *Background Information, Op. Cit.*, (1965) pp. 106-7.
14. *Background Information, Op. Cit.*, pp. 109-110; and *BULLETIN, Op. Cit.*, April 6, 1964, pp. 522-3.
15. *Loc. Cit.*
16. *Background Information, Op. Cit.*, pp. 120-1.
17. *New York Times*, November 6, 1964, Letter to the Editor.
18. Hsin Hua News Agency, *Dispatches*, August 6 and 7, 1964.
19. Department of State, *Aggression from the North: The Record of North Viet Nam's Campaign to Conquer South Viet Nam* (Washington, February 1965), p. 1-ff.
20. *Ibid.*, p. 1.
21. *Ibid.*, p. 29.
22. *Loc. Cit.*
23. *Loc. Cit.*
24. *U.S. News & World Report*, February 15, 1965, pp. 68-72.
25. Department of State, *Bulletin*, Washington, February 24, 1964, pp. 278-80, and *Background Information, Op. Cit.*, pp. 107-8.
26. *New York Times*, March 2, 1966.

CHAPTER IX

THE TEACH-INS AND THEIR IMPLICATIONS

1. *Their Origin and Developments*

College students in most East Asian countries have long taken a personal interest in politics, almost as a matter of necessity. Their lives and livelihood depend largely on the political situation in their respective countries. Students of higher education in the United States, on the other hand, have shown a remarkable indifference to politics. To some extent this is still quite true today, but recent events indicate that American students are becoming more interested in politics and international problems than ever before.

The United States first shelled North Viet Nam in August, 1964, in retaliation against the Viet Cong attack on U.S. warships. On several college campuses, students began demonstrating against America's policy in Viet Nam. The Viet Cong further increased the tempo of their terroristic attack against South Viet Nam, bombing military installations, civilian and military personnel, and even the United States Embassy in Saigon. On February 1, 1965, the United States and South Viet Nam largely abolished the policy of granting privileged sanctuary to the aggressor. Left-wing elements led the protests against the bombings. They carried their demonstrations to the White House and the Pentagon. The movement soon spread to thirty or forty different colleges, including teachers as well as students. Liberal and leftist speakers took the position that the United States was an aggressor in Viet Nam, and that American Forces have no right to be there. Some pointed to Ho Chi Minh as a national hero, and urged that the United States should not obstruct his take-over of Viet Nam.

J. Edgar Hoover, the Director of the Federal Bureau of Investigation, wrote to all law enforcement officials, on June 1, 1965:

"Tremendous pressure and criticism are being leveled against the President and the Congress to confuse and mislead the American public. Irresponsible charges . . . are used to discredit our Government in hopes it will be forced to abandon its role as defender of freedom. Some of this protest comes from legitimate peace groups and others who are opposed to the course of action being followed in Viet Nam and the Dominican Republic. However, much of the agitation is part of a diabolical scheme contrived by the Communist Party, U.S.A. (CPUSA), an integral arm of the international conspiracy, the materialistic, Godless ideology dedicated to ruling the world. . . .

"The CPUSA encouraged and endorsed the student march on the Nation's Capitol on April 17, 1965, protesting U.S. intervention in Viet Nam . . . Communist marchers from all over the Country were present, and Communist leaders claimed a major role in the demonstration.

"This is a typical example of the party's widespread campaign to influence our Country's foreign policies. The strategy is not new, but it is effective. The party is working through non-Communist groups and front organizations to embarrass our Government and disrupt its efforts. Communist leaders are striving to initiate other marches and demonstrations to keep their campaign of fear and terror rolling. We can expect that the party will push for some type of nationwide action similar to "peace" strikes or work stoppages to emphasize their aims.

"Party leaders hope, of course, that more and more Americans will be duped and misled by these tactics. They envision a commanding wave of hostility against American policies abroad. The goal is to incite citizens to the point that they will demand American Forces be withdrawn from Viet Nam and other places, allowing international Communism to take over and engulf more defenseless countries." [1]

Although the American Government was aware that considerable Communist influence was behind the various "sit-ins," "teach-ins," and other demonstrations, it did not stop them. The demonstrations recall a resolution passed by the

Oxford Union, in 1933. The Oxford Union is a student debating society at Oxford University. Its debates have been a training ground for many eminent British politicians and public servants. The famous resolution of 1933 declared: "This house refuses to fight for King and country." It was adopted by the students by a vote of 275 to 153. Prime Minister Winston Churchill described it as "ever shameful." He also wrote that "it was easy to laugh off such an episode in England, but in Germany, in Russia, in Italy, in Japan, the idea of a decadent degenerate Britain took deep root and swayed many calculations. Little did the foolish boys who passed the resolution dream that they were destined quite soon to conquer or fall gloriously in the ensuing war and prove themselves the finest generation ever bred in Britain." [2]

Similarly, until 1941 there was a very strong peace movement in Great Britain and the United States, one that Germany and Japan contributed to. There were hundreds of "peace organizations" under various names which insisted that Britain and the United States must keep out of war. Hitler, Mussolini, and Tojo took interest and comfort in the movement. After Hitler attacked the Soviet Union in June, 1941, the international Communists then maintained that the United States should no longer remain neutral.

The Teach-in Movement and the various anti-war demonstrations in the United States since May 1965 have been conducted on a much larger scale than the anti-war movement carried out by the Oxford Union in 1933. These demonstrations were considered by Hanoi and Peking as the "second front" of their "war of liberation" in Viet Nam. Such well planned and well organized efforts could not have occurred without international encouragement and support.

Senator Thomas J. Dodd, Vice-Chairman of the Internal Security Sub-Committee of the United States Senate, who helped to conduct the investigation of the Teach-ins, noted that they originated at the beginning of March, 1965, at the University of Michigan.[3] They were launched by Eric J. Wolf, Professor of Anthropology, William A. Gamson, Assistant Professor of Sociology, and Arnold S. Kaufman, Associate Professor of Philosophy. No officers were announced, but the contacts listed were Professor Arnold Kaufman and Marshall Sahlins. The first meeting contained a series of lectures and seminars, punctuated by folksongs and bomb scares. Viet Cong films were also shown at the meeting, and pro-Communist literature was distributed.

2. *The First National Teach-In*

When the Headquarters of this movement announced that a National Teach-in would take place in Washington with a high official of the Johnson administration to make its defense, it immediately acquired national significance. Without the recognition of the American Government, whose policy it attacked, the Washington Teach-in would never have had such an impact. As it was, 129 colleges and universities carried it on television.

The United States has been very tolerant of the "peace movements". Instead of trying to discourage the demonstrations, the Government has taken the stand that it would be better to explain its own position to the students and faculty of these institutions, rather than remaining silent when attacked. The Government sent some of its own officials and other intellectuals sympathetic with the present policies in Viet Nam to try to clarify the situation and correct misleading information. The opposition leaders challenged the Administration and asked to debate with some of its officials, including McGeorge Bundy, then Special Assistant to President Johnson on American Policy in Viet Nam. The Teach-in lasted the entire day on Saturday, May 15, 1965. It was televised from Washington, D.C.

The National Teach-in seems to have been conceived by Richard Mann and a few other members of the faculty of the University of Michigan. They decided to form an "Inter-University Committee for a public hearing on Viet Nam," which later became the official organ handling the arrangements of the debate in Washington.

This debate was held in the Sheraton-Park Hotel. All-day live television coverage was made by the TV educational stations in New York, Washington, and Boston. Highlights of the program were carried for several hours by many stations throughout the country.

The principal speakers included the following:

1. *Those defending American Policy:*
   Arthur J. Schlesinger, Jr., Harvard University
   Robert A. Scalapino, University of California
   Walt W. Rostow, Chairman, Policy Planning Council, State Department
   Zbigniew Brzezinski, Columbia (now on White House staff)
   Michael F. M. Lindsay, American University
   P. J. Honey, British scholar on Viet Nam
   Paul Kattenberg, Policy Planning Staff, State Department

Samuel Huntington, Harvard University
Benjamin Schwartz, Harvard University
Wesley Fishel, Michigan State University

2. *Those attacking American Policy:*

Hans J. Morgenthau, University of Chicago
Isaac Deutscher, writer on Communism
George M. Kahin, Cornell University
Stanley Millet, Briarcliff College
Mary Wright, Yale University
William A. Williams, University of Wisconsin
Bernard Fall, Howard University
Felix Greene, Stanford University
Stanley Hoffman, Harvard University
Robert Browne, Farleigh-Dickinson University.

When the moderator, Ernest Nagel of Columbia University, read the telegram sent by McGeorge Bundy, expressing his regret that he was unable to participate in the discussion on Viet Nam, laughter, boos, and applause came from the audience. Throughout the day various speakers made derogatory remarks about Bundy's avoidance of the debate. The moderator of the night session, at the conclusion of the meeting, reprimanded Bundy for his failure to be present. In his earlier telegram, Bundy had explained that he might not be able to attend. After the Teach-in was adjourned, it was learned that Bundy had been sent by the President to Santo Domingo on an urgent fact-finding mission.

Since it was impossible for Bundy to be present, Walt W. Rostow was the highest ranking official at the debate. There were a few other officials from the State Department of medium rank, together with some officers from West Point.

Speakers for the government side included:

Robert A. Scalapino, professor at the University of California. Some years ago he and a few others wrote what is known as the "Conlon Report."[4] Its official title is "The Studies of the United States Foreign Policy in Asia." About $300,000 was allocated for this report by the United States Senate Foreign Relations Committee, under the Chairmanship of Senator J. William Fulbright. It was published in November, 1959.

The report made several recommendations for the consideration of the Committee. It suggested the abolition of SEATO which expressly provides in its "Protocol" that South Viet Nam be included in its "Treaty Area" and that it be under the protection of the signatories. It also recommended that the United States should cooperate with the Soviet Union and other Communist bloc members to extend economic and technical assistance to the underdeveloped countries in Southeast Asia. It recommended that Red China become a member of the United Nations Security Council, and that the Republic of China be cast aside and replaced by a Republic of Taiwan.

The Conlon Report further suggested that the United States embargo against Communist China be lifted, and that the United States grant recognition to Red China. The report also proposed that the large American military forces in Taiwan, Viet Nam, and Korea be reduced, and that a new reassessment be made of United States military policies in Asia. It is interesting to see Scalapino defending quite different views later.

It is also interesting to note that Paul Kattenberg, now a member of the policy planning staff of the State Department and a defender of American policy at the Teach-in, was reported by the *Washington World*, Oct. 14, 1963, as "The United States official masterminding the move to oust Diem." In 1963, when he was director of the Working Group of the State Department in Viet Nam, he strongly urged that Diem be removed. Perhaps Scalapino and Kattenberg have changed their viewpoints. In any case, Ernest Nagel, the moderator, announced that Professor Scalapino had agreed to speak in the place of McGeorge Bundy, and that George M. Kahin would give the principal opposing statement.

Kahin's basic attack on American policy in Viet Nam was that our "most consistent failure has been an inability both to appreciate the importance of Asian nationalism and to work with rather than against this powerful force. . . ." [5] He further condemned "the obsession of American policymakers with what they still see as monolithic Communism, which has blinded them to the fact that Communism in Asia has adapted itself to nationalism." He charged United States policy makers with having "confused the broad but nationally differentiated force and potential of Communism with the threat of especially Chinese power." [6] In particular, Kahin thought that it had been a mistake for the United States to support the Government of Ngo Dinh Diem with economic aid and military assistance.

Kahin stated that "non-Communist governments of Southeast Asia will not automatically collapse" if the Communists should come to control all of Viet Nam. He asserted that if the United States really wants to negotiate unconditionally, she should not insist that the Viet Cong cease all operations immediately. He urged that the United States negotiate with "the National Liberation Front," the political arm of the Viet Cong. He wanted the United States to halt her bombardment of North Viet Nam as the first genuine indication of an interest in negotiations. In conclusion, he again urged Bundy's participation in the future debates on American policy in Viet Nam.

In reply to Kahin's critical statement on American policy in Viet Nam, Scalapino at the outset declared that he was not there as "a spokesman for the Government," and that he did not know what Bundy would have said. Scalapino stated that the Viet Cong is not an indigenous force in South Viet Nam. He pointed out that the real leaders of the Viet Cong have always been the small hard-core members of the Communist Party. He declared that although there may have been differences in tactics between the National Liberation Front in the South, and the Labor Party, or Lao Dong Group, in the North, there has been no difference on the question of basic policies or fundamental programs.

Scalapino contended that the Communists in South Viet Nam follow the Chinese revolutionary tactics of a five-stage development. The first stage is to have a tightly disciplined Communist Party, closed to penetration from the outside. The second stage is the United Front, which enlists the support of the peasantry, the intelligentsia, and the petit bourgeoisie. The third stage is the use of guerrilla warfare. The fourth stage is from guerrilla to positional warfare. The fifth and final stage is the establishment of a "People's Democracy."

Scalapino also contended that the Viet Cong do not command the support and allegiance of the people of South Viet Nam. He maintained that very few, if any, significant anti-Diem leaders in the South joined the Viet Cong. Very few Catholics, Buddhists, Cao Dai or Hoa Hao sects have joined the Communist-led National Liberation Front in South Viet Nam. He pointed out that through a long period of war and suffering, the vast majority of the people in the South have not joined the Communist movement.

Scalapino said that Communist states could not afford to allow free elections, and he did not think that Hanoi was interested in elections in the North. Free elections are meaningful to democratic countries, but would be meaningless to the Communists. The Geneva Agreements providing for free elections in the North and South were fraudulent from the very beginning. In a society dominated by men who regard class enemies as susceptible to control by any means possible, free elections are impossible.

Scalapino maintained that if the United States withdraws from Viet Nam, the Communist-led Thai National Liberation Movement would certainly spread far and wide. It would also prove that Peking's hard line towards the United States is more successful than the comparatively soft Moscow line.

Scalapino charged that Peking has refused every chance and channel to negotiate. He hoped that Hanoi would be more independent from Peking by coming to a conference table to talk for a cease-fire. Scalapino clearly repudiated Kahin's theory that the Viet Cong are indigenous forces. The Viet Cong forces under Ho Chi Minh cannot represent nationalism on the part of the people in Viet Nam, either in the North or the South. The so-called *National Liberation Front* in South Viet Nam has not been a spontaneous movement, but has been infiltrated, subverted, and directed by the Communists from the North, with very substantial economic and military aid from Peking and Moscow.

In discussing what he called "nationalism" in Viet Nam and in Southeast Asia, it not known whether Professor Kahin meant nationalism in the American or Communist sense. Nationalism to the Communist means one thing and to the average American another. Ho Chi Minh used the word prior to 1954, but only as a means to his own ulterior end. As a thorough-going Marxist-Leninist, Ho Chi Minh believes that "nation" or "state" is only a bridge toward world socialism or Communism. Scalapino correctly refuted Kahin when he pointed out:

> "The evidence thus far shows that most of the true South Vietnamese anti- or non-Communist leaders do not regard the Viet Cong as a nationalist movement." [7]

Hans Morgenthau, who fled to the United States as a refugee from Hitler, declared that there is "something basically wrong in the modes of thought and action" of the United States Government. He warned that present American policy in Viet Nam will lead to war with Red China. He said that the United States Government "does not have the courage to retreat" and "does not dare advance too far." He maintained that "from the point of view of Peking nothing better could happen than the United States waging a war in Viet Nam, which it is not able to win and which it cannot afford to lose." He alleged that Peking will simply extend its cultural and political influence to Southeast Asia, and would not be interested in territorial or military conquests. Morgenthau urged that the United States allow Ho Chi Minh to take over South Viet Nam, a betrayal which the United States has opposed for nearly a generation.

Isaac Deutscher analyzed the armed conflict in Viet Nam as a long-range capitalist-communist conflict, but he justified the use of force by the Viet Cong and the Chinese Communists. He said that all revolutions, including the American and French revolutions, used force to overthrow unjust regimes. This, he asserted, is what the Communists are doing in South Viet Nam. Deutscher pronounced the war in Viet Nam irresistible and unconquerable.

Zbigniew Brzezinski of Columbia University pointed out that the revolution in South Viet Nam is not indigenous and nationalistic. He quoted Robert Kleiman, an editorial writer of the *New York Times,* who stated that the "war of liberation in South Viet Nam still retains its original characteristics as an armed conspiracy. . . . The Viet Cong has scored military successes and entrenched itself politically in many rural areas. But there has never been any sign of a mass uprising, and there is a relative absence of popular support for the Viet Cong."

Brzezinski pointed out that some say Red China will be the dominant power in Asia, and that the United States should accept this. According to such a theory, he said, the United States should not have resisted Japan's domination in Asia in 1940, nor Germany's domination of Europe in the same year. Nor, according to that theory, should the United States have tried to contain Soviet Russia subsequent to 1947 in Europe.

Mary Wright of Yale University considered Brzezinski's parallels very dangerous intellectual exercises. She accused him of advocating a war to save Asia from Communism. She maintained that the best thing for the United States to do was to face reality, to give diplomatic recognition to Red China, and to accommodate itself to the Communist government there. She also asserted that Japan and India do not want the United States to be in Asia. Scalapino objected to this latter charge.

Michael Lindsay, of American University, pointed out that there has been a small but determined minority in Viet Nam using force and terrorism to get themselves in power. He declared that if your enemy is not going to follow any rules, you have to face the realities of the situation. Stanley Millet of Briarcliff University said that the truth about the

Vietnamese is that in 1960 the National Liberation Front in South Viet Nam wanted "universal suffrage to elect a new national assembly." Scalapino then asked Millet: "How can you have meaningful elections unless the opponents have full access to mass media, or at least sufficient access to get their position expressed?"

Patrick J. Honey, a noted British authority who has spent considerable time in North Viet Nam, was better informed about the situation in Hanoi and its environs than anyone else there. However, he was not given time to make a statement about Viet Nam. He was only allowed to ask a few questions or to make very brief comments.

Some of the remarks made by other participants in this historic Teach-in should also be mentioned briefly. Arthur Schlesinger, former special assistant to President Kennedy, was originally opposed to bombing the Viet Cong. But in this debate he was assigned to defend American policy in Viet Nam. He said that the American decision in 1954 to give aid to defend Viet Nam may have been wrong, but he enumerated three alternatives for the United States:

i. To withdraw from Viet Nam;
ii. To extend the war theatre;
iii. To negotiate with honor.

Schlesinger said that American withdrawal from Viet Nam would inevitably mean Communist domination, and that from then on no Asian nation would ever trust the United States. It is wishful thinking, he said, to hope that Ho Chi Minh would become another Tito, as Morgenthau never tires of saying he would. Viet Nam is geographically adjacent to China, while Yugoslavia is a great distance away from Soviet Russia. He conceded that the domino theory might not necessarily follow immediately, that perhaps not all the Southeast Asian countries would fall under Communist control. But he insisted that for the United States to abandon South Viet Nam through voluntary withdrawal, without a struggle or meaningful negotiation, would be immoral and unethical.

Regarding the second point, Schlesinger objected to any extension or escalation of the war, either into North Viet Nam or Red China. He said that such military action would cause more American sacrifices in men and material, and that it would force Moscow and Peking to come to terms with each other on the Viet Nam issue.

Concerning negotiations, Schlesinger said there was no doubt that the American Government under President Johnson has been very anxious to negotiate with the Communists for a cease-fire. It may be that the people in Hanoi also want to stop fighting. He pointed out, however, that Hanoi cannot rid itself of Peking's influence. He thought that if the United States could successfully help the Vietnamese Government repel the Viet Cong forces in South Viet Nam, and if the Communist nations begin to realize that they cannot control South Viet Nam, then they will be willing to talk peace.

William A. Williams, Professor of History at the University of Wisconsin, said that any reliance on force is dangerous, and that the United States is relying on force in Viet Nam. Michael F. M. Lindsay, Professor of Far Eastern Studies at American University, stated that when the Communists carry on their revolutions or guerrilla warfare in a country, they pretend that such movements are nationalistic and indigenous. But when they are in control, they change color. The United States, he said, should have stopped the Chinese Communists at the Chinese-Korean border during the Korean War in 1950-51. He explained that if Hitler had been stopped in 1938, and if Tojo had been stopped in 1941, World War II might have been avoided.

Wesley Fishel of Michigan State University said that the Republic of Viet Nam is not only an established fact, it has been recognized by 55 nations as an independent country. He also said that 28 countries had given aid to the government of that country*. He said that it was unfair to condemn the United States for her recognition and aid to the Republic of Viet Nam as a violation of the Geneva Agreements of 1954, as George Kahin had charged. Kahin commented on the Fishel statement by charging that South Viet Nam is not a sovereign state, because, he said the division of Viet Nam, as provided by the Geneva Agreements, was only a temporary measure. He seemed to feel that the people of South Viet Nam could never have a legitimate government unless some group meeting in Geneva first gives them permission.

Walt W. Rostow, Chairman of the Policy Planning Council of the State Department, gave a lengthy statement on the broad aspects of American policy, with an emphasis on its principles as applied in Viet Nam. He pointed out that, according to the constitution, United States foreign policy is conducted by the President, with the consent and approval of Congress. He brought out the fact that the United States now has treaty-obligations to protect 42 nations

* By February 1966, the number of countries giving aid to Viet Nam had increased to 39.

against aggression. Since 1946, shortly after World War II, Communist threats have occurred against Iran, Greece, China, Italy, Korea, Malaya, and India, as well as Viet Nam. The United States has signed various security pacts with free nations in Europe, Asia, and Australia to ward off Communist aggression and the threat of aggression. Signing these treaties or agreements was deemed in the best national interests of the United States, as well as for the freedom of peoples the world over.

Samuel Huntington of Harvard University said that the Viet Cong have followed the five phases of war strategy of Mao Tse-tung quite closely. The first phase or stage was the use of terrorism, from 1957 to 1960. The second phase was organized military action from 1960 to 1961. The third was the increasing use of guerrilla forces in South Viet Nam, from 1961 to 1963. The fourth was to intensify the guerrilla forces and to destroy the strategic hamlets in South Viet Nam from the spring of 1963 to August 1964. Now the war is in the fifth stage, which means further intensification of guerrilla warfare by means of sabotage, subversion, and large scale forces. He termed the Viet Cong military action in South Viet Nam a serious challenge to the freedom of the Vietnamese people.

Stanley Hoffman, also from Harvard University, attacked American policy in Viet Nam in other areas. He said that the United States has over-extended her capacity to defend other countries. The American Government has often asked other Governments or allies to share her burden for the defense of other areas without defining what the burden is. He also charged that the American Government often uses force without waiting for consultation with other nations or international organizations. He termed American policy in Viet Nam completely unsuccessful. He questioned whether the United States is prepared to use force to intervene whenever and wherever there is a Communist threat.

Oliver Clubb, Jr., of Syracuse, was against the bombing of the military targets in North Viet Nam. He said that bombing is never really effective. He suggested that a coalition government should be formed by North and South Viet Nam. He thought that neutralization of South Viet Nam would be acceptable to Moscow and Hanoi, and possibly to Peking. The most important thing, he said, was to stop the war in Viet Nam immediately. How this would be possible without a complete surrender he did not say, nor did he seem to care.

Before the debate was adjourned, Scalapino, the principal

defender of American policy in Viet Nam, and Rostow, the leading State Department official present, left the meeting. Most of the speakers and the audience remaining were against American policy. The atmosphere became more antagonistic to the Johnson administration. The chairman resolved that hereafter the National Teach-in should become a permanent organization.

After the Teach-in was over, the press began discussing the merits and demerits of such a large-scale discussion of American foreign policy. Many believe that this type of debate is beneficial and it should be continued. They maintain that it is a healthy sign to have citizens and government officials exchanging their ideas on vital issues, such as the war in Viet Nam. They insist that since it is a question of peace or war, the general public is entitled to know what their government is doing about it.

George Meany, the President of the American Federation of Labor and the Congress of Industrial Organizations, sharply criticized the "academic" opponents of President Johnson's policy in Viet Nam. He told the delegates at the national convention of the Utility Workers Union that "the surest way to bring about World War III is to appease dictators. The place to stop a third world war is when they take the first step." He told the reporters after his speech that "there are a good many people in this country who do not know what is happening." He further stated:

"I think the President has made it clear that he would rather negotiate in Viet Nam than continue to use force. But there are people who are still trying to get him to pull out. What they don't realize is that there is no one in Viet Nam who wants to negotiate. . . ." [8]

Presidential Assistant McGeorge Bundy expressed approval for such a national debate, explaining that he had genuinely desired to participate in it. He stated in his telegram to the panel:

"It has been argued that debate of this kind should be avoided because it can give encouragement to the adversaries of our country. There is some ground for this argument, since it is true that Communists have little understanding of the meaning of debate in a free society. The Chinese will continue to pretend, and perhaps to believe, that American policy is weaker because

700 faculty members have made a protest against our policy in Viet Nam. . . .

"The American people, whatever their opinions, know better. They know those who are protesting are only a minority, indeed a small minority, of American teachers and students." [9]

The *Tass* News Agency and *Radio Moscow* reported that the National Teach-in was attended by more than 100,000 academic people, and the majority were against American involvement in Viet Nam. Less than 5,000 actually attended. *Radio Hanoi* said that American intellectuals have denounced the policy of their government for its aggressive actions in Viet Nam. The *Hsin Hua* News Agency in Red China and *Radio Peking,* as well as Chinese Communist newspapers in Hong Kong, stated that United States barbaric and aggressive acts in Viet Nam and Southeast Asia have been denounced by more than 100,000 professors and students. The same sources also said that McGeorge Bundy failed to keep his promise to face his critics because he was afraid to confront them.

President Johnson took the opportunity to warn the Communists of their mistake in taking the public debate over American foreign policy in Viet Nam as a sign of weakness or division on the part of the United States. Smaller discussion groups have been conducted by various student organizations on the Viet Nam issue. Since these discussions are mainly organized by critics of the Government policy, they usually follow a pattern like this:

a. Leftist and socialist literature, including petitions, are distributed.

b. Whenever a pro-government speaker has made a remark for the defense of President Johnson, some in the audience hiss and boo, but when a speaker attacks the United States policy, there is applause. The moderator at such discussions usually favors those who attack American policy in Viet Nam. Those points were common to most of the teach-ins attended by the authors of this book.

David Lawrence wrote that the teach-ins

"encourage the Communist Chinese to believe that if they stick to their present strategy long enough and hold on indefinitely the United States Government will grow tired and will eventually find a face-saving device, by means of negotiation, which will be actually equivalent to withdrawal." [10]

The teach-in spread to different countries, with varying degrees of Communist support. On June 11, 1965, one thousand students went into the cafeteria at the University College, London, to attend a teach-in for six hours. Out of 20 speakers, only three approved the United States policy in Viet Nam. The other speakers denounced the United States as the "aggressor," and as the "oppressor" of the Vietnamese people. They compared Viet Nam to Ethiopia and Algeria. They expressed their disappointment with the British Labor Government for its support of the United States.

Isaac Deutscher and Hans Morgenthau made special trips to England to speak at the teach-in in London. President Johnson was described as the gendarme of world counterrevolution, and Prime Minister Wilson as the assistant gendarme. Morgenthau told the British audience that everywhere he went in the United States he was asked: "Why does your Labor Government betray us?"

3. *The Second National Teach-In*

The national teach-in debate on Viet Nam was followed by "Viet Nam Dialogue—Bundy and the Professors," an hour-long debate at Georgetown University on June 21, 1965, over the Columbia Broadcasting System, with Eric Sevareid as moderator. McGeorge Bundy was the principal speaker for the defense. Supporting him were Zbigniew Brzezinski, Director of the Research Institute on Communist Affairs at Columbia University, and Guy G. Pauker of the Rand Corporation.

The chief critic was Hans Morgenthau. He was supported by C. Edmund Clubb, a former United States Foreign Service officer now lecturing at Columbia University, and John Donoghue of the Department of Anthropology at Michigan State College.

The Moderator posed the question why the American forces are in Viet Nam—the legal, moral, and political reasons. Bundy quoted extensively from President Johnson's speech at John Hopkins as follows:

"We are there because we have a promise to keep. Since 1954 every American President has offered support to the people of South Viet Nam. We have helped to build, we have helped to defend. Thus, over many years we have made a national pledge to help South Viet Nam defend its independence. And I intend to keep that promise.

"To dishonor that pledge, to abandon this small and brave nation to its enemies, and to the terror that must follow would be an unforgiveable wrong.

"We are also there to strengthen world order . . . to leave Viet Nam to its fate would shake the confidence of all these people in the value of an American commitment; and in the value of America's word. The result would be increased unrest and instability—and even wider war.

"We are there because there are great stakes in the balance. Let no one think for a moment that retreat from Viet Nam would bring to end to conflict. The battle would be renewed in one country and then another. The central lesson of our time is that the appetite of aggression is never satisfied."

He said the American objective was the independence of South Viet Nam, that America wanted nothing for herself.

O. Edmund Clubb alleged that the United States has violated the Kellogg Briand Pact of 1928, which was designed to outlaw war forever and which renounced war as an instrument of national policy. He charged that the United Nations Charter provides pacific means for the settlement of international disputes, and condemned the United States for not consulting the SEATO members before helping South Viet Nam.

Bundy refuted these statements, maintaining that none of these international documents prohibits the use of force, and that the U.S. was acting within the legal and moral commitments of the Kellogg-Briand pact and the U.N. Charter, as they both provide for individual and collective self-defense. He pointed out that the SEATO signatories do not have to consult each other before acting. The United States, he said, is fulfilling its treaty obligations.

Morgenthau tried to repudiate the Administration's stand that it has made a national pledge to help South Viet Nam defend its independence. He said that the State of Viet Nam is "our own creation" and that we "installed the first government in Saigon," that is, the Diem Government. He alleged that the so-called commitments made by the United

States to Viet Nam were actually a contract between the Administration and its agency, or itself.

Morgenthau seemed completely unaware that Diem was appointed Prime Minister by Bao Dai, the Chief of State of Viet Nam, in 1954. He was the choice of Bao Dai, and it was in the following year, as the result of a national referendum, that the State of Viet Nam was changed to the Republic of Viet Nam, when Diem was elected as first President of Viet Nam by an overwhelming majority in an open and free election.

It is erroneous for Morgenthau to assert that the Diem Government was the creation of the United States. It is unfortunate that even in a national debate Morgenthau is swayed by imagination and sentiment. Morgenthau has been accepted in many quarters as the "great authority" on Viet Nam, but his statements are often misleading, and in this case, simply not true.

Morgenthau also contended that it was "obvious" the United States is unwelcome in South Viet Nam, and that the Vietnamese wished that the United States would find wars to fight elsewhere. Brzezinski could not believe that Viet Nam wants a Communist takeover. The proof of their commitment and loyalty, he said, was the fact that they are dying in the defense of their country.

Pauker testified that there were guerrilla attacks as early as 1954. He said also that after the war with the French had ended, 90,000 South Vietnamese soldiers wanted to go home but were not permitted to do so. Instead they were sent to the North, and indoctrinated thoroughly with Communist beliefs. Almost half of them became party members. They now form the hard core of the Viet Cong in South Viet Nam. He also contended that captured documents and interviews with guerrillas, together with other evidence, indicated that the Viet Cong are operating on a long-range plan of conquest on behalf of the Communist Government in Hanoi.

Professor Donaghue maintained that this was civil war, and that the South Vietnamese were alienated from their government. He said that the officials and village chiefs were neither trusted nor liked, and that this was a war of the peasants against the government.

Morgenthau insisted that the problem in Asia was primarily political, and that the United States could never succeed in Viet Nam. He asserted that the military containment of Communism in Asia is bound to fail. Brzezinski said Morgenthau was wrong both in Europe and in Asia, that

173

the European threat had also been primarily political. He said that the Viet Nam conflict was not a local issue, but would have far-reaching consequences on the stability of the world. Unless stability could be achieved in Asia, he said, there would be no end to wars there. He further predicted that if the United States did not help Viet Nam defend herself from aggression, Red China would win her argument with Moscow by insisting that the best way to oppose the United States is to foment more wars of liberation in Asia, Africa and the Western Hemisphere.

Morgenthau concluded that the United States cannot win in Viet Nam, nor can she continue to stay there. If she stays and continues to use force, he said, she will eventually have to fight the Chinese Communists. This is exactly what Peking wants, he said. His personal conviction was that the United States should adopt Fulbright's position: "Our aim should be to get out, but to get out with honor."

Before the adjournment of the debate, McGeorge Bundy quoted statements from Morgenthau's own writings in 1956 which declared that the Marshall plan was a failure, while he now said that the American policy of containment in Europe was a success. He quoted contradictory remarks Morgenthau had made on Laos and on Viet Nam, and recalled that Morgenthau had once described the accomplishments of former President Diem as "a miracle."

When the moderator gave time to Morgenthau to reply, he admitted that nobody could be right all the time, that he had made mistakes in the past, but that such mistakes should not negate his arguments, and that he thought he was right on the present issue. One of the authors shared a platform with Morgenthau six weeks later, only to find that he had changed his mind again.

Subsequent to these two national debates on Viet Nam, the Gallup Poll reported that the majority of the American people supported the American Government's policy on Viet Nam. Reports from Hanoi and Peking indicated that the Communists regarded these debates as signs of dissension, indecision, and weakness in the United States. The people in Communist countries can never understand this democratic practice.

4. *Appraisal of the National Teach-Ins*

According to Senator Thomas J. Dodd, who played an important role in the investigation of the Teach-in Movement by the Senate Judiciary Sub-Committee, there are four classes of people who have participated in such demonstrations:

    i Honest critics who oppose Communism, but disagree with the methods of fighting the Viet Nam War;

    ii Honest critics who believe that Communism is not a real threat, and who think that the United States should not be involved in any war in Viet Nam;

    iii Pacifists who oppose the use of any kind of force;

    iv Critics who follow the Communist line.[11]

In his introduction to the Senate report, Senator Dodd drew the following conclusions:

    a. The criticism ranged from strategic considerations to pacifism.

    b. The Communist Party, U.S.A., and its affiliates gave full support to the Teach-in Movement and the various demonstrations.

    c. Pacifist organizations such as the National Committee for a Sane Nuclear Policy derived their position from the Communists.

    d. Certain persons of known Communist background played a prominent role in the movement.

    e. Extreme elements openly burned their draft cards and tried to stop troop trains after October 15, 1965.

    f. Most of the demonstrations have been characterized by extreme statements and the distribution of pro-Communist literature.

    g. The National Teach-in of May 15, 1965, gave the general impression of condemning American policy in Viet Nam.

    h. The World Communist apparatus has been able to exploit the anti-Viet Nam agitation and the Teach-in movement to confuse world opinion and to attack the morale of the United States forces in Viet Nam.[12]

A televised national debate on Viet Nam for a whole day is a novel project, something that could occur only in a democratic country. It could never happen in a totalitarian state, such as the Soviet Union or Communist China. If it took place in an unstable country, the government might collapse. It is a forum to express the opinion of the people on a particular issue, depending on how the speakers are selected. It can never be said to represent the public opinion of a country, as it is at best merely the expression of a minority group.

There is the danger that the Teach-in program might have the effect of the Oxford Union Resolution of 1933, which was interpreted by Nazi Germany, Fascist Italy, and Imperial Japan as a sign of weakness and a lack of will to resist on the part of the English. A warning against this was made by President Johnson when he told President Chung Hee Park of the Republic of Korea, on May 17, 1965, that debates in a free country do not mean a divided country. This should be fully understood at home and abroad. It is interesting to note, however, that Ho Chi Minh stated to the world that he is "encouraged by the criticism of United States policy in Viet Nam among the western allies and the Americans themselves." He made this remark to *Pravda. Radio Peking* expressed a similar view.

In the United States, Congress represents the people and their opinion. The Joint Congressional Resolution of August 10, 1964, with only two dissenting votes, authorized the President to take whatever measures he deems proper to repel the aggression and subversion in Viet Nam. The recent increase in the military budget in Viet Nam, together with the recent budgets for economic and technical aid for Viet Nam, indicate that Congress supports the President and his policy in Viet Nam as much as ever. The Teach-in represents the well-organized expression of the opinion of a minority of American intellectuals, whose opinions are then challenged by their colleagues.

Much publicity has been given the Teach-ins by the news media, but they have not substantially altered public opinion, nor the attitude of Congress, and is far from being able to change the determination of the President. However, a well organized minority in any country can exert a great deal of influence. Fluent speakers can swing the opinions of people who have not yet made up their minds. Mass psychology can be used for spreading emotional arguments. Well-meaning persons can often be induced to sign petitions about which they know little, either as to their significance or their consequence.

During the televised debates, the defenders of the Government position did not give sufficient emphasis to the political, economic, and military importance of Viet Nam in relation to the United States and other countries. Little mention was made about the commitments of the United States to the Vietnamese Government. Critics omitted the fact that President Eisenhower and President Kennedy had already made pledges to give economic and military aid to that country, and that President Johnson was also there in response to a direct request of the Vietnamese Government.

They overlooked the declaration of Walter Bedell Smith, the United States delegate at the Geneva Conference in July, 1954, that "any renewal of Communist aggression would be viewed by the United States as a matter of grave concern." Practically no mention was made about the fact that according to the Protocol of SEATO, South Viet Nam is within the "Treaty Area" of its signatories—which means the United States has treaty obligations to protect Viet Nam from aggression.

Some critics accused President Johnson of making decisions and taking action in Viet Nam without consulting Congress. They overlooked the Congressional authority and directive given him under the Joint Congressional Resolution of 1964.

This Resolution clearly authorized the President "to take all necessary steps, including the use of armed force, to assist any member or protocol state of the Southeast Asia Collective Defense Treaty requesting assistance in defense of its freedom." Before the President decided to bomb the military targets in North Viet Nam he consulted with Congressional leaders of both major parties, as well as with the Security Council, his Cabinet members, and his military advisors.

The "Teach-in" should have a balanced list of speakers, and it should not be extended beyond its proper scope. Thousands of American lives and many billions of dollars, as well as the fate of millions of people in Asia and throughout the world, depend on the outcome of this vital struggle in Viet Nam. The outcome depends more on the result of the cold war being waged in the United States than on anything else.

FOOTNOTES

CHAPTER IX: THE TEACH-INS AND
THEIR IMPLICATIONS

1. The Edgar Hoover Directive entitled "Communists behind Peace Demonstrations" was quoted in toto by Congressman W. J. Bryan Dorn (S.D. in the *Congressional Record*, June 7, 1965, p. A-2930-1.
2. Winston S. Churchill, *The Second World War: The Gathering Storm* (Boston, 1948), p. 85.

3. U.S. Senate Committee on the Judiciary, *The Anti-Vietnam Agitation and the Teach-in Movement, the Problem of Communist Infiltration and Exploitation*, (Washington, Oct. 1965).

4. Senate Document, *The Studies of the United States Foreign Policy in Asia* (Washington, 1959).

5. Excerpts from National Teach-In on Vietnam Policy and Text of Bundy Statement, in the *N.Y. Times*, May 17, 1965, p. 30.

6. *Loc. Cit.*

7. *New York Times*, May 17, 1965.

8. *New York Times*, May 15, 1965.

9. *New York Times*, May 18, 1965.

10. David Lawrence in his column, "U.S. Viet Nam RoleA—nd Appeasement," in *N.Y. Herald Tribune*, May 20, 1965.

11. Senate Committee on the Judiciary, *The Anti-Vietnam Agitation and the Teach-in Movement, Op. Cit.*, p. vii.

12. *Ibid.*, pp. xiv and xv.

CHAPTER X

MORE AGITATION AND
COUNTER-MEASURES

Following the two National Teach-ins in Washington, many other student demonstrations took place. Two of the most drastic anti-war-in-Viet Nam agitations occurred in Berkeley on October 15 and 16, and in Washington on November 27, 1965. In the California demonstration, some of the demonstrators challenged police authorities. Some tried to block the departure of servicemen for Viet Nam. Others distributed pro-Communist literature and handbills. Viet Cong flags were displayed by a few. Under the leadership of the Viet Nam Day Committee, the Du Bois Club, and others, several thousand students and non-students physically blocked the gates of the Oakland Army Terminal, as munitions and personnel were being sent to Viet Nam. Some arrests were made by the police, but the demonstrators were released within a short while.

Among those involved were Communists, pacifists, conscientious objectors, and clergymen. About 300 faculty members of the University of California at Berkeley condemned the Viet Nam Day Committee for its actions, but the press gave little space to their protest. Similar but smaller demonstrations occurred in Argentina, England, Italy, Japan, Mexico, and Senegal, and in such a way as to indicate that the effort had coordinated world-wide support.*

While the demonstrations were going on in California, a

* On March 26, 1966, thousands of anti-war demonstrators paraded on Fifth Avenue between 95th and 72nd Streets in New York City. There were some counter-demonstrations on the scene. Similar demonstrations on the same day took place in Washington, D.C., Chicago, Boston, Philadelphia, San Francisco, Madison (Wisconsin), and Oklahoma City. Demonstrations against American war-efforts in Viet Nam also occurred in London, Rome, Stockholm, and Tokyo. There was evidence of a well-organized international effort behind them. More demonstrations of this kind will take place in the United States and elsewhere, as long as the war in Viet Nam exists.

similar demonstration took place in New York on October 15, 1965.[1] In addition to protesting against the United States war efforts in Viet Nam, the demonstrators urged that the American troops be unilaterally withdrawn. They encouraged American youth to refuse to be drafted into the armed services. Draftees were openly encouraged to destroy their draft cards. On the same day David J. Miller, a 20-year-old student from Le Moyne College in Syracuse, New York, stood on a platform and burned his draft card in front of a large group of spectators. The whole event was televised throughout the United States and retelevised throughout other parts of the world, especially in Asia.

By a federal law passed on August 30, 1965, any draftee who intentionally destroys his draft card may receive five years in prison or up to a $10,000 fine, or both. Young Miller publicly defied this law by burning his draft card. When he struck a match, it went out almost immediately. Then a cigarette lighter was passed to him from someone in the crowd, and his card blazed. During this performance his supporters cheered, but many hostile spectators shouted "Treason". On October 18, 1965, Miller was arrested by the Federal Bureau of Investigation in New Hampshire for burning his draft card, which is a criminal offense. He was recently convicted and received a sentence of three years imprisonment. Sentence was suspended and Miller was placed under probation for five years with three conditions:[2]

i. Within two weeks of entry of judgment Miller will apply for and hereafter carry with him a new draft card.

ii. Miller will obey all valid orders issued by his local draft board.

iii. Probation will terminate if and when Miller is inducted.

Miller announced on leaving the court that he has no intention of complying with the conditions laid down by the judge.

James E. Wilson, from New Hampshire, a 21-year-old pacifist, pleaded guilty to burning his draft card and received a two-year suspended sentence and two years probation from Federal Judge Edward Weinfeld on March 4, 1966.[3]

On October 22, 1965, Stephen Smith, 20 years old from Marion, Iowa, also burned his draft card before 100 persons, and was subsequently arrested.[4] Shortly after this arrest, Stan Witkowski, a student from Iowa University, walked into the *Daily Iowan* office with the charred remains of his draft card, declaring that he had "burned it privately this afternoon." Witkowski was also placed under arrest.

There has been an organized effort to avoid the draft, and there has been a movement to extend the anti-war-in-Viet Nam protest from the college campuses to the high schools. More than one session for "beating the draft" was recently held at the Free University at 20 East 14th Street, New York City. An officer from the Columbia University Chapter of the May 2 Movement informed the students that they could duck the draft by declaring themselves homosexuals, conscientious objectors, or by forming an "ad hoc" church and ordaining themselves to be ministers. Anti-war clinics ranging from legitimate pacifist counselling sessions to the teaching of draft dodging techniques have been deluged with inquiries. The *Students for a Democratic Society* announced plans to indoctrinate high school students against military service in Viet Nam. The *Progressive Labor Party* announced that it was printing an anti-draft manual.

Shortly after the draft-card burnings occurred, Attorney General Nicholas Katzenbach declared that an investigation of the anti-draft movement indicated there was Communist involvement. Federal Bureau of Investigation Director J. Edgar Hoover reported that Communists are exploiting the anti-war-in Viet Nam protests and demonstrations.[5]

On Capitol Hill, Senate Majority Leader Mike Mansfield said that some of the demonstrators reflected a "sense of utter irresponsibility," and that the net effect would be to "undermine the President in his efforts to end the war in Viet Nam." Senate Minority Leader Everett M. Dirksen described the demonstrations as "enough to make any person loyal to this country weep."

In both houses of Congress, both Republicans and Democrats denounced the destruction of the draft cards as public defiance of a federal law. Senator Thomas Kuchel of California urged a congressional investigation of the anti-draft movement at Berkeley and elsewhere, declaring that such acts contain the "seed of treason."

Former President Eisenhower considered the demonstrators "mistaken people," and pointed out that "none of us is so stupid that he can't see that if we don't stop Communism . . . then indeed we are ready to engage in another Munich."

In commenting on the pacifist demonstrators, former President Truman told the press on December 27, 1965: "They don't know what's going on." [6] Billy Graham, the noted evangelist, repeatedly declared that "the United States has a moral obligation to defend freedom in Southeast Asia." He stated that "if we do not defend the freedom of the people of Viet Nam, the other nations with which we have treaties will never believe our word again." He also pointed out that the Bible does not advocate pacifism. Dr. Graham told the audience at the Presidential Prayer Breakfast in Washington, on February 17, 1966, that peace should be based on justice, order, and charity and that "Jesus Christ never advocated peace at any price."

1. Self-Immolation and More Agitation

The anti-war-in-Viet Nam demonstrations also seem to have brought about a few Buddhist-style suicides-by-burning in the United States. At a Quaker meeting in Westminster, Maryland, Norman R. Morrison participated in a discussion about a Buddhist monk who had turned himself into a human torch in Viet Nam. Noting that Morrison became greatly upset, David Greene, an instructor at a Baltimore community center, approached him and asked whether he was "all right." Morrison replied that he was.

On November 2, 1965, Morrison suddenly left his home for Washington, D. C. In front of the Pentagon he held his infant daughter, Emily, in one hand, soaked himself with kerosene with the other, and lit a match. When a few persons shouted at him to save the baby, he threw his daughter aside and burned himself to death. An official spokesman for the Quakers told newsmen that Morrison burned himself to death as a protest against American war efforts in Viet Nam. Morrison was much honored in Hanoi. Special meetings commemorating him were held in North Viet Nam and Red China. A special postage stamp has been issued at Hanoi in his honor.

A second public immolation took place when Roger La Porte, a 22-year-old pacifist living at the *Catholic Worker* offices in New York, set fire to himself in front of the United Nations headquarters on Tuesday, November 9, at about 5:30 a.m.[7] He drenched himself with two gallons of gasoline and set himself afire. A United Nations guard immediately called the U.N. Security Room, then snatched a hand fire extinguisher and rushed to the street to try to put out the flames. Three firemen arrived and extinguished the fire. Young La Porte cried out, "Water, give me water." He later said his act was a protest against the war in Viet Nam. He was taken to Bellevue Hospital, where he died of burns, shock, and kidney failure two days later. La Porte was a student at Hunter College.

The world Communist movement was much encouraged by

the anti-draft movement and the cases of self-destruction in the United States. Both Hanoi and Peking expressed their "profound thankfulness" to those Americans who participated in these protests against the American war effort in Viet Nam. The Communists consider all of this an important part of the cold war, the "second front" for Viet Nam. Peking and Hanoi have repeatedly said that the mobilization of public opinion would inevitably force the United States Government to halt its bombing of North Viet Nam and end the presence of American troops in the South.

This has been the principal theme in the polemics employed by Peking to convince Hanoi to reject peace offers from many directions, including Washington and the Vatican. For instance, *Nhan Dan,* the organ of *Lao Dong,* the Communist Party in North Viet Nam, gave a front page report on the Berkeley and Washington demonstrations. Special significance was given to the Washington march. The Viet Cong official paper highly praised the "courage" of the American demonstrators. Both Peking and Hanoi radio broadcasts and editorials declared:

"The American people by their angry protests, have given the lie to President Johnson and his like who have time and again boasted that Washington's policy of aggression in Viet Nam had the support of the American people."

In the fall of 1965, the agitation against America's war effort in Viet Nam became more widespread and more violent. For a while it looked as though an organized minority might succeed in dominating a segment of the press. Gradually, however, the general American public realized the danger. Students, professors, experts on East Asia, and ordinary citizens organized counter-measures against the agitators. Rallies, parades, and counter teach-ins were held in major American cities and on many college campuses. Blood donations called "bleed-ins," letters, and gift packages were sent overseas by the thousand. The peace-nik demonstrations had boomeranged.

2. *East Asian Experts Support Johnson*

On October 20, 1965, a group of scholars and specialists on Viet Nam made a strong declaration supporting the American war effort in that country.[8] This declaration was carried in major newspapers across the country, denouncing the distortion of fact and the emotional allegations made by certain "intellectuals, students and faculty members," pointing out that those involved had very little knowledge of

Viet Nam. This declaration made it clear that the Viet Cong initiated the war in South Viet Nam by terrorism, guerrilla warfare, subversion, and armed attacks, in order to communize South Viet Nam and force it to become part of the Hanoi regime. It explained that the war in South Viet Nam is not a colonial war because the United States has no territorial or political designs in Viet Nam. They declared that the Viet Cong have committed acts of terror, torture, and murder rivaling on a smaller scale the atrocities of the axis powers in World War II.

These Asian experts pointed out that the Hanoi regime is the most brutal and cruel in all Asia, whereas the Republic of Viet Nam was well on the way towards prosperity and democracy until the attacks against her were intensified. The Geneva Agreements of 1954 were violated by the Viet Communists since the time of their signing. If South Viet Nam were permitted to fall into the hands of the Communists, they concluded, it would open the gate to the further spread of Communism in Southeast Asia. President Johnson, they pointed out, repeatedly sought for unconditional discussions with the Viet Communists, but Hanoi has constantly refused to negotiate with Washington. The signers included Wesley R. Fishel, Michigan State University; P. J. Honey, University of London; William P. Maddox, New York City; Ralph L. Turner, Michigan State University; Charles Wolf, Jr., The Rand Corporation; George E. Taylor, University of Washington; William Dunn, University of the State of New York; J. D. Montgomery, Harvard University; Charles A. Joiner, Temple University; William Henderson, Socony Mobil Oil Company; Frank N. Trager, New York University; Rev. F. J. Corley, S.J., St. Louis University; Chester Hunt, Western Michigan University; Lucian Pye, Massachusetts Institute of Technology; David Wilson, University of California; John T. Dorsey, Vanderbilt University; T. M. Sacks, Brandeis University; R. H. Smuckler, Michigan State University; and George K. Tanham, the Rand Corporation.

Two large counter-demonstrations were held in New York on October 30 and 31, 1965, expressing support of America's war efforts in Viet Nam.[9] The "Patriotic Parade" of October 30 had 50,000 marchers, together with bands, the colorful uniforms of the Veterans of Foreign Wars and the American Legion, and thousands of high school students. Patriotic slogans and handbills were displayed, endorsing the government's policy.

The October 31 demonstration in New York City was truly a citizen's parade, composed primarily of residents of the various boroughs. It criticized the anti-draft movement, and supported the Johnson Administration's policy in Viet Nam. About 45,000 people participated, led by New York City Councilman Matthew T. Troy, Jr. Troy explained that the main purpose of the parade was to counteract the false impression created by the October 15 and 16 demonstrations in New York City.

In California, on November 3, Stanford University students told the press that within two days they had obtained 1,500 signatures on the campus stating that they had "basic agreement with United States policy in Viet Nam." This was a counter-measure to the activities and agitations of the Viet Nam Day Committee. On November 3 and 4, over 100,000 college students took part in a blood donation drive on behalf of the American armed forces in Viet Nam, and to indicate their support of the American war effort. Blood donations were collected from 75 colleges and universities by the American Red Cross and turned over to the United States Defense Department.

In New Haven, at the beginning of November, 1965, five hundred Yale students signed a petition deploring civil disobedience. They submitted a petition to Vice-President Hubert Humphrey indicating their support of the war efforts of the United States in Viet Nam. At Michigan State University, 15,000 students signed a declaration endorsing United States policy in Viet Nam and Southeast Asia as a measure against aggression. Undergraduates at Villanova, Washington State, Manhattan College, and Georgetown University collected blood, Christmas gifts, and cards for the fighting forces in South Viet Nam. In March, 1966, several thousand tons of Christmas gifts for American servicemen in Viet Nam were still in storage in Idaho, so many had been collected.

In commenting on the demonstrations, Joseph C. Harsch wrote in the *Christian Science Monitor* on November 3, 1965:

"In all wars fought by the United States there has been some opposition, some demonstrating against the central authority, and some avoidance of the draft. . . . Loyalist and patriotic groups have now staged bigger demonstrations in support of the war in Viet Nam than had earlier been put on by those who disapprove of that war. More men were in the pro- than in the anti-parades."

Viet Nam was the main theme on Veteran's Day, November 11, 1965. The occasion was celebrated by patriotic organizations throughout the United States, particularly in New York City and Washington, D.C. Strong pleas were made for assuring the American fighting forces in Viet Nam that their countrymen were solidly behind them, despite minority protests against American war efforts there. In New York some speakers labeled the anti-draft exponents as "cowards" and "traitors." Others called them "misguided daydreamers."

In Washington, Vice-President Hubert Humphrey greeted the crowds with a speech about war heroes. Referring to the pacifist protesters, Humphrey said their voices "must be rejected. Theirs is the counsel of despair and defeat." He added that the United States "will remain in Viet Nam until a just and lasting peace has been established there."

During the march on Washington on November 27, nearly a hundred bus drivers from New York and New Jersey refused to drive the demonstrators to Washington. The crowd gathered in front of the White House to protest, and then proceeded to the Washington Monument for their meeting. The main speakers for the occasion were Norman Thomas, several times Socialist candidate for the American Presidency, and Mrs. Martin Luther King. Communist and pro-Communist literature was widely distributed. The slogans were "Unconditional withdrawal from Viet Nam," and "Get out from Viet Nam." Flags of the Hanoi regime and also flags of the National Liberation Front in South Viet Nam were displayed.

During the meeting, counter demonstrations were held side by side with the pacifists. The counter demonstrators displayed signs and slogans such as "Pacifism does not insure peace or immunity from aggression," "Oppose Asian Munich," and "Red and Peace Creeps." About 15 persons were arrested.

Shortly after the Washington march, John W. Chancellor, Director of the *Voice of America,* commented on the protests and demonstrations, pointing out that they are "hurting the United States with unsophisticated audiences around the world." He further declared that *Radio Moscow* and *Radio Peking* have been using them to give the false impression that the United States is divided, and will pull out of Viet Nam.

According to a *Reuter News Agency* dispatch from Peking, February 27, 1966, a big demonstration entitled "Demonstration in Support of the American People" took place at the *Peace Square* in Peking. General Chu Teh, a father of the Red Army and a member of the Politburo, and Liao

Cheng-chi, President of the Overseas Affairs Commission, and many other Communist leaders were present. Liao told the 16,000 persons in the audience:

> Stormy revolution is about to occur in the United States of America. The Chinese people highly respect the heroic and patriotic effort of those Americans who participated in the demonstrations in their country. We support with determination their struggle for justice. Our demonstration here is to give unreserved support to all those Americans who oppose their government's imperialist aggression in Viet Nam.

3. *Labor Unions Support Johnson*

Labor unions have given strong support to the American war effort in Viet Nam. George Meany, the International President of the *American Federation of Labor* and the *Congress of Industrial Organizations,* has repeatedly endorsed President Johnson's policy in Viet Nam. The AFL-CIO, on December 2, 1965, voted for full support of President Johnson's war efforts in Southeast Asia, recognizing it as necessary for the preservation of freedom.[10] The national labor convention also resolved that it would bring a full understanding and endorsement of American military action in Viet Nam through its 8,000 local unions and its 525 state and regional councils to their 13½ million members. In a unanimous resolution, it declared that the defeat of American efforts in Viet Nam would cause a loss of confidence by all small nations in American ability to protect them from Communist aggression, and that such a defeat would seriously imperil Southeast Asia and the security of the United States. The United Auto Workers Union also gave warm support to the United States action in Viet Nam. Walter Reuther, the International President of the Union, told the press that the UAW unanimously resolved to support America's resistance to the aggression in Viet Nam. The UAW particularly condemned Peking's aggressive policy and actions in Viet Nam.

In putting their policy into action, the AFL-CIO labor union picketed shipping lines which had visited or might have visited the territorial waters of North Viet Nam. On Friday, February 25, 1966, 500 longshoremen [11] with picket signs marched along the dock at Pier 92 on the Hudson River where the *S.S. Queen Mary* was docked in the Cunard Luxury Line Row. Some of the placards read "British shipping helps Viet Cong," "Keep British Flag ships out of Viet Cong Trade," "We have sons in Viet Nam—Don't want British ships to help kill them," and "We are with LBJ all the way in Viet Nam." The picketers were from the members of Locals 82 and 824. They succeeded in obtaining assurance from the British Line that its company would not enter into North Viet Nam waters.

John Bowers, President of Local 82 and also Executive Vice-President of the 60,000-member International Longshoremen's Association Union, told the press that his men would also act against other lines if they were engaged in trading with North Viet Nam. When asked by newsmen whether dockers in other ports would boycott foreign ships that had touched North Vietnamese ports, he declared that he was "quite certain that every member of the union would react the same way to any ship that stopped in North Viet Nam." The I.L.A. members work at piers from Maine to Texas, an area that includes every key port along the Atlantic and the Gulf of Mexico.

Similar picketings against the French lines in New York occurred, and the French companies also assured the picketers that their ships would not touch North Vietnamese waters. The State Department also announced that foreign ships which are on the black list were not eligible to carry American foreign aid cargoes.

4. *Prominent Americans Support the President*

On November 28, 1965, one hundred and four prominent Americans gave strong public support to American policy in Viet Nam. Their declaration was widely published in the United States and extensively quoted in other countries. Besides Dean Acheson, former Secretary of State, the signers included Frank R. Barnett, President of the National Strategy Information Center; Vannevar Bush, former President of the Carnegie Institute; Leo Cherne, Executive Director of the Research Institute of America; General Lucius Clay, former United States Governor in West Germany; James B. Conant, President Emeritus of Harvard University; Douglas Dillon, former Secretary of the Treasury; Michael V. di Salle, former Governor of Ohio; Roscoe Drummond, syndicated columnist; William van den Heuvel, President of the International Rescue Committee; Harry Gideonse, then Brooklyn College (now New School for Social Research); Sidney Hook, Professor at New York University; Max Lerner, Professor at Brandeis University; Richard Nixon, former United States Vice-President; John dos Passos, author; Whitelaw Reid, former editor and publisher of the *New York Herald Tribune;* Samuel I. Rosenman, President of the New York City Bar Association; Whitney North Seymour, former President of the American Bar Association; Frank N. Trager, Professor at New York University; Milton Waldor, National Commander of Jewish Veterans, and many others.

On December 9, 1965, one hundred ninety professors in New England universities and colleges pledged their support to American war efforts in Viet Nam.[12] They declared that a Viet Cong victory "would spell disaster for millions of South Vietnamese and other millions in Southeast Asia." They also hoped that the Vietnamese would "have the opportunity to determine their own destiny through free elections, protection from opposition parties, and a free press." They were "seriously disturbed by that small minority of the intellectual community whose tactics have led to highly exaggerated estimates of their members." They feared that "these tactics may lead both Peking and Hanoi to underestimate seriously American commitment and hence to reduce the possibility of ending the war in Viet Nam in the shortest possible time."

Among the signers of this declaration were Samuel H. Beer, of the Department of Government, Harvard University, and John Roche, of the Department of Political Science, Brandeis University. Both were former National Chairmen of Americans for Democratic Action. Other prominent signers included Henry A. Kissinger, Harvard, and Harold Isaacs and Max Milliken of Massachusetts Institute of Technology. Sixteen universities and colleges were represented among the signers.

Half the signers of this declaration are in the fields of government, history, or social science. About one-fourth are political scientists. This is in sharp contrast to the academic signers of petitions opposing United States policy in Viet Nam, where most of them are teachers in fields unrelated to social science or world politics, and who presumably have a limited professional knowledge of Viet Nam. The 25 experts on Viet Nam quoted earlier pointed out that of all those who had signed ads in the *New York Times* against U.S. policy, they had never seen the name of one expert.

5. *American Bar Association Supports Johnson*

Substantial legal support was given the Johnson policy in

Viet Nam by the American Bar Association, which has 120,-000 members, at meetings of its delegates in Chicago on February 21, 1966. The association discussed the legality of the American position in Viet Nam, which has been challenged by Senator Morse and others. The 250 attending members of the policy-making House of delegates *unanimously* declared that the American position in Viet Nam is legal under international law, the United Nations Charter, and treaty obligations. A copy of the resolution was sent to the Chairman of the Senate Foreign Relations Committee. Since this resolution is of legal significance, it deserves quoting at length:

"Whereas, in recent hearings before the Foreign Relations Committee of the United States Senate, it has been stated that international lawyers are agreed that the United States position in Viet Nam is illegal and in violation of the Charter of the United Nations; and

"Whereas, Articles 51 and 52 of the Charter sanction steps for self-defense and collective and regional security arrangements such as the Southeast Asia Treaty Organization to which the United States is a party;

"Whereas, in the course of these hearings it has been suggested that an expression on this subject by the American Bar Association would be appropriate;

"Now, therefore, be it resolved by the American Bar Association that the position of the United States in Viet Nam is legal under international law, and is in accordance with the Charter of the United Nations and the Southeast Asia Treaty." [13]

Edward W. Kuhn, President of the American Bar Association, told reporters that this resolution is a strong repudiation of those who allege that the American position and action in Viet Nam are illegal.

In order to reaffirm its legal ground for action in Viet Nam, the State Department presented a 52-page brief entitled "The Legality of United States Participation in the Defense of Viet Nam" to the Senate Foreign Relations Committee.[14] It is a rebuttal to those such as Senators Morse and Fulbright, who have challenged the legality of American military involvement in Viet Nam. This brief states that South Viet Nam has been under "armed attack" by the North through infiltration of armed personnel, military equipment, and combat troops. Such aggressive acts, started long before February, 1965, caused the United States to extend more military aid to the Republic of Viet Nam and to cease granting sanctuary to North Viet Nam on February 7, 1965. It "has long recognized the right of individual and collective defense consistent with international law and with United States obligations under the United Nations Charter." The same document maintained that South Viet Nam, though not a member of the United Nations, still has an inherent right to defense. Although Viet Nam is a temporarily divided state, such a situation should not diminish her right to individual and collective defense, since she has been recognized by more than fifty nations as a sovereign and independent state. Thus, under Article 51 of the United Nations Charter, South Viet Nam should not be prevented from self-defense or asking for aid from other friendly states.

South Viet Nam, declared the State Department, has "the same right that South Korea had to defend itself and to organize collective defense against an armed attack from the North." The United States, though not a signatory of the Geneva Agreements of 1954, declared that any renewal of aggression in Viet Nam or Indo-China would be viewed with "grave concern." Added to this, the American Government has acted in Viet Nam in accordance with the repeated assurances given by three Presidents. In upholding her treaty obligations, the United States should not shrink from her duties to give aid to South Viet Nam. The Republic of Viet Nam is within the "Protocol states," under the Southeast Asia Collective Defense Treaty of 1954, and all the signatories, including the United States, "undertook an obligation to defend South Viet Nam against Communist armed aggression." Such an obligation does "not depend on a collective decision" by all the signatories of the treaty. Any one of the signatories may choose independent and individual action, if it deems there is an aggression in any one of the "Protocol states," such as Cambodia, Laos, and Viet Nam. The Southeast Asia Collective Organization (SEATO) Treaty was signed in accordance with the United Nations Charter under the title of "Regional Agreements."

6. *Forty-one Governors Support Johnson's Policy*

On March 12, 1966, thirty-eight state governors and the Governors of Puerto Rico, Guam, and the Virgin Islands unanimously adopted a resolution endorsing President Johnson's policy in Viet Nam. The resolution was offered by Governor James A. Rhodes, Republican of Ohio, and seconded by Governor Nelson Rockefeller of New York. There was no dissenting vote, with 38 state governors present. Since this resolution is significant, it is quoted at some length:

"Whereas, the Governors have been given the greatest freedom in the expression of their convictions and the exchange of their views of the Viet Nam situation; and

"Whereas, it is the unanimous opinion of the Governors here assembled that the pursuit of our national objectives in Viet Nam is sound and the only rational policies to be followed under the circumstances; now therefore, be it

"Resolved, by the Governors of the states assembled in Washington, D.C., on this 12th day of March, 1966, that they do wholeheartedly support and endorse the policies and programs in Viet Nam being pursued by the United States of America under the leadership of President Lyndon B. Johnson." [15]

Since governors of the various states and territories of the United States are elected by the people directly, their opinion can be considered as representative expression of the nation at large. Almost immediately after the Governors' Conference, President Johnson told the press that he had no idea that Governor Rhodes had planned to offer the resolution, but that he was glad the Governors felt as they did. President Johnson then added, "I hope it's not too displeasing to anyone; it's very pleasing to me."

7. Other Patriotic Actions

A movement known as "Affirmation: Viet Nam" was started on December 2, 1965. It was a spontaneous patriotic movement to counteract false impressions made at home and abroad by leftist-pacifist agitators, and it was started by Remar "Bubba" Sutton, former President of the Student Council of the University of the Seven Seas and later a student at Emory University in Atlanta, Georgia. He and Don Brunson, also from Emory, acquired the endorsement of their fellow students, and rapidly gained the support of students from other Georgia colleges.

On February 12, 1966, a big "Affirmation: Viet Nam"

rally was held in the Atlanta Stadium.[16] Despite wet and stormy weather, 15,000 students attended the rally. Also present were Secretary Dean Rusk, Senator Richard Russell, Senator Herman Talmadge and General Lucius Clay, who were the main speakers. This meeting was also attended by the Ambassadors from Australia, the Republic of China, the Netherlands, New Zealand, and Spain, the Vietnamese Observer at the United Nations (with ambassadorial rank,) and the Ministers of Korea, Malaysia, and Thailand, together with other distinguished guests. More than 50 universities and colleges were represented at this expression of endorsement of American policy in Viet Nam. The Student President presented a document to the Vietnamese Observer at the U.N., Ambassador Nguyen Duy Lien, with more than 221,000 signatures supporting the Vietnamese war effort against aggression.

8. Public Polls

Since the American Government has tried every political and diplomatic means to urge Hanoi and Peking to give up their plan for subjugating South Viet Nam and to sit down at the conference table to negotiate, and since both Hanoi and Peking have consistently refused such peace overtures, American public opinion is swinging more and more in favor of their Government's position. The Gallup Poll in December, 1965, revealed that about 65 percent of the American people support the President's policy in Viet Nam, while only about 20 percent were opposed to it. The rest gave no opinion. Another public opinion poll in January, 1966, indicated that 71 percent of Americans believe that American troops must remain in South Viet Nam and keep fighting until Hanoi and the Viet Cong are willing to participate in *bona fide* peace talks. Only 4 percent believe that American forces should be withdrawn.

In commenting on the Harris Poll, published February 28, 1966, which indicated that support for the President's policy in Viet Nam dropped from 63 to 49 percent, Robert H. Fleming, Presidential Press Secretary, said on March 9 that it was "not an accurate reflection" of the true situation. On the contrary, Fleming maintained that "any relaxation" of American military pressure in Viet Nam brings a drop in the support of the President's stand. He further noted that the "dove" group remains steadily at about 10 percent, whereas the recent rise of President Johnson's policy has reinforced the proportion of "hawks," not "doves". He insisted that when public opinion polls show a drop in those supporting the Johnson policy in Viet Nam, it is because the American people do not think he is pressing the war hard enough.

A Gallup Poll of March 9 showed that 50 percent of those interviewed approved the President's policy, while 33 percent disapproved and 17 percent expressed no opinion.[17]

Another poll was conducted by National Public Opinion Research Center at the University of Chicago, with the aid of some academicians from Stanford in late February and early March. It was released on March 14, 1966. One thousand, four hundred seventy-four persons, a national cross-section in age, sex, and employment, were questioned. Thirty questions were asked. However, some of the questions were vague and misleading. For instance, one of the most important questions was: "Would you favor negotiations with the Viet Cong if they were willing to negotiate?" It was not brought out whether the Viet Cong would sit as part of the delegation of the Hanoi regime or as a separate and independent political entity. Eighty-eight percent replied "yes", eight percent "no". But other answers definitely indicated that the public opposed abandoning the defense of South Viet Nam. For example:

"Would you approve of withdrawing American troops immediately from South Viet Nam?"

Yes, 15 percent; No, 81 percent.

"Would you favor gradual withdrawal?"

Yes, 39 percent; No, 56 percent.

"Would you withdraw even if it meant the loss of Laos and Thailand?"

Yes, 13 percent; No, 77 percent.[18]

After it became known that the United States had mobilized her high-ranking diplomats to contact the Soviet Union, Poland, Hungary, France, England, Canada, Japan, the Philippines, the Republic of China, the Vatican, and many other countries, as well as North Viet Nam directly, more and more Americans felt that the United States has done everything possible to seek peace. This is particularly so since Hanoi and Peking kept insisting that peace must be accepted on Communist terms. There is no doubt that the American nation supports its country's policy in Viet Nam.

9. *Aid from Other Nations*

The number of allies now giving support to South Viet Nam has tripled since the Saigon Government first appealed for help from non-Communist countries. The Vietnamese themselves, with armed forces of more than 600,000, bear the main brunt of the war, but American forces are not the only ones sharing the burden. The Republic of Korea has 42,000 well-trained jungle fighters in South Viet Nam. Seoul has also sent combat engineers, a surgical hospital, and some instructors in guerrilla warfare. Australia sent 1,500 combat infantrymen with logistic support. She then trebled her military forces by June, 1966, to 4,500. Thailand started sending troops in mid-1966. Australia has also sent 3,300 tons of roofing, 6 windmills, 400 radios, a 50-kilowatt broadcasting station, 16,000 blankets, and 15,750 sets of tools. New Zealand has sent a battery of 150 howitzers to South Viet Nam, and has contributed surgical teams, a $200,000 science building, and some large scientific instruments.

The Republic of China is very willing to aid Saigon, but her offers so far have not met with the approval of the United States, even though it has signed a mutual security treaty with her. This treaty provides for advance consultation and approval from Washington prior to an attack on the China Mainland. So far, the Republic of China has given considerable economic, agricultural, and technical aid to Saigon. The United States has not accepted her offer of troops, and the State Department is reported to fear that if Chinese Nationalist troops were in South Viet Nam, Peking might use this as a pretext to send Red Chinese troops there. However, as General Maxwell Taylor has pointed out, Communists are not provoked into acting. They act according to policy.

Other nations have given aid to South Viet Nam in various ways.[19] Austria gave blankets and medicine. Belgium donated medicine. Brazil gave coffee and medical supplies. Canada gave $850,000 worth of flour and butter, plus medicine, scientific equipment, and a science building for the University at Hue. Denmark and Ecuador contributed medical supplies. France sent over 600 educators, physicians, and technicians. West Germany sent 30 ambulances, 25 professors, physicians, and technical advisers, a 3,000-ton hospital ship, and radio batteries. The Bonn Government also gave more than $20 million in credit to the Saigon Government.

Greece donated medical supplies. Guatemala sent 15,000 doses of typhoid vaccine. Although India is suffering from natural calamities and internal riots, the New Delhi Government contributed clothing to help the Vietnamese people. Iran sent 1,500 tons of petroleum, plus a medical team of 22 men. Ireland donated $2,800 for relief. Israel gave pharmaceutical supplies. Italy gave scholarships to Vietnamese students, as well as medicine and a surgical team in Saigon.

The new Japanese Constitution prohibits Japan from having an army, navy, or air force in any form, so she is unable to send any armed forces to help. But Japan has recently paid South Viet Nam $55,000,000 as reparations for damages in South Viet Nam during World War II. Tokyo has contributed substantially to the Asian Development Bank, which is helping South Viet Nam. Tokyo has also helped Saigon in many other ways. She has helped repair bridges destroyed by the Viet Cong. She has sent hundreds of electricians and much equipment, such as 20,000 radios, 25 ambulances, and many electrical accessories. Laos gave $4,167 in cash for Vietnamese flood relief. Luxembourg gave plasma and blood-transfusion equipment. Malaysia sent experts in counter-insurgency and guerrilla warfare to help train the South Vietnamese.

The Netherlands sent two surgical teams, one dredge, and $2,000 worth of antibiotics. Pakistan has not fully recovered from her war with India, but she did send clothing and $10,000 for flood relief to Saigon. The Philippine Government has long been undecided about sending troops to Viet Nam, but it has already sent psychological and guerrilla warfare teams and equipment. The new Filipino President, Ferdinand Marcos, and the new Foreign Minister, Narciso Ramos, have already requested the Philippine Congress to approve the sending of some 2,000 troops to Saigon. Spain sent a medical team with physicians and equipment, and also blankets for the South Vietnamese. Switzerland donated thirty miscroscopes and technical equipment. Thailand sent pilots, cement, and roofing materials. Turkey sent medical supplies and a promise of cement. The United Kingdom dispatched police instructors, professors, and technicians. Venezuela donated 500 tons of rice. Non-military aid has been either given or pledged by Argentina, Costa Rica, the Dominican Republic, El Salvador, Honduras and Nicaragua.

By comparison, after the United Nations had officially condemned North Korea and Red China as aggressors in the Korean War, only 16 nations participated in the actual fighting in the Korean war, and about 39 nations gave emergency relief to South Korea. During the Korean War there were only two kinds of aid: military and relief. But in the war in the Viet Nam, the aid has taken many forms. Though not many nations have sent troops to South Viet Nam, the aid that has been given is helpful, and it implies agreement and sympathy. No country in the free world has given any military aid to North Viet Nam.

The question remains whether or not the United States, as the leader of the free world, has the determination and courage to bring the Viet Nam War against subversion and aggression to a successful end. It appears that President Johnson will continue his policy of resistance to aggression and bring the war to a just and reasonable settlement, provided there is not too much pressure at home and abroad to force too many concessions, nor too much political turmoil in South Viet Nam.

FOOTNOTES

CHAPTER X: MORE AGITATION AND COUNTER-MEASURES

1. All American newspapers reported this story at length on October 16, 17, 1965.
2. *New York Times,* and *Herald Tribune,* March 16, 1966.
3. *New York Times,* March 5, 1966.
4. *New York Times,* October 23, 1965.
5. "Communists Behind Peace Demonstrations," in *Congressional Record,* June 7, 1965, A-2930-1.
6. *New York Times,* December 28, 1965.
7. *New York Times,* November 10, 1965.
8. Printed in all the leading newspapers in the United States.
9. *Journal American* and *World Telegram,* October 30 and 31, 1965.
10. *New York Times* and *Herald Tribune,* December 3, 1965.
11. *New York Times,* February 26, 1966.
12. Voice of America *Broadcasts,* December 9 and 10, 1965.
13. *New York Times,* February 22, 1966.
14. *New York Times,* March 10, 1966.
15. *New York Times,* March 13, 1966.
16. All major newspapers in the United States including the *New York Times* reported about this rally, on February 12, either on the same day or the following day. The *Cheng Hsin Daily News* in Taipei on March 2, 1966 gave almost a full page report about the rally of Affirmation: Vietnam.
17. *New York Times,* March 10, 1966.
18. *Ibid.*
19. *U.S. News & World Report,* March 14, 1966, pp. 32-3.

CHAPTER XI

BETWEEN WAR AND PEACE: THE UNITED STATES AT THE CROSSROADS

Ever since the end of World War II, South Viet Nam has suffered from Communist terror and subversion. After Viet Nam became a member of the French Union in 1950, she fought against the Viet Minh guerrillas, with the help of France, until the French surrendered in May, 1954. Ngo Dinh Diem became Prime Minister in June 1954, and the Geneva Agreements were signed by France and North Viet Nam the following month. A brief period of comparative calm ensued, but after Diem became President of the Republic of Viet Nam, the Viet Communists became actively engaged in subversion and infiltration in South Viet Nam. The Viet Minh cadres left behind those guerrillas who were already members of the Communist Party. The others were taken to the North for training and indoctrination. This gave the Communists a ready fifth column in the South, plus future infiltrators from the North. From 1955 until 1963, there were thousands of clashes between the Government forces and the Viet Communists in different villages and mountains. Both sides won small battles from time to time. However, such conflicts were primarily confined to the villages and suburbs of the cities, and the battles were on a comparatively small scale. After the assassination of Diem and his brother, Nhu, in November, 1963, the situation "unquestionably worsened," as Secretary McNamara declared on March 26, 1964.[1]

No one knows exactly how many Viet Cong forces there are in the "Liberation Front" in South Viet Nam. The Communist forces do not wear uniforms, with the exception of a few regular divisions of the *People's Army of the Democratic Republic of Viet Nam* that have been found in South Viet Nam. According to the United States Defense Department, there were about 65,000 regular Communist forces in

South Viet Nam in June, 1965, an increase of 18,000 from May. There were also from 80,000 to 100,000 part-time guerrillas, plus 30,000 professional propagandists.[2] In North Viet Nam, the Hanoi regime has concentrated about 200,-000 Viet Cong armed forces, posting them at the borders of the demarcation line between the North and South, together with about 60 Soviet Mig fighters, 7,000 anti-aircraft installations and 70 surface-to-air missile sites. The Communists have no naval forces to speak of, except some PT boats and torpedo boats.

The South Vietnamese Government has about 635,000 regular army troops, para-military and police forces, including air and naval forces. The Government of the *Republic of Viet Nam* has little time to think of the legality of the war. Those in power in Saigon are fighting on the side of freedom, and there is every reason to believe that they have the backing of the people much more than the people in the North back their government, which has never even had the pretext of a Communist-type election.

International law is binding only under the mutual consent of the signatories. Neither side is bound by the various agreements concerning the rules of war. They neither know about nor do they necessarily observe the Geneva Protocol of 1925 concerning the treatment of war prisoners. On both sides there have undoubtedly been instances of inhuman and cruel treatment of prisoners. The torturing, kidnaping, and murdering of innocent civilians, however, has been done only by the Communists, and done by them on a mass scale that rivals, in a smaller way, the tortures of the Nazis in World War II. The war has been going on since 1955. South Viet Nam has suffered with patience and dignity, and she fought a defensive war. Until February, 1965, the war was comparable to that of individuals fighting in their own homes to resist gangsters, but who were not permitted to retaliate by attacking the sronghold of the enemy.

Shortly after the American Government began bombing military targets in North Viet Nam on February 7, 1965, rumors of peace feelers began to be heard. Many nations began to fear that this undeclared "war" might develop into a very large-scale conflict.

1. *Hanoi's Four Demands for a Cease-fire*

According to Radio Hanoi, received through Tokyo, the terms laid down by the Communists on April 12, 1965, were as follows:

i. Recognition of the basic national rights of the Vietnamese people—peace, independence, sovereignty, unity and territorial integrity. According to the Geneva agreements, the U.S. Government must withdraw from South Vietnam U.S. troops, military personnel, and weapons of all kinds, dismantle all U.S. military bases there, and cancel its 'military alliance' with South Vietnam. It must end its policy of intervention and aggression in South Viet Nam. According to the Geneva agreements, the U.S. Government must stop its acts of war against North Viet Nam, completely cease all encroachments on the territory and sovereignty of the DRV.

ii. Pending the peaceful reunification of Viet Nam, while Viet Nam is still temporarily divided into two zones, the military provisions of the 1954 Geneva agreements on Viet Nam must be strictly respected—the two zones must refrain from joining any military alliance with foreign countries, there must be no foreign military bases, or military personnel in their respective territory.

iii. The internal affairs of South Viet Nam must be settled by the South Vietnamese people themselves in accordance with the program of the NFLSV without any foreign interference.

iv. The peaceful reunification of Viet Nam is to be settled by the Vietnamese people in both zones, without any foreign interference.[3]

The above conditions have been repeated by Ho Chi Minh, Prime Minister Pham Van Dong, and also by *Radio Hanoi* and *Radio Peking* on many occasions. Even as late as February 27, 1966, a *United Press International* dispatch from Tokyo quoted Communist China as saying that unofficially "the United States was willing to allow National Liberation Front participation in any future South Vietnamese Government," but that "the Communists would accept only complete control."

The Hanoi regime, backed by Peking and Moscow, behaves as though the Communists are going to win the war. Acceptance of any of the four conditions would mean a Communist victory. Accepting any one of them would mean surrender and capitulation on the part of South Viet Nam, the United States, and other countries of the Free World. The reasons for this are manifest:

a. American bombings on military targets and communication lines in North Viet Nam have damaged the Hanoi regime materially and psychologically. Viet Cong defectors and prisoners of war have made it clear that the people in North Viet Nam are very much afraid of American bombing attacks.

b. If the American and other allied forces withdraw from South Viet Nam, the dominant forces of North Viet Nam would completely take over the country. Saigon would be unable to resist, even if it had the will to do so. Even with the presence of American and allied troops, it is difficult for South Viet Nam to withstand the subversion and aggression of the Communists. It is not difficult to imagine what would occur if American forces were withdrawn.

c. If the above conditions were accepted or used as a basis for future terms of settlement, it would mean that the parties to the agreement would acknowledge the sole authority of the *National Liberation Front* and have to act "in accordance with the program of the Viet Cong's political representation." This would mean surrendering South Viet Nam to the Viet Cong.

d. If the fourth condition were accepted, it would mean that South Viet Nam would have to submit to the control and rule of Hanoi. In the North there is no freedom, and no possibility of holding a free election, while in the South there are many Viet Communists already organized and armed by their comrades from the North. Furthermore, the North outnumber the South by more than a million people. When Hanoi stipulates that the unification of the North and South be "without foreign interference," it means that unification be without any international supervision. Even if there should be some sort of United Nations supervision, it would include representatives from Communist countries who would favor their comrades from the North. The previously organized *International Control Commission* consisting of Canada, India, and Poland, has been almost completely ineffective during the twelve years since its inception.

The Hanoi regime has repeatedly turned down every peace overture from any source, and insisted that its own terms must be accepted before Hanoi will come to any conference. An indirect but official reply to the various peace overtures, including Pope Paul's, was broadcast in English by Hanoi on January 4, 1966. The statement merely reaffirmed, in more detail, the four conditions enumerated above. These conditions were also demanded by the *National Liberation Front* in South Viet Nam (NFLSVN) on the fifth anniversary of the formation of the Viet Cong, on December 20, 1965, reiterating the terms proposed by the NFLSVN spokesman.[4]

2. *U Thant's Intervention*

As early as February 24, 1965, U Thant, Secretary-General of the United Nations, told a press conference:

"I have been conducting private discussions on this question of Viet Nam for a long time, as you all know. Of course, it will not be very helpful at this stage to reveal even some parts or some features of the negotiations I have conducted. I just want to say that I have the greatest respect for the great American leader, President Johnson, whose wisdom, moderation and sensitivity to world public opinion are well known. I am sure the great *American people, if only they know the true facts and the background to the developments in South Viet Nam, will agree with me that further bloodshed is unnecessary.* And also that the political and diplomatic method of discussions and negotiations alone can create conditions which will enable the *United States to withdraw gracefully from that part of the world . . ."* [5] (Italics added)

U Thant told the Press Conference that he had "presented certain ideas on his own to some of the principal parties directly involved in the question of Viet Nam." He did not reveal these ideas, but it is obvious that he wants the United States "to withdraw gracefully from that part of the world." He implied that the American people are not fully informed. It was learned from very reliable sources that at that time neither President Johnson nor Secretary of State Rusk appreciated U Thant's remarks about the "American people . . ." Their feelings were conveyed to U Thant through the American Mission at the United Nations. The reaction of the American press to his remarks was also cold. U Thant himself then became very concerned about the response to his comments.

In order to placate U Thant, Harlan Cleveland, the Assistant Secretary of State for International Organization Affairs, told a gathering in New York on March 31, 1965, that the United Nations might be able to provide a channel for mediation in Viet Nam, and that the Secretary-General may have a role to play.[6] This was the first time the State Department expressed the opinion, indirectly, that it would not object to Thant's proposed trip to Hanoi and Peking.

In his speech at Johns Hopkins University on April 7, 1965, President Johnson mentioned future economic and technical aid to Viet Nam and Southeast Asia. He said the United Nations Secretary-General could be useful in the "plan for cooperation in increased development." U Thant, on the following day, praised President Johnson for his conciliatory speech, implying that President Johnson had opened the door for negotiations on Viet Nam.

Hanoi indicated that the American forces in Viet Nam must withdraw as a condition for any accord. Radio Peking said U Thant had "knocked at the wrong door," insisting that Viet Nam had nothing to do with the United Nations. The objection from Hanoi and Peking killed U Thant's advocacy, at least for the time being, and he is temporarily not very active about his plan. Since then, the U.N. Secretary-General has been secretly engaged in contacting diplomats and statesmen regarding negotiations over Viet Nam. He had intended to advocate a cease-fire at the 20th Anniversary of the signing of the U.N. Charter at San Francisco on June 26, 1964, but he gradually realized that the United States was not ready to compromise or capitulate on the rights of the South Vietnamese. Many of his actions are inconsistent with the spirit and letter of the United Nations Charter.

Article 97 of the Charter states that "the Secretary-General . . . shall be the *Chief Administrative Officer* of the Organization." He is not a policy maker or supervisor of the United Nations. He is merely supposed to be in charge of the secretariat for administrative purposes. Article 98 provides that the Secretary-General "shall perform such other functions as are entrusted to him by these organs (the General Assembly, the Security Council, the Economic and Social Council, and the Trusteeship Council). He is supposed to be impartial, above politics and controversies, and not involved in political questions unless he is authorized either by the Security Council or the General Assembly to handle certain political and controversial matters. Article 99 stipulates that "the Secretary-General may bring to the attention of the Security Council any matter which in his opinion may threaten the maintenance of international peace and security." If U Thant believes that the Vietnamese situation threatens the maintenance of international peace and security, he should bring it to the attention of the Security Council. Section 2 of Article 100 states that ". . . The Secretary-General and the staff . . . shall refrain from any action which might reflect on their position as international officials responsible only to the Organization." U Thant is not entitled to use his Office as a forum to handle a very controversial and political subject. It is true that Dag Hammarskjold played a role in the Congo crisis, but he was authorized by the Security Council to handle the dispute.

Until February 1, 1966, when Ambassador Goldberg officially brought the case of Viet Nam to the Security Council and the Council included it on the agenda, U Thant had no right to meddle in this highly controversial issue, nor to use his office as a forum to influence the opinion of the governments of the world.

At his press conference on February 24, 1965, U Thant himself said that he did not "see any immediate prospect of a useful discussion in the Security Council." In what capacity, then, is he acting in trying to mediate in Viet Nam? He has no right to use his prestigious office for furthering his individual desire to serve as a peace-maker, or for enhancing his popularity in order to insure his re-election as Secretary-General.

U Thant has repeatedly recommended that the "Big Five" help North and South Viet Nam negotiate a cease-fire. By the "Big Five" he meant Russia, Communist China, Britain, France, and the United States. It would mean overlooking the U.N. condemnation of Red China as an aggressor in the Korean War, a resolution which is still in the U.N. records. It would also mean a defeat of the American nonrecognition policy toward that aggressive regime. On several occasions, U Thant has publicly said that Red China should be admitted to the United Nations. He communicated his views to the press, highly commending Edgar Snow's book on Red China. When reminded that as the "Chief Administrative Officer" of the United Nations, he should not be partial in highly controversial questions, he explained that he was expressing his personal opinion. How can the general public in the United States, and indeed the whole world, distinguish on what occasion U Thant speaks as Secretary-General of this international organization, and under what circumstances he speaks as a private individual?

As the chief administrative officer of the United Nations, U Thant is a guest of the United States Government, living on American territory, enjoying diplomatic immunity. It was highly improper that he should arouse the doubts and fears of the American public by saying "if they only know the true facts . . . they will agree that further bloodshed is unnecessary." Secretary of State Rusk refuted him when he pointed out that the American public is one of the best informed in the world. U Thant realized that he had blundered, and he authorized a spokesman to say that he did not mean to insult the American public, and that he had not intended to suggest that the United States public was uninformed. Both the President and the Secretary of State disapproved of his statement, and the State Department politely declined to accept his mediation offer at that time.

In addressing the *American Newspaper Publishers Convention* in New York on April 21, U Thant urged the publishers and press of the world to help "in creating an atmosphere in which solutions become possible," [7] in Viet Nam. He further warned that when newspapers emphasize military victories and defeats, it "inevitably creates a heated atmosphere which is unfavorable to reason and conciliation." He did not like to see newspapers report the military situation, he said, as he wants to create a more favorable climate in order to secure a cease-fire. His stand would hardly help to inform the American people. U Thant never became concerned about the war until the Communists started to lose.

3. *Appeal of 17 Nations For Negotiations*

On March 15, 1965, the representatives of Afghanistan, Algeria, Cyprus, Ceylon, Ethiopia, Ghana, Guinea, India, Iraq, Kenya, Nepal, Syria, Tunisia, the United Arab Republic, Uganda, Yugoslavia, and Zambia met at Belgrade, Yugoslavia. They sent an appeal to all the nations directly concerned with the war in Viet Nam to try and achieve a political solution. The Ambassadors of Yugoslavia, Afghanistan, Ethiopia, and Ghana went to see the Secretary of State, urging him to present the appeal to President Johnson. Secretary Rusk stated that the appeal would be studied "with great interest." He added that peace would be restored in Viet Nam "very quickly" if the Communist aggression would cease. The 17 nations call themselves "non-aligned states," but at least one of them, Yugoslavia, is Communist controlled, while many of the others are closer to Moscow or Peking than to Washington.[8]

In his speech at Johns Hopkins University on April 7, 1965, President Johnson in his opening remarks said:

"Last week 17 nations sent their views to some two dozen countries having an interest in southeast Asia. We are joing those 17 countries and stating our American policy tonight, which we believe will contribute toward peace in this area of the world." [9]

President Johnson sent his official reply to these 17 nations by stating that Washington would cease its attack on the military targets in North Viet Nam if Hanoi would stop its support and direction of "terror and military action" in South Viet Nam. He stated that "the basic cause of the conflict in Viet Nam is the attack by North Viet Nam on the independent nation of South Viet Nam. The object of that attack is total conquest." [10] He explained that Viet Nam requested the United States to help her defend herself against attack, and that in fulfillment of long standing United States commitments, the American Government would continue to give aid as long as it is needed.

President Johnson pointed out that "peace in Southeast Asia demands an independent South Viet Nam—security guaranteed and able to shape its own relationships to all others—free from outside interference—tied to no alliance—a military base for no other country. These are the final essentials of any final settlement." [11] He declared that negotiations could be with large or small groups, with reaffirmation of old agreements, or by strengthening them with new provisions, but that the Viet Cong must cease their bombing of compounds by night and embassies by day—murdering civilians, secretaries, and soldiers alike. He made it clear that the Viet Cong terrorism and military actions in South Viet Nam must cease before American military action could be ended and American forces in Viet Nam withdrawn. President Johnson offered large-scale economic aid to Viet Nam and Southeast Asia, a plan in which he hoped that other industrialized nations would join.

After President Johnson made his speech at Johns Hopkins, the Foreign Minister at Saigon, Tran Van Do, was concerned about a possible misunderstanding of it. In a special interview to the *Christian Science Monitor* he said that President Johnson had spoken neither of negotiations nor cease-fire, but only of discussions. He said further:

"We can't negotiate while fighting. This isn't a conventional war with established fronts and troops openly crossing boundaries. It is a war of subversion. We can agree to negotiate only if Hanoi first withdraws its troops, its cadres, its arms and munitions from our territory." [12]

He continued that an unconditional cease-fire would be unacceptable to South Viet Nam because it would permit the Communists to build their strength, with no guarantee that they would not attack again. He also stated:

"It is no use negotiating if we know in advance that the negotiations will fail. But if, as conversations go on, we discover some hope for negotiations, then negotiations may follow. This is how I interpret the President's statement." [13]

Chou En Lai, the Premier of Red China, told former Algerian President Ben Bella that Peking believed the Viet Cong forces are winning, despite American air and naval superiority. Because of this, Red China has not been interested in a cease-fire or in anything short of complete American withdrawal from Viet Nam. The message was relayed to U Thant by Tewfik Bouattoura, the Algerian Delegate at the United Nations, on April 6, 1965. Almost immediately after President Johnson delivered his speech, Peking termed it "full of lies and deception," while Moscow called it "a smoke screen."

On April 19, Hanoi officially rejected the appeal of the 17 nations. This rejection came through a broadcast of the *Viet Nam News Agency*. Their reason was that "any approach tending to secure a U.N. intervention in the Viet Nam situation is inappropriate because such an approach would be basically at variance with the 1954 Geneva Agreements on Viet Nam." [14] Two days later, the *Peking People's Daily* described Johnson as a "hangman," and accused him of hypocrisy in announcing his willingness to enter unconditional discussions, yet actually going "a step further along the path of war, escalation." [15]

The British, Canadian, and French Governments tried earnestly to have the Soviet Union exert her influence on Hanoi to talk peace, but it was to no avail. When Secretary Rusk met Soviet Minister Andrei Gromyko in Vienna, in April, 1965, Rusk tried to talk about a possible cease-fire in Viet Nam, but Gromyko was curt and disinterested.

4. *Pope Paul VI's Repeated Appeals For Peace*

As the spiritual Father of five hundred million Catholics,

Pope Paul has repeatedly appealed to the world for a cessation of war. On March 28, 1965, he declared to a large assembly: "We pray . . . for a cessation of war . . . we want an end to the state of tension which keeps peoples bound, which divides them and sets them against each other."

Lest anyone should think that Pope Paul wants anything less than a just peace, he added on the following day: "We pray also for those who do not want peace, so that a sense of responsibility may recall them to better purposes and feelings." [16] In his Easter message, he declared: "Let every war and guerrilla operation give way to constructive collaboration." [17]

In his *Encyclical* of April 30, 1965, the Pope deplored armed conflicts, cautioning that,

> "the world is darker and more uncertain than ever, now that grave new threats are endangering the supreme benefit of world peace. . . . Today as if no lesson had been learned from the tragic experiences of the two conflicts which shed blood on the first half of our century, we have the dreadful spectacle in certain parts of the world of antagonism on the increase between peoples, and see repeated the dangerous phenomenon of recourse to arms, instead of negotiations, to settle the disputes of the opposing parties. . . . This means that populations of entire nations are subject to unspeakable sufferings caused by agitation, *guerrilla warfare,* acts of war ever growing in extent and intensity, which could now at any movement produce the spark for a terrible fresh conflict." [18]

The Pope declared "with heavy heart" that too often respect for "the sacred and inviolable character of human life" was sacrificed. He condemned the terrors of "guerrilla warfare," the holding of hostages, the reprisals, kidnapping, and murder of unarmed civilians. The *Encyclical* clearly gives the moral support of the Catholic Church to President Johnson's urge for "unconditional discussions" regarding Viet Nam.

Pope Paul's *Easter Message,* together with his appeal to stop the sufferings caused by guerrilla warfare with all its terror, might possibly move the hearts of political leaders in many chanceries. The papal messages, however, have never been able to penetrate the deaf ears of Communist leaders in Peking, Hanoi, and Moscow.

Pope Paul VI's visit to the United Nations on October 4, 1965, was of much significance to the world organization. It was reported that U Thant himself initiated the invitation. The Communist countries made no objection, since the Pope's plea for peace could be utilized by them, and has been distorted ever since to make the United States look as though it is not peace-loving, and that it is wrong to fight, even in a defensive war. All the Communist delegates to the United Nations were present during the Pope's speech, with the conspicuous exception of Albania, which echoes Peking. Red China carried no news about the Papal visit. Hardly anyone in Communist China knew of Pope Paul's message. The Pope pleaded for general peace and urged "no more war." Leftist writers and politicians misinterpreted his remarks, construing them to advocate begging for peace from the Communist countries. Although Pope Paul had condemned aggressive wars and guerrilla warfare previously, he reiterated the traditional Christian teaching that defensive wars are often necessary and justified.

Some people think that Pope Paul is for peace at any price and for universal membership in the United Nations. But in his speech to the United Nations General Assembly on October 4, 1965, he declared:

> "You do not confer existence upon states, but you qualify each single nation as fit to sit in the orderly congress of peoples: you grant recognition, of high ethical and juridical value, to each sovereign national community, guaranteeing it an honourable international citizenship. This in itself is a great service to the cause of humanity—namely, to define clearly and to honour the national subjects of the world community, and to confirm their juridical status, which entitles them to be recognized and respected by all and from which there may derive an orderly and stable system of international life. You give sanction to the great principle that relations between peoples should be regulated by reason, by justice, by law, by negotiation; not by force or by violence, not by war, not by fear, not by deceit." [19]

Pope Paul also justified the righteousness of a defensive war. He told the United Nations Assembly in unmistakable terms:

> "As long as man remains that weak, changeable and even wicked being that he often shows himself to be, defensive arms will, unfortunately, be necessary."

5. Peace Talks at Cambodia Conference Unobtainable

As a neighboring State of Viet Nam and a "non-aligned" nation, Cambodia is greatly interested in the peace and security of Viet Nam. The Cambodian Chief of State, Prince Norodom Sihanouk, realizes the seriousness of the Vietnamese situation in relation to his own country. He has long sought a Cambodian Conference, and hopes to guarantee Cambodia's neutrality, in case the war should widen. Prince Sihanouk asked the Soviet Union, Communist China, the United Kingdom, France, the United States of America, the Democratic Republic of Viet Nam, Laos, the Republic of Viet Nam, and Thailand to attend an informal conference at Pnom Penh, Cambodia, to be held in the latter part of April, 1965. The British were hoping that such a conference would be a forum for informal discussions concerning Viet Nam. On April 23, 1965, the American Government expressed its readiness to participate.

The Soviet press also indicated Russia's interest. When the Mongolian Prime Minister, Yumzhagiin Tsedenbal, visited Moscow, Soviet Prime Minister Alexei Kosygin and the Mongolian Prime Minister issued a joint statement, on April 23, 1965, stating that the two governments supported Prince Sihanouk's proposal for the Cambodian conference, and that they favored an international conference on Laos as well. Saigon's Foreign Minister, Tran Van Do, wrote to the Cambodian Government that Viet Nam was ready to participate in an international conference for guaranteeing the independence and neutrality of Cambodia. He expressed the desire that Cambodia might some day play the role of Switzerland in Southeast Asia.

On April 25, 1965, Secretary of State Rusk announced that the American Government has "informed a number of interested governments that if such a conference is called we will gladly participate." Prince Sihanouk immediately announced that there was no need to have the United States, Thailand, and South Viet Nam guarantee Cambodia's neutrality. He said that if the conference were used as a pretext to discuss the Vietnamese crisis, he would refuse to attend. Prince Sihanouk accused the United States of "aggression" in Asia, and indicated that he would soon break diplomatic relations with the American Government, except for a Consul in Pnom Penh. This sudden change in the attitude of Prince Sihanouk seems to have been due to pressure from Peking. Red China wanted to be sure there would be no settlement of the Vietnamese war under the guise of a Cambodian Conference.

The Cambodian Chief of State was compelled to forgo the opportunity of solving Cambodia's neutrality status, and the conference was cancelled. This was later confirmed by Chou En-Lai's own statement to the press that Prince Sihanouk had changed his attitude after he had conferred with him during their visit in Jakarta, Indonesia. The Prince was quoted by the *Hsin Hua News Agency* of Peking and Hong Kong on April 26, 1965, as saying: "We categorically refuse a Conference on Cambodia which would only be a pretext for talks on South Viet Nam or Viet Nam." Such a conference, he said, should not be used "by certain powers to bait their adversaries." All hope of using the Cambodian Conference as a means for holding cease-fire discussions on Viet Nam was killed. By the first week of May, Cambodia broke off diplomatic relations with the United States. On May 9, 1965, Secretary of State Rusk made it clear that the United States would not be interested in establishing a consulate in Pnom Penh, the capital of Cambodia.

6. *Offers to Mediate by India and Others*

Under Jawaharal Nehru, India had been very friendly toward Red China, and became her most ardent spokesman for admission into the United Nations. Even after the Chinese Communist forces attacked India, the New Delhi Government did not openly reverse its stand. The late Prime Minister, Lal Bahadur Shastri, feared the renewal of Red Chinese aggression against India, so did not dare become unfriendly toward Peking. India hopes to remain a non-aligned nation, with friendly tendencies toward the Soviet Union and the Afro-Asian Nations and a rather critical attitude toward the United States. She realizes that the United States is a democratic country, and will accept criticism without turning against her. In this way India and others practice non-alignment, and sometimes influence American policy. This also helps the Indian leaders to silence critics at home, thereby gaining internal unity.

India is anxious lest Red China's influence spread too far in Asia. She hopes to see it confined to Indo-China, far from her own borders. The Shastri Government sent a proposal to about 20 leading Afro-Asian and non-aligned countries. The proposal was also sent to London, Moscow, and Washington. The plan was also reportedly sent to both North and South Viet Nam.

India does not intend to offer a permanent solution for Viet Nam; she only hopes to get around the current diplomatic and political deadlock. India is still the Chairman of the *International Control Commission* in Viet Nam, and as such is supposed to be neutral in the present dispute. India proposed an immediate cease-fire, hoping to make the disputants talk peace. To supervise the enforcement of the cease-fire, India proposed that the United Arab Republic, Japan, Nigeria, and perhaps other Afro-Asian nations should form a commission to police the area.

In the early part of May, 1965, Shastri paid a visit to Moscow. He was accorded a great welcome, and a joint communique was issued by him and Soviet Premier Kosygin denouncing "the Imperialist countries, first of all the United States of America," which had imposed their will on foreign nations and caused "a sharp aggravation" of tension in Southeast Asia.[20] The joint communique further stated that these two nations adhered to the policy of "the principles of peaceful co-existence," an attitude scorned by Peking. It continued: "These two governments urge once again that the bombings of the *Democratic Republic of Viet Nam* should be stopped immediately. The solution of the problem of Viet Nam can be found only within the framework of the Geneva agreements of 1954 on Indochina."[21]

Shastri intended to visit Washington in early May, 1965, hoping to convince President Johnson to accept his cease-fire plan. But the White House announced that the President would not be able to see him until fall. Early in June of the same year, during Shastri's visit to Ottawa, he announced that he would not have time to visit Washington in the fall. The fatal blow to Shastri's ambition came from Peking, which flatly turned down the Indian proposal.

Many other nations made various attempts to start discussions or negotiations on Viet Nam. The British Government appointed Patrick Gordon Walker, the former Foreign Secretary, to visit Southeast Asia as a special representative to make a survey on the possibility of arranging for political negotiations in Viet Nam. He was to visit Saigon, Hanoi, Peking, Moscow, and probably Washington, to convince them to come to peace terms. Washington welcomed this proposed trip as a means to further the possibility of negotiation; but Moscow maintained silence, and Peking quickly declared that the former British Foreign Secretary's suggested mission would be unwelcome. This was a severe blow to the British peace overture.

Canada's Prime Minister Lester Pearson, during his visit

to Washington in the early part of April, urged that the bombing of North Viet Nam be halted. Senator J. William Fulbright also asked the American Government to suspend its bombings in order to seek peace. Responding to these pressures, President Johnson ordered suspension of the bombing for six days, starting April 13, 1965. This decision was relayed to Paul Martin, Canadian Minister of External Affairs. The Canadian Government then instructed its representative on the *International Control Commission* to contact both North and South Viet Nam, hoping that Hanoi would be willing to talk rather than fight. Hanoi's reply to the Canadians was both negative and full of scorn.

One of the co-authors of this book was slated to share the same platform with Chester Ronning in a Seminar on "The Explosive Orient," at Brandon College, Brandon, Manitoba, Canada, on January 29, 1966. But during the conference it was reported that Ronning was called to Ottawa by Paul Martin, Minister of External Affairs, to an important diplomatic mission in the Far East. This retired Canadian diplomat was sent to both North and South Viet Nam because he was a member of the *International Control Commission* in Viet Nam. He carried a letter from Canada's Prime Minister Pearson to Ho Chi Minh, urging him to send his representative to a cease-fire conference. Later, on March 16, 1966, the Ottawa correspondent of the *New York Times* quoted Ronning on his return to Canada that "the time for negotiations was not ripe." [22] This was still another indication that Hanoi is more interested in fighting than talking.

Peking denounced the American suspension of bombing as a trick and a deceit. The Soviet Union paid no attention to President Johnson's appeal to ask Hanoi for negotiations or even discussion. Despite all the discouragement and the many obstacles to cease-fire talks, American efforts to seek peace have not relaxed. Senator Fulbright, Chairman of the Foreign Relations Committee, made a major speech on Viet Nam on May 15, 1965. He opposed both immediate American withdrawal and extension of the war. The gist of his speech was clearly expressed in his opening remarks:

"A complete military victory in Viet Nam, though theoretically attainable, can in fact be attained only at a cost far exceeding the requirements of our interest and our honor. [American policy] has been—and should remain—one of determination to end the war at the earliest possible time by a negotiated settlement involving major concessions by both sides." [23]

7. *Peace Effort of British Commonwealth Nations*

The Conference of the *British Commonwealth Nations* decided to send a Commission to Peking, Moscow, Hanoi, Washington, and Saigon, to make arrangements for a cease-fire in Viet Nam. The commission, headed by Britain's Prime Minister Wilson, is composed of 21 nations, mostly from Asia and Africa. Participating members included Ghana, Nigeria, Trinidad, Togo, and Ceylon. It was to start its trip after the adjournment of the Conference on June 25, 1965. If the mission were not successful they hoped to continue their efforts at the *Afro-Asian Conference* opening in Algiers on June 29. About 13 Commonwealth nations belong to the Afro-Asian Conference. Seven of the 17 nations which had previously appealed to President Johnson for a cease-fire talk were also Commonwealth countries, viz. Ceylon, Cyprus, Ghana, India, Kenya, Uganda, and Zambia.

Long before the proposed mission of the British Commonwealth started on its trip, Red China's Premier, Chou En-lai, denounced it as a "hoax" intended to help the United States to "hang on in South Viet Nam." He condemned both Washington and London for their policy, and said that "as co-chairman of the Geneva Conference, Britain has not only failed to check United States acts of aggression in fulfillment of her duty, but has consistently supported them." Both Moscow and Hanoi indicated that the peace mission was unwelcome. The Communist nations, particularly Peking and Hanoi, have repeatedly rejected every kind of peace overture from any source. Supplementing the peace efforts of the Commonwealth Nations, the British Government sent Michael Stewart, Foreign Secretary, to Moscow from November 29 to December 3, 1965, to urge the Soviet Government to act as Co-Chairman of the Geneva Conference of 1954 and to reconvene the conference for discussions on Viet Nam.

The British Foreign Secretary saw Soviet Foreign Minister Andrei Gromyko and Soviet Premier Aleksei N. Kosygin, but he failed utterly in his peace mission. The only statement he obtained from Moscow was that the United States should stop bombing North Viet Nam before any cease-fire discussion could take place. During the entire course of the war, the United States has tried to neutralize the Soviet Union, and attempt to persuade Moscow to influence Hanoi to come to the conference table. But all the efforts of America, as well as those of the rest of the world, have come to nothing. This is partially because Moscow fears that Peking will accuse her of collusion with Washington and betraying the socialist nations. It is primarily because Moscow is solidly on the side of world Communism.

Prime Minister Harold Wilson made a personal appeal for peace at the United Nations Assembly on December 16, 1965. Hanoi snubbed the British effort within twenty-four hours. Radio Hanoi relayed the following statement by one of her officials:

> "The Government of the Democratic Republic of Viet Nam (DRVN) energetically protests against the wrongful acts of the British Government and its policy of tailing after the United States. The DRVN categorically rejects all British 'plans' and 'proposals' made under the pretense of peace."

The broadcast from North Viet Nam also condemned a proposal by Britain's Foreign Secretary that had requested a conference in Geneva. Despite the fact that the British Foreign Secretary accomplished nothing toward another Geneva Conference, the English papers reported that Britain was going to send Prime Minister Harold Wilson himself to break the Viet Nam deadlock. The visit of Wilson to Moscow in February, 1966, was cordial, but again failed to convince Moscow it should join London in serving as co-chairman to reconvene the Geneva Conference of 1954.

8. *The Viet Cong's Reported Willingness to Discuss*

Eric Sevareid reported on November 30, 1965, that Adlai Stevenson told him that in the early autumn of 1964, U Thant had privately made arrangements with the Hanoi authorities to meet the American Emissary in Rangoon, Burma. Stevenson reportedly said that Washington felt such an attempt could not be made during the Presidential election campaign. Sevareid said in his news broadcast, in August, 1965, that after the election was over Defense Secretary Robert McNamara and Secretary of State Dean Rusk opposed the suggestion on the ground that such an effort would demoralize the Saigon Government, which was already weak. Sevareid also indicated that Stevenson did not agree with the President's policy on Viet Nam, and that he was planning to resign as the U. S. Ambassador to the United Nations. These charges were made by Sevareid shortly after Stevenson's death on July 17, 1965, and were related in more detail in a subsequent article in *Look* magazine (November 30, 1965). As a result of Sevareid's charges, Presidential Press Secretary Bill Moyers responded rather angrily that "it was a disservice to Stevenson's memory when he was dead and could not answer."

In recalling the peace feelers to Hanoi in 1964, U Thant declared on November 16, 1965, that if "bold steps" had been taken in 1964, much of today's tragic developments in Viet Nam could have been avoided. The United States Government was quickly condemned by the press without examining the merits of the case. The Special Assistant to Stevenson, Clayton Fritchey, who was also Director of Public Affairs of the U. S. Mission at the U. N., wrote in *Newsday* that Stevenson supported U. S. policy in Viet Nam right up to his death, and that he had had no intention of resigning. Fritchey quoted from an unposted letter written by Stevenson just a few days prior to his death to a group of artists, writers, and scientists, rejecting their suggestion that he resign. Stevenson's letter concluded:

"I do not believe the policy of retreat in Asia or anywhere else would make any contribution whatsoever to the idea that violence cannot be the formal arbitrator in world affairs." *

Adlai E. Stevenson III made public the full text of his father's letter to Paul Goodman, who had asked Stevenson to resign from the United Nations. The late Stevenson wrote:

"So far, the new Communist 'Dynasty' (in Peking) has been very aggressive. Tibet was swallowed, India attacked, the Malays had to fight 12 years to resist a 'national liberation' they could receive from the British by a more peaceful route. Today, the apparatus of infiltration and aggression is already at work in North Thailand. Chinese maps show to the world's chagrin the furthest limits of the old Chinese empire marked as Chinese. I do not think the idea of Chinese expansionism is so fanciful that the effort to check it is irrational."

Young Stevenson issued a statement in Chicago on December 14, 1965, saying that his father had told him in June that there were some suggestions that he should resign from his post, but his father, "on the contrary, intended to restate publicly and firmly his support of our [U.S.] Viet Nam

* December 14, 1965. This letter has been deposited at Princeton University as part of the Stevenson Papers.

policy in a letter to Paul Goodman of North Stratford, N. J."

Concerning the charges that the United States did not respond to the peace overtures offered by Hanoi through U Thant, there appears to have been an organized effort to blame the U.S.A., as indicated by various demonstrations, slogans, and outcries made by writers and critics of the Johnson Administration. The State Department rejected such charges by pointing out that at the time, in August, 1964, there was no indication that the Viet Cong were seriously thinking about a cease-fire. On the contrary, they were preparing to increase their war efforts in South Viet Nam.

In answering charges that the United States was at fault for turning down Hanoi's suggestion that its diplomats meet at Rangoon with American representatives, Robert J. Mc-Closkey, spokesman for the State Department, said that "there was no interest on the other side in what we would have considered to have been serious peace talks." He further denied that U Thant ever had said that Hanoi would accept "any formulation" for a cease-fire "that the United States would propose." He added that Secretary McNamara did not participate in the American decision on this matter. McNamara also flatly denied the remarks made about him in the Sevareid article in *Look*, regarding U Thant's private promotion of a meeting between Viet Cong and American diplomats in Rangoon.

Former Vice-President Richard Nixon supported President Johnson's decision of non-acceptance of the Hanoi 1964 peace overture. He told the Bond Club of New York on November 22, 1965, that "if the United States had gone to the conference table then, the North Vietnamese would have been able to dictate terms." It should be borne in mind that U Thant, as Chief Administrative Officer of the U. N., was not authorized in 1964 either by the Security Council or the Assembly to promote such an important international conference. U Thant was also not authorized by the United States. He also acted behind the back of the Republic of Viet Nam.

An editorial in the *New York Herald Tribune* on November 18, 1965, entitled "Vietnamese Peace Talks," stated:

". . . it is [or should be] elementary that truce or peace negotiations are intimately related to and reflect positions currently held by belligerents on the battlefield. When Mr. Thant proposed negotiations [acting on his own initiative or on an idea inspired by another party], the Communists were holding most of South Viet Nam and were advancing. South Vietnamese forces were becoming demoralized and the political situation in Saigon was chaotic . . .

"Negotiations under circumstances prevailing in Viet Nam in 1964 would have represented a betrayal of those who aspire to freedom from Asian Communist conquest. There was no indication at that time that Hanoi was interested in anything other than a U. S. and South Vietnamese surrender; and for the United States even to have entered into talks then might have been enough to complete the demoralization of South Viet Nam and break whatever was left of Saigon's back."

Even President de Gaulle, who recognized the Communist regime in Peking in January, 1964, and whose Government has been very critical of American policy in Viet Nam and East Asia, endorsed the American attitude toward Hanoi's peace feelers.

9. *The Fanfani Affair*

In November, 1965, two Italians involved Amintore Fanfani, who was then the Italian Foreign Minister and President of the U. N. Assembly, as an official intermediary between Hanoi and Washington to contact the American Government. The incident caused a sensation, not only in the United States but in many other countries. The contents of the documents had been partly disclosed in an article by Richard Dudman of the *St. Louis Post-Dispatch*. If the American Government had maintained silence, it could have been accused of hiding important political information from its people, and of not taking advantage of the alleged overtures to negotiate with the Hanoi regime. Hence the State Department revealed all the important documents concerning the peace feelers.

The story claimed that Giorgio La Pira, former Mayor of Florence and now Professor of Roman Law at the University of Florence, and a Professor Mario Primicerio, who allegedly visited Ho Chi Minh on November 11, 1965, initiated attempts to bring about a meeting between representatives of Hanoi and the United States. Pira wrote to Fanfani that Ho Chi Minh told them he was "prepared to go anywhere to meet anyone." Fanfani, then President of the U. N. Assembly, relayed this message to Ambassador Goldberg on November 20, 1965, requesting him to forward it to President Johnson. On December 4, Secretary Dean Rusk replied to Fanfani that the United States did not agree with the "elements" or conditions of Hanoi's four points for a peace settlement, but that the United States was prepared to include them for consideration in peace talks. He also asked Fanfani to obtain clarification from Hanoi. On November 13, Fanfani wrote to Rusk saying that a summary of his reply had reached Hanoi and as soon as he received an answer he would immediately inform Rusk. On December 17, after careful consideration, the related documents were released for publication.

The Fanfani letter to President Johnson included the following conditions for negotiations:

i. There must be a cease-fire (air, sea, and land) in the entire territory of Viet Nam (North and South); there must be a cessation of all belligerent operations (including any further debarkation of American troops).

ii. The four points formulated and announced by Hanoi should be considered as "in reality the explanation of the Geneva text, and which therefore can be reduced to a single point: application of the Geneva Accords." If these conditions were accepted, Ho Chi Minh and Prime Minister Pham Van Dong would be willing to "go anywhere and meet anyone."

The reply of Secretary Rusk on December 4 consisted of the following important points:

a. The United States is willing to enter into any unconditional discussions for ending armed hostilities in Viet Nam.

b. The United States would be willing to engage in negotiations based on the Geneva Agreements of 1954 without any qualifications or conditions, although there is some ambiguity in the Hanoi conditions regarding the Geneva Agreements.

c. The United States would not consider the four points laid down by Hanoi as an authentic interpretation of the Geneva Agreements, but would be willing to consider and discuss them along with any other proposals that may be advanced at the conference table.

d. The United States desires negotiations without any conditions. If there are any conditions, one of them should be the prevention of any more troops and equipment infiltrating into South Viet Nam.

e. The United States seeks a clarification on whether the withdrawal of American troops is a prior condition to the initiation of negotiations.

Secretary Rusk told Fanfani that from the Italian sources quoted, the United States was still far from persuaded that there is sufficient evidence that Hanoi has any "real willingness of unconditional negotiations." Fanfani replied, on December 13, that the contents of his letter had been forwarded to the proper authorities at Hanoi, and that as soon as he received any reaction therefrom, he would immediately inform Secretary Rusk. Within twenty-four hours, Radio Hanoi disavowed the allegations of peace feelers. It stated:

"The Viet Nam press agency is authorized to declare that those news reports spread by the United States State Department are sheer, groundless fabrication."

The same press agency commented: (i) The two Italians were received by Ho Chi Minh and Premier Pham Van Dong, but they were told by the Viet Cong leaders that the U.S. had violated the Geneva Agreements of 1954. The offer by the United States of "unconditional discussions" was only aimed at covering up the acts of the U.S. imperialists.

(ii) Hanoi's insistence that the Four Points as previously laid down must be used as a basis for future settlements of the Viet Nam problem was reiterated.

(iii) It reaffirmed the unswerving stand of Hanoi, demanding that "the United States must stop at once their air raids against North Viet Nam, put an immediate end to their aggressive war in South Viet Nam, withdraw all troops and weapons of the United States and its satellites from South Viet Nam, and let the Vietnamese people solve their affairs by themselves."

(iv) Radio Hanoi called the U.S. release of these news reports "part of its peace hoax." It charged that "each time the United States imperialists jabbered about 'peaceful negotiations,' they intensified and expanded the war in Viet Nam." It condemned the United States "imperialists," alleging that "they are now trying by hook or by crook to increase their forces in South Viet Nam and further 'escalate' their bombing raids on North Viet Nam."

Since Hanoi completely denied the truth of Fanfani's report that Hanoi was advancing a peace feeler, Fanfani was severely criticized by the Italian press and his colleagues in the Italian Parliament as having shown "poor judgment" on the whole incident. But the final blow was when Mrs. Fanfani arranged for La Pira, one of the two principals in the purported negotiations, to receive Mrs. Gianna Preda, editor of *The Borghese,* in her home. The published interview in this conservative weekly quoted La Pira as having expressed great affection for Benito Mussolini, and active admiration for President Charles de Gaulle. He declared that Italian Premier Aldo Moro was "sad and soft," that Vice-Premier Pietro Nenni was "extinct," and that Secretary Dean Rusk "doesn't know anything, doesn't understand much." Fanfani had to offer his resignation [24] and it was accepted by Italian Premier Moro. The Fanfani affair still constitutes a political issue in internal Italian politics, but its significance on the outcome of the Viet Nam problem is probably very little.*

10. *U. S. Efforts to have the Soviet Union Help Secure Negotiations*

President Johnson has repeatedly tried to win over the people in North Viet Nam by promising them economic and technical aid if they would discontinue fighting. He has prepared proposals for granting such assistance. These tempting promises have never succeeded in getting the support of North Viet Nam. In Communist countries it is impossible for the people to do anything about such offers unless their rulers concur.

President Johnson also appealed to the Soviet Union to see if it would use its influence to help secure negotiations. The U. S. S. R. replied with scorn, criticism, and sweeping condemnation of America's position. On May 8, 1965, the First Secretary of the Soviet Communist Party, Leonid I. Brezhnev, accused the United States of "imperialist aggression" in Viet Nam. He denounced the American Government for its action "to usurp the role of a supreme judge over the destinies of nations." He condemned President Johnson for his "policy of dictatorship," which, according to Brezhnev, would bring "neither glory nor respect" [25] to the United States. Supplementary to these accusations, the Soviet Union, on May 19, 1965, warned the United States against the use of force. In regard to the Dominican Republic, *Tass* reported:

"No one should expect that it is possible to interfere

---

* In February 1966, Moro resumed his Prime Ministership and Fanfani again became his Foreign Minister.

in the internal affairs of independent states, provoke armed conflicts—now here, now there—commit acts of aggression against the Socialist countries and at the same time talk about some kind of agreements with the Soviet Union about 'ending tension.' " [26]

The day after the release of this dispatch denouncing American policy in Viet Nam and the Dominican Republic, Nikolai V. Podgorny, one of the most influential of the Soviet secretaries, accused President Johnson of grossly violating "the rights of the peace-loving people." [27] Subsequently, Moscow warned Red China that the Communists of the world must be united. By the beginning of June, the Soviet Communist Party shifted its ground in dealing with Red China and other Communist countries. Instead of adhering to ideological disputes with Peking, the Soviet Union used Viet Nam as a practical and concrete issue. Moscow then stressed her aid to the Viet Cong as a bid for Communist support from different socialist countries, saying that it was Peking that had tried to split them. Peking declared that Moscow's gestures towards Hanoi were hypocritical and only symbolic, and that Moscow merely used the Viet Nam issue in order to exercise leadership over the Socialist parties throughout the world.

Bearing in mind the split between Moscow and Peking, President Johnson appealed to the people and the leaders of the Communist countries in June, 1965, by saying: "Come now, let us reason together. Our door is unlatched. Out table is set. We are ready—we believe mankind is ready with us." [28] Neither Moscow nor Peking responded to his appeal. On June 8, while signing a bill establishing a National Institute for the Deaf, President Johnson said that "sometimes it seems that deafness is not simply an affliction of individuals, but an affliction of nations, as well."

Since late December, 1965, the American Government has intensified its peace efforts. It has also instructed its Ambassador in Moscow to urge the Soviet Government repeatedly to cooperate with the United States in solving the Viet Nam problem in order to avoid further fighting in that country. Ambassador Harriman made a special trip to Moscow to induce the Soviet Government to put pressure on Hanoi to come to the conference table. On the occasion of the funeral of the late Indian Prime Minister, Lal Bahadar Shastri, Vice-President Humphrey and Secretary Dean Rusk had lengthy talks with the Soviet Premier, Aleksei Kosygin, and Foreign Minister Gromyko in New Delhi. Peking charged Moscow and Washington with having engaged in "funeral diplomacy" at the expense of a dead man. Despite every American effort to lure Moscow away from Peking and into a position of co-operation with the United States toward a cease-fire in Viet Nam and toward peaceful solutions in Southeast Asia, the Soviet Union remains deaf to all of America's entreaties.

There are various explanations offered by authorities on Communism about the cold relationship between Moscow and Washington. The Soviet Union does not want Peking to accuse her of being a "tool of American imperialism by betraying the war of liberation" in Viet Nam. The Soviet Union seems to favor the war in Viet Nam, at least as long as it is localized, and she aids Hanoi substantially, partly in order to maintain her prestige in that country and throughout Southeast Asia, and partly because the U. S. S. R. is always on the side of Communism and against the Free World. Some authorities believe that Moscow would like to see the war in Viet Nam spread to the China Mainland in order to weaken the Peking regime, so that China will have to turn to the Soviet Union for help. Some think that if the war of liberation in Viet Nam drags on for several years, it will weaken both Red China and the United States, a situation that would benefit the U. S. S. R.

The Soviet Union still considers herself the leader against "imperialism" and for world revolution. She holds that her tactics towards the United States and Viet Nam are correct and prudent, while Red China's approach embodies dangerous risks. By letting the war drag on, the Soviet Union hopes for American concessions before a cease-fire is arranged, thereby benefiting the side of World Communism. The difference between Moscow and Peking in dealing with the United States is mainly tactical. Moscow's attitude towards Washington has recently hardened, but Peking will never agree that the Soviet policy towards the United States is stern enough.

There are a considerable number of Japanese who are against American policy in Viet Nam. The former Japanese envoy to Britain, Shunichi Matsumoto, wrote an article for the *Asahi* newspaper in Tokyo on April 6, 1965, that was very critical of American policy. But the Japanese party in power, the Liberal-Democratic, strongly supports American policy in Viet Nam. On June 8, 1965, the Japanese Government, under Prime Minister Eisaku Sato, explained to the Japanese people that "the Vietnamese conflict should be evaluated in its entirety and historically." He stated that "it is simply one-sided to start discussing the merits and demerits of the problem beginning with the American bombings of Viet Nam." The Japanese Government party concluded that "self-defense and retaliation is perfectly within the bounds of reason," [29] in view of the Viet Cong attacks on the Vietnamese Government and American forces.

In Manila, the Philippine House and Senate voted, by an overwhelming majority, to send an engineer-battalion to South Viet Nam with Filipino security support. The Philippine legislators believe that their country must help fight the Communists in Viet Nam in order to keep them from spreading to the Philippine Islands and other areas of the Pacific. Salvador P. Lopez, the Philippine representative to the United Nations, told the 114-Nation Disarmament Commission on May 19, 1965: "The truth of the matter is that armed aggression against the Republic of Viet Nam is being and has been for a long time organized, directed, and supported by Communist North Viet Nam." He concluded that "Southeast Asia has become the testing ground for the free world's will and determination to resist Communist aggression and expansion." Both President Marcos and Foreign Minister Ramos are in favor of sending Philippine troops to South Viet Nam. They expect to do so sometime in 1966.

Concerning the Republic of China, her 600,000 well-trained and well-equipped forces are one of the factors deterring Red China from openly participating in the war. President Chiang Kai-shek has recently made several declarations that his troops are ready to attack the China Mainland at any time, with the permission and cooperation of the American Government, without committing any American troops on the China Mainland. It might require only American logistic support. President Chiang has ordered the Chinese Nationalist Army to accelerate the training of army divisions for amphibious operations around China's sea coasts. Peking is quite aware of this, and has responded by preparing to meet any possible attacks from Free China.

Chiang Kai-shek has repeatedly said that as long as the Peking regime remains in the hands of the Communists, it will continue to threaten the security and independence of the whole of Asia. Compromises or concessions to the Chinese Communists would simply lead to a larger war in the future. He believes that this is the best time to defeat the Chinese Communists in Viet Nam, while they are still quarrelling with Moscow, and while their atomic weapons are not ready to be used. If Chinese Communist aggression is not checked, it will spread to other parts of the world.

The Chinese Nationalists have repeatedly urged the United

States to let them attack the Chinese coastal cities. In accordance with the Sino-American Security Pact of 1955, the Chinese Government is required to consult with the American Government before launching any major military operations against the Chinese Mainland. American policy has thus far discouraged any such Nationalist undertaking. But Chiang and other Nationalist leaders feel that the best way to save Viet Nam and to uproot the Chinese Communist forces is to attack other parts of Red China. They believe that the present American policy in Viet Nam is just hoping for a peaceful settlement without having any definite goal, and that this is not the best solution to a war. They feel that whether one likes it or not, there is a war, and a very serious one, in Viet Nam, and that General Douglas MacArthur was right when he said: "There is no substitute for victory."

Many people think that Communist China is very strong, but compared to the United States or the U.S.S.R., Red China is extremely weak. The editor of the scholarly *China News Analysis,* the Rev. Ladislas La Dany, S.J., recently testified that the people on the Chinese Mainland desperately want a change. When asked about landing the Nationalist troops from Taiwan on the Mainland, he replied that "there is an 80 per cent probability that the whole country would be shaken. It would change people's outlook." [30]

It is hopeless today for anyone in Red China to try to overthrow their Communist oppressors. In the words of Father La Dany: "Very rarely do you have one single friend to whom you can say what you really think. So there is a great artificial silence." But if the Nationalists from Taiwan were to establish a large beachhead on the Mainland, a place where the oppressed people of China could flee to, and from which they could strike back at their oppressor, the whole picture would be changed. American air support for such a venture would be essential. The more America threatens to do this, the more Red China will stay out of the Vietnamese war, or any other war where America is involved. Communist China did not enter South Viet Nam with troops last year, as she threatened, precisely because President Johnson let them know that they would not have any sanctuary this time, like they enjoyed during the Korean War.[31]

Australia, New Zealand, and Thailand are all signatories of SEATO, and under that treaty they are supposed to render aid to Viet Nam, since Viet Nam is within the Protocol area of SEATO. Australia has sent 4,500 troops to Saigon, while New Zealand has sent a few hundred. South Korea has sent more than 42,000. Because she may be the next

Communist target, Thailand is concentrating on stemming the spread of Communism on her own soil. Thailand had a 9% rate of economic growth in 1965, and is now the world's leading exporter of rice. Countries that prosper under a free economy, as South Viet Nam did from 1954 to 1963, become the object of envy and avarice on the part of Communist countries, which have seldom even been able to feed themselves. Thailand is deeply concerned about the outcome of the war, and has sent both material and technical assistance to South Viet Nam.

The importance of the struggle in Viet Nam is very well understood by the Asian peoples and their governments. It is also appreciated by the British. The Labor Government has given strong moral support to American policy in that area. Ludwig Erhard, the West German Chancellor, also issued a joint communique with President Johnson on June 5, 1965, emphasizing the importance of mutual solidarity in dealing with Communist aggression. He promised that his Government would participate in the Asian Development Bank proposed by President Johnson. The German people have also contributed generously to relief and welfare work in South Viet Nam. Germany's Chancellor declared:

"The German people fully understand the American concern with Saigon. They are fully aware that if freedom is protected there, this means an assurance for the German people that the United States stands by their commitment to protect freedom all over the world."

Many vital problems confront the Communist nations. Hanoi is caught between Moscow and Peking. Ho Chi Minh himself has had a life-long relationship with both the Chinese and the Soviet Communists. Peking and Moscow have each claimed to be the only reliable friend of the *Democratic Republic of Viet Nam*. Many Americans had predicted that if America escalated the war it would drive China and Soviet Russia together. Exactly the opposite has happened. The ideological disputes between Moscow and Peking have grown with the intensity of the war.

The Soviet Union did ask Red China to put aside their differences and take "united action" in Viet Nam. But Peng Chen, Secretary to the Chinese Communist Party and Mayor of Peking, strongly attacked Soviet policy in Viet Nam on May 25, 1965. He condemned the Soviet Union by declaring that the kind of united action advocated by Moscow "can only be sought with United States imperialism and its lack-

eys, with the Indian reactionaries and with the Tito clique.*
To seek such united action with Marxist-Leninists is to knock
at the wrong door." [32]

In response to the Peking charges, the Soviet Communist
Party organ, *Pravda,* in a 4,000-word editorial, launched
an official attack on Red China. This editorial, issued in
Moscow on June 20, 1965, accused the Peking regime and its
party of violating their "sacred international duty" toward
another Socialist State by her refusal to take part in "a
joint action" to oppose American military moves in Viet
Nam. However, the *Pravda* editorial expressed the fervent
hope that in spite of the existence of serious political differences in both theory and practice, Moscow and Peking
can still be united for joint action against the "imperialist
United States."

The United States seems determined not to withdraw
from Viet Nam. Despite objections from various quarters
within and without, she is increasing her military personnel
and equipment. This is a most crucial period for the outcome of the war in Viet Nam. The United States is at a crossroads between war and peace. The American people must
realize that the Communist nations may insist on obtaining
more concessions from South Viet Nam and the United
States. However, it is possible the war may end quietly by
having North Viet Nam gradually decrease its aid to the
Communist troops in the South, and by engaging merely in
prolonged guerrilla warfare.

Thousands of Viet Cong will eventually settle in the South
as farmers, exchanging their bullets for ballots, as rifles are
turned into plough-shares. The mortal remains of all too
many thousands have returned to dust. War is the cruelest
of follies, and the billions of dollars it is costing could always have been put to a better purpose, except that those
who are fighting to preserve their freedom have usually had
no other rational choice. The most foolish of all follies is to
condemn defending one's country when the only alternative
is succumbing to the slavery of Communism.

* Tito clique—This refers to the 17 Nations Peace Appeal made in
Belgrade.

FOOTNOTES

CHAPTER XI: BETWEEN WAR AND PEACE: THE UNITED STATES AT THE CROSSROADS

1. Dept. of State, *Bulletin* (Washington, Apr. 13, 1964), pp. 566-7. Also quoted in *Background Information Relating to Southeast Asia and Viet Nam* (Washington, 1965), p. 115.
2. A dispatch quoted by the A.P. from the Defense Department in *The Christian Science Monitor,* June 18, 1965.
3. Senate Foreign Relations Committee, *Background Information Relating to Southeast Asia and Viet Nam,* (Washington, March 1966), p. 295.
4. Text given by Nguyen Huu Tho to the Japanese newspaper, *Mainichi,* in Japanese on Dec. 19 in Peking and published by that paper on Dec. 22, 1965.
5. United Nations, *Press Services,* Note No. 3075, Feb. 24, 1965, p. 5.
6. *New York Times,* Apr. 2, 1965.
7. U.N. Press Services, Press Releases, SG/SM/283, entitled "Mass Media and Public Opinion," p. 7.
8. *N.Y. Times,* Apr. 2, 1965.
9. *N.Y. Times,* Apr. 8, 1965. *Text of the President's Address on U.S. Policies in Viet Nam.*
10. *N.Y. Times,* Apr. 9, 1965.
11. *N.Y. Times,* Apr. 9, 1965.
12. *Christian Science Monitor,* Apr. 10, 1965.
13. *Ibid.*
14. *World Telegram and Sun,* Apr. 19, 1965, quoting the Associated Press.
15. *N.Y. World Telegram and Sun,* Apr. 21, 1965.
16. *N.Y. Times,* Mar. 29, 1965.
17. *N.Y. Times,* Apr. 19, 1965. Easter Message of Pope Paul.
18. "Text of Encyclical by Pope Paul Deploring Armed Conflicts," in *N.Y. Times,* May 1, 1965.
19. *U.N. Document, Provisional*: A/PV 1347, Oct. 4, 1965.
20. *N.Y. Times,* May 13, 1965
21. *N.Y. Times,* May 20, 1965.
22. *N.Y. Times,* March 17, 1966.
23. *N.Y. Times,* June 16, 1965; *Congressional Record,* June 16, 1965.
24. Aldo Moro again was authorized in February, 1966 to organize a new cabinet which again includes Fanfani as Foreign Minister.
25. *N.Y. Times,* May 9, 1965.
26. *N.Y. Times,* May 20, 1965.
27. *Tass* dispatch, dated May 21, 1965, released by the Tass News Agency.
28. *N.Y. Herald Tribune,* June 7, 1965. (N.Y. Times did not report President Johnson's speech on that occasion.)
29. *N.Y. Times,* June 9, 1965.
30. *U.S. News and World Report,* Feb. 28, 1966.
31. *Look,* February 22, 1966 "Why I quit China" by Morris Wills.
32. *Hsin Hua News Agency* Dispatches (Hong Kong edition) June 13, 1965.

CHAPTER XII

U. S. PEACE OFFENSIVE AND REACTIONS

To supplement the Christmas truce of 1965, the United States made an all-out effort to launch a peaceful settlement in Viet Nam. In order to more fully understand this peace offensive it is necessary to have a clear picture of the Christmas truce, its origin, the decisive factors, and the outcome.

1. *The Christmas Truce and Its Aftermath*

In the second week of December, 1965, the Viet Cong broadcast a statement that they would stop attacking for twelve hours during Christmas in South Viet Nam so that the native Christians could observe their holiday. The United States was skeptical about the proposal, thinking that it might be propaganda. The American Government waited for further clarification of the situation before it made a decision. Meanwhile, on Sunday, December 19, Pope Paul VI, while addressing 20,000 pilgrims in St. Peter's Square, appealed for a peaceful Christmas in the following words:

"We wish that at least—at least!—the proposal for a truce is accepted and put into effect so that Christmas may be for all a day of peace! We recommend this to the wisdom and hearts of the leaders responsible. We hope that after the truce will come reflection, then negotiation, then finally equilibrium, concord, and peace." [1]

The United States and South Viet Nam had been considering the Viet Cong proposal for a 12-hour suspension of hostilities, and the Pope's message for a Christmas truce may have helped in accepting a cessation of fighting for

Christmas Day. The decision and execution of the Christmas truce was left by the White House to the American Command in Viet Nam. On December 22, General William Westmoreland, the U. S. Commander in Viet Nam, directed that "U. S. forces will not fire at or on the enemy except in self defense" for 30 hours between Friday, December 24, at 6 p.m., and Saturday midnight, December 25, Saigon time. A similar announcement by the Vietnamese Commander said it was "in response to the call of the Pope for a truce during the Christmas holidays." This was accepted by the Viet Cong through radio announcements.

With a 30-hour Yuletide truce, Francis Cardinal Spellman was able to celebrate Mass for the servicemen in Da Nang and in a suburb of Saigon rather quietly. Bob Hope and other American motion picture stars and musicians entertained American servicemen and civilians in Viet Nam during the Holy Season, with little interruption from the war. According to *Associated Press* reports, dated December 26, 1965, however, the Viet Cong chopped up a U. S. Marine patrol on Christmas Day, during the cease-fire. One U. S. military spokesman declared that the truce was never really in effect. Although no major military operation occurred during that period, there was every indication of preparation for further fighting on the part of the Viet Cong. The same U. S. spokesman said that there were 84 significant Viet Cong violations of the truce. As a result of the Viet Cong military activities, the U. S. Command and the Vietnamese Command gave orders on Sunday morning, December 26, for full resumption of air and ground operations within South Viet Nam, although there was still a halt of bombing in the North. At this juncture, the *New York Times,* on December 26, had a front-page story headlined: "Viet Nam Truce is ended; Allies resume operations after Viet Cong attacks."

Pope Paul's peace plea has sometimes been misinterpreted. Some maintain that the Pope advocated peace at any price. Others said that the Pope was willing to make substantial concessions to the Viet Cong and other Communist nations. The Pope's Christmas message "to all men" clearly stated:

"Peace is in fact the first and chief good of any society. It is *based on justice, freedom and order;* it opens the way to every other value in human life . . .

"Fresh schemes, which the tragic experiences of the last war had given rise to, are now joined by old and deep-rooted nationalistic tendencies, *along with newer ideologies of subversion and domination* . . .

"No one ought to set about disturbing the peace of others by means of underhanded schemes and contrive disorder. No one *ought to force his neighbor* (and today we are all neighbors) *to resort to armed defense,* and no one ought to shirk just and sincere negotiation to restore order and friendship." (Italics added.)

Concerning a true foundation for peace, Pope Paul pointed out that religious freedom and freedom of conscience should be respected and safeguarded. He also declared:

"Peace needs to be built on a courageous revision of the inadequate ideology of egoism, strife and national superiority. Relationships between men will not be determined by power and force, nor simply by economic gain or the state of civic development, but by a higher concept of equality and solidarity, which in the long run, only the fatherliness of God, manifested in Christ, reveals as logical, easy and worthwhile."

The Pope also asked that religious freedom and freedom of conscience be respected and safeguarded. In his New Year's message to President Johnson, he asked the President "not to overlook any favorable occasion, however slight," to bring about peace in Viet Nam. On January 8, 1966, Robert D. Doty, reporting for the *New York Times* from Rome, explained why the Pope dispatched messages to both Communist and non-Communist leaders of the nations involved. The Pope said that his efforts were entirely independent from "the competitions of this world." This did not mean that the Pope or the Church he represents is indifferent to the errors of those ignorant of the "ambiguities of world values." But he pointed out that the Church keeps its distance from worldly concerns in order to be better able to "penetrate society . . . to put itself at the service of the common good, to offer to all its aid and 'its means of salvation.' "

Some writers and critics wonder why Pope Paul communicated directly with the authorities in Communist capitals of Moscow, Peking, and Hanoi, while his predecessors for more than a quarter of a century have been denouncing Communism. He did so only after referring to the Church's sensitivity to "errors," and "ambiguities" in modern values.

By this he meant to make it clear that he is not a "neutralist" when it comes to such important moral values as freedom, justice, and liberty. He pointed out that "even outside the generally accepted protocol forms, every time we believe that the Church can usefully bring to world leaders the weight of its moral authority for the maintenance and progress of a just peace among men and peoples . . ." it will do so. On Sunday, January 2, 1966, the Pope told an audience: "This is all we can do; it is very little indeed compared with the end to be achieved." On January 3, 1966, Pope Paul told Ambassador Goldberg of his satisfaction over "the truce in Viet Nam" since Christmas Eve.

Ho Chi Minh's reply to Pope Paul was broadcast by *Radio Hanoi* on December 29, 1965. His lengthy statement was mostly an accusation of "barbarity" and aggressiveness on the part of the United States. He charged:

"The U. S. leaders want war and not peace. The talks about unconditional negotiations made by the U. S. President are merely a maneuver to cover up his plan for war intensification and extension in Viet Nam."

Ho Chi Minh insisted that the United States must accept the four points demanded by the Hanoi Government in order to obtain peace.

On January 1, 1966, Pope Paul sent New Year's messages to the political leaders in Moscow, Peking, Hanoi, Saigon, and Washington, appealing for peace. In his message to Nikolai V. Podgorrny of the Soviet Union, the Pontiff asked him "to favor a just solution of the Viet Nam problem." In addressing Mao Tse-tung of Red China, the Pope appealed to him "in the hope that you will want in this painful crisis to help favor a just resolution safeguarding the independence of the country." In even more specific terms, the Pope told Mao that "an intervention on China's part would honor her in the eyes of humanity and would permit a hardtested people to resume in peace the work of reconstruction made impossible by the continuation of the war." To Ho Chi Minh in Hanoi, Pope Paul simply said: "We beseech all who are responsible to take no steps which could lead to the resumption of violent combat and bombardment."

To Nguyen Van Thieu, the Chief of State in Saigon, who is a Catholic, the Pope spoke of "the possibility of frank, serene negotiations marked by care for justice and charity to bring an equitable solution of the conflict while safeguarding the country's independence." The Holy Father simply asked

President Johnson to continue to seek for a just peace in Viet Nam. Yet despite the Pope's earnest efforts for peace, there was no indication from Hanoi, Peking, or Moscow, expressing willingness to enter into a discussion or negotiation for a settlement. On January 19-20, 1966, the *Associated Press* reported from Rome that the Pope had abandoned, for the time being, his efforts to end the conflict.

2. *U. S. Peace Offensive*

Never in the history of the United States has the American Government made so great an effort to seek for a peaceful settlement of an armed conflict. From the latter part of December, 1965, and continuing until the end of January and beyond, the Johnson Administration mobilized its highest diplomats, including Vice-President Hubert Humphrey, to travel all over the world urging a cease-fire in Viet Nam.

Arthur J. Goldberg, American Ambassador to the United Nations, was sent to Pope Paul, to the Italian President, Giuseppe Saragat, to Italy's Premier Moro, to the French President, Charles de Gaulle, and to the British Prime Minister, Harold Wilson. America's roving Ambassador, W. Averell Harriman, flew to Cairo, Belgrade, Teheran, Moscow, Tokyo, Manila, New Delhi, Canberra, Bangkok, and Saigon, to further the cause of President Johnson's peace offensive. Vice-President Humphrey was sent to Tokyo, Manila, and Taipei to explain to these capitals the sincerity of American peace efforts in Viet Nam. McGeorge Bundy, the Special Assistant for Security to President Johnson, was sent to Ottawa to convey his country's interest in a just peace to the Canadian Government. G. Mennen Williams, then Assistant Secretary of State for African Affairs, was sent to visit a number of African nations for the same purpose: explaining and promoting America's interest in obtaining a ceasefire. Thomas Mann went to Mexico and other Latin American countries for the same purpose.

On December 29, 1965, Moscow summoned Foy Kohler, the American Ambassador there, to an hour's meeting with Nickolai Podgorny, the new Soviet President. This was just a few hours after the Soviet Union announced that the Communist Party Secretary, Alexander Shelepin, would soon leave for Hanoi. This was Podgorny's second meeting with a member of the diplomatic corps since he became President on December 10, 1965. The other was with the dean of the diplomatic corps in Moscow, who also happens to be the Ambassador from Hanoi. Ambassador Kohler said that he had requested a meeting with the new Soviet President, but so had every other ambassador in Moscow. Little transpired at the meeting, although Kohler was told of the Soviet mission to Hanoi.

Upon the arrival of Shelepin, the Hanoi regime publicly acknowledged the aid given by the Soviet Union. He was accompanied by Soviet experts on anti-aircraft defense. The Soviet diplomat denounced the "United States aggression" in Viet Nam, counteracting U. S. hopes that Moscow might help to mediate the war. Peking denounced what it terms Soviet "double dealings" with Hanoi and Washington at the same time. Radio Peking and the Chinese press called Shelepin a "peace peddler," plotting to help the United States bring a temporary halt to the war, in order to escalate the war to North Viet Nam and possibly beyond its borders.

Shelepin praised the war aims of the Viet Cong, declaring that the Communist Party and the Soviet Union hold that the cause for which North Viet Nam is fighting is a righteous one. The Viet Cong, he said, will triumph and defeat the American imperialists. Similarly, Pham Van Dong, the Premier of the Hanoi regime, praised both the Soviet and Red Chinese aid to Hanoi. He declared that the American imperialists are stepping up the war of aggression against Viet Nam, and at the same time conducting a so-called "peace seeking" campaign in order to condition public opinion to extremely dangerous steps on the road of escalation.

Max Frankel, correspondent of the *New York Times,* reported from Washington on January 5, 1966:

"One of the most interesting but least apparent aspects of President Johnson's worldwide diplomatic campaign to demonstrate good faith on Viet Nam Policy has been its lack of appeal to his principal diplomat, Secretary of State Dean Rusk . . .

"It is the Secretary's awareness of the difficulties that appears to have made him chary of the risks, and one of the most rigid advocates of a more traditional diplomacy and an uncompromising posture toward aggression."

Senator Majority Leader Mike Mansfield acknowledged that negotiation at this time might not be satisfactory, but that it would be the best the United States could do in order to avoid a general war in Asia. In his report on Viet Nam, he concluded in these words:

"Negotiations at this time, if they do come about . . . would serve to stabilize a situation in which the majority of the population remains under nominal Government control but in which dominance of the countryside rests largely in the hands of the Viet Cong. What might eventually materialize through negotiations from this situation cannot be foreseen at this time with any degree of certainty . . .

"The visible alternative at this time and under present terms of reference is the indefinite expansion and intensification of the war which will require the continuous introduction of additional U. S. forces. The end to that course cannot be foreseen, either . . .

"The situation as it now appears, offers only the very slim prospect of a just settlement by negotiations or the alternative prospect of a continuance of the conflict in the direction of a general war on the Asian mainland." [2]

U. N. Ambassador Goldberg wrote to the U. N. Secretary-General and to all the members of the United Nations on January 4, 1966, informing them of U. S. peace objectives and efforts for Viet Nam. Ambassador Goldberg outlined the points in the American messages sent to various governments as follows:

i. The U. S. is prepared for "unconditional discussions" or using the Geneva Agreements of 1954 and 1962 as a basis for discussions.

ii. Reciprocal reduction of hostilities.

iii. Cease-fire.

iv. Gradual withdrawal of American forces from South Viet Nam as soon as the "external interference" ceases.

v. The U. S. does not desire to continue her military presence in South Viet Nam when the South Vietnamese can decide their own "political structure" through democratic processes.

vi. The "reunification of the two Viet Nams should be decided by the free decision of their two peoples."

The American Ambassador presented this as a matter of record as sincere indication of America's desire to collaborate unconditionally with every or all member states "in the search for an acceptable formula to restore peace and security to that area of the world." [3]

The Mansfield Mission was originated by Senator Mike Mansfield and supported by President Johnson. Other members of the mission were Edmund Muskie (D-Maine), Daniel Inouye (D-Hawaii), George Aiken (R-Vt.) and Caleb Boggs (R-Del.). They were assisted by aides from the State and Defense Departments. They visited France, Poland, Romania, the Soviet Union, and the Far East including Viet Nam.

The Mansfield report concluded that the situation in Viet Nam "offers only the very slim prospect of a just settlement by negotiations," and "no prospect of a rapid solution" to the conflict. It stated that the war has already expanded significantly into Laos and is beginning to lap over into the Cambodian border, while pressures are increasing in northeast Thailand. It also stated that "what might eventually materialize through negotiations from this situation cannot be foreseen at this time with any degree of certainty . . . there are no grounds for optimism that the end is likely to be reached within the confines of South Viet Nam or within the very near future." Vice-President Humphrey, in a television interview, said that the report was too pessimistic and that he did not share its conclusions.

3. Congressional Reactions

Senator Everett H. Dirksen of Illinois, the Minority Leader of the Senate, has supported President Johnson's policy in Viet Nam. The long halt in the bombing of military targets in North Viet Nam, however, caused Senator Dirksen to have misgivings about the wisdom of that policy. He told the press that when in April, 1951, General MacArthur said "there is no substitute for victory," he planted a phrase that is never to be forgotten. Dirksen said that the U. S. should achieve a complete victory before entering into peace negotiations. He thought that unless the Viet Cong lay down their arms, there will be no peace in South Viet Nam.

The Dirksen remark has been interpreted as indicating that he is preparing to join the House Republican leaders, Gerald Ford of Michigan and Melvin R. Laird of Wisconsin, in their repeated calls for intensified air attacks on North Viet Nam, and less investment of American ground forces in the war, in order to end the war more quickly and to save more American and South Vietnamese lives. Dirksen advocated the bombing of Hanoi, the blockading of

Haiphong, and the bombing of other military targets. He explained that Haiphong is the big port of entry for war supplies for the Viet Cong, and that since its shallow canal must be constantly dredged, it is highly vulnerable. He expressed the conviction that the blockade of Haiphong "is the just, proper and necessary thing to do." He later had misgivings about bombing Hanoi, fearing it might cause the Viet Cong to bomb Saigon. The Illinois Senator read a sentence from the Mansfield report: "It is considered by some that Saigon with its many vulnerabilities to sabotage and terrorism and Hanoi with its exposure to air attack are mutually hostages, one for the other." In response to questions, Dirksen said that he previously had simply wanted to "quarantine" the North Vietnamese harbors, but he did not propose bombing Hanoi.

In addition to Senator Dirksen's and Congressman Ford's criticism that the Johnson limited war effort in Viet Nam is insufficient, Barry Goldwater has said several times that President Johnson is doing what he advocated during the election campaign. He urged the bombing of Hanoi, Haiphong, and other military and industrial targets in North Viet Nam. Former Vice-President Nixon said that unless the Viet Cong withdrew their forces from South Viet Nam and let the South Vietnamese alone, the United States should not stop bombing the North and should not negotiate with the Viet Communists.

Congressman L. Mendel Rivers, Chairman of the House Armed Services Committee, and Senator Richard B. Russell, Chairman of the Senate Armed Forces Committee, have repeatedly advocated extension of U. S. bombing attacks on North Viet Nam. Both of them have appeared on television and radio programs, as well as in the press. They maintain that neither Hanoi nor Haiphong should be immune from bombing. They remain convinced that heavier bombing of those cities and military targets would bring the war to an end and thus reduce casualties. They concur with General Curtis B. LeMay, former Air Force Chief of Staff, who has advocated a substantial increase in the bombing of North Viet Nam. Congressman Rivers expressed himself in this way:

"It is folly to continue to let the port of Haiphong and military targets of Hanoi remain untouched and unscathed while war supplies being used against our troops are pouring into that port . . ."

Rivers also feels that the U. S. "can never hope to match

the Chinese and North Vietnamese man for man and it is ridiculous to pursue this policy." [4]

Reaction from Peking towards the American peace offensive was very critical. On January 5, 1966, the *People's Daily*, a Communist Party publication, denounced the movement: "How could the Johnson Administration fool the clear-sighted people with its tricks?" It asserted that Washington has been engaged in a "peace-talks hoax" as a prelude to expansion of the war, with the goal of an indefinite occupation of South Viet Nam. Hanoi followed the same line, adding that the U. S. peace offensive was "an attempt to appease public opinion at home and abroad."

Vice-President Hubert Humphrey asked Premier Eisaku Sato for "the help of Japan or any other government" in bringing about peace in Viet Nam. Pursuant to this request, the Japanese Government sent its Foreign Minister, Etsusaburo Shiina, to Moscow, ostensibly to sign an air accord with Soviet Russia. The Japanese diplomat revealed that he tried to urge the Soviet Union to use its influence on Hanoi to open diplomatic negotiations between Saigon and Washington. The Soviet Union reported that it maintained diplomatic aloofness from Vietnamese peace efforts, and declined to meet the Japanese request. Premier Sato told American Ambassador Edwin O. Reischauer in Tokyo that his government was concerned about the Viet Nam war, and asked whether or not the American Government could "continue the bombing pause in North Viet Nam," while Japan pursued her peace effort.

Although the United States was very patiently and persistently waiting for a positive sign from Hanoi for peace talks, U Thant, on January 20, 1966, maintained that "the political climate for negotiations today is more favorable than the political climate last year," and urged the United States to be more patient and more lenient towards the Hanoi regime. He then urged, for the first time, the inclusion of the Communist National Liberation Front in the reconstructed Saigon Government. He also urged that the Liberation Front, which is an arm of the Hanoi regime, be invited as a separate entity to participate at any peace negotiations. He described this as "the only sensible approach." Whenever U Thant makes a suggestion toward a settlement in Viet Nam, he always urges the United States to make great concessions to the Hanoi regime and to try to please the latter as much as possible. While he was discussing the Viet Nam question on this occasion, he again seemed to have forgotten that he is only the "Chief Administrative Officer of the United Nations." He repeatedly abuses his position with the United Nations when he urges such policy-making recommendations as admission of Red China into the United Nations. He wants Red China put on the Security Council, and wants Nationalist China put off. U Thant's own country of Burma is a police state, and has just expelled several hundred missionaries.

The dramatic American peace offensive in Viet Nam has both advantages and risks. On the positive side, the American Government can tell its people and those in other countries that the American move is sincere and earnest, and that the Government has done everything possible to seek for cease-fire talks with the Hanoi regime and other Communist governments. This is proof that it is the Communist bloc which does not want peace. By so doing, the American Government will certainly get more support from the American people and from allies on other continents. It also weakens the position of those critics who do not want America to win, or who are unwilling to face the facts.

The risks are numerous. The most obvious is a setback in the morale of the American forces, and even more the morale of the South Vietnamese forces. Similarly, the morale of the South Korean, Australian, and New Zealand forces have suffered considerably because they cannot see the necessity of continuing to fight if a cease-fire might come at any time. This is a parallel situation to the Chinese Nationalists fighting the Chinese Communists from 1944 to 1949 while "peace talks" were being conducted with the United States. The Chinese Communist forces knew perfectly well that a "cease-fire" and "peace talks" were for them an implement of war to defeat their enemies. But the Nationalist forces naively thought that there would be a truce. It is hoped that this sad lesson, inscribed in the pages of history with the blood of those who fought for freedom, will not be forgotten soon.

Hanoi is still badly in need of Peking's help, and the aid will be more easily forthcoming because they share the same borders. Hanoi is also seeking more Soviet aid, both economic and military. This does not mean that either Hanoi or Peking wants an all-out war with the United States. Both prefer to fight through others, and to wear down the United States while keeping a safe distance.

Two days after the Christmas truce, the Viet Cong *Liberation Radio* announced a four-day cease-fire in honor of the Chinese (lunar) New Year. The broadcast, addressed to the Saigon Government, said the cease-fire would last from midnight, January 19, until midnight, January 23, 1966. The Viet Cong took this initiative because they realized the traditional importance that had been attached for many centuries to this special season, and that the Vietnamese people would not want to fight during their celebrations. Meanwhile, Peking commented on President John's peace campaign in an article entitled "The Johnson's Administration's Gigantic Conspiracy." On January 7, 1966, *The People's Daily* declared:

"A gigantic fraud, a carefully planned conspiracy, is being feverishly enacted around the question of Viet Nam. Two cards have recently been played by the Johnson administration. The first is the 'pause in the bombing' of North Viet Nam, which has continued for many days running. The second is the '14 point' proposition allegedly made 'in the search for a peaceful settlement' of the Viet Nam question." [5]

Both Hanoi and Peking still believe that time is in their favor. They are confident that they can wear down the American people through anti-war demonstrations in America and through other left-wing propaganda, and finally force America to abandon the struggle. They also interpret the American peace offensive as a sign of weakness. To them it is a strong indication that the American people are eager to get out of Viet Nam on any sort of face-saving proposition. They also think that enough international pressure has been put on Washington to make her seek peace at any price. They exaggerate the role of such undistinguished and uninfluential senators as Wayne Morse of Oregon, Frank Church of Idaho, and Ernest Gruening of Alaska. They seriously overestimate the influence of Hans Morgenthau and Walter Lippmann, both of whom have lost considerable influence precisely because of their unsound positions on Viet Nam.

The people behind the Bamboo Curtain have no access to the real-life situation beyond their borders. Even their leaders are blinded by their self-imposed isolationism and their self-inflicted prejudices. The Communists feel it is to their advantage to wait for more favorable military conditions, not realizing that these will only get steadily worse for them.

During the truce for the Chinese New Year, in January, 1966, the Viet Cong made many attacks on unsuspecting troops. By official United States tabulation, the guerrillas mounted 45 attacks on South Vietnamese or other Allied forces, six against Vietnamese civilians, and 15 against gov-

240

ernment military units. Apparently under instructions from Washington, the spokesman tried to softpeddle the facts to the American public by calling them "clashes" instead of "violations."

It was revealed by Bill Moyer, the Presidential Press Secretary, on January 10, 1966, that an American representative delivered a message to Hanoi laying down the conditions for a cease-fire in Viet Nam. The message was delivered by an American officer in Rangoon, Burma, on December 29, 1965. The Hanoi Government did not refuse to accept the note, as it had in May, 1965, when a Canadian diplomat delivered the American message. The Ho Chi Minh regime never replied, however, nor did it ever acknowledge receipt of the note.

In spite of the obstacles created by the Communists, President Johnson, in his "State of the Union Message" on January 12, 1966, declared:

"In 1965 alone we had 300 private talks for peace in Viet Nam with friends and adversaries throughout the world.

"Since Christmas . . . for 20 days now we and our Vietnamese allies have dropped no bombs in North Viet Nam. . . .

"Able and experienced spokesmen have visited on behalf of America more than 40 countries. We have talked to more than a hundred Governments—all 113 that we have relations with and some that we don't. We've talked to the United Nations and we've called upon all of its members to make any contribution that they can towards helping obtain peace." [6]

4. America's 14 Points for Peace

Since Hanoi's terms for peace, as outlined in its "Four Points" described in the previous chapter, amount to the surrender of South Viet Nam, they are completely unacceptable. The United States, on January 7, 1966, made her official position on Viet Nam as clear as possible. As early as December 27, 1965, the *United States Information Service* had released partial conditions of the peace terms of the American Government. In a document issued by the White House on January 2, 1966, entitled "The Heart of the Matter in Viet Nam," these terms were reiterated. On the same day, the *New York Times* called them the "14 Points" of the

American Government on Viet Nam. On January 7, 1966, the State Department in a press release issued the following detailed peace terms:

"United States Official Position On Viet Nam"

"The following statements are on the public record about the elements which the United States believes can go into peace in Southeast Asia:

1. The Geneva Agreements of 1954 and 1962 are an adequate basis for peace in Southeast Asia;

2. We would welcome a conference on Southeast Asia or any part thereof;

3. We would welcome 'negotiations without pre-conditions' as the 17 Nations put it;

4. We would welcome 'unconditional discussions' as President Johnson put it;

5. A cessation of hostilities could be the first order of business at a conference or could be the subject of preliminary discussions;

6. Hanoi's four points could be discussed along with other points which others might wish to propose;

7. We want no United States bases in Southeast Asia;

8. We do not desire to retain United States troops in South Viet Nam after peace is assured;

9. We support free elections in South Viet Nam to give the South Vietnamese a government of their own choice;

10. The question of reunification of Viet Nam should be determined by the Vietnamese through their own free decision;

11. The countries of Southeast Asia can be non-aligned or neutral if that be their option;

12. We would much prefer to use our resources for the economic reconstruction of Southeast Asia than in war. If there is peace, North Viet Nam could participate in a regional effort to which we would be prepared to contribute at least one billion dollars;

13. The President has said 'the Viet Cong would not have difficulty being represented if for a moment Hanoi decided she wanted to cease aggression. I don't think that would be an insurmountable problem.'

14. We have said publicly and privately that we could stop the bombing of North Viet Nam as a step toward peace, although there has not been the slightest hint or

suggestion from the other side as to what they would do if the bombing stopped." [7]

The Chinese Communists in Peking did not even wait for the official issuance of America's 14 points before they denounced the American terms. The official issuance date of the American terms was January 7, Washington time. But *The People's Daily* in Peking, on January 7, 1966, Peking time, which is 13 hours ahead of Washington time, printed a full front page under the name, "Observer," denouncing the principles and detailed terms of these 14 points as one of the two cards being played by the Johnson Administration, the other being the pause in the bombing. The Chinese Communist attack consisted of 5600 words against the 14 points. Its substance is reported here briefly. Replied the Communists:

i. As to the first point relating to the Geneva Agreements of 1954 and 1962, the U.S. has already violated them: "A little analysis of the 14 points proves the U.S. has not a particle of good faith about returning to the Geneva Agreements as the 'basis'. Point one of the 14 points contradicts the other 13 points. The latter negate the former."

ii. Points two, three and four of the Johnson Administration would mean that they would use the Geneva Agreements as a basis for discussion, but other questions would be brought to the conference table, which means U.S. forces would continue to stay in Viet Nam.

iii. "Point five says 'a cessation of hostilities would be a suitable first order of business in any negotiation or discussion,' but it is the United States who is the aggressor in South Viet Nam; thus unless the United States withdraws from that area and ceases hostilities, there cannot be any negotiations or discussions."

iv. "Point six says 'Hanoi's four points could be discussed.' This is a gesture by the Johnson Administration to mislead peace. In fact, it is a sinister plot with ulterior motives."

v. Points seven, eight, nine, ten and eleven of the Johnson Administration sound as if the United States were "sincere and magnanimous," but "these are all empty promises." This is because the Administration has repeatedly said that "Hanoi should stop 'conquering' South Viet Nam . . ." and this "shows that the Johnson Administration is not prepared to withdraw its troops."

vi. Point twelve says that after peace should be restored the United States would be willing to contribute one billion dollars for the reconstruction and development of Southeast Asia. This sort of thing has long been called by the Vietnamese "the calculations of these stupid marauders." "Money could not succeed to buy the people in Viet Nam."

vii. Point thirteen says that "the Viet Cong would have no trouble having its views heard if Hanoi ended aggression to the South." But

". . . so long as U.S. imperialism does not change its policy of aggression against South Viet Nam and does not withdraw all its troops, the people in the South will never stop their just struggle. In these circumstances, it is an unalterable principle for the people in the North to help the people in the South."

viii. "The last point—fourteen—says: The United States 'could stop bombing the North if it could get an indication of what such a cessation would bring about.' Here we have the essence of the 14-points proposition. The so-called stop-the-bombing 'offer' is obvious blackmail."

In conclusion, *The People's Daily* in Peking wrote:

"Why is the Johnson Administration in such a hurry to sell its 14-point proposition?

"The United States now finds itself unable to win in South Viet Nam, but does not want to withdraw. At home, the antiwar movement is rapidly spreading among different sections of the people, and in ruling circles there is endless internal bickering. Abroad, the Johnson administration's policy of aggression against Viet Nam is under attack on all sides, and very few of its allies are willing to lend a helping hand.

"Both at home and abroad the Johnson administration is in dire straits. It is going through a most trying time.

"Beaten to pieces on the battlefield, it seeks a way out through its 'peace talks' swindle. Still seeking a way out when the swindle fails, it reverts to escalation of the war. For a year now, the Johnson administration has been oscillating back and forth in this blind alley. This has become its law of motion."

Finally this Communist Chinese paper quoted a statement

made by the Foreign Affairs Ministry in Hanoi on January 4, 1966, by saying that the United States Government "calls black white and poses as peace-lover to slander the Vietnamese people, and thus to create a pretext for taking new steps in the implementation of its scheme to intensify and expand the war."

Echoing the same tone of condemnation, the *Peking Review*, mouthpiece of the Peking regime, devoted much space on January 14, 1966, to its feature article, entitled: "The '14-point' Proposition: Johnson Administration's Big Conspiracy: Background and Objective of Washington's Much-Trumpeted 'Peace-offensive'." This article called the 14-points, a "Basket of Peace," a "Smokescreen," a "Hoax" and "Variation in Blackmail."

5. *Viet Nam and the State of the Union Message*

The question of Viet Nam occupied an important place in President Johnson's State of the Union Message to a joint session of Congress on January 12, 1966. Johnson stressed the fact that it is in order to preserve freedom that "the United States has had to defend Berlin, Korea, Cuba, and tonight, Viet Nam." He outlined American choices in Viet Nam by saying:

"We could leave, abandoning South Viet Nam to its attackers and to certain conquest—or we could stay and fight beside the people of South Viet Nam.

"We stayed, and we will stay until aggression has stopped.

"We will stay because a just nation cannot leave to the cruelty of its enemies a people who have staked their lives and independence on America's solemn pledge, a pledge which has grown through the commitments of three American Presidents.

"We will stay because in Asia, and around the world, are countries whose independence rests in large measure on confidence in America's word and in America's protection.

"To yield to force in Viet Nam would weaken that confidence, would undermine the independence of many lands, and would whet the appetite of aggression.

"We would have to fight in one land, and then fight in another or abandon much of Asia to the domination of the Communists. And we do not intend to abandon Asia to conquest." [8]

The general reception to the State of the Union message by the United States news media was favorable, although some publications maintained that Johnson's enticement to the Viet Cong was not enough. Some even urged suspension of the bombing of North Viet Nam indefinitely, an end to sending more troops to South Viet Nam, and above all, more favorable terms for North Viet Nam, including recognition of the Viet Cong.

The ranking Republicans of the Senate and the House on January 17, 1966, made their own "State of the Union" message in the historic old Supreme Court Chamber in the Capitol. Senator Everett Dirksen and House Minority Leader Gerald Ford expressed their views on foreign and domestic problems respectively. Senator Dirksen generally supported the Johnson policy in Viet Nam. He favored continuation of the policy of seeking peace while at the same time continuing the war, and intensifying it "as sound military judgment dictates." His radio-broadcast speech stressed the fact that "to retreat and get out would be deemed a confession that we are a paper tiger . . . to forsake our pledges would shatter confidence in us and further diminish our prestige."

Senator Dirksen urged that United States war-aims in Viet Nam be definite: "Let the objective be kept crystal clear at all times, and that is guaranteed freedom and independence for the Vietnamese." This was in line with what President Johnson had said in his speech: "We fight for the principle of self-determination—that the people of South Vietnam should be able to choose their own course, in free elections, without violence, terror and fear."

Senator Dirksen declared that "to negotiate from weakness would mean defeat before we ever reached the negotiation table. There is, after all, no substitute for victory," and "we will not embrace any settlement that fails to satisfy the above condition." Dirksen's comments on Viet Nam were mildly criticized by some members of Congress for their generalities, but President Johnson told the press that he was pleased with the Senator's comments.

Peking was not slow to attack President Johnson's State of the Union message. In a lengthy commentary broadcast by the *New China News Agency* (Hsin Hua) on January 13, Peking strongly denounced the current U.S. peace offensive in Viet Nam, accusing President Johnson of resorting to blackmail against the Chinese people "who have long since made preparations to deal with the American aggressor." The Peking broadcast, which was monitored in Tokyo, stated in part:

"Johnson's remarks show clearly that the U.S. Government's 'peace offensive' is nothing but a smokescreen spread to cover up its scheme for a wider war . . .

"Johnson's message sheds additional light on the true colors of the U.S. imperialist gangster. It is a glaring case that the United States, which is thousands of miles away, has launched intervention and aggression against South Viet Nam and extended the war to North Viet Nam . . .

"Johnson let loose his war blackmail against the Vietnamese people who are engaged in the heroic war of resistance to U.S. aggression and against the Chinese people who have long since made preparation to deal with the American aggressor. He said 'for others it must now be clear the choice is not between peace and victory. It lies between peace and the ravages of a conflict from which they can only lose.' " [9]

6. *Saigon's View on Peace Terms*

The government and people of the Republic of Viet Nam have been concerned since President Johnson announced his "unconditional discussions." Tran Van Do, the Vietnamese Foreign Minister, immediately distinguished between "discussion" and "negotiations." He said that the fighting forces in South Viet Nam should not negotiate until the situation became more favorable to South Viet Nam and less advantageous to the Communist aggressors. Prime Minister Nguyen Cao Ky of Saigon has repeatedly said that he would not sit down at a conference table with the Viet Cong. To do so would be to recognize them as a political entity separate from the North. This would not only do violence to the truth, as U.S. Undersecretary of State George Ball has pointed out, but would pave the way for a coalition government after the war.

On October 13, 1965, Nguyen Duy Lien, Permanent Observer of South Viet Nam to the United Nations, told the press that his country has to "bear the brunt of the aggression," and should be fully consulted prior to any cease-fire conference. He also stressed the fact that his country never signed the Geneva Agreements of 1954 and should not be required to observe their terms and suffer from aggression without defending itself, while the Hanoi regime has actually violated the provisions of these accords. The United States forces came to South Viet Nam, other than as advisors, only in 1965—about five years after North Viet Nam had intensified its subversion and aggression. South Viet Nam's Permanent Observer at the United Nations also laid down four conditions as peace terms for the settlement of the war in his country:

i. Subversive and military activities from Hanoi in South Viet Nam must cease. The Hanoi regime must dissolve all puppet organizations in the South and withdraw all its troops and its political and military cadres which have illegally entered South Viet Nam.

ii. South Viet Nam must be left alone to choose and shape for itself its own destiny in accordance with established democratic processes, without intervention from the outside.

iii. The United States and allied forces should remain in South Viet Nam temporarily, until order is restored there.

iv. The independence and liberty of the Vietnamese people must be effectively guaranteed.

Since the United States peace offensive started, Saigon reports have indicated that the morale of the people there has been affected. Rumors have spread that the United States might compromise with the Viet Cong at the expense of South Viet Nam. The Saigon Government disliked the all-out efforts to seek peace from Hanoi. The Vietnamese were dismayed at the long suspension of the bombing of military targets in the North, as they realized that this gave an opportunity to the Communists to recuperate, to obtain reinforcements, to repair means of communication, to add anti-aircraft equipment, and to make other military and political preparations. Premier Ky reportedly told Ambassador Lodge that if negotiations with Hanoi took place under such circumstances, his Government would not participate in the conference. Similar views were expressed to other high American officials in Saigon and in Washington by other leading Vietnamese officials.

Premier Ky told his country that until the Viet Cong abandon their subversion and aggression in South Viet Nam, there should be no negotiations.* Tran Van Do, the Foreign Minister in Saigon, repeatedly declared that under present conditions it would be inadvisable to seek peace from Hanoi. The South Vietnamese contend that they were not properly consulted about the outcome of the Viet Nam war prior to the American peace offensive, even though such an outcome

---

* At the Honolulu Conference, Prime Minister Ky publicly declared that he would not negotiate with the Viet Cong or the National Liberation Front.

would greatly affect their fate for centuries to come. That they resent not being told what the United States is planning in Viet Nam is well known.

Realizing that South Viet Nam is to be the most affected by what may be the outcome of the American peace offensive, and therefore is the most concerned, Secretary Dean Rusk and Ambassador W. Averell Harriman flew to Saigon on January 15, 1966, to talk with the leaders of the Saigon Government in order to ease their fear of peace at any price. Tran Van Do, Saigon's Foreign Minister declared:

> "There is only one way left. We have to fight, and fight hard. Our position remains the same. The Communists are the aggressors. If they really want to negotiate, if they really want this war to end, they must stop their aggression and withdraw their troops . . .
> "These are very reasonable conditions. The Allies could not have negotiated with the Germans in World War II while German troops remained on French soil." [10]

At the same time, Premier Ky made a speech at the closing ceremony of the Second Armed Forces Day Congress on January 15, 1966:

> "We have accepted and are grateful for the moral and material, military and economic assistance from the friendly countries. But never can we tolerate any interference harmful to our nation's sovereignty or any decision at variance with our people's aspirations . . . no other nation is qualified and able to decide our destiny, independent or our own will." [11]

It was reported in Saigon that on January 14 and 15, 1966, there was considerable army activity, and that Ky was threatened with a *coup d'etat* if he were to yield to American pressure to accept peace then. Dean Rusk assured Nguyen Van Thieu, the Chief of State of Viet Nam, Premier Ky, and Foreign Minister Tran Van Do that President Johnson's peace offensive would not mean "peace at any price and undercut the Saigon Government." According to reports, it was upon the insistence of Ambassador Lodge and General Westmoreland that Ambassador Harriman and Secretary of State Rusk came to Saigon, to ease the fears of the Vietnamese Government and its people. During their visit, the United States and South Viet Nam reconfirmed their readiness to "take all necessary military measures" against Communist aggression in South Viet Nam.

One of the most effective weapons Saigon has obtained from the United States was the joint communique issued by Prime Minister Ky and Secretary of State Rusk on Sunday, January 16, 1966. The communique was worked out with the assistance of Ambassadors Harriman and Lodge. This historic document is of great importance to the progress of war and peace in South Viet Nam. It merits quoting at length:

> "Secretary Rusk reiterated the firm determination of the United States to continue its full support for the Government of Viet Nam in its struggle against external aggression, as most recently re-stated by President Johnson in his State of the Union Message. The Prime Minister reaffirmed the unflinching resolve of the people and Government of the Republic of Viet Nam to pursue that struggle so that aggression would be brought to an end. Prime Minister Ky also emphasized his Government's deep concern with measures to improve the welfare of the South Vietnamese people, and Secretary Rusk made clear that the United States would do all in its power to assist in these efforts . . .
>
> "The Government of the Republic of Viet Nam once again reaffirms that peace in Viet Nam must:
>
> A. Accord with the pledges and desires of the Vietnamese people: an end to aggression, independence and liberty, in order to permit eventually unification of Viet Nam;
>
> B. Be accompanied by guarantees in the absence of which there could be resumption of aggression which would endanger both Southeast Asia and the peace of the world."

The communique declared at its conclusion:

> ". . . the Prime Minister and Secretary Rusk reviewed the extensive efforts made in capitals throughout the world to initiate steps toward a peaceful settlement of the conflict in Viet Nam. It was noted that there was at present no indication that North Viet Nam was prepared to take positive steps to peace.
>
> "The Prime Minister and Secretary Rusk agreed that the Vietnamese Government and its allies must continue to take all necessary measures, while remaining

alert to all proposals and initiatives that might lead to peace." [12]

This joint communique somewhat relaxed the concern over the differences between the American and Vietnamese Governments regarding the United States peace offensive. The Saigon Government feels that the time is not ripe for negotiations with Hanoi, since many of the villages in South Viet Nam are still in the hands of Hanoi. Saigon believes that negotiations cannot be conducted now to the advantage of South Viet Nam. Some of Saigon's officials feel that the American Government launched the "unconditional discussions" and "peace offensive" maneuvers, then used rather high-handed diplomacy to tell Saigon what to say and what to do. American officials maintain, however, that there have been constant consultations with Saigon at all times. Yet Tran Van Do, the Foreign Minister, declared that "the United States had not informed his ministry of the direct, although brief, contact between American and North Vietnamese representatives announced from the White House on January 10." [13]

The problem of communication and consultation is of great importance, lest South Viet Nam consider she has been treated as a "colony" or a "satellite."

7. U.S. at the Crossroads

Despite the U.S. peace offensive, there was no evidence that Hanoi, under strong pressure from Peking, was in any way willing to come to the conference table. Facing this dim prospect, President Johnson declared on January 20, 1966:

"The door of peace must be kept wide open for all who wish to avoid the scourge of war, but the door of aggression must be closed and be bolted if man himself is to survive.

"It seems clear that what is holding up peace in the world today is not the United States . . . What is holding up peace is the mistaken view on the part of the aggressors that the United States is going to give up our principles, that we will yield to pressure, or abandon our allies, or finally get tired and get out."

President Johnson reiterated that the United States wants "a peace with honor and with justice that will endure":

"On the day that the others decide to substitute reason for terror, when they will use the pen instead of the hand grenade, when they will replace rational logic for inflamatory invective, then on that very day, the journey toward peace can readily begin." [14]

On the following day, Secretary Rusk, after his return from Asia, told a news conference:

"The Christmas cease-fire was therefore extended, as far as the bombing was concerned, until now the suspension is in its 29th day. The question posed to the other side: 'Are you interested in peace?' is the same question which has been posed for months and indeed years by all available means.
"We have been waiting for some word from Hanoi that goes beyond bitter invective or charges that talk of peace is a trick or a deceit or a swindle. We have been listening to sounds of bombs and grenades and mortars in South Viet Nam. I regret that I cannot report to you any positive and encouraging response to the hopes of the overwhelming majority of mankind."

In reply to a question from the press, Secretary Rusk declared:

"The simple issue is the apparent determination of Hanoi to impose a political solution upon South Viet Nam by force. If they abandon that determination . . . adopt another policy, then many things could fall into line and peace could be readily established. But this is the heart of the matter." [15]

FOOTNOTES

CHAPTER XII: U. S. PEACE OFFENSIVE AND REACTIONS

1. *New York Times* and *New York Herald Tribune*, December 20, 1965.
2. Senators Mansfield, Impuye, Muskie, Aiken and Bogg's Report on *The Viet Nam Conflict: The Substance and the Shadow to the Senate Committee on Foreign Relations* (Washington, 1966) pp. 12-13.
3. *U.N. Document* S/7067, January 5, 1966.
4. *New York Times*, December 23, 1965.
5. Quoted in Chinese News Service, *Background on China* (New York, January 12, 1966).

6. *Congressional Record*, January 13, 1966.
7. This quotation is from the original *Press Release* issued by the State Department on January 7, 1966. The *New York Times* again on January 17 reprinted its version of the 14 points, which is in substance similar to that official version which is just quoted. This document was furnished by the Public Relations Department of the U.S. Mission to the United Nations.
8. *N.Y. Times*, January 13, 1966.
9. Quoted in Chinese News Service, *Background on China* (New York, January 14, 1966).
10. *Christian Science Monitor*, January 15, 1966.
11. *New York Journal-American*, January 15, 1966.
12. *Associated Press Dispatch*, Saigon, January 16, 1966.
13. *Christian Science Monitor*, January 20, 1966.
14. *New York Times*, January 21, 1966.
15. *New York Times*, January 22, 1966.

CHAPTER XIII

RESUMPTION OF BOMBING NORTH VIET NAM

—The Honolulu Conference and Its Aftermath—

The suspension of the bombing of North Viet Nam began with the 1965 Christmas Eve Truce. The 37 day suspension gave considerable military advantage to the Hanoi regime. General William Westmoreland, the U.S. Commander in South Viet Nam, Ambassador Henry Cabot Lodge, and other Americans in Southeast Asia urged the American Government to resume the bombing. The South Vietnamese Government became particularly impatient, as it saw the military strength of North Viet Nam increase considerably during the lull. When sufficient evidence had accumulated to indicate serious danger to the lives and security of South Viet Nam, President Johnson, on January 25, 1966, called the key members of Congress from both parties for a two-and-one-half hour conference at the White House.

The meeting was also attended by the Secretary of State, the Secretary of Defense, members of the Cabinet, and the Security Council. The Administration reported that during the long suspension of the bombing of North Viet Nam, the North Vietnamese Communists built up their military position in South Viet Nam, repaired the military roads, widened the Ho Chi Minh Trail, strengthened certain military installations, and increased military personnel. During the meeting most of the members of Congress were satisfied with the reports of the Administration and were "relaxed and confident" regarding the recommendations. Senators Fulbright and Mansfield, however, still favored "indefinite prolongation of the pause in bombings." Aerial photographs taken since the bombing halted on Christmas Eve, 1965, showed that where military trucks had previously moved only at night, they traveled in the daytime during the suspension of the bombing. There was evidence of infiltrators from Hanoi into Quant Tri Province, in the northern part of South Viet Nam.

Both President Johnson and his Secretary of State reported to the key members of Congress at the meeting that there was no indication Hanoi was willing to come to a conference table. Through all possible diplomatic sources, allied and neutral, official and private, Hanoi and Peking had done nothing but denounce the peace efforts. Moscow had also shown itself completely uncooperative, and kept on supplying approximately as much military aid to North Viet Nam as Peking did.

Both the Joint Chiefs of Staff and General Maxwell D. Taylor attended the White House meeting. It was reported that all the Joint Chiefs and the senior diplomatic advisers were in favor of a resumption of the bombing of North Viet Nam. General Taylor, the following day, pointed out "the obvious disadvantages" of the bombing lull. He felt that it had been justified for a time, but that continuation of it would serve no good purpose. Taylor stated that the United States had shown her friends and foes the sincerity of her peaceful purposes, and yet no favorable response had been received from the Communist camps. Admiral Arthur W. Radford, former chairman of the Joint Chiefs of Staff, suggested the blockade of all seaports supplying North Viet Nam. General Taylor advocated mining the harbor of Hanoi, a few weeks later.

In both Houses of Congress there still remained a minority who favored indefinite suspension of bombing any part of North Viet Nam. Seventy-six members of the House of Representatives signed a letter that was made public by the White House on January 22, 1966. The letter stated that despite the "continuing hostility and aggressiveness in Hanoi and an insistence on the abandonment of South Viet Nam to Communist take-over," the American Government would not abandon its peace efforts. President Johnson then quoted from his own letter to House Speaker John W. McCormack: "Whether the present effort is successful or not, our purpose of peace will be constant; we will continue to press on every door." He concluded his letter by stating:

"For a month we have held our hand in an important area of military action. But the infiltration of the aggressor's forces had continued, and so have his attacks on our allies and on our own men. I am sure you will agree that we have a heavy obligation not to add lightly to the dangers our troops must face. We must give them the support they need in fulfillment of the commitment so accurately stated in your letter: 'The determination of our Government to resist the terror and aggression which deny the people of South Viet Nam the right freely to determine their own future.' " [1]

Fifteen senators signed a letter to President Johnson asking him to extend the pause in bombing North Viet Nam's military targets. The senators were Eugene J. McCarthy of Minnesota, E. L. Bartlett of Alaska, Lee Metcalf of Montana, Vance Hartke of Indiana, Maurine B. Neuberger of Oregon, Frank Church of Idaho, Quentin N. Burdick of North Dakota, William Proxmire of Wisconsin, Stephen M. Young of Ohio, Ernest Gruening of Alaska, Joseph Clark of Pennsylvania, Wayne Morse of Oregon, Gaylord Nelson of Wisconsin, George McGovern of South Dakota, and Harrison Williams of New Jersey. Senator Frank Moss of Utah was in London and did not sign the letter, but he subscribed to its contents. The substance of the letter was to urge the President to think carefully before making his decision regarding the possible resumption of bombing the military targets of North Viet Nam. The letter urged the President to consult "collective judgment"—meaning Congress—before he made his decision.

President Johnson did not object to the exchange of opinions and discussions on Viet Nam, having been a member of Congress so long himself. He listened patiently and open-mindedly to arguments and criticism, yet avoided giving any impression to the enemy that congressional dissent was weakening his decisions in the conduct of diplomacy concerning the war.

For 37 days, because of internal and external pressures, the United States suspended bombing North Viet Nam. While the American Government was considering what to do next with the Hanoi regime, a great majority of the representatives and the majority of senators were in favor of supporting the Administration's policy to defend South Viet Nam against aggression from the North. According to a tally compiled January 31, 1966, by *U.S. News and World Report*, 272 members of Congress, including thirty-five senators and 237 representatives, thought the United States should fight to win in Viet Nam.

The President had more support from the House of Representatives than from the Senate. In the House, 76 of the congressmen simply raised minor questions as to the conduct of the Viet Nam war. In the Senate, the most severe critics were Senators William Fulbright, Wayne Morse, and Ernest Gruening. Besides Morse and Gruening, thirteen other senators wrote to President Johnson in a joint letter, on January 27, criticising the Administration's policy in Viet Nam. Senators Morse and Fulbright thought that the American Government had little or no legal right to be involved in a war in Southeast Asia. The President replied on January 28, 1966:

"I continue to be guided in these matters by the resolution of Congress approved on August 10, 1964—Public Law 86-408—by a vote of 504 to 2. My views of the present situation remain as stated in my recent reply to a group of members of the House, of which I enclose a copy." [2]

President Johnson's message to the House members said evidence indicated that there was

". . . only continuing hostility and aggressiveness in Hanoi, and an insistence on the abandonment of South Viet Nam to Communist takeover . . .

"Even though it is increasingly clear that we have had only a hostile response to the present pause in bombing North Viet Nam, you can be sure that our unflagging pursuit of peace will continue." [3]

1. *Hanoi's Rejection of the U. S. Peace Drive*

Ho Chi Minh's letter to the chiefs of some states and to others "interested in the Viet Nam situation," was monitored in Washington on January 28, 1966. It denounced the American threat and "aggression" in Viet Nam. The attack was a clear rejection of the American peace offensive. It especially mentioned the 14-points for peace presented by Washington as "an excuse for its war of aggression in South Viet Nam." This note insisted on the previous conditions laid down by Hanoi, but changed the order of precedence. Its tone was stern and definite. It demanded as prerequisite conditions for a cease-fire talk:

i. "If the United States really respects the Geneva

Agreements, she must withdraw all U.S. and satellite troops from South Viet Nam.

ii. "If the United States really wants peace, it must recognize the N.F.L.S.V. (National Front of Liberation in South Viet Nam) as the sole genuine representative of the People of South Viet Nam, and engage in negotiations with it.

iii. "If the United States really respects the right to self-determination of the people of South Viet Nam, it cannot but approve this correct program of the National Front of Liberation.

iv. "So long as the U.S. Army of aggression still remains on our soil, our people will resolutely fight against it. If the U.S. Government really wants a peaceful settlement, it must accept the four-point stand of the Democratic Republic of Viet Nam Government, and prove this by actual deeds."

The note from Ho Chi Minh also concluded that the United States

"must end unconditionally and for good all bombing raids and other war acts against the Democratic Republic of Viet Nam. Only in this way can a political solution to the Viet Nam problem be envisaged."

Hanoi rejected the peace offers of the United States, and Liu Shao-Chi, chairman of the "People's Republic of China," on January 30, 1966 (Peking time), after endorsing the Hanoi demands, declared:

"To whatever extent U.S. imperialism may expand its war and whatever may be the price we [Red China] have to pay, the 650 million Chinese people will stand by the fraternal Vietnamese people in a joint struggle to thoroughly defeat the U.S. aggressors." [4]

A few days later, on March 4, 1966, the *Reuters News Agency* reported that President Ho Chi Minh of North Viet Nam had rejected an Indian proposal for an Asian or African peace-keeping force in Viet Nam. President Sarvepalli Radhakrishnan of India had suggested that such a peace force would replace American troops in Viet Nam, but the

North Vietnamese President had turned down the suggestion.

2. *Resumption of Bombing North Viet Nam*

Since Hanoi and Peking had totally ignored the peace offers of the United States and taken this opportunity to strengthen their military build-up in South Viet Nam, there was no alternative for the United States but to take appropriate action to cope with this situation. On Monday morning, January 31, 1966, President Johnson solemnly addressed a press conference at the White House in these words:

"For 37 days no bombs fell on North Viet Nam. During that time we have made a most intense and determined effort to enlist the help and support of all the world in order to persuade the Government in Hanoi that peace is better than war, that talking is better than fighting, and that the road to peace is open . . .

"In these 37 days the efforts of our allies have been rebuffed. The efforts of neutral nations have come to nothing. We have sought without success to learn of any response to efforts made by the governments of Eastern Europe. There has been no answer to the enlightened efforts of the Vatican. Our own direct private approaches have all been in vain . . .

"It is therefore very plain that there is no readiness or willingness to talk. No readiness for peace in that regime today . . .

"In the light of the words and actions of the Government in Hanoi, for more than 37 days now, it is our clear duty to do what we can to limit these costs. So on this Monday morning in Viet Nam, at my direction, after complete and thorough consultation and agreement with the Government of South Viet Nam, United States aircraft have resumed action in North Viet Nam." [5]

While the United States resumed the aerial bombings in North Viet Nam, President Johnson instructed Ambassador Arthur J. Goldberg to ask the United Nations Security Council to call an immediate meeting. Ambassador Goldberg presented a resolution to the U. N. Security Council, stressing the following points:

a. To immediately call for a Security Council meeting without pre-conditions.

b. To seek for a cease-fire under effective supervision.

c. To provide arbitrators and mediators.

d. To call on all concerned for cooperation to implement this resolution.

e. To request the Secretary General to assist, as appropriate, in the implementation of this resolution.

When the United States resolution was submitted to the Security Council, it had a tepid reception. It was not put into the agenda at the first day's session. The Soviet and French delegates opposed including the resolution in the agenda. Finally, with the support of the delegate from Jordan, the U. S. resolution was adopted in the agenda, with the barely sufficient votes of nine of the fifteen members. But the search for discussion of peace in Viet Nam was kept "private and secret," for fear that open discussions might lead to "open clashes," which could be undesirable.

In spite of America's desire and readiness for a cease-fire through the efforts of the United Nations, both Hanoi and Peking denounced the American attempt to negotiate through the U. N. *Radio Hanoi* declared that any discussion or decision made by the United Nations concerning Viet Nam was invalid and improper. The only proper place for discussing Viet Nam, it said, was Geneva, and by enforcing the Geneva Agreements of 1954. Peking announced that the United Nations was now a tool of American imperialism, and that Peking would have nothing to do with it under those conditions.

The United Nations Security Council handled the Viet Nam issue as follows: After it was put on the agenda it was decided that there should be no formal discussion, but that only "informal and private consultations be held." Akira Matsui of Japan, as President for the month of February, 1966, arranged a number of informal and private meetings for the Council Members "both individually and collectively." However, in his letter to the Council Members on February 26, 1966, he reported to them that "some serious differences of views remain unresolved." Even without revealing the substantial differences among the 15 Council Members, Matsui stated that "on the procedural question at issue," some Members questioned "the wisdom of the Council" to consider the Viet Nam issue. Others disagreed. At least four Members: Bulgaria, France, Mali, and the Soviet Union chose not to participate in the consultations. The Council President maintained that he detected "a certain degree of common feeling among some Members of the Council," that they hoped "for the early cessation of hostilities and a peaceful solution of the Viet Nam problems," and that they hoped for negotiations "in order to work out the implementation of the Geneva Accords." The Council President concluded that "it would be inopportune for the Council to hold further debate or a formal meeting of the Council." [6]

In spite of the mild tone and contents of the Council President's letter to the Members, Bulgaria and the Soviet Union refused to accept the letter and marked it, "Return." This meant that these two nations did not want to reply to the Council President. Hence the Viet Nam issue has been at least temporarily shelved at the United Nations. Secretary-General U Thant, however, continues to work personally and secretly for a peace conference by urging all those concerned to give more concessions to North Viet Nam and Communist China.

3. *The Honolulu Conference and its Aftermath*

During the presidential press conference on February 4, 1966, President Johnson suddenly revealed his plan to meet with South Vietnamese leaders in Honolulu. The announcement was sensational.[7] He explained that he wanted to meet General Westmoreland, Ambassador Lodge, General Nguyen Van Thieu, the Chief of State of the Republic of Viet Nam, and General Nguyen Cao Ky, the Prime Minister. Much emphasis was placed at the conference on economic and social reforms in Viet Nam. It had long been alleged that American policy was failing to reach the native people, or to improve their living conditions. It was hoped that by stressing non-military reforms, the villagers would have a much better alternative to the Communist way of life. The non-military reforms were to concentrate on rural pacification and agricultural improvements, land reform, development of the villages, and the establishment of popular civilian government, both national and local. In addition to the Secretary of State, the Secretary of Defense, aides on security matters, Far East experts, and the Secretaries of Agriculture, and Health, Education and Welfare were included in the Presidential Mission.

President Johnson declared in his opening remarks on February 7:

"Our stand must be firm as ever . . .
"If we allow the Communists to win in Viet Nam, it

will become easier and more appetizing for them to take over other countries in other parts of the world. We will have to fight again in some place else—at what cost no one knows. That is why it is vitally important to every American family that we stop the Communists in South Viet Nam." [8]

Both the American and Vietnamese delegations comprised the highest officers of both countries. The American delegation included Dean Rusk, Secretary of State; Robert McNamara, Secretary of Defense; Orville L. Freeman, Secretary of Agriculture; General Earl G. Wheeler, Chairman of the Joint Chiefs of Staff; Henry Cabot Lodge, U.S. Ambassador to South Viet Nam; David E. Bell, Administrator of Agency for International Development; U. Alexis Johnson, Deputy Under-Secretary of State for Political Affairs; John W. Gardner, Secretary of Health, Education and Welfare; General Maxwell D. Taylor, Presidential Consultant on Southeast Asia; McGeorge Bundy, Special Assistant to the President on Security; Walt N. Rostow, Assistant Secretary of State; and Bill Moyer, Press Secretary.

The South Vietnamese delegation included Lt. General Nguyen Van Thieu, Chief of State; General Nguyen Cao Ky, the Prime Minister; Tran Van Do, Foreign Minister; Nguyen Ba Kha, Minister of Health; and Lt. General Nguyen Huu Co, the Minister of Defense.

On February 7, Premier Ky offered his pledges to the American delegation by saying:

"We pledge to cooperate with the United States and the Allied forces in South Viet Nam to continue to fight against the Communist aggression as long as necessary, to accept sacrifice and death as long as this war requires it.

"We pledge our determination not to surrender or to compromise with the Communists, whether in the North or South.

"We pledge to cooperate with you in the American quest for an *honorable* and *just* peace, and we pledge not to betray those valiant sons of America who have given their lives to this sacred cause.[9]

General Thieu expressed the plan of the Vietnamese Government to "build up a very solid democratic basis from the hamlet level up." Premier Ky also expressed his strong advocacy of social reforms and social improvements as well as other non-military remedies. The Joint Declaration and Communique issued by President Johnson and Nguyen Van Thieu, Chief of State, and Nguyen Cao Ky, the Premier of South Viet Nam, at Honolulu on February 8, 1966, definitely dramatized the commitments of the United States to help South Viet Nam. It also placed the emphasis on winning the war through a combination of military action and expanded civic reform programs. These documents are of great historic importance to the freedom of South Viet Nam and Southeast Asia, a solemn declaration of the mutual determination of both countries to check Communist aggression.

Part I of the Honolulu Declaration reaffirmed the commitments of both the Republic of Viet Nam and the United States.[10] Part II stated that the purposes of the Government of Viet Nam are "a government—indeed a generation —of revolutionary transformation." It also indicated that the Vietnamese people "are caught up in a mortal struggle." This struggle has four sides:

i. The defeat of the aggression directed by Hanoi through the Viet Cong or the "National Liberation Front" is "vital for the future of our people of South Viet Nam."

ii. The South Vietnamese and their Government must be dedicated to the eradication of social injustice among themselves, and must bring about a true social revolution and construct a modern society.

iii. There must be a stable, viable economy and a better life for the South Vietnamese people.

iv. There must be a true democracy for the people of South Viet Nam. There should be a free, independent, strong, and peaceful Viet Nam, with a democratic constitution. In its concluding paragraph, the South Vietnamese declaration stated that their effort means:

"To win the war of independence; to build while we fight; to reconstruct and develop our nation when terror ceases . . .
"Thus, we are fighting this war. It is a military war, a war for the hearts of our people. We cannot win one without winning the other. But the war for the hearts of the people is more than a military tactic. It is a moral principle. For this, we shall strive as we fight to bring about a true social revolution."

Part III, the Declaration by the United States, was divided into four parts:

(a) The United States reaffirmed the determined effort of the American armed forces now engaged in Viet Nam. It declared that the United States seeks no bases, no colonial presence, no alliance or alignment in South Viet Nam. "It aims simply to help a people and government who are determined to help themselves."

(b.) The United States pledged to support the principles of self determination, and the purpose of free elections proclaimed by South Viet Nam. It also pledged to give support to measures of social revolution there.

(c.) The United States will support South Viet Nam to stabilize its economy, to increase the production of food, to spread the light of education, to stamp out disease while they are fighting.

(d.) The United States will continue to seek for peace in Viet Nam and Southeast Asia, "which will permit the governments and peoples of the region to devote themselves to lifting the condition of man."

Part IV was "the Common Commitment," wherein the United States and South Viet Nam jointly pledged again:

Defense against aggression.

Work toward social revolution.

The goal of free self-government.

An attack on hunger, ignorance and disease.

An unending quest for peace.

Besides their declarations, a Joint Communique was also issued which expressed the views of the Chiefs of the Governments and their cabinet ministers. This Communique contained ten points:

(1) The results of three days of intense discussions and their fundamental accords have been expressed in the Declaration and the Joint Communique.

(2) Both the United States and South Viet Nam regretted "the total absence of a present interest in peace" on the part of the Hanoi regime. They reviewed the diplomatic situation in the United Nations and elsewhere, and "agreed upon continued diplomatic efforts for peace."

(3) Both the United States and South Viet Nam agreed to "take further concrete steps to combat inflation in Viet Nam."

(4) The United States pledged to give prompt support to the rural construction in South Viet Nam.

(5) Emphasis is to be placed on democracy in rural areas, the improvement of the livelihood of the people, and protection from disruption by the enemy.

(6) American agricultural experts were to be sent to South

Viet Nam to help the Vietnamese farmers improve and enlarge their agriculture there.

(7) American experts on education and health were to be sent to South Viet Nam to raise the standards of education and public health.

(8) The United States promised full support and assistance to the programs for the refugees in South Viet Nam.

(9) There shall be closer cooperation between the military forces of the Americans and the Vietnamese. Both are determined to respect the rights of innocent civilians and to adhere to the Geneva Convention of 1949 in the treatment of prisoners of war.

(10) Similar kinds of meetings, that is a meeting of the leaders of both countries, will be held in the future for the continued execution of the policies and purposes of the Honolulu Conference.

Shortly after the arrival of President Johnson at Los Angeles on February 8, he issued a statement on the Honolulu Conference:

"We went to Honolulu to meet the leaders of the Government of South Viet Nam. They and other people understand—and we understand—that the war we are helping them fight must be won on two fronts.

"One front is military. The other is the struggle against social injustice; against hunger, disease and ignorance, against political apathy and indifference." [11]

President Johnson pointed out that the South Vietnamese leaders admitted that their Government is "indeed a generation— of revolutionary transformation."

During and subsequent to the Honolulu Conference, Chief of State Thieu and Premier Ky were adamantly opposed to any talks with the Viet Cong as such. They made it clear that they would not negotiate with the "National Liberation Front," except as part and parcel of North Viet Nam. Both of them so declared in unmistakable terms at a press conference in Honolulu on February 8, at the close of the conference. When Premier Ky was asked about the Liberation Front, he replied: "It is the National Enslavement Front." The national Liberation Front, he said, is made up of "criminals and assassins." He made it clear, however, that he was willing to talk with Hanoi, and to cooperate with U. S. peace efforts. President Johnson also announced at the end of the Conference that he would send Vice-President

Hubert Humphrey and several other American officials to South Viet Nam in order to implement the decisions of the Honolulu Conference.

Even before the Honolulu Conference began, both Peking and Hanoi denounced it. On February 6, both *Radio Peking* and *Radio Hanoi* said that "the gathering in Honolulu of American and South Vietnamese leaders was a proof that the United States was facing difficulties in Viet Nam." They stated that the United States has been isolated from the other nations. *Nhan Dan*, the official organ of the Viet Communist party, asserted that the conference was called "to cope with repeated and heavy defeats suffered by the United States," both militarily and politically.

The *Hsin Hua News Agency* and the *Peking Review* stated in Peking that the United States was preparing to escalate the war in Southeast Asia and possibly in China. It denounced the conference, calling it a result of the failure of both the American peace offensive and American military policy. The press and radio of Peking and Hanoi became even more violent at the conclusion of the Honolulu Conference, denouncing the declaration and communique, calling them further steps of the American imperialist escalation of the war in East Asia.

4. *Senate Foreign Relations Committee Hearings*

A few senators who were opposed to the resumption of the bombing of the North Vietnamese communication lines and military targets endeavored to use both the Senate floor and the Senate Foreign Relations Committee as forums to influence the public against the Johnson policy. They also hoped to hold up the budget which President Johnson had asked for foreign aid, and especially for Viet Nam. Senator Fulbright, the chairman of the Committee on Foreign Relations, insisted on an extended and critical hearing of the administration's policy. Senator Wayne Morse, the most severe and unorthodox critic of all, tried to rescind the Congressional resolution of August 10, 1964. It had been adopted then with only two dissenting votes, one of them his. That was the measure which authorized the President to take "all necessary measures to prevent aggression in Viet Nam and Southeast Asia." Everyone including Senator Morse knew that his policy of harassment had no hope whatsoever of adoption. Apparently he wanted to embarrass the President, but there is an old saying in politics that if you throw enough mud you will end up scraping it off yourself.

Senator Fulbright wanted Robert McNamara, the Secretary of Defense, to testify at the public hearings of the Foreign Relations Committee, but the Secretary felt that a public hearing might jeopardize the nation's security.

After the American resumption of bombing of North Viet Nam on January 31, 1966, and during the Honolulu Conference, February 6 to 8, as well as subsequently, Senator Fulbright intensified the hearings on Viet Nam. A statement was given by Lt. General James M. Gavin, (retired) who was critical of American strategy in Viet Nam. He wrote a letter to *Harper's* magazine, published in February, 1966, in which he outlined a new policy for Viet Nam. His views against United States policy in Viet Nam were widely publicized. Gavin urged a permanent end to the bombing, the withdrawal of American forces to coastal enclaves, and mediation of the war by the United Nations.

Gavin's theory received such publicity and caused such agitation by various "peace groups" supporting him that the Chiefs of Staff could not maintain silence. General Earl G. Wheeler, the Chairman of the Joint Chiefs, found six points in the Gavin article "worthy of comment" and repudiated all of them, when he testified at the Senate Hearings on military budgets.[12] In the first place, he pointed out, General Gavin had implied that France had had the same objectives as the United States now had in Viet Nam. "This is not so," said General Wheeler, "France had colonial objectives, and the issue was whether or not the Vietnamese would get their freedom from France. The issue now is whether the Vietnamese can remain free." Gavin had written that the American forces are "endeavoring to secure the entire country from the Viet Cong." Again Wheeler commented: "This is not so." He said that our objective is to defeat both the Viet Cong units and the North Vietnamese forces that have invaded the country. He pointed out that this was primarily a police-type action, and that we need to assist the Vietnamese in establishing security for the population so that they can maintain a free government.

Discussing the proposal to stop bombing North Viet Nam, General Wheeler said that the purpose of the aerial attacks was to reduce the availability of men and material which could be moved to the South, and by attacking the lines of communications to reduce the capability of the North Vietnamese to move men and supplies within their own country and from the North to the South. He stated that the bombing of North Viet Nam, the presence of the United States troops in South Viet Nam, and the possibility of a future ultimate troop withdrawal were "three blue chips" for negotiation of the war. He added, "If you stop bombing North Viet Nam, in effect you throw one of your blue chips over your shoulder."

General Gavin had proposed that the United States forces withdraw into several bases or "enclaves". General Wheeler said this would surrender the initiative to the enemy and would surrender the rest of the country as well, since the result would be to give South Viet Nam to the North Vietnamese.

Gavin had proposed that, having suspended bombing and having withdrawn to the enclaves, we should then seek negotiations in the United Nations or another Geneva Conference. General Wheeler suggested that if Gavin's first two steps were undertaken, namely, stopping the bombing and withdrawing to enclaves, there would be little point in negotiations, as the country would have already been surrendered before the negotiations were started. Under these circumstances there would be no pressure on the North Vietnamese to negotiate.

Another suggestion made by General Gavin was that the United States might hold the Kra peninsula, which includes Malaya and Singapore, and also defend Thailand the Philippines. If the United States turned South Viet Nam over to North Viet Nam, said General Wheeler, no one could expect the Malaysians, the Thailanders, or the Filipinos to be enthusiastic about being engaged in a defense activity on their soil and with their assistance. General Wheeler also declared that "if we lose this war, which we do not have to lose, we will have more wars of national liberation to face up to, with the prospect of greater losses under less favorable circumstances.

As an indirect reply to General Gavin's enclave theory, General Maxwell Taylor, former Chairman of the Joint Chiefs of Staff and former Ambassador at Saigon, criticized Gavin's theory as "acceptance of a crushing defeat of international proportions." It would be a vindication, he said, of the Communist policy of wars of liberation. Senator Fulbright insisted on bringing the views of General Gavin before the whole country and most of the world, in spite of the fact that the Gavin theory had been unanimously repudiated by the Joint Chiefs of Staff, as Defense Secretary McNamara had revealed to the press.

Since Gavin had already been retired from the army for almost eight years, his information and understanding of the military situation in Viet Nam could not compare with that of the chiefs of staff, with their intimate knowledge and experience of the present war, and the comparable strength of the allied forces and that of the enemy. Gavin had very little knowledge or experience in the Far East. His enclave theory was practiced by the French forces to a great extent in Indo-China during and before their defeat at Dien Bien Phu. Right after World War II, the Chinese Nationalist forces held most of the coastal cities and towns, which were their "enclaves," but which they were forced to abandon to the Chinese Communists in 1948 and 1949. General Gavin might well read the military history of the French from 1951 to 1954, and that of the Chinese Nationalists from 1946 to 1949. He might also have given some thought to the Maginot Line and its collapse.

General Matthew B. Ridgway, (retired) former U. S. Commander in Korea, wrote an article in *Look* magazine, on April 5, 1966, giving conditional endorsement to Gavin's "enclave theory." But Ridgway did not want to pull out of Viet Nam. He emphatically rejected the two extreme courses —"Pullout" or "All-out war." He also advocated giving full support to the President's determined efforts to fulfill the American pledges and treaty obligations. He did nevertheless favor a "Stand Fast" cause in Viet Nam.

As a supplement to Gavin's theory, George F. Kennan, former United States Ambassador to Moscow and Belgrade, told the Senate Foreign Relations Committee on February 10 that the United States should adopt "a dig in" theory and await talks with the enemy. There is no basic difference between Gavin's "enclave theory" and Kennan's "dig in" theory. Both entail surrendering most of the country, and then standing still and waiting for negotiations.

In his testimony, Kennan presented several points, primarily the following:

i. "Viet Nam is not a region of major industrial-military importance," and the United States should not be involved in Viet Nam.[13]

From this one can conclude that only highly industrialized and militarily important places should be defended, that all other regions are not important and could be given up to Communists or other aggressors. He also seemed oblivious of the various commitments made by the United States through her presidents and government spokesmen, as well as through her mutual defense treaties, such as NATO,

SEATO, and the Congressional Resolution of August 10, 1964, on Viet Nam.

ii. Kennan expressed the opinion that

"there is every likelihood a Communist regime in South Viet Nam would follow a fairly independent course. There is no reason to expect that such a regime would find it either necessary or desirable, in present circumstances, to function simply as a passive puppet and instrument of Chinese power."

This means that Ho Chi Minh or his successor would become another Tito. If it had been possible for Tito to act with some minor degree of independence of Moscow, it has been partially because he is so isolated geographically from the Soviet Union. But Viet Nam is adjacent to Red China. The geographical propinquity and cultural and racial similarity of Viet Nam would make it extremely difficult for a Communist regime in Hanoi or Saigon to act differently from the Peking line of thinking and action.

iii. Kennan considered that American involvement in Viet Nam is "unfortunate," and he advocated that the United States "liquidate this involvement just as soon as this can be done, without inordinate damage to our own prestige or to the stability of conditions in that area."

He seemed oblivious of the fact that American involvement in Viet Nam is not of its own volition, but that it was forced upon Washington by the North Vietnamese Communists themselves. If the United States does not defend Viet Nam, she will soon find herself involved elsewhere, perhaps on a larger scale.

iv. Kennan said he hoped that the United States would restrict her "military operations in Viet Nam to the minimum necessary to assure the security" of American forces. He also advocated that the United States "continue to pursue vigorously and consistently the quest for such resolution," even if this involves some moderation of American "stated objectives." It all sounded like a scholar's description of compromise, appeasement, and capitulation.

v. Continued Kennan: "Nor do I understand the argument that our allies will lose confidence in us if we fail to press forward aggressively in Viet Nam."

Since Kennan has no experience in Southeast Asia, it might be difficult for him to understand, but he should be able to comprehend the basic psychology of the people in that area. Either South Viet Nam will win the war and remain free, or lose the war and be taken over by the Communists. The deciding factor is whether or not Washington keeps her commitment. With due respect for Kennan's experience as a diplomat, his judgment on Viet Nam is far from accurate, and his suggestions would lead to a hopeless situation.

General Maxwell D. Taylor testified on February 17, 1966, before the Senate Foreign Relations Committee, that in the Viet Nam war the United States has a limited objective. He strongly emphasized the fact that the American forces do not intend to destroy the regime in Hanoi, or to occupy North Viet Nam. He assured the Committee that the United States simply wants to attack the "main line enemy units." He also indicated that the United States hopes to preserve the freedom of the Vietnamese to choose their own form of government in a fair and internationally supervised election after a stable peace has been established. He summarized his own testimony by saying:

a. "A simple statement of what we are doing in South Viet Nam is to say that we are engaged in a clash of purpose and interest with the militant wing of the Communist movement represented by Hanoi, the Viet Cong and Peking . . ."

b. As to how the United States is doing in Viet Nam, Taylor said that the immediate American aim is to fight a limited war to protect and safeguard the people in South Viet Nam, who are the real target of the enemy.

c. Regarding ways to improve the war efforts in Viet Nam, Taylor said:

". . . the Hanoi leadership is not yet convinced that it must mend its ways. Perhaps they still hope for some kind of military victory in the South. Certainly they are not convinced that in some way the United States cannot be detached from the support of South Viet Nam.

". . . They have not forgotten that the Viet Minh won

more in Paris than in Dien Bien Phu, and believe that the Viet Cong may be as fortunate in Washington." [14]

Taylor outlined the American strategy in Viet Nam in the following concise terms:

"In summary then, our strategy consists of a complex but coherent package of measures designed to improve the effectiveness of our forces on the ground in South Viet Nam, to exploit our air superiority by attacking military targets in North Viet Nam, to stabilize the political, social and economic systems in South Viet Nam, and to seek an honorable negotiated statement of the conflict." [15]

During the question period, when Senator Fulbright asked General Taylor what he meant when he said the Viet Minh won more in Paris in 1954 than in Dien Bien Phu, the general replied:

"It was the weakening will (of the French) to continue the conflict which had been growing over the months and years and the fact that the home front and political front had reached the conclusion that the struggle was hopeless, and hence they must end it very rapidly." [16]

When Senator Fulbright further questioned General Taylor, asking him if he did not consider Dien Bien Phu a decisive battle, General Taylor answered, "It was in a sense; it tilted the scale of decision, but actually the French had strong military forces which were not involved at Dien Bien Phu at all and could have continued the conflict."

Senator Wayne Morse remarked: "It isn't going to be too long before the American people as a people will repudiate our war in Southeast Asia," to which General Taylor replied, "that, of course, is good news to Hanoi, Senator."

Senator Russell Long, the Democratic whip in the Senate debate, remarked:

"Speeches on the floor of the Senate and on television advocating that our boys not fight for their country and that the people back off from the effort to help their country . . . do nothing but encourage the Communists to prolong the war." [17]

The critics of the Administration justified their debates and hearings, however, on the ground that the aims and conduct of the war in Viet Nam will be clarified by discussion, and that this will outweight any injurious effect that the criticisms might have on the war.

5. Robert Kennedy's Proposal for a Coalition Government

Senator Robert F. Kennedy made a televised statement on Viet Nam on Saturday, February 19, which became very controversial and which had far reaching repercussions on both domestic politics and foreign relations. He presented his views at a press conference of his own, after the Senate had already conducted six days of intensive hearings:

> "Whatever the exact status of the National Liberation Front—puppet or partly independent—any negotiated settlement must accept the fact that there are discontented elements in South Viet Nam, Communist and non-Communist, who desire to change the existing political and economic system of the country." [18]

Senator Robert Kennedy forgets that the "National Liberation Front" was organized entirely by Hanoi in 1960, and that it is the political and military arm of the Communists in North Viet Nam. It is merely a Communist "front," and is so called by the Communists themselves. There was nothing spontaneous or indigenous about it. To refer to it as a "discontented element" is grossly misleading. Yet Senator Kennedy suggested that the best thing for the United States to do would be to deal with the "Liberation Front," i.e., the Viet Cong, in this way:

> ". . . to admit them to a share of power and responsibility . . . is at the heart of the hope for a negotiated settlement. It is not the easy way or the sure way; nor can the manner or the degree of participation now be described with any precision." [19]

Senator Kennedy added that the United States ". . . must be willing to face the uncertainties of election, and the possibility of an eventual vote on reunification." Senator Kennedy's remarks were highly praised by the left-of-center press media. His proposal to offer the Liberation Front a role in South Viet Nam was immediately and severely criticized by

George W. Ball, Under-Secretary of State; McGeorge Bundy, Special Assistant to the President for National Security Affairs; Senator George D. Aiken of Vermont, and many others. They pointed out that he was giving in to aggression, and sacrificing the rights of the allies. Perhaps the most forceful critic of the Kennedy proposal was Vice-President Hubert Humphrey, long a liberal Democratic leader. Humphrey was in Wellington, New Zealand, when Kennedy made his remarks. On February 21, 1966, at Wellington, Humphrey described Kennedy's suggestion for a coalition government in Saigon as "a prescription for the ills of South Viet Nam which includes a dose of arsenic."

Humphrey commented that recognizing the Viet Cong "would not bring about a settlement that would result in establishment or continuity of a democratic government." He further said that coalition governments of the past have been "either paralyzed or taken over by the Communists working from within." He compared the inclusion of the Viet Cong in the South Vietnamese Government as "a fox in a chicken coop; soon there wouldn't be any chickens left." In summing up his criticism of Kennedy's suggestion, Humphrey said that to suggest that the Viet Cong be included in the South Vietnamese Government would mean "to impose on them the very forces that have been destroying them." Vice-President Humphrey shared his press interview with Keith J. Holyoake, Prime Minister of New Zealand, who described the Viet Cong as "law-breakers."

Premier Ky also criticized Kennedy's proposal as soon as he heard about it:

> "I think now is too soon to begin the campaign (meaning the American Presidential election). It is not good if you use the destiny of 20 million people as an issue in the campaign . . ." [20]

Premier Ky said he intended to write to Senator Kennedy himself, giving him the true picture of Viet Nam so that he would not be confused. On February 21, two days after the Kennedy proposal, a *New York Times* correspondent, E. W. Kenworthy, interviewed Senator Fulbright, who "backed Kennedy on a role for the Viet Cong." Fulbright told the reporter that since the Viet Cong "are mounting the principal military effort" on the Communist side, the National Liberation Front "must be one of the principal parties" at the bargaining table. This viewpoint of Fulbright is not as surprising as it sounds. Fulbright had previously held such a theory. He was pleased, therefore, to express his support.

The *New York Times* on February 22, 1966, printed a lengthy editorial entitled "Coalition in Viet Nam." The editorial insisted that the situation:

> ". . . requires acceptance of Viet Cong participation both in negotiations and in the future political life of South Viet Nam. . . . In the absence of a leader capable of forming a neutral administration, such a government in Saigon will have to include all the main factions: the South Vietnamese Army, the Viet Cong, the Buddhists, the Catholics, the Cao Dai, and other elements . . . there is no basis for the widespread assumption that a coalition government inevitably means a Communist takeover."

Yet on the front page of the *New York Times* for the same day, Under-Secretary of State George Ball is quoted as saying, in regard to a coalition government: "What we would have would be, only in a very short time, a Communist Government in Saigon." Ball merits confidence much more than an unnamed editorial writer of the *Times*. In complete disagreement with the *Times*' editorial, C. L. Sulzberger wrote in the *Times* three days later, February 25, 1966, on the editorial page:

> "Senator R. Kennedy proposes Communists be included in the Saigon Government. It would be more honest to suggest abandoning Viet Nam without even bothering to negotiate."

Sulzberger, who is a cousin to the publisher of the *New York Times,* went on to say:

> "There has been thought among strategists who don't understand what 'revolutionary warfare' is all about that we might stay in South Viet Nam—but restrict our troops to limited enclaves. This is even more naive than France's hope of squashing Germany by sitting on the Maginot Line."

He went on to quote George Kennan:

> "We should show ourselves a little more relaxed and less terrified of what happens in the smaller countries of

Asia and Africa, and not jump around like an elephant frightened by a mouse . . ."

To which Sulzberger replied:

"I would scarcely consider the menace of expanding Chinese dynamism as mouselike. . . .

"The totem of Johnson's liberal opponents is Lippman, whose pronouncements from the ivory-towered eminence of a public philosopher carry particular authority. On May 19, 1933, after reading a speech by Chancellor Hitler, Lippmann advised: 'We have heard once more . . . the authentic voice of a genuinely civilized people. I am not only willing to believe that, but it seems to me that all historical experience compels one to believe it.'

"Lippmann already knew Europe and German well, so there was a basis for such lucid reassuring prescience. He knows Asia little, and Viet Nam not at all. His jungle stories parable comparing Chinese and American power to an elephant and a whale is pleasant nonsense. Were the Southeast Asian peninsula to fall under Chinese suzerainty, as Lippmann seems almost to recommend, island Indonesia would patently go along. Australia and the Philippines would be directly menaced.

"One must only hope the counsel President Johnson receives in private is superior to that he gets in public. Senator Gruening suggests no draftees should be sent to Viet Nam—as if to make certain we ape France's Indo-China disaster in detail.

"What has emerged so far in our Great Debate is a deep-seated doubt about ourselves and deep-seated ignorance of the world we inhabit. Elegant platitudes found on myth are offered to the President as substitutes for policy.

"There is an old Chinese adage: 'If you know yourself and know your enemy, in 100 battles you will win 100 times.' We don't know ourselves very well and it is questionable whether we know our enemy at all."

Vice-President Humphrey said of the Kennedy proposal:

"I am not going to be any part of suggesting to the South Vietnamese or any government that you should reward the kind of banditry and murder which has characterized the Viet Cong by giving it legitimacy in a position of government. I just don't believe it." [21]

There is no room for compromise with wrongdoing. Either a person must resist it, or capitulate. This is the point Senator Robert Kennedy missed entirely when he said:

"I think that statements that are made that we will never deal with assassins or murderers make it difficult for them [Viet Cong] to believe that they are being asked to come to the negotiating table for anything other than to surrender."

It is not necessary for North Viet Nam to surrender, or to come to the negotiating table at all. All the North has to do is to quit its aggression.

Senator Robert Kennedy later declared that he favored only recognition of the Viet Cong until an election is held. But recognition of a Communist party almost invariably leads to a coalition government and a subsequent Communist takeover. That is why Premier Ky delcared in a TV interview in Honolulu that if the Viet Cong are to be recognized, South Viet Nam should stop fighting now, that the war to defend his country would be fought in vain. As far back as 1954, Senator John F. Kennedy had said that a coalition government is "like trying to ride a tiger." However, Senator Edward M. Kennedy has said that he agrees with Senator Robert Kennedy's position.

6. *The Humphrey Mission to East Asia*

On his return to Los Angeles, on February 8, 1966, President Johnson told the press: "I come back to the mainland refreshed and confident." In addition to praising the South Vietnamese leaders as brave and determined young men, he went on to say:

"The road ahead may be long and difficult. But we shall fight the battle against aggression in Viet Nam; we shall fight the battle for social construction; and throughout the world we shall fight the battle for peace. And we shall prevail." [22]

The President stopped over in Los Angeles in order to confer with Vice-President Humphrey, whom he instructed to visit Viet Nam and other Asian countries. The Vice-President's mission was announced just before the Honolulu Conference came to an end. Humphrey's first conferences were with the South Vietnamese leaders who travelled with him from Honolulu to Saigon. After leaving Viet Nam he visited Thailand, Laos, India, Pakistan, the Philippines, Australia, New Zealand, Japan and South Korea.

While in Saigon, Vice-President Humphrey and Secretary of Agriculture Orville L. Freeman, together with other agricultural experts, visited villages and military centers. His visit to South Viet Nam has strengthened the morale of the government and the people. In Bangkok, Humphrey acquired a new understanding of Thailand's fear of the threat of Communist infiltration and subversion. In Manila, he learned that the Philippine Government was about to send an engineering battalion of 2,000 men to South Viet Nam. In Seoul, he learned that the South Korean Government was ready to send another 20,000 crack troops. In both Australia and New Zealand he found the governments ready to increase their military and technical aid to South Viet Nam. The nations he visited, and some which he omitted visiting, were relieved to learn from Vice-President Humphrey that the United States rests firm in her commitments, and is determined to continue her stand against aggression.

Upon his return to the United States, Vice-President Humphrey expressed renewed confidence over the outcome of the war in South Viet Nam.[23] This was clearly demonstrated during his briefing to some 200 congressional leaders in the East Room of the White House on February 23, after returning from his trip.

Concerning the Great Debate and all its ramifications, President Johnson delcared, when it was about over:

"In these last days there have been questions about what we're doing in Viet Nam, and these questions have been answered loudly and clearly for every citizen to see and to hear. The strength of America can never be sapped by discussion, and we have no better nor stronger tradition than open debate—free debate in hours of danger. We believe with Macauley that men are never so likely to settle a question rightly as when they discuss it freely.

"We are united in our commitment to free discussion. So also we're united in our determination that no foe anywhere should ever mistake our arguments for indecision nor our debates for weakness." [24]

Despite some dissenting opinions before the Senate Foreign Relations Committee and on the floors of both Houses, and the severe criticism of a very few Senators, Congress turned out to be very favorable to President Johnson's requests for military and foreign aid. On March 1, 1966, the Senate tabled (i.e. killed) the Morse Amendment by 93 to 5. The Amendment had been intended to rescind the 1964 Congressional resolution authorizing the President to repel aggression in Southeast Asia.

The Senate action, overwhelmingly endorsing the 1964 Congressional Resolution was due primarily to the following factors: Senator Richard B. Russell, chairman of the Armed Services Committee, planned to offer a substitute for the Morse Amendment. The substitute would have meant reaffirming the 1964 resolution. Senator Fulbright himself realized that it would not be possible to obtain more than a few votes to rescind the 1964 resolution. Although he was the floor manager at the time, he knew that it was useless for him to continue the fight against the 1964 resolution.

Whether one liked it or not, there was a war going on in Viet Nam. It would have been unpopular and imprudent for any member of Congress to repudiate, in time of war, the authority that Congress had already given to the President almost unanimously. If the Morse Amendment had not been tabled it would have provided the opportunity for the Senate to adopt the Russell Amendment reaffirming the 1964 resolution. That would have backed the President all the more. As it was, both Houses of Congress approved the President's foreign aid programs nearly unanimously, and Viet Nam was in the forefront of the requests.

The Senate Foreign Relations Committee, on March 7, approved a bill authorizing an appropriation of $415 million more for economic aid. Out of this amount, $275 million was to be used for South Viet Nam between March and July 1. When the bill was presented to the Committee, Senator Fulbright presented a rider saying that the adoption of this bill was "not to be construed as a commitment to use armed forces of the United States for the defense of such a country." [25] This was defeated in the Committee by a vote of 13 to 6.

Concerning the same bill, for economic aid mainly to

South Viet Nam, Senator Frank Church (D.-Idaho) on behalf of Senator George McGovern (D.-South Dakota) presented another rider to the effect that the adoption of this bill "shall not be construed as a ratification of any policy decision heretofore made with respect to hostilities in Viet Nam, or as an endorsement of any future commitment with respect to such hostilities." [26] But the Church rider was also tabled by the Senate Foreign Relations Committee. Consequently, President Johnson's policy in Viet Nam still enjoyed the overwhelming support of Congress, the representatives of the people. Winston Churchill once said that "democracy is the worst form of government—except for all the rest." It is costly and time-consuming to have these Great Debates, but they help inform the people, and this is of the essence of democracy, particularly when the propaganda of the cold war has to be penetrated. The decision made by the people and their Congress was unquestionably the right one.

When the $4.8-billion supplemental defense authorization bill for South Viet Nam and Southeast Asia was voted upon in the House of Representatives, it was approved by a vote of 389 to 3, and approved in the Senate by 95 to 2. In signing the bill on March 15, 1966, President Johnson asserted that the overwhelming approval of the bill indicated the Congress's "support of the fighting men in Viet Nam." The President expressed sadness that such a sum of money had to be spent for war, and reiterated his offer of economic aid to North Viet Nam after peace had been restored. He declared that most of the world leaders desired peace. Yet he warned:

> "But there are still a few who do not . . . So to those who ask what our present struggle in Viet Nam really means, let me say: our purpose is to demonstrate to the remaining advocates of violence that there is more human profit to be had from peace than there is from war." [27]

The overwhelming congressional approval of President Johnson's policy in Viet Nam is a clear indication that, in spite of certain minor congressional opposition, the majority of the representatives of the people strongly support the President on his policies in Viet Nam.

FOOTNOTES

CHAPTER XIII: RESUMPTION OF BOMBING OF NORTH VIET NAM

1. Photostat of President Johnson's letter to House Speaker McCormack is in the authors' possession.
2. Photostat copy of President Johnson's letter to the senators is also in the authors' possession.
3. Johnson's letter to McCormack.
4. *Peking Review*, February 4, 1966.
5. Quoted by all newspapers in the United States on Jan. 31 and Feb. 1, 1966.
6. United Nations Document, S/7168, Feb. 26, 1966.
7. *N.Y. Times* and *Herald Tribune*, Feb. 5, 1966.
8. *Journal American and World Telegram*, Feb. 7 and 8, 1966.
9. *N.Y. Times* and *Herald Tribune*, Feb. 8, 1966.
10. *N.Y. Times*, Feb. 9, 1966.
11. *Ibid.*
12. Photostat copy of partial release of General Wheeler's statement is in the authors' possession.
13. Excerpt of Kennan's testimony in *N.Y. Times*, Feb. 11 and 12, 1966.
14. *N.Y. Times*, Feb. 18 and 19, 1966.
15. *Ibid.*
16. *Ibid.*
17. *Ibid.*
18. *N.Y. Times* and *Herald Tribune*, Feb. 20, 1966.
19. *Ibid.*
20. *Radio Saigon*, Feb. 21, 1966.
21. *N.Y. Times*, Feb. 25, 1966.
22. *N.Y. Times*, Feb. 9, 1966.
23. *N.Y. Times*, Feb. 24, 1966.
24. *Ibid.*
25. *N.Y. Times*, March 8, 1966.
26. *Ibid.*
27. *N.Y. Times*, March 16, 1966.

CHAPTER XIV

THE HEART OF THE MATTER

1. Viet Nam: A Test Case

The Viet Nam crisis has become a test of resistance to Communist subversion and aggression. Its outcome will decide the fate of the people of Asia for many years to come. It will also affect the rights and interest of the United States and the free world. Viet Nam is a test of the effectiveness of deterring aggression through international effort, with or without the United Nations. Such critics as Walter Lippmann, Hans Morgenthau, and Senator Frank Church have described the task as impossible.

During its long history, Viet Nam was subjugated by the Chinese for more than a thousand years. Yet the Vietnamese continued during this long period to fight for their independence. The name of that territory has varied from time to time, and its political and administrative divisions have differed. It was divided into two and sometimes three political entities under different dynasties. When France made Indo-China her protectorate, it was again divided by the French into two or three administrative units.

Viet Nam's strategic importance in Southeast Asia cannot be overemphasized. Her richness in mineral and agricultural production is well known, and her production of such an essential strategic material as rubber has long been recognized by statesmen and industrialists.

As early as 1832, the American Government was interested in that part of the world, and sent its first diplomatic mission to Cochin China, Siam and Muscat. It was not Presidents Eisenhower, Kennedy, or Johnson who first created an interest in Viet Nam on the part of the United States.

2. Nationalism Abused

Restive for centuries under Chinese domination, the Vietnamese were also restive under the French. In the early

1920's a movement for independence was started by Vietnamese living abroad, particularly in China and France. The movement was shared by Vietnamese intellectuals, who at that time were mostly nationalists. Only a handful were Communists. During World War II, Indo-China was mainly under the control of the Vichy regime until March, 1944, when the Japanese militarists gained almost complete control. During this period Nationalist China, the United States, and Great Britain helped the underground forces in Viet Nam to undermine both the Vichy and the Japanese puppet regimes.

Ho Chi Minh was an important underground leader, and received support from China, Britain, and the United States. Ho himself was well known as a Communist, having been trained in Moscow. He had been secretary to Michael Borodin, the Soviet representative in Canton, China, from 1925 to 1927, and had long been associated with Mao Tsetung and Chou En-lai. It was because of his resistance to Japanese rule, which was supported by the Vichy government, that the Chinese, British, and American governments in turn supported Ho. They looked with a certain favor on his growing strength in Northern Viet Nam, especially along the China borders.

While World War II was still going on, Ho Chi Minh expanded his own forces and liquidated other non-Communist leaders. He quickly established his government under the name of the "Democratic Republic of Viet Nam" on September 2, 1945, at the end of the war, and forced Emperor Bao Dai to abdicate. He also succeeded in gaining tactical recognition from the French in 1946. He was not satisfied with this, however, and he began attacking the French in many parts of Indo-China that same year. He insisted at this time that he was just a student of Marxism, although he continued to head the Communist Party in Viet Nam.

3. *From Dien Bien Phu to Geneva*

During the Korean War the Chinese Communists sent outstanding military strategists and political workers in large numbers to form a joint staff Committee with the Vietnamese in order to direct the war against the French. The Chinese were disguised as Vietnamese, and they joined the Soviet military and political advisers already there to help the Viet Minh forces fight against the French. The war against the French continued under the general political leadership of Ho Chi Minh, and the military direction of General Vo

Nguyen Giap, who was a disciple of Mao Tse tung's strategy of guerrilla warfare. Guerrilla warfare was new to the French, who were fighting to maintain their colonies. As the Viet Minh forces became stronger, the French kept suffering losses, the accumulation of which were very heavy. The French Command in Indo-China had concentrated its forces in fortified places, thus isolating itself from the villages and cities that furnished them with food and other supplies.

The Viet Minh forces lured the French into the central part of Viet Nam, pretending that they were going to attack Laos. This is how the French became encircled at Dien Bien Phu. When the French finally realized they were being trapped, they asked the United States for large-scale military support. President Eisenhower thought that unless the United States entered into the actual fighting with the Communists in Viet Nam, French defeat was inevitable. He was unwilling to supply air support unless some other country, preferably Britain, was willing to make it a joint venture. Britain declined, and the defeat of the French in 1954 at Dien Bien Phu ended the French rule in Indo-China that had begun in 1885. Because of this defeat and the lack of French determination to continue fighting, France had no alternative but to sign a costly truce at Geneva on July 20, 1954. The participants in this Geneva Conference included France, the United Kingdom, the Soviet Union, Communist China, Laos, Cambodia, the "Democratic Republic of Viet Nam," the State of Viet Nam (which was succeeded by the Republic of Viet Nam) and the United States.

In addition to a general declaration, there were separate agreements concerning Laos, Cambodia, and Viet Nam. The United States considered that the agreements amounted to appeasement of the Communist nations, and would not consent to them. Hence the United States was unwilling to sign any of the agreements. However, the American representative at the Geneva Conference said that if there was any renewal of aggression in Viet Nam, it would be considered a matter of "grave concern" to the United States. The representative from the State of Viet Nam flatly refused to sign the agreement concerning Viet Nam, and also refused to put his signature to the general declaration.

The provisions of "The Agreement Concerning Viet Nam" are complicated, and its provision for an *International Supervisory Commission* has been very ineffective. India, Canada, and Poland have not been able to agree. Nor have the co-chairmen, Great Britain and the Soviet Union.

Hanoi and Washington now say that they would like to

adhere to the Geneva Agreements of 1954, but have charged each other with violating the agreements. The interpretation of the Geneva truce will be an important issue in any future conference. Although the United States and the Republic of Viet Nam are not signatories of these agreements and are not legally bound by them, yet responsible American statesmen repeatedly say they would not object to using the Geneva Agreements of 1954 as a basis of discussions over Viet Nam. Senator Fulbright has gone further, calling for adherence to the Geneva Agreements "in all their details." Perhaps this is part of the "major concessions" he favors giving to North Viet Nam.

4. *Why SEATO*

The main purpose of the SEATO pact, which was signed in September, 1954, was to deter Communist subversion and aggression in Southeast Asia. Signatories of this Southeast Asia Collective Defense Treaty were Australia, France, New Zealand, Pakistan, the Philippines, Thailand, the United Kingdom, and the United States. It was the first time in the conduct of international relations that an international treaty provided for ". . . continuous and effective self-help and mutual aid," to its signatories, and to "maintain and develop their *individual and collective capacity to resist* armed attack and *to prevent and counter subversive activities* directed from without . . ." (Article II). (Italics added.)

It was unanimously agreed that the "Treaty or Protocol Area" should cover "the States of Cambodia and Laos and the free territory under the jurisdiction of the State of Viet Nam." Article II of SEATO provided that the signatories may *"separately and jointly"* take effective measures to resist armed attack or subversion from outside the country. As an initial promoter and signatory, the United States could and perhaps should invoke the SEATO provisions to resist the external subversion and aggression against South Viet Nam. This is perhaps the only international treaty that the United States could invoke without being outnumbered by Communist or pro-Communist countries, and which provides a solid legal ground against the Viet Cong and the Chinese Communists. The United States would have better legal grounds here than with the Geneva Agreements of 1954, to which it was not a signatory. Also, there are several provisions in the Geneva Agreement concerning Viet Nam that are more favorable to the Communists, since it was signed shortly after the Communists won their big battle at Dien Bien Phu.

Concerning the three principal characters: Bao Dai, Ho Chi Minh, and Ngo Dinh Diem, each played a decisive role in the political and military situation of North and South Viet Nam. Without an understanding of these three it is difficult to understand the Viet Nam situation, either yesterday or today. In dealing with a man like Ngo Dinh Diem, it is not scholarly either to defend or to attack him prejudicially. An evaluation of his merits and demerits should be made from the facts, as much as possible. The Buddhist crisis of May, 1963, was certainly the spark which lighted the fire culminating in the political coup d'etat in November of the same year. The detailed and objective account presented herein, based on the testimony of experts and eye-witnesses, enables the reader to understand how the Diem Government was overthrown. While the stability of that government was criticized, all subsequent governments have been attacked for their instability.

How did the United States become involved in Viet Nam, and why were American commitments made by Presidents Eisenhower, Kennedy, and Johnson? First, an indirect pledge was made by the American delegate at the Geneva Conference of 1954 when he stated that any renewal of aggression in that area would be considered a matter of "grave concern" to the United States. Next, various commitments were made to Saigon in response to requests of the Government of the Republic of Viet Nam for help.

The provisions of SEATO obligated the United States to protect South Viet Nam and to help it resist subversion and armed attack from without. The Congressional Resolution of August 10, 1964, directed the President of the United States to use whatever measures are necessary to repel aggression in Viet Nam and Southeast Asia.

5. Viet Nam and the UN

The United States presented the case of Viet Nam to the United Nations Security Council, but the move was rather unrewarding for a number of reasons. The initial difficulty was having it adopted in the agenda. After its adoption, most members thought that public discussions would bring no fruitful results, that on the contrary it might aggravate the situation as a result of denunciation from both sides. Even if the United Nations should get down to business and try to determine who is the aggressor and what should be done, it still would be extremely difficult for the UN to decide what "aggression" is, and whether or not it is "war" or "civil war" in Viet Nam. The Communist countries prefer to call it "liberation" when they want to conquer a free country. The term "aggression" has never been defined by the General Assembly or the Security Council of the United Nations. Neither have the words "war" or "civil war."

An outstanding case at the United Nations was presented by the Chinese delegation in 1949 accusing the Soviet Union of violation of treaty obligations by aiding the Chinese Communists to overthrow the Chinese National Government. This accusation became Item 68 on the agenda of its General Assembly in 1949, under the title:

> "Threats to the political independence and territorial integrity of China and to the peace of the Far East, resulting from Soviet violations of the Sino-Soviet Treaty of Friendship and Alliance of 14 August 1945 and Soviet violations of the Charter of the United Nations."

Philip Jessup, the American delegate at the Political Committee of the General Assembly, together with some other officials of the State Department, considered that the war between the Chinese National Government and the Communists was internal politics, that it was a "civil war," and not aggression on the part of the Soviet Union. Jessup, a long-time member of the Institute of Pacific Relations, pleaded on behalf of the State Department that the principle of "self-determination" should be enforced in China. It was not until 1952, three years after China, with enormous help from Russia, had fallen to the Communists, that the U.N. General Assembly finally decided that the Soviet Union had "not acted in accordance with the Sino-Soviet Treaty of Friendship and Alliance of 1945."

On February 1, 1952, the General Assembly at last adopted a resolution which concluded:

> "The Union of Soviet Socialist Republics obstructed the efforts of the National Government of China in reestablishing Chinese national authority in the Three Eastern Provinces (Manchuria) after the surrender of Japan, and *has failed to carry out* the Treaty of Friendship and Alliance between China and the Union of Soviet Socialist Republics of 14 August 1945."

This post-mortem resolution could not alter the political or military situation of the China Mainland. It was just another lesson in the conduct of international relations written into the pages of history. But the world will never be the same because of it.

Some critics of American policy say that this is a "civil war" because Vietnamese are fighting Vietnamese. Some contend that it is a war against the tyranny of misrule of the Vietnamese Government. But the guerrilla forces represent a foreign government in South Viet Nam and nothing else, since North Viet Nam completely directs and controls them. That is why it is a war of aggression, a war of conquest, a war to deny to the South Vietnamese their basic human rights, as well as their political right to self-determination. The classical notion of "civil war" is completely different from the Communist concept.

President Johnson and Secretary of State Rusk have not refused to talk with the "National Liberation Front"; they have only refused to recognize it as something separate from the Hanoi regime. The "Front" is not a government. If it has anything to say, it can say it through the Hanoi Government, by whom it is employed. Otherwise a precedent would be established whereby any dissident persons could form a group and insist on having a voice in the government of a nation. Concerning the term "aggression," from the time of the drafting of the future charter of the International Organization at the Dumbarton Oaks Conference in 1944 through the San Francisco Conference in 1945 and up to the present time, the United Nations has never agreed on any definition of aggression. In April, 1962, at the second session of the General Assembly of the United Nations, "a Committee on Drafting Aggression" was established. Many meetings and debates have taken place since then, but it is not expected that an agreement will be obtained at any time in the near future. Hence the United Nations is unable to decide whether there is aggression or a civil war in Viet Nam.

As late as February 26, 1966, Akira Matsui of Japan, the President of the Security Council for the month of February, notified all the Council members that he had been unable to obtain any agreement on a precise course of action that might bring the Viet Nam case to a conference table. He reported that among its 15 members, the Soviet Union, France, Mali, and Bulgaria declined to discuss the Viet Nam issue. Although nine members favored a peace effort of the United Nations, and two expressed no opinion, there is no immediate hope of getting an amended compromise resolution adopted. The Soviet Union delegation even refused to accept the notice sent them by the Security Council President. By the spring of 1966 it was reported that the United Nations had lost interest in the Viet Nam question, as far as taking any action is concerned. U Thant, however, is still privately active concerning it.

The Communist nations insist on another Geneva Conference for the settlement of the Vietnamese war. The United States does not object to such a conference. But it should be borne in mind that in such a case the American Government would face a much less favorable situation than in 1954. The United States has already committed itself to the reconvening of another Geneva Conference. Peking, Hanoi, and Moscow will probably choose a strategic time for them to attend. The participants at such a conference would be more in favor of the cause of Hanoi and Peking than of Washington. The alignment of nations at the Geneva Conference in 1954 was as follows:

LEFT	RIGHT
U.S.S.R.	United Kingdom
Red China	United States
North Viet Nam	France
	South Viet Nam
	Laos
	Cambodia

The line-up in 1966 would be as follows:

LEFT	RIGHT
U.S.S.R.	United Kingdom
Red China	United States
North Viet Nam	South Viet Nam
France	Laos?
Cambodia	
National Liberation Front (if recognized)	

SEATO is still the best international forum the United States could have. The United States should call for an emergency SEATO meeting to deal with the Viet Nam war, since Viet Nam is within the protective umbrella of the SEATO signatories. American treaty obligations under SEATO commit it to take effective measures in Viet Nam "to resist armed attack and to prevent and counter subversive activities directed from without." The President of the United States has also been fully authorized by the Joint Congressional Resolution on Southeast Asia on August 10,

1964, "to take all necessary steps, including the use of armed force, to assist any member or protocol state of the Southeast Asia Collective Defense Treaty Organization requesting assistance in defense of freedom." This resolution became U.S. Public Law 88-408, and it is mandatory for the President to carry it out. As long as this resolution is valid, it is incumbent on the President of the United States to execute the spirit and principles of the resolution to the best of his ability.

The National Teach-in Movement could take place only in democratic countries, such as the United States and the United Kingdom, without undermining the morale of the fighting forces at the front. It is a good idea to bring the issues to the general public, as long as it does not become an organized, one-sided demonstration. The opposition forces and the forces of confusion and dissent are often better organized than the defenders of the Government's position. This was evident during the May 15, 1965 televised national debate on Viet Nam. But in the second televised debate, when McGeorge Bundy appeared and made an effective and well-documented defense against Hans Morganthau's rather emotional attack, the Government appeared stronger than its critics. The extent to which the Communist countries think the United States is divided as a result of these public debates is difficult to estimate. A government representative defending American policy cannot reveal everything concerning the background and future planning of government.

As counter-measures to the demonstrations for withdrawal took shape, there were many pro-government rallies, particularly by student organizations. Outstanding among these were the *Young Americans for Freedom,* which has chapters on more than 300 college campuses and is rapidly growing. The YAF went all out in their support of the troops in Viet Nam. They donated blood, collected petitions, wrote letters, and gathered books, soap, and gifts by the ton. In January, 1966, they sponsored an *International Youth Crusade for Freedom in Viet Nam,* holding eight mass rallies in this country and ten such rallies overseas. The authors have often spoke at YAF-sponsored talks around the country, from Princeton to Houston, from Yale to California, from Washington, D.C. to the University of Alaska. *The New Guard,* official organ of the *Young Americans for Freedom,* has carried factual and well-informed articles on Viet Nam consistently to the 700 campuses where it circulates.

As early as February 25, 1965, just two weeks after the

war was carried to the North, Secretary Rusk declared that the United States was actively interested in exploring "the possibilities of a peaceful solution" in Viet Nam. On March 25, 1965, President Johnson said that he was "ready to go anywhere at any time and meet with anyone wherever there is promise of progress toward an honorable peace." On April 7, 1965, President Johnson again declared that the United States "would never be second in the search for a peaceful settlement in Viet Nam." He pointed out that there are many ways to arrive at peace: in discussion or negotiation with the governments themselves; in large groups or in small ones; in the reaffirmation of old agreements or in the strengthening of new ones. The President, the Secretary of State, and other high American officials have been persistent in seeking discussions or negotiations with the governments concerned, directly or indirectly.

Along with American efforts for a peaceful solution in Viet Nam, there was the 17 Nations' proposal for peace, and the Canadian, Indian, and British attempts for arranging a cease-fire conference. U Thant, the Secretary-General of the United Nations, has tried and is still trying to play a role in peace promotion. Pope Paul, though he has justified defensive war, has also repeatedly appealed for cessation of war and especially for an end to "guerrilla warfare." The British Commonwealth nations have very recently been trying to send a peace mission to Hanoi, Peking, Moscow, and Washington. The effort has already been denounced by Red China's Premier, Chou En-lai, as a "hoax" to help "the imperialist United States to hang on" in Viet Nam.

All through 1965, the United States has tried, through indirect and direct approaches, to influence the Hanoi regime to come to a conference table in order to reach a cease-fire agreement. In May of that year, for about six days, the United States suspended bombing North Viet Nam with the hope that Hanoi would rather talk than fight. This American attempt failed. For more than a month, beginning at Christmas, 1965, the United States launched a "peace offensive" in a very dramatic way by sending outstanding diplomats to five continents. It also ordered its envoys in more than a hundred different countries to contact their respective governments in its all-out effort for peace. The U.S. used private and informal sources in neutral, Communist, and non-Communist nations to seek a conference with the Hanoi regime. At home, President Johnson made every effort to convince the American people that he would not seek a "blind escalation" of the war. Similarly, he informed the Communist nations in unmistakable terms of his peaceful intentions.

Other nations, including the Vatican, exerted their moral influence by appealing to Mao Tse-tung, Ho Chi Minh, and the Soviet leaders, urging them to talk rather than to see the war in Viet Nam continue. All such appeals and peace offers brought back to Washington nothing but denunciation and scornful accusations of bluffing. Added to their wordy denunciations of the United States' peace offensive, the Viet Communists strengthened their military build-up in North Viet Nam. They widened the Ho Chi-Minh Trail, accelerated infiltration through Laos and Cambodia, and increased their infiltration both on the South China Sea and on the Gulf of Siam. They also crossed over the neutral zone of the 17th parallel in their all-out effort to reinforce their military personnel in South Viet Nam. It has been reliably reported that a new Ho Chi Minh Trail has been built through the demilitarized zone between the North and the South. In order to safeguard the lives of the American and Allied fighting forces in South Viet Nam, the President had no alternative but to resume the bombing of military targets in North Viet Nam.

While the bombing was suspended in North Viet Nam, the Saigon Government repeatedly urged the American Government to intensify its war efforts against the North. It was repeatedly suggested that in order to win the war more non-military means must be employed. To meet these and other issues, and for the principals in both Washington and Saigon to meet each other, the Honolulu Conference was called from February 6 to 8, 1966. A Declaration and a Communique were issued in order to coordinate and intensify the war effort in Viet Nam along both military and non-military lines. In order to supplement and implement the spirit and decisions of the conference, Vice-President Humphrey and other government officials and technical experts were sent to Viet Nam. They were to continue to work out detailed programs for improving the economic, social, educational, and agricultural conditions there while the war goes on. Both governments pledged that the war effort, both military and non-military, will be increased.

6. *The Basis for Negotiations*

The following are the basic principles which should be the guidelines for the American delegates at the case-fire table:

(1) The United States should start any cease-fire with "unconditional discussions" with the participants of the Conference. There should not be any pre-conditions attached to a conference for negotiation.

(2) Since the United States and South Viet Nam never signed the Geneva Conference Agreements of 1954, these nations are not legally bound to the terms of the Agreements. If the United States should accept such terms after turning them down 12 years ago, and after she had made such a sacrifice in human lives and money, it would mean a great defeat for the American Government and people.

(3) The present line-up of the possible Geneva Conference in terms of Communist and non-Communist nations would certainly be in favor of the Communist and pro-Communist nations, as indicated previously. The contents of the original agreements resulted from the French defeat and the Viet Minh victory. Any new agreement based on its contents would not be favorable to the United States, particularly since this time the majority of the countries would be stacked against the United States.

(4) If the Viet Cong, i.e. the National Liberation Front, were admitted to a future cease-fire conference as a separate political entity, it would mean that the United States recognizes the war as partially a civil war, and not as a war of aggression, as America has so often maintained. It would be a direct reversal of the American stand.

(5) Since this has been primarily a war for and in Viet Nam, it is of the utmost concern to the Vietnamese themselves. The United States should not act as if it were her own war. America should stop using the word "we" unless it is truly speaking for South Viet Nam and its allies. The United States has often taken a different stand from the Government of South Viet Nam. The United States has offered to negotiate any time, blithely ignoring the fact that it has no right to do so, and that the Premier of South Viet Nam has officially declared that his government will not negotiate as long as North Viet Nam keeps up her aggression.

(6) A neutralization plan, as advocated by President De Gaulle and others, was denounced as unacceptable by the Secretary of Defense on March 26, 1964. Similar statements were made subsequently by other high American officials. Any neutralization plan for Viet Nam, in name or in fact, would be in direct violation of these statements. Senator Fulbright, however, went a step further and advocated a neutralization plan for all of Southeast Asia, ignoring the sovereign rights of these countries.

(7) Under Communist rule there is no freedom of political action. No one can expect a fair or impartial election in any country, whether in Asia or Europe, if it is under Communist control. Moreover, there are about two million more people in North Viet Nam than in the South. Even if ninety per cent of the people in South Viet Nam voted against Communist rule, Hanoi would still receive a majority in an over-all election. The Communist regime controls the entire vote in the North, and could also exert some influence in the South. Communism can exert some influence even in the United States.

(8) It is extremely difficult for a coalition government with Communist participation to succeed in maintaining its identity. A well-organized international plot can make a coalition pro-Communist, and then Communist-controlled. It is naive to compare the situation in Viet Nam with a coalition government in post-war France and Italy. France and Italy have a long democratic tradition. They have a sound economy, political stability, and a high level of education. Nor do they have a powerful Red Army and an aggressive Communist China next door to them.

(9) The Viet Cong aggression should cease, and the people of South Viet Nam should be allowed to decide their own form of government, and whether or not they want unification with the North at this time, or at any time. The South Vietnamese are not bound by the suggestions or dictates of France, Britain, or Soviet Russia, nor do the South Vietnamese need permission from other countries in order to have their own government. Americans and others who would like to force a Communist regime on the South Vietnamese people in the name of "unification" seem strangely silent about a divided Korea, a divided Germany, or a divided Ireland. Many people cease to concern themselves with the civil rights and basic human rights of persons once they are incarcerated behind the Communist curtains, such as in East Germany, Tibet, or in any of the other colonies of Communism.

(10) The SEATO agreements are applicable to South Viet Nam, since it falls within the "protocol" area of the treaty. They can be applied individually, or collectively without a veto. The formal application of SEATO might increase the number of voices friendly to the United States. It should have been invoked long ago.

(11) Cease-fire talks should not be permitted to become delaying tactics so that the Communists might be able to make further aggressive preparations. Nor should

military advantage be given to bring about or continue negotiations. If an actual cease-fire is accomplished, it should be supervised by a truly impartial international mission, more justly and prudently formed than the previous *International Control Commisson* for Viet Nam.

(12) After the cease-fire there will be many urgent problems, such as those of rehabilitation. The highly developed countries should be willing to assist Viet Nam and Southeast Asia. President Johnson has set good general directions for economic and technical aid to this part of the world. Thousands of administrators, educators, doctors, nurses and technicians will be needed to help with the job of rehabilitation after so many Vietnamese soldiers have been killed by the Communists, and after so many thousands of civilian leaders have been killed or kidnapped by the Viet Cong. The extent of democracy in South Viet Nam will continue to depend on the degree to which the Communists leave the South Vietnamese alone. It will also depend on how much human help the country receives from the outside world.

Some people allege that the United States cannot do what France failed to do in Viet Nam from 1945 to 1954. They overlook the essential differences between France and the United States in their respective positions in Viet Nam. France never claimed to be stemming Communist aggression. She was fighting as a colonial power, whereas the United States is fighting as an ally to help the Republic of Viet Nam maintain her political independence. Unlike France at that time, the United States has no territorial or political designs in that part of the world.

In 1954, France was militarily weak and politically divided. The United States is militarily very strong and politically united. The dissident voices in Congress are few. In 1954, the Vietnamese people thought that the war was between the French colonialists and the Viet Minh, and they were told that the Viet Minh were nationalists and patriots, not Communists. The Vietnamese today know that the Americans are not colonialists, and that Ho Chi Minh and his followers are Communists. Ho Chi Minh has been the head of the Communist Party in all of Indochina since 1924.

When the French were fighting in Viet Nam, they had no troops from other countries, although Korea three times offered to contribute troops. Today, beside the United States, there are fighting forces from several other allied countries, while approximately forty nations have given material aid and moral support to the Republic of Viet Nam in its fight against Communism. Only one-third of the troops for France were Vietnamese. Today, the Vietnamese forces far outnumber all of the other forces combined.

The air power of the French was very limited, whereas the United States has an air power in Viet Nam today such as the world has never seen. It provides for the greatest possible mobility of troops, plus destructive power that is proving to be a very decisive factor in defeating the enemy. The French Premier, Pierre Mendes-France, was eager to put an end to the fighting in Indo-China and was willing to give "peace and independence" to Viet Nam. In 1954, the French "doves" clearly triumphed over the "hawks". The French were very reluctant to support their war in Indo-China. Many of their officers and officials in Viet Nam were corrupt, and they lacked the support of the native people. Politically divided, The French government was militarily too weak to cope with the situation.

One of the main reasons why the Viet Minh accepted a truce in Viet Nam was that they had also suffered very heavily, and needed time to recover. They were convinced that if they signed a favorable truce it would be only a matter of two years or so before they could completely control South Viet Nam, either through a Communist-held election or through direct military action. It is unlikely today that Hanoi or Peking would be willing to negotiate with Washington as they did with Paris in 1954.

CHAPTER XV

PROBLEMS AND POSSIBILITIES

1. *Attitude Toward Communism*

A great deal of the confusion about the war in Viet Nam hinges on one's attitude toward Communism itself. Communism can only be defined and identified as the governments of Soviet Russia, Red China, and their satellites. A person's attitude toward this reality determines his attitude toward the war in Viet Nam, and what should be done about it. It is precisely the difference in this attitude that makes a man like Senator Fulbright disagree with the vast majority of his colleagues. In his first Senate speech, in 1945, he termed fear of Communism "a powerful prejudice." He has said that Communism in Russia "is scarcely more radical under modern conditions than the Declaration of Independence was in the days of George III." This blind spot has been chronic throughout his career. His attitude has been described by *Time* as "an emotional and intellectual reluctance to believe that Communism is a monolithic doctrine of belligerence based on a fanatical dream of world domination." [1]

One of the strongest forces in the United States against winning the war and against the belief that Communism is a dangerous threat is the *Center for the Study of Democratic Institutions* (an instrument of the *Fund for the Republic*) in Santa Barbara, California. The Vice-President of the *Center*, W. H. Ferry, has accused J. Edgar Hoover of creating a false picture of Communism's strength. This Ferry branded "sententious poppycock." He termed Hoover's warnings of Communist subversion "a mischief-making tapestry of legend and illusion . . ." [2] The *Center* employs Robert Scheer as its expert on Viet Nam, and has joined forces with the *Fellowship of Reconciliation* to promote American withdrawal from Viet Nam. Together they are currently sponsoring one hundred convocations around the United

States, supposedly based on Pope John's Encyclical, *Pacem in Terris*. Commented one of the nation's leading newspapers:

> Any seminars promoted by these outfits will certainly preach the wickedness of the United States and the nobility of the Viet Cong and North Vietnamese Communists. The Hutchins group (the *Center*) has already distributed a screed entitled, *'How the United States Got Involved in Viet Nam,'* which says that American anti-communism is just plain fascism and no more respectable than communism itself.[3]

In an article entitled, *Hang Down Your Head, Tom Dooley,* Scheer blamed the war in Viet Nam on the late Dr. Thomas Dooley. Scheer wrote a pamphlet describing Ho Chi Minh as a modern-day George Washington. He also repeated the allegations of Drew Pearson that America entered the war through the machinations of Cardinal Spellman.

Congressman Richard Ichord investigated Scheer's background, as did the *House Committee on Un-American Activities.* Scheer was an official of the Castro-backed *Fair Play for Cuba Committee.* He participated in an illegal tour of Cuba sponsored by the pro-Peking *Progressive Labor Movement.* He has been active in such organizations as the radical *Women Strike for Peace,* and helped sponsor the *International Days of Protest.* Scheer was also affiliated with the *Viet Nam Day Committee,* the group in California that sought to halt troop trains carrying soldiers bound for Viet Nam. The *Center* described Sheer's pamphlet on Viet Nam as "the best short treatment of this subject we have ever seen."

Chairman of the *Center* is Supreme Court Justice William O. Douglas, who maintained recently that America should disarm Taiwan.* The *Center's* President, Robert Maynard Hutchins, holds that America should never give a dollar in foreign aid, or send a single soldier anywhere, except through the United Nations. This would mean that such organizations as NATO and SEATO would have to be scrapped, and that the United States would lose all control over its foreign aid. W. H. Ferry, the *Center's* Vice-President, advocates the unilateral disarmament of the United States.

The *Center for the Study of Democratic Institutions* and the *Fellowship of Reconciliation* have been exploiting the

---

* Throughout this chapter, "we" includes the whole free world.

encyclical *Pacem in Terris* by Pope John XXIII to promote pacifism and withdrawal from Viet Nam. As a consequence, the top Communist publication in the United States, *Political Affairs,* boasts that *Pacem in Terris* has been responsible for many and "possibly most" of the peace actions, petitions, ads, mass meetings, union resolutions, picket lines for peace, teach-ins and other actions throughout the country. For example, this leading Communist journal declares: "Undoubtedly the encyclical has been a major factor in achieving the signatures of some 3,000 religious leaders to a full-page ad in the *New York Times* and other newspapers, calling on President Johnson to stop the war in Viet Nam." [4]

Dr. John C. Bennett, the President of Union Theological Seminary, maintains that it was all right to defend the world against Nazism, but that it is not all right to defend the world against Communism because Communism is "changing." The opposite would have been more true. Nazism was more of a one-man operation, and gradually the German people would have changed it, but Communism is an iron-clad system that is almost totally independent of the individual in power. Hitler lasted for only a few years. Communism has already lasted for two generations. Yet Dr. Bennett recently referred to "the obsession with anti-Communism." Similarly, Rabbi Jacob Weinstein, President of the Central Conference of American Rabbis, speaks of the "obsessional neurosis about Communism." The question of whether one feels there is a danger in both the hot and cold war, a danger in propaganda and infiltration as well as in straight Communist aggression, is paramount. Dr. Fern Stukenbrocker, administrative assistant to FBI Director J. Edgar Hoover, recently pointed out: "The people who dismiss the threat of Communism have been psychologically disarmed."

It was America's total commitment to freedom in World War II that saved Western Europe and much of Asia twenty-five years ago. Leaders of some of those countries today criticize America for helping to preserve freedom in Southeast Asia. Yet human freedom means just as much to the inhabitants there as it did in Europe in the early 1940's. Alliances like NATO have been weakening, and the very reasons for them have been fading from our memories. People like Senator Joseph Clark have described Viet Nam as "only an incident," but defeat there would reverberate around the world, demoralizing our allies and driving our friends into the enemy camp. General Matthew Ridgway recently declared that if we would retreat to the enclaves we would "fulfill our obligation to our Vietnamese allies." [5]

Yet the enclave theory would protect only the Vietnamese troops, surrendering the rest of the country and its 15 million people. All that would be left to negotiate would be the enclaves themselves.

How serious would the loss of Viet Nam be? The late President Kennedy wrote, as a Senator, in 1956:

> "Viet Nam represents the cornerstone of the Free World in Southeast Asia, the keystone to the arch, the finger in the dike. Burma, Thailand, India, Japan, the Philippines and obviously Laos and Cambodia are among those whose security would be threatened if the red tide of communism overflowed into Viet Nam." [6]

2. America's Indecision

When confronted with an aggressor who has already attacked, the peace-at-any-price mentality provokes war, whereas war itself in defense of freedom is the key to peace. The war in Viet Nam is being prolonged by America's indecision. Logically, the war should be carried to targets in the North in order to reduce the ability of North Viet Nam to carry on the war. The battleground should be shifted from South Viet Nam to the North. Yet very few targets in the North have been hit. This is the reason why North Viet Nam continues to fight. It was not until April, 1966, that a B-52 was allowed to bomb the North. Nor has anyone been permitted to bomb the vital areas. The Joint Chiefs of Staff have long urged that the port of Haiphong be blockaded. The President recently told a top congressional leader: "If Moscow continues to escalate the war by increasing military shipments to Hanoi, Haiphong will be shut down completely. I'll have no other choice." [7] At the same time, Chairman Mendel Rivers of the House Armed Services Committee warned Defense Secretary McNamara:

> "The American people will not stand for our fighting men being wounded and killed in Viet Nam while we do nothing to halt the flow of arms to the enemy. If this policy isn't changed soon, I plan to hold public hearings to ascertain why we are not taking such necessary measures to protect our fighting men, and to find out which officials are responsible for forcing our troops to fight under these conditions." [8]

There is no need to acquiesce in the theory that this

will be a "long war". World War II was wrapped up in three years. But we have to adopt a policy of victory, and we have to convince our enemy we fully intend to win. When we ask the North to get out of the South, we are asking them to that extent to accept defeat. In order to do that we have to defeat them. It is not necessary to blockade the harbor of Haiphong. All we have to do is let the South Vietnamese mine that harbor. A blockade may be interpreted as an act of war, and whereas we have not declared war on North Viet Nam, South Viet Nam has. Once the mines are dropped into the harbor, no ship that goes there will be able to get insurance. Soviet Russia could keep sending ships into Haiphong, but it would be doing so at its peril. Dean Rusk has said that the war would end in a matter of months if we could prevent the supplies from coming down the Ho Chi Minh Trail. Eighty-five percent of them first go into the harbor at Haiphong.

The Communist bloc realizes that United States' policy is not aimed at defeating the enemy, that we are not seeking victory, but negotiations. Both Peking and Moscow are counting on this fact. Consequently, they do not worry about the war being extended.

We have no choice but to adopt a firm policy of winning. Otherwise we will have fallen into the trap of a ground war in Asia. A prolonged war is an open invitation. And how many fronts can we be confronted with at the same time? Whether it be in Korea or Laos, in Cuba or Berlin, in the Congo or Santo Domingo, it is the same enemy, an enemy who wants to get us in a weak position. As sure as night follows day, that is just what the enemy will do if we let him drag out the war.

The best way to prevent World War III, the only real way to bring peace to the world, is to stop aggression in its tracks. We watched the Communists take Central Europe, but we stopped them in Greece and Turkey by decisive military action. And we prevented them from taking western Europe by arming our allies. It was the strength of NATO, rather than a powerless UN or a Russian "detente," that kept them from further aggression in Europe.

But in the other half of the world we have let them take China, then North Korea, then North Viet Nam, then most of Laos. It is no wonder they think they can gain by their aggression! Appeasement, weakness, and diplomatic compromise are useless against such an enemy. Victory is the only answer, and victory comes only by defeating the other side. In order to win the war, somebody has to lose. This basic fact seems to have escaped our civilian leadership. For 20 years we have been seeking substitutes for victory, but we have sought in vain. The President has men who can tell him how to win the war, but they are not in the State Department, nor are they the civilians in the Defense Department.

As head of the Joint Chiefs of Staff, General Wheeler recently stated that U.S. forces can impose an effective blockade on North Viet Nam and against the Chinese Communists if so ordered. General John McConnell, Air Force Chief, recently said that the air force has done everything it has been asked to do, and that it can do anything it will be asked to do. These men and their associates are trying to say that they can win the war, "if so ordered".

The American people want the war won. Before the President resumed the bombing, the Louis Harris public opinion poll showed that the people would support the resumption of bombing by more than two to one. His survey showed that 60 percent of the country would back a U.S. force of 500,-000 troops in South Vietnam. But before we send many more, we should remove the ban on using Formosan troops, and we should remove the privileged sanctuaries around Hanoi and Haiphong. When polled early in 1966, 206 in the House of Representatives said they judged it a vital issue to save South Viet Nam from a Communist takeover. Only 20 said they did not think it vital. Again, 219 U.S. Congressmen declared that the U.S. has a vital interest in the future of Southeast Asia. Only 10 thought that it did not.

The most important step to be taken is to seal off outside reinforcements to the guerrillas. The bombing has not been nearly as effective as it should have been. The restrictions have been much too tight, and so have been the direct controls imposed from Washington. These restrictions have made it impossible to cut off the reinforcements to the Viet Cong. For some reason, we have not even disrupted the railroads leading from Hanoi to China and to Haiphong. We finally started to cut off ships trading with the North from hauling U.S. foreign aid. But here again, we do after several years what we should have done long before.

Secretaries Dean Rusk and Robert McNamara have both been strongly opposed to a blockade of the harbor at Haiphong. They fear this would lead to a direct confrontation between the United States and Russia, since Russian ships would be involved. But if the government of South Viet Nam mined the harbor, this would not be the case. The harbor must be closed, the railroad lines from Hanoi to Red

China must be permanently disabled, the storage depots, power plants, air fields, and industry around Hanoi must be put out of commission, and the earthen dikes in the Red River Delta need to be hit.

When these things have been done the North will be able to wage her war of aggression no longer. These things need to be done, and they should be done sooner rather than later, in order to bring the war to a successful conclusion sooner. As a further step, the troops from Free China should be brought into the struggle. One of the authors heard Hedley Donovan, Editor-in-Chief of *Time,* say in Seattle that the troops from Taiwan could not be used in Viet Nam "because the Vietnamese hate the Chinese." But there are a million Chinese living in South Viet Nam now, and there is no basis for the fear that the two armies could not get along. Mr. Donovan admitted that the source of his remark was hearsay. It is a remark that is often made, but has never been proven. The Vietnamese readily distinguish between Red China and Free China.

Secretary Rusk testified before the Fulbright Committee that a vote for withdrawal from Viet Nam is a vote for war. It is essential to international peace that Red China be taught she cannot continue to pursue her wars of aggression, and that in spite of the nuclear age we are not going to give in to her wars of "liberation". America can never win at the conference table what she does not win on the battlefield. The only thing that can defeat us in Viet Nam is a no-win policy, and that will defeat us anywhere in the world. We are slowly winning the war militarily, but we are bound to lose it politically, if we continue our policy of stalemate. America's superiority is on the sea and in the air. As long as the enemy is permitted to carry the conflict into South Viet Nam, and as long as we are unwilling to destroy the source of his strength in the North, the war will continue until the South gives up. America keeps talking of negotiating with anyone anytime, without any pre-conditions, but the government of South Viet Nam has already said they will not negotiate with the Viet Cong, they will not use the Geneva Accords as a basis for any negotiations, and they will not negotiate until the North stops its aggression. What America has to realize is that we have no right whatsoever to negotiate for the South Vietnamese government.

In a recent issue of the *Spectator,* London's Professor Patrick J. Honey described how the Communist leaders are pinning their hopes on the 'Peace in Viet Nam' campaigns around the world. Groups like the *Fellowship of Reconcilia-*

303

tion are in the forefront of such a movement. The *Fellowship* continually creates such groups as the *Catholic Peace Fellowship*, the *International Committee of Conscience on Vietnam*, and the *Clergymen Concerned about Vietnam*. The Communists spread similar propaganda in France for several years before 1954, thus forcing France to capitulate. The *Clergymen Concerned* want the war brought to the conference table, but they have already written the terms of settlement, with no heed of the consequences. Their statements call for a complete withdrawal of U.S. troops, a return to the Geneva Accords of 1954, and a coalition with the Viet Cong. This amounts to outright capitulation in South Viet Nam.[10]

Senator William Fulbright, Senator Robert Kennedy, Walter Lippmann, and the *New York Times* have all come out in favor of a coalition with the Viet Cong. But as General Thomas A. Lane has pointed out, just to talk with the National Liberation Front and thereby recognize them would be to surrender South Viet Nam.[11]

3. *Recognize the Viet Cong?*

As early as 1961, the U.S. State Department reported that the National Liberation Front, or the Viet Cong, was under the direction and control of the Central Committee of the Lao-Dong Party, i.e. the Communist Party of North Viet Nam. Under this Central Committee a special *Committee for Subversion of the South* was organized. In order to promote the idea that the Viet Cong and the Communist Party were separate, a pseudo-conference of "representatives of Marxist-Leninists in South Vietnam" was held on December 19, 1961. Hanoi then announced that the conference had established the *Viet Nam People's Revolutionary Party*. This "new" party came into existence, said Hanoi, on January 1, 1962. Its program was identical to that of the Lao-Dong, the Communist Party. In fact, for several months the new party did not even have officers to run it. Even today, there is only one headquarters for the Viet Cong, and that is Hanoi. The only leaders with whom we can negotiate are in Hanoi. The facile advice that we "talk to the Viet Cong" is erroneous and misleading.

When we fail to see that the Viet Cong represent only the North, we are compromising the freedom of South Viet Nam. Undersecretary of State George Ball has warned that recognition of the National Liberation Front "would do violence to the truth and betray the very people whose liberty we are fighting to secure." The NLF was created to confuse the issue and establish the myth that the war of conquest in South Viet Nam is partially a civil war.

The strategy of North Viet Nam all along has been to have the Viet Cong recognized as something separate from the North. This would mean they represent a minority in the South, and that they would be entitled to a place in the postwar government. Thus the Communists could achieve their coalition. As David Lawrence recently explained, this is exactly what happened in China when a coalition was formed in which the Communists were given a substantial part. They would end up by taking over the control of the entire government.

We are beginning to see a breach in our position all along the line. United Nations Secretary-General U Thant urges both recognition for the Viet Cong and a Communist coalition after the war. Under his tutelage, the U.N. news releases now refer to the "Viet Cong rebels." Walter Lippmann writes that "a peace cannot be negotiated if the Viet Cong does not participate in the negotiations." Averell Harriman came out in favor of recognizing the Viet Cong. Secretary of State Rusk recently declared that "the Viet Cong are only one and a relatively small element in a very large population in South Viet Nam." Since they are completely directed and controlled by the North, they do not represent any element in the South at all. The *New York Times* stated: "The Johnson Administration's view is that the NLF could have at least a secondary status at any peace conference." There is no such thing in international law as "secondary status." Either we do not recognize them, or we do. They can sit at the conference table, but only as a part of North Viet Nam.

There is much talk about some day having an international sovereignty of nations, but we have to live in the world as it is. The policy maker lives in a very real world, and if churchmen and moralists speak to him, they must do so within the framework of that world. When the *World Council of Churches* called on the United States to stop bombing North Viet Nam, it also asked Hanoi to stop sending troops to the South. But if it expected unilateral action on our part, it was being unrealistic. Meeting in Geneva last February 16, the *World Council of Churches* criticized the United States for its policy of containing Communist aggression, as well as condemning Communism for its wars of "liberation." In urging that the policy of containment be modified, the *World Council* singled out the United States by name. In asking Communism to reconsider its policy of wars of liberation, it mentioned no particular country.[12] The *World Council* went on to demand international acceptance of the government of Red China, and insisted that Western nations must accept the fact that what is happening in Viet Nam "is essentially a social revolution." It declared that military force is futile in trying to deal with this "revolution". Dr. Eugene Carson Blake, the head of the *World Council of Churches,* stated that if the United States wins the war in Viet Nam it would "create more problems than it would solve."

In contrast to this type of thinking is that of the policy maker, as seen in recent statements by House Minority Leader Gerald Ford, and by Senator Thomas Dodd. Congressman Ford insists: "It is obvious that until the Communists are convinced of our unbearable power and our will to use it, real and lasting peace cannot be negotiated under any circumstances. History teaches us that appeasement in dealing with dictatorships and aggressors is a proven way to touch off a general war." [13]

Writes Senator Dodd:

There is a growing accumulation of evidence that Moscow has no interest in encouraging or permitting an honorable settlement of the Viet Nam war. The USSR has given and continues to give massive support to the Viet Cong. . . . There are men in high administrative positions who persist in believing that Soviet actions in Vietnam are a facade and that, deep down in their hearts, Kremlin leaders are as anxious as we are to see the Viet Nam war settled on terms that would be acceptable to the West. This is an exceedingly dangerous form of wishful thinking.

We shall have to face up to the harsh inescapable fact that the Communists will not call off their aggression in Viet Nam until we have made the cost of continuing it prohibitive. The more costly we make the war for the Communists . . . the sooner we can hope for an end to the conflict.

I do not believe that any single measure can, by itself, prevail in this situation. On the contrary, I am convinced that we must bring to bear on the Communists the most potent possible combination of measures and pressures, both military and diplomatic. If we take half measures or if, out of deference to those who do not understand the issues, we take certain measures but do not take others, we thereby make peace that much more remote and difficult to achieve . . .

The hard lesson of history is that, in dealing with totalitarian dictators, gentleness, professions of good faith, concessions, and conciliatory actions in general are construed as manifestations of weakness. Conversely, the policy of firmness has been successful against them whenever it has been tried.[14]

4. *A Policy of Weakness*

The first major war America ever entered that it did not win was in Korea. The Korean War gave great encouragement to our enemy. Our surrender of most of Laos since then has encouraged the enemy even more, and we are paying the consequences in South Viet Nam today. Just as the American forces were to make their final breakthrough in Korea, President Truman ordered a standstill because the other side had agreed to start negotiations. His order not only led to a less satisfactory peace, it prolonged the war for two more years, years in which 95,000 Americans were killed, wounded, or reported missing. Yet our roving Ambassador, Averell Harriman, returned from Moscow in June of 1965 to say that he told the Russians we would not stop bombing the North "until negotiations started." If we stop bombing the North, the negotiations will continue on indefinitely. The lesson of Korea is that two-thirds of all the Americans killed were killed after negotiations started.

Our policy of weakness is seen by the statement of the State Department that it opposed a blockade of Haiphong because such an action would not win the war. Then Defense Secretary McNamara told a congressional committee that he saw no point in bombing the industry in the North because "it is so small and most of the war goods are imported." The solution is not to be found in weak excuses, but in the testimony of General Maxwell Taylor before the Fulbright committee: "The key, I believe, is inexorable pressure at all points, directed at the will, the ability, and the means of the Communist aggressors . . ."

The Communists chose South Viet Nam as their springboard to the conquest of all Southeast Asia. It is a test case of free world resolve. Unaggressive as we are, we are inclined to think that fighting is evil but negotiations are good. The issue is not so simple. If de Gaulle had negotiated with Hitler when France was conquered, if Churchill had negotiated when London was losing the war, if the United

States had negotiated with Japan right after Pearl Harbor, the negotiations would have been good for tyranny but bad for freedom. Max Lerner of the *New York Post*, for example, proposed a two year moratorium in Viet Nam, followed by elections. With the country still occupied by Communist troops, the elections would be anything but free. Yet Mr. Lerner remarks: "If they voted for Communism it would be their privilege." Others propose a simple cease-fire, but the proposal is not that simple. Conventional armies can have a cease-fire, but in guerrilla warfare it is impossible to administer. That is the basic difference between Korea and Viet Nam.

Our policy in Viet Nam is being controlled by civilians and diplomats. The decisions of the military aimed at winning the war are often overruled. Civilians seldom realize that in order to win, your enemy has to lose. Diplomats do not think in terms of winning but of concessions, negotiations, and promises. To solve the problem with a paper of some sort, whether it be an agreement, a treaty, or a pact, has often seemed important in the past, but promises of this kind with Russia have seldom been of any value. The Administration continues to have negotiations instead of victory as its goal, and this is the crucial mistake in our entire policy that has to be reversed. Words like "good faith" and "mutual self-interest" are meaningless when applied to the Communist world, whose avowed purpose is military conquest of any country we let them conquer.

No international supervisory body half-way acceptable to the United States or South Viet Nam would ever be acceptable to Peking or Hanoi. Washington is not trying to make Ho Chi Minh admit defeat. But peace and freedom around the world demand that Ho Chi Minh be defeated in his efforts to conquer the South. Whether Ho can find a face-saving maneuver is up to him. The war may just gradually peter out, as did the guerrilla wars in Greece, the Philippines, Malaya, and the Congo. The only thing that really counts is that South Viet Nam be kept free, and that Hanoi, Peking, and Moscow learn that their attempts to take over free countries will be stopped wherever they start them. Unless this is proved, the war in Viet Nam will have been a criminal waste.

If the war is not won with speed and dispatch perhaps half of the lives lost will have been lost unnecessarily. As Senator Jack Miller pointed out, all the port facilities in Haiphong are not worth the life of one American soldier. In the words of Congressman Robert Sikes of Florida:

"The ground rules under which U.S. forces fight will

have to be changed. It is necessary that the North Vietnamese port, power and industrial complex which supplies Communist forces be neutralized. Continuation of the sanctuary now provided those facilities in North Vietnam will mean continued escalation of the conflict and more American deaths." [15]

Another House member remarked that someone must impress upon the State Department that we are not going to make friends with Moscow by refraining from bombing Haiphong or from using the Navy to throw a blockade around the harbor. We are at war. American boys are dying. This is no time to 'play footsie' with one group of Communists. Said Congressman Martin of Alabama: "It is unthinkable to refrain from cutting off the sources of supply to the enemy." Congressman John Rhodes of Arizona summed it up: "We will have to put them in a situation in which continuance of the war is unthinkable." [16]

Why is there so much confusion about the war in Viet Nam? The Communists know that there is no better weapon for defeating us. Confusion is a normal tactic for them. A total of 30,000 persons demonstrated against the government in Viet Nam in the spring of 1966, and the majority of them were teenagers. But after the stories were reported in the press a number of American congressmen suggested that we were no longer wanted there. Said Senator Cooper of Kentucky: "If they do not want us, we will leave." But surrender is no solution. It is easier to save our face than to save our freedom. When Congress passed the Southeast Asia Resolution, in 1964, it made it very clear that it is America's freedom that is threatened, as well as that of South Viet Nam's. When President Truman asked Congress to help Greece and Turkey in 1947, he made it clear that must be our policy because otherwise "the security of the United States" would be imperiled. "If we falter in our leadership," he said, "we may endanger the peace of the world—and we shall surely endanger the welfare of this Nation." This became known as the Truman Doctrine. This is the Doctrine we are applying belatedly in Southeast Asia today. If we are there because our own freedom demands it, then we are not there just to help our neighbor. If our own safety demands that we be there, can we afford to pull out?

5. Thich Tri Quang

The man behind the demonstrations in the spring of 1966 was Tri Quang, a leftwing Buddhist agitator who has been behind the fall of eight of the past nine governments in Viet Nam. Had Ambassador Lodge not prevented President Diem from arresting Tri Quang in 1963, there would probably not have been any *coups* at all. The only government Tri Quang did not help considerably to destroy was that of Dr. Quat. Quat was forced out by the Catholics, the Hoa Hao, and the Cao Daist sects, after Quat had fired fifty of their officials at Buddhist instigation.

Tri Quang seems drunk in his quest for power. When you visit him at his headquarters in Saigon, at the Xa Loi Pagoda which Diem helped build, you find printing presses all around you, humming with material attacking whatever government is in power. He thinks that he can handle the Communists. Twice arrested by the French for collaborating with Ho Chi Minh, his brother is one of the top Communist officials in Hanoi. He says he wants a "neutralist" government, even though the government in South Viet Nam agrees with President Johnson that a neutralist government would only be another name for a Communist takeover. He wants a coalition government, even though President Kennedy warned long ago that a coalition with the Communists is "like riding a tiger."

On April 13 the Senate Internal Security subcommittee released a report prepared by the China experts at the Library of Congress. The report showed how the Communists have used the Buddhist Association to stir up anti-American sentiment in Southeast Asia. At a news conference in Saigon in April, 1966, Buddhist leaders were asked if they envisioned an elected civil government seeking peace with the Viet Cong and asking the American forces to pull out. A Buddhist spokesman replied: "If that is what the people want, then that is what they will get. We want to fulfill the aspirations of the people." Officials both in Washington and Saigon figure that is exactly what a new regime might very well do if it is controlled by Tri Quang.[17]

The Vietnamese people are among the most anti-Communist in the world. In a free and fair election there is no fear they will vote for Communism. One million of them fled from the tyranny in the North, and several million more, currently 100,000 a month, have fled from the tyranny of the Viet Cong-held areas in the South. No one fears the outcome of a *bona fide* election. What they fear is that the election will be neither fair nor free. Ambassador Henry Cabot Lodge expressed such fear shortly before his visit to the United States in April, 1966. He wisely pointed out:

If there is intimidation, if people, as so often happens in this part of the world, are threatened with assassination, with kidnapping, with torture, with maiming, which is a very common thing in Southeast Asia—if the count is not honest, if there is interference with the ballot boxes, then of course it won't be a success.[18]

Mr. Lodge then implied that he thought the Vietnamese voters would be intimidated by violence. He pointed out that the Viet Cong were trying to shift the brunt of the struggle for control from the military and economic fronts to the political front. We should realize what has happened, something with which we are not familiar in the West. If America loses the war because of an unjust election it will be just as big a loss as a military defeat, and it will be just as encouraging to the enemy. The danger is precisely that we will not recognize the danger, and that if we get defeated through such manipulations, we will be fed excuses and not even recognize that we were defeated. As Ambassador Lodge explained further:

This is the kind of war—you have a military side of it, which goes quite well, as a matter of fact goes well, then they try the economic side, and try to bring about starvation. If we can meet them on that, then they try the political side, the subversive side, and they switch to and fro all the time, and that's very baffling and very complicated for people in the United States.[19]

If America is to continue as the leader of the free world it has to realize that its own freedom is in jeopardy whenever a part of the free world is lost. We are not in Viet Nam primarily to help the Vietnamese. We have much more to lose than they do. Freedom is the great goal to be achieved. But to think that a country must have the American type of government in order to achieve it is unrealistic and naive. Even England did not have elections for nine years because of World War II. Yet her country was not occupied, and she had had democracy for centuries.

The war in Viet Nam can be won only if the United States backs the government in South Viet Nam—particularly when it is in trouble. The war can be won only if we make up our mind to win it. This may mean declaring war on North Viet Nam. It certainly means that we will have to put the harbor at Haiphong out of commission, and it means we will have to stop granting sanctuary to the enemy. It also means that we will have to stop fooling ourselves about how easy it is in time of war to export our form of democracy abroad. South Viet Nam has been in ferment mainly because of agitation by Tri Quang and his followers. Yet we seem to condone the rioting. The government there is tottering, yet our Secretary of Defense seems to praise the chaos. Commented Mr. McNamara on the political disorder in May of 1966:

> South Viet Nam is in the midst of a political ferment, and we should expect a ferment at a time when a nation is seeking to form institutions that had been absent in the society.

The followers of Tri Quang are demanding a constitution and an assembly, both of which the country had from 1955 until 1963, when the government was overthrown with the help of the United States Government at the instigation of Tri Quang. We need to recall the age-old admonition: once bitten, twice shy.

6. *A Just and Lasting Peace*

If the recent unrest in South Viet Nam means anything, it means that we cannot keep on with a stalemate without losing Viet Nam in the end. To think that Soviet Russia would ever help us get peace in Viet Nam is folly, yet the State Department has repeatedly tried to get Russia to do just that. As far as American analysts can tell from studying Soviet statements, the Russians would like a peace in Viet Nam that would give the Viet Cong autonomy in wide areas. Moscow and Peking want the Viet Cong placed in positions which will insure the instability of the South Vietnamese Government.[20] The talk of a "detente" with the USSR has a hollow ring when we consider how much Russia is trading with Hanoi. Communist Russia is giving enormous support to North Viet Nam. She has refused to do anything about peace talks, and has given us nothing but stinging abuse when we have asked for her help to bring about peace. All we have received in reply is missiles aimed at our planes.

The Communists are not going to cease their aggression in Viet Nam unless they are forced to. They can justify anything they want to do, and they want to conquer whatever countries they can. Every reasonable measure must be employed in order to win. Above all, America has to convince the enemy that she intends to win. It is a terrible mis-

312

take to keep on bombing bits and pieces of equipment as they come down the Ho Chi Minh Trail and to have hundreds of American and South Vietnamese lives lost in the process when we permit every nation on earth to supply Hanoi with the necessities for carrying on the war.

Premier Ky has made it clear that Haiphong should be bombed. He has made it clear that Saigon will never negotiate with the Viet Cong, and that it will not use the Geneva Accords as a basis for negotiations. For several years the United States seemed to point the finger at South Viet Nam, saying that unless that nation wanted to win the war nothing could be done to save it. The shoe now is on the other foot. Perhaps it always was. Premier Ky advocates a much stronger action than the United States does, and it is America's policy which restricts his government's action and which is aimed at negotiation instead of victory.

One of America's greatest mistakes is to forget that the United States is only an ally. It should stop talking about how "we will negotiate". America has no right to negotiate for another country. If South Viet Nam wants to use the troops from Taiwan, blockade Haiphong, or hit the industry around Hanoi, it should be free to do so. Only the details should be worked out with the United States. The tables seem to be turned. South Viet Nam wants nothing more than to win the war. As soon as America determines to do so, the war will rapidly commence to be won.

Various leaders in the United States, including the Chairman of the Senate Foreign Relations Committee, have urged a return to the Geneva Accords of 1954. But a close study of these Agreements proves that we should not return to them. To quote Dr. Frank Trager, Professor of International Affairs at New York University:

> The Geneva Accords were written in haste and ended in compromises with, and concessions to, the Communist powers. They add up to political folly. These Agreements aided Communist North Vietnam to *initiate* further struggle against South Viet Nam and prevented an objective peace-keeping machinery from performing its assigned function. They also fed the Pathet Lao in Laos and helped to bring that country almost to ruin.[21]

Less than ten percent of the U.S. population favor a policy that would abandon Viet Nam to the Communists. But this minority have had an impact out of all proportion to their numbers. They invoke freedom, but would see it abolished. They want the war to end, but their incessant clamor prolongs the war. Like everyone else, they want the killing stopped. But their continual and irresponsible clamor can only result in more people being killed. It is easy to urge that America negotiate, but it is destructive to imply that meaningful negotiations can be brought about just for the asking. General Edward Lansdale (Ret.), who is now a special assistant to Ambassador Lodge with the rank of Minister, maintains that the war effort is badly hurt every time that U.S. political leaders speak of "negotiations." The very word, he feels, sends shudders through the government of Viet Nam. General Wallace M. Greene, Jr., Commandant of the U.S. Marine Corps, has made the observation that America must not permit critics of its basic policy to deter us from continuing our efforts toward a just peace and against "wars of liberation". Asia, he pointed out, can be won or lost depending on the outcome of the cold war in the United States.

The vast majority of Americans support their government's goal of defeating aggressors, but many doubt if present tactics will achieve that goal. As former Vice-President Richard Nixon observed, the Communists want a ground war, and they want a long war. He pointed out that the South Vietnamese need to see the prospect of winning, since they have been fighting for so many years. Nixon averred that present U.S. policies can lead to defeat "through South Vietnamese disintegration." But even then American troops could not leave, he said, because disintegration would mean that U.S. forces would have to be sent to Thailand, the Philippines, and all the other areas where the aggressors would be encouraged to go.

America's superiority is not on the ground. It is on the sea and in the air. No nation can win when it grants sanctuary to the enemy. Even Canada could attack the United States without ever being defeated, if we failed to invade her. Yet America still grants sanctuary to the important targets in North Viet Nam. Both China and North Viet Nam realize that present U.S. policy is one of stalemate. They realize that if they keep up their aggression for a while, South Viet Nam will lose its will to fight, that then nothing could prevent a Communist takeover. They realize that just four years ago America took the easy way out by giving up in Laos. They recall that the anti-Communist forces were defeated in China by means of a cease-fire.

The military commanders in Viet Nam are virtually unanimous in urging a more intensified, selective pattern. None suggest bombing population centers. But they point out that the United States has hardly 300 planes to bomb a 7,310 square mile area, whereas the Air Force in World War II used 1,700 planes to bomb a 2,900 square mile area in northern and central Italy. They are dismayed, as are much of the U.S. civilian population, when they hear the Secretary of Defense maintain that bombers should be replaced by missiles. They realize that no missiles have been used in Viet Nam, nor would they be useful there. Air Force planners insist that far more bombers should be built, and they point out that the North can be bombed effectively only if source targets can be hit, e.g. oil dumps instead of trucks, ammunition factories instead of little ammo dumps, hydroelectric plants that supply small workshops, instead of hitting the scattered workshops themselves. As *Time* pointed out at the beginning of February, 1966, resumption of bombing the North would not produce victory because the bombing is only used to harass the enemy, not to defeat him.[22]

Early in 1965 America was faced with a very critical decision. The decision was whether to abolish sanctuary or lose the war. The decision was made on February 7, 1965, but it was only partial: abolish sanctuary except for the important targets. Today America is faced with an equally serious decision. The decision is whether or not to win the war. To do so, the sanctuary on important targets has to be abolished. Upon this decision rests the hope for peace in the world tomorrow.

America has to adopt a policy of winning or it will find itself overextended. The United States has commitments to defend 41 other nations, in addition to Viet Nam. If it allows this war to drag on indefinitely as the Communists want it to do, the United States is sure to have a series of other Viet Nams to fight at the same time. America's hesitancy and indecision encourage trouble around the world. So does Defense Secretary McNamara's decision to phase out most of America's bombers. America used to count its bombers in the thousands. Now it can only count them in the hundreds. Such a situation is an open invitation to aggression. The United States may never have an all-out war. It is certain to have a series of guerrilla wars from time to time. Unless they are won with dispatch, they will be started faster than America can handle them.

Peace cannot be bought with kindness, with compromise, or by securing promises from a ruthless atheistic enemy who has neither qualms nor conscience. The danger of an all-out war with the Communist world depends on one thing only: when and if the Communists are able to defeat the United States. The policy of deterrents is the only justifiable policy in a world where there is no sanction to international law except by the aggrieved nation itself, and where the United States is the only effective obstacle to the Communist desire to take over the world. Test bans and promises of disarmament are deliberately intended by the enemy to lull the free world into a state of somnolence that can only lead to our destruction or surrender. The only sound policy is the policy of preparedness. As a part of that policy, the United States should be building an anti-missile defense system. Thus far the Department of Defense has refused to do so, even though the noted scientist, Edward Teller, has pointed out that a defense against missiles would save the lives of 75 million Americans, in case of an attack.

Such a defense would not only save that many lives, it might save that many more because it would serve as a powerful deterrent to attack. Dr. Teller further points out that the development of such a system would help greatly in containing Communist China. He urges that the United States begin now to build such a system, and give simplified versions of it to the free nations in Asia in order to deter a nuclear attack by Red China on its neighbors a few years from now. Yet the White House Committee headed by Jerome Wiesner of M.I.T. has strongly recommended that the United States declare a moratorium on any anti-missile defense, in order to build up a "rapport" with Russia. The committee argues that Russia would consider it an "unfriendly act" if the United States tried to defend itself by such a system. Russia, of course, has an anti-missile defense system. When the Defense Department polled Americans in May, 1966, it found that two-thirds of them thought the United States already had such a defense. Some people seem to have an unerring instinct for surrender. America's pacifists, for instance, are also opposed to civil defense against a nuclear attack.

America became the leader of the free world by defeating Germany and Japan in World War II. The world needed America then, but it needs her even more today. Without the United States the free world would be without a leader. If America loses in Viet Nam, it will be the greatest defeat in the history of the United States. It will also be the beginning of the decline and fall of the United States as a great nation. If America remains strong and continues to strengthen her position, if America maintains its position as the leader of the free world, the forces of Communism will gradually decline. This is the theory behind the policy of containment, and the theory is sound. As President Kennedy pointed out, America has not assumed her role of greatness, greatness has been thrust upon her. If America fulfills its obligations, if it lives up to its responsibilities, the free world will enjoy freedom, prosperity, and progress that will be unprecedented in the history of the world. But it cannot accomplish this through irresolution and inaction. America has to cut through the fog and smoke of cold war confusion and realize its true position. It has to adopt a policy of winning the war, a policy that it has been unwilling to adopt since World War II.

It was the policy of winning that made America the leader of the free world. Only by such a policy can she continue as its leader. Only by such a policy can America give aid and comfort to the inhabitants of the captive nations comprising a third of the world. Only by a firm determination to defeat aggression wherever it rears its head, only by the policy of winning can America keep the free world free. Diplomats should not be making the bulk of military decisions, nor setting the basic military policy, because diplomats never think in terms of winning. They are trained in a different school of thought. They think in terms of concession and compromise, appeasement and capitulation. They want at all cost to avoid a "confrontation." They seldom think of using military means of settling a military dispute, even against a ruthless, militant aggressor. They are too inclined to think in terms of settling any war at any price. They tend to favor peace at whatever price.

America's policy of restraint has caused a lot of wars in the past. It was her lack of resolve, her indetermination, her failure to want to win that cost the loss of Central Europe, then China, then North Korea, then North Viet Nam, then Cuba, then most of Laos. America is ill-advised and ill-informed. If South Viet Nam is lost it will be because of this policy of undue restraint. If South Viet Nam is lost it will terrify America's allies and the free peoples all over the world. It will also bring despair to the hearts of the hundreds of millions of people behind the Iron and Bamboo Curtains, most of whom are also allies in the cause of freedom. It is false to think that America's power is resented by other free countries. If America wins in Viet Nam there will be rejoicing the whole world over. The stakes are high indeed. They are higher than they were against both Germany and Japan. The whole free world is up for grabs. This is a once-and-for-all struggle. South Viet Nam is the test case *par excellence,* and if America cannot succeed in defending it, neither can America hope to defend the rest of Asia, nor anywhere else.

If South Viet Nam is lost, America will have served notice on the rest of the world that they cannot count on the United States, that they will have to come to terms with atheistic Communism. This is not primarily South Viet Nam's war. It is primarily our own. If the United States should lose, it will have proven Red China's contention that America cannot win against a combination of guerrilla war and cold war propaganda. America lost Laos in 1962 through concessions and compromise. America lost the only stable regime South Viet Nam ever had by swallowing false propaganda. Whether South Viet Nam is lost by succumbing to the clamor for "instant democracy," whether it is lost through the clamor of the teach-ins at home, or whether it is lost simply because America lacked the will to win—whatever the cause and however we try to excuse ourselves or explain it away—it will still be the greatest defeat in the history of the United States, and the world will never forget it. America will not lose the war on the field of battle. But if it prolongs its policy of stalemate it is certain to lose through the ultimate demoralization and despair of its allies. The war in Viet Nam is indeed a "dirty war," as the Communists call it. But it would be much dirtier if the South Vietnamese and the Americans lay down their arms. In the words of Dean Rusk: "If you tell the other side, 'We don't want trouble, take Viet Nam,' that is a step toward war." [23]

The Vietnamese in Saigon, particularly those from the North who form forty percent of South Viet Nam's officer corps, do not expect Ho Chi Minh to give up until he absolutely has to. They give three reasons: 1) Hanoi has no other alternative. It has worked for thirty years to conquer all of Viet Nam, and it wants the South's resources, without which it would face a very dreary future. 2) The North cannot call off the war unless the Chinese Communists agree, and Red China seems as determined as ever to keep the war in Viet Nam going. 3) North Viet Nam still thinks it will achieve final victory. They believe that America will gradually give up or get tricked into doing so in the face of an increasingly expensive and frustrating war.[24]

Communist China is beginning to look like a loser, and its position is deteriorating almost everywhere. Mao Tse-tung banished 160,000 artists and writers during the winter of 1965–1966.[25] He lost his grip on Indonesia, on Cuba, and on most of Africa. Paranoia is the main affliction of Red China's leaders, paranoia caused by the realization that the Communist system there has been a flop. Lenin's doctrines were applied as though Lenin knew the Chinese people, when he did not understand people at all. The paranoia has resulted from the fact that the aged leaders of Red China would not admit that the Chinese did not respond to the godless theories of Marx and Lenin like those theoreticians thought they would.

What about the split between Russia and Red China? There is a split, but one should know the reasons behind it. Both Russia and China agree that Communism should dominate the world. They have proclaimed this year after year, and they have always acted accordingly. People unwilling to admit this are indulging in dangerous wishful thinking.

The basic difference between the two Communist hierarchies is that Russia seeks to accomplish world domination primarily through a *detente,* i.e. by cold-war propaganda and by boring from within. China seeks the same identical goal of Communist domination of the world, but she seeks it through revolution, through wars of "liberation". This difference of opinion may cause the split between Russia and China to widen. It may lead to border clashes between them. If this happens, many will forget that they both have the same objective. They will conclude that we can win Russia over to our side. Some of America's diplomats already think that Russia is somewhat on our side, but this is a wanton disregard of the facts. As long as these two big powers are ruled by Communists, they will both attempt to control the rest of the world. They are irrevocably committed to extending their domain over all the non-Communist nations.

As this goes to press on May 16, the troops of South Viet Nam have taken action at Da Nang and Hue against some rebel uprisings. For quite a while Tri Quang, the leftist Buddhist monk, has been arming youths in Hue, training them to act against the legal government. Much of the American press seemed not to understand the issue. Asked Raymond Coffey, in the *Chicago Daily News:* "How can Premier Ky possibly win this sort of showdown where he forces Vietnamese to run against Vietnamese?" In a civil war that is just what happens in any country. Ky did not force the Buddhists to fight him. They were the aggressors against the legitimate government. They forced him to fight them, which he did with great restraint.

The practicing Buddhists in Viet Nam make up just 25% of the population.[26] Only a minority of this 25 percent are controlled by the militant Buddhist group. In ousting General Nguyen Chanh Thi in March, Ky had shown that he would not continue to let the first corps area around Da Nang and Hue be run as an autonomous and anti-government domain. The Government of South Viet Nam also began to realize that quick elections would only lead to a legislature controlled by the Unified Buddhist church, which has been penetrated by Communists and neutralists.[27]

Some American officials thought they should start issuing orders, but the United States is not a neo-colonialist power in full command. It was learned after Diem had been assassinated that his greatest mistake was to listen to the American officials who told him to let the rebels riot, because the Americans thought they were well-meaning Buddhists. Similarly, in the current crisis, America seemed to drop its support of the only legitimate government. American officials were instructed "to make every effort to persuade the various South Vietnamese leaders to consult together to resolve their differences." Our officials apparently made no distinction between the government leaders, and the rebels who were Communist-infiltrated. The Buddhist Struggle Committee even got encouragement from Uncle Sam when the State Department stressed U.S. desires for a transition from military to civilian rule in South Viet Nam. State Department officials could talk all they wanted about "a broad-based civilian rule," but in the 1965 provincial and municipal council elections in South Viet Nam only 38.8 percent of the estimated 9,408,000 persons eligible to vote cast ballots.[28] More than half of the eligible voters were in areas where voting was physically impossible. To think that voters even in the so-called safe areas were not exposed to undue pressure by the Viet Cong or Buddhist-directed "struggle committees" would be naive.[29] Early in the spring of 1966, demonstrators were denouncing the United States, alleging that the U.S. embassy was hindering the formation of a national assembly. This helped scare U.S. officials into hasty acceptance of the Buddhist demands.

The Chief of State, General Nguyen Van Thieu, kept calling on the population to keep calm and disciplined: "The action in the north was not to oppress the people but to restore order and democracy," he explained. "Democracy and security will be implemented. The law and sovereignty of the nation must be respected," he continued. The government's military action in Da Nang and Hue was prompted by recurrent defiance of its authority in the northern areas. Even some of the army regiments there were antigovernment, and the population obeyed local chieftains who were under Buddhist control. [30]

Officials in Washington were gravely concerned about this latest turn of events, but it probably saved the situation. Strength on the side of law and order is the only thing that will produce results, and if Premier Ky succeeds in using it he will have established a very successful regime. The idea that beneficial universal elections can be held within a few months is very questionable. The country is still held largely by Communist troops. The war in Viet Nam can be won only if the United States backs the government in South Viet Nam, particularly when it is in trouble.

Officials in Washington seem to lament the failure of Premier Ky to tell them before he acted against the communist-infiltrated Buddhist Struggle Committee. Early in April of 1966 Ky was restrained by American pressure from occupying Da Nang. His failure to assert his government's authority at that time encouraged the rebellious Buddhists and prolonged the political crisis. Ky acted the next time when Ambassador Lodge was in Washington, General Westmoreland was in Honolulu, and General Lansdale was also out of Viet Nam. Had he taken the United States into his confidence in all probability he would have had to act against U.S. advice, or do nothing and let his country drift further into anarchy and chaos.

The *Chicago Sun-Times* criticized Ky in its leading editorial on May 17 for "his sudden and unannounced drive against his political enemies." Ky leads the government of South Viet Nam. It is folly to imply that those who would destroy that government are just his personal enemies. Ky is acting, not to protect himself, but to save his country from the inevitable Communist takeover that would follow if he let law and order give way to mobocracy and confusion. Ky's government is the only one that has shown political stability since the death of President Diem three years ago. If he lets the militant Buddhist minority take over the country, or if a Buddhist-dominated neutralist regime gains power, the sacrifice of thousands of lives on the battlefield will have been in vain. Ky is no great statesman, by classical standards. But he is a courageous and patriotic leader, and has the staunch support of at least eight of the ten generals of the directory. He is strongly anti-Communist, and if he has a weakness, it is his reluctance to control the political Buddhists. Indeed, this is the main complaint against him from the younger officers. The opposition to him was confined to the first and second divisions in the first corps area.

The Buddhists threatened mass suicides and civil war, but there is little danger of either one. They held a protest meeting at Vien Hoa Dao, the Buddhist Institute in Saigon, but the meeting failed. Ky handled the situation better without American advice than he might have with it, and America would do well to let him work it out. If he succeeds here he has the makings of a statesman, and he will have gained self-confidence and learned a great deal.[31]

President Johnson declared on February 11, 1965, that he believes the American people and Congress "overwhelmingly" support the Administration's position of "neither escalating the war in Viet Nam, nor withdrawing." There are very few in favor of withdrawing, but the vast majority want a policy of winning. They want the President to adopt a firm policy of winning with all deliberate speed. If we are the stronger side we should go ahead and win. If we are not the stronger side, we have no business there.

American policy has been not to escalate, but to send more troops. That is escalation, but in the wrong direction. The enemy can match us on the ground. Our real superiority is on the sea and in the air. There is where America can escalate but the enemy cannot. The idea that somehow we will provoke Communist China into the war by a show of strength was answered by General Maxwell Taylor, when he pointed out: "One does not provoke Communists to do things. They will do things whenever they feel it is both timely and in their interest. When it's not in their interest, they won't do it." The great fear we have of Red China is hard to understand. China has no modern bombers, no long-range missiles, no modern air power, no modern sea power, very little plane fuel, no way to carry on an aggressive war against a modern enemy.

The recent rise in the proportion opposing the policies of the Administration was an increase in the number of "hawks," not "doves." [32] The President watches these polls closely. The White House revealed on March 9, 1966, that when public opinion polls showed a drop in support for the President's policy in Viet Nam, it was because people did not think that he was pressing the war hard enough. When bad weather has forced the United States to reduce its military effort, public support has gone down, revealed Robert H. Fleming, deputy Presidential press secretary.[33]

The Administration has often pointed out that America must stand fast in Viet Nam, that if it does not, no one else will trust its guarantees. The damage to U.S. commitments could spread around the world. But that is not the main thing to be gained in Viet Nam. This ugly, maddening war, that is so small on the battlefront and so large on logistics, may one day be remembered as the turning point in history. Not only Asia but all the world may come to realize with gratitude that America's efforts turned the tide against Communism by fighting in Viet Nam. For that beleaguered country is the key to the freedom and safety of 330 million people, a population fifty percent greater than all of North America, a population possessing some of the greatest riches in the world. "The road to Paris lies through Peking," wrote Lenin long ago. The Communists will never take Paris unless they first take Southeast Asia. The tyranny in Communist China has been worse than Stalin at his worst. China's economy under Communism has failed just as much as the economy of Free China has succeeded. The diplomatic programs of Red China have flopped around the world largely because their economy at home has been too poor to support their promises.

Red China failed miserably in its efforts to conquer South Korea. The supreme test for conquering Southeast Asia is the war in Viet Nam. If Red China fails in its aggressive purposes there, the free world will have proved that Communist China can be contained. If Red China is contained it will wither on the vine. The stakes indeed are high. But they are not only against the spread of tyranny and evil. If Communist China is contained, if Southeast Asia is kept free, the whole free world will share in that freedom. So eventually will that twenty percent of the world still enslaved on the Chinese Mainland.

FOOTNOTES

CHAPTER XV: PROBLEMS AND POSSIBILITIES

1. *Time,* Feb. 18, 1966.
2. *Church League of America,* Oct. 1965.
3. *Chicago Tribune,* Sept. 29, 1965, p. 22.
4. *Mindszenty Foundation Release,* Dec. 15, 1965.
5. *Look,* April 5, 1966.
6. *New Guard,* Feb. 1966, p. 13.
7. *Allen-Scott Report,* March 18, 1966.
8. *Ibid.*
9. *U.S. News and World Report,* Jan. 31, 1966.
10. *America,* Feb. 5, 1966.
11. *St. Louis Globe-Democrat,* Feb. 27, 1966.
12. *New York Times,* Feb. 17, 1966.

13. *Political,* July, 1965, p. 15.
14. *Washington Report,* American Security Council, Feb. 9, 1966.
15. *U.S. News and World Report,* Jan. 31, 1966.
16. *Ibid.*
17. *New York Journal-American,* April 12, 1966.
18. *New York Times,* April 23, 1966.
19. *Ibid.*
20. Ray Cromley, *New York World Telegram,* April 4, 1966.
21. *Viet Nam Perspectives,* August, 1965, p. 1.
22. *Time,* Feb. 4, 1966.
23. *Time,* Feb. 25, 1966.
24. *U.S. News and World Report,* Jan. 31, 1966, p. 25.
25. *Time,* Feb. 25, 1966, p. 28.
26. Rev. Patrick O'Connor, *Brooklyn Tablet,* May 5, 1966.
27. *Chicago American,* May 16, 1966.
28. O'Connor, *ibid.*
29. *Ibid.*
30. *Chicago Sun-Times,* May 16, 1966.
31. *Chicago Tribune,* May 16, 1966.
32. *New York Times,* March 10, 1966.
33. *Ibid.*

INDEX

Acheson, Dean, 188
Affirmation: Viet Nam, 192, 290
Afghanistan, 123, 205
Afro-Asian Conference, 212, 214
Aggression, 197, 288
Aiken, George, 236, 274
Alliance of the Viets, 4
American Bar Association, 190
American Federation of Labor–CIO, 187
American 14 Points for Peace, 241
American Military Assistance Advisory Group (MAAG), 71
America's First Diplomatic Mission, 4
An Nam, v, 2, 3, 7, 9, 19, 81
Animism, 114
Appeal of 17 Nations, 205
Armed Services Committee, 279
Asahi (Newspaper), 223
Asia, 168
"Asian Munich," xv
Asian Speakers Bureau, vii
Association for the Study of Marxism, 21
Atlee, Clement, 20

Australia, 13, 49, 50, 51, 60, 62, 167, 193, 195, 225, 239, 278, 285
Australia, New Zealand and United States Security Treaty (ANZUS), 60

Ball, George, 247, 274, 275
Bamboo Curtain, xii, 240, 317
Bangkok, 58, 60, 61, 233
Bao Dai (Nguyen Vinh Thuy), 3, 12, 19, 22, 23, 24, 29, 65, 173, 285
Bay of Bengal, 18
Belgium, 83
Belgrade, 233, 269
Berkeley campus, x
Berlin, Berlin blockade, xiii, 32, 301
Berlin-Rome-Tokyo Axis, 18
Bhutto, Zulfikar Ali, 62
Bidault, Georges, 33, 35, 83
Binh Xuyen, 84, 86
Bonn Government, 195
Borodin, Michael, 19, 73
Bouscaren, Dr. Anthony T., 76
Brandon College (Canada), 213
Brazil, 123

French Socialists, 73
French Union, 198
Fulbright, J. William, xii, xiii, xv, xvi, 43, 44, 145, 214, 254, 267, 272, 274, 285, 304. (Fulbright Committee, see Senate Foreign Relations Comm.)

Gallup Poll, 193, 194
Gavin, James M., 267, 269
General Buddhist Association, 118
Geneva, xiv, xv, 13, 15, 32, 33, 37, 38, 39, 40, 41, 42, 43, 44, 45, 48, 55, 58, 76, 84, 90, 105, 106, 148, 163, 177, 184, 191, 199, 214, 215, 219, 242, 243, 257, 260, 284, 285, 286, 288, 289, 293, 313. (See also Ch. III on the Geneva Agreements.)
Geopolitical Factors, 9
George VI, 67
German-Italian-Japanese Axis Alliance, 17
Germany, 12, 13, 18, 55, 294, 175
Ghana, 205, 214
Gia Long, 7
Goldberg, Arthur, 230, 233, 235
Goldwater, Barry, 154, 237
Graham (Rev.), Billy, 181, 182
Great Debate, 276
Great Dictator of China, 2
Greater East Asia Co-Prosperity Sphere, 17
Greece, 48, 168, 308, 309
Greene, Felix, 161
Greene, Wallace M. Jr., 314
Gromyko, Andrei A., 214, 222
Gruening, Earnest, 240, 256, 276
Guerrilla forces, 12, 40, 46, 74, 84, 91, 98, 153, 199, 208, 283
Gulf of Siam, 13
Ha Tien, 94

Haiphong, 237, 300, 311, 313
Halberstam, David, 115, 125
Hanoi's four demands for a cease fire, 199, 220
Hanoi rejection of U. S. peace drive, 257
Harkins, Paul D., 115, 129
Harriman, Averell, xv, 62, 125, 233, 249
Hawks, 322, 296
Hickenlooper, Bourke B., 150
Higgins, Marguerite, 124
Hilsman, Roger, 125
Hirota, Koki, 17
Hitler, 18, 23, 36, 42, 46, 159, 226
Ho Chi Minh, v, ix, x, xiii, 3, 4, 12, 13, 19, 20, 21, 22, 23, 26, 27, 149, 152, 164, 200, 213, 219, 220, 232, 258, 270, 283, 286, 292, 295, 308, 317
Ho Chi Minh, also known as: Lee Shui, Lee Shun, Yuong Son Nhi, Houng*Son, Wong San Yi, Nguyen Bih-sinh, Nguyen Ai Quoc.
Ho Chi Minh Trail, 254, 301, 313
Hoa Hao, 4, 86, 114, 163, 309
Holyoake, Keith J., 274
Honey, P. J., 160, 166
Hong Kong, 51, 69, 82, 102
Honolulu Conference (see Ch. XIII), 248, 265, 261, 278, 292, 321
Hoover, J. Edgar, 157, 181, 297, 299
House Armed Services Committee, 300
House Subcommittee on the Far East and the Pacific, xii
Hue, 3, 7, 9, 12, 65, 66, 79, 81, 95, 96, 195, 318, 320
Hull, Cordell, 18
Hume, Alex, 154
Humphrey, Hubert, 185, 222, 233, 266, 274, 276, 277, 278
Hungary, 55, 194
Hunt, Chester, 184

United States (America, Washington), 4, 13, 15, 39, 44, 51, 60, 67, 83, 149, 155, 164, 194, 210, 211, 218, 223, 227, 248, 264, 271, 283, 284, 285, 286, 289, 311, 315

U. S. Official Position on Viet Nam, 242, 244, 245, 246, 247

U. S. Military Command in Viet Nam (USMACV), 115

USOM (United States Overseas Mission Building), 116, 120

University of Seven Seas, vi, 192

U. S. News and World Report, 104, 256

USS Maddox, 145

U Thant, xv, 202, 203, 205, 207, 209, 217, 238, 239, 260, 291, 305

Vatican, 194

Vichy Government, 18, 283

Viet Cong, 4, 13, 14, 23, 45, 46, 49, 57, 61, 84, 97, 103, 110, 139, 140, 149, 154, 157, 163, 165, 188, 193, 194, 199, 201, 206, 215, 217, 222, 227, 239, 244, 248, 267, 271, 272, 277, 293, 294, 304, 305, 306, 310, 312

Viet Cong Liberation Radio, 239

Viet Minh, 4, 19, 21, 22, 24, 26, 30, 36, 41, 68, 70, 106, 271, 284, 293

Viet Nam Day Committee, 179

Viet Nam Hon (the Soul of Viet Nam), 73

Vietnamese Empire, 3

Vietnamese Mission the U. N., vii

VJ Day, 81

Vo Nguyen Giap, 27-29

Walker, Gordon, 212

Wan Waithayakon, 53

Washington, D. C., 44, 211, 223

Westmoreland, William (General), 230, 261

Wheeler, Earl G., 262, 267, 302

White Paper, 14, 45, 147, 148

Williams, G. Mennen, 233

Williams, William A., 161, 167

Wilson, Harold, 215, 233

Witkowski, Stan, 180

Wolf, Eric J., 159, 184

World Council of Churches, 305

World War II, 4, 17, 49, 135, 198, 199, 249, 283, 301, 317

Xa Loi Pagoda, 116, 120, 310

Yalta Agreements, 42

Yeh, George, 101

Young Americans for Freedom (YAF), 290

Yugoslavia, 55, 166, 205

Yunnan, 3, 9, 11, 26

Yu-pin, Paul (Archbishop), ix, 82